Crazy Ji

Chinese Religion and Popular Literature

Harvard-Yenching Institute Monograph Series, 48

Crazy Ji

Chinese Religion and Popular Literature

Meir Shahar

Published by the Harvard University Asia Center
and distributed by Harvard University Press
Cambridge (Massachusetts) and London
1998

Printed in the United States of America

The Harvard-Yenching Institute, founded in 1928 and headquartered at Harvard University, is a foundation dedicated to the advancement of higher education in the humanities and social sciences in East and Southeast Asia. The Institute supports advanced research at Harvard by faculty members of certain Asian universities and doctoral studies at Harvard and other universities by junior faculty at the same universities. It also supports East Asian studies at Harvard through contributions to the Harvard-Yenching Library and publication of the *Harvard Journal of Asiatic Studies* and books on premodern East Asian history and literature.

Library of Congress Cataloging-in-Publication Data

Shahar, Meir, 1959–
Crazy Ji : Chinese religion and popular literature / Meir Shahar.
p. cm. -- (Harvard-Yenching Institute monograph series ; 48)
Includes bibliographical references and index.
ISBN 0-674-17562-X (alk. paper). -- ISBN 0-674-17563-8 (pbk. : alk. paper)
1. Tao-chi, 1148–1209--Folklore. 2. China--Religious life and customs. I. Title. II. Series.
GR335.4T35S45 1998
299'.51--dc21 98-18864
CIP

Index by Mark Gamsa

Printed on acid-free paper

Last figure below indicates year of this printing

07 06 05 04 03 02 01 00 99 98

For the elevation of the soul of my father

David Shahar

Acknowledgments

Two persons have contributed most to this study. My teacher Patrick Hanan introduced me to Chinese literature and to the fictionalized character of Crazy Ji. My friend Huang Chunsen showed me Chinese religion as practiced in Taiwan and revealed to me that Crazy Ji is not only the protagonist of novels but also the object of religious worship. My debt of gratitude to both of them is hard to express in words.

Numerous other teachers, colleagues, and friends have generously shared with me their knowledge and advice. I am grateful, among others, to Chen Pingyuan, Glen Dudbridge, Vincent Durand-Dastès, Andrea Goldman, John Christopher Hamm, Jiang Wuchang, David Johnson, Li Fengmao, Masatoshi Nagatomi, Andrew Plaks, P. Steven Sangren, Shang Quan, Hugh Shapiro, Donald Sutton, Tu Wei-ming, Wang Ch'iu-kuei, Robert Weller, Zhang Ping, and Zhou Chunyi. I would also like to express my thanks to the Taiwanese puppeteers Xu Wang, Huang Haidai, and Huang Junxiong, as well as to the Chen family of the Taiwanese Minghuayuan opera company for the insight into Crazy Ji's role in Taiwanese drama. I also thank the sprit-medium Chen Wenshan of Pingdong county, Taiwan, for permission to use a photograph of him as the cover illustration. Jean DeBernardi and John Kieshnick read the entire manuscript, and I am most grateful for their detailed comments. My thanks are also due to my student, Mark Gamsa, who prepared the index. John Ziemer, my editor at the Harvard University Asia Center, provided invaluable help throughout the preparation of the manuscript for printing.

A major portion of Chapter 3 was published under the title "Enlightened Monk or Arch-Magician? The Portrayal of the God Jigong in the Sixteenth-Century Novel *Jidian yulu,*" in *Proceedings of International Conference on Popular Beliefs and Chinese Culture* (Taipei: Center for Chinese Studies, 1994). An earlier version of the introductory essay was published under the title "Vernacular Fiction and the Transmission of Gods' Cults in Late Imperial China," in *Unruly Gods: Divinity and Society in China,* edited by Meir Shahar and Robert Weller (Honolulu: University of Hawai'i Press, 1996).

Research for the dissertation that served as the starting point for this book benefited from fellowships from the Charlotte Newcombe Doctoral Dissertation Foundation, the Center for the Study of World Religions at Harvard University, and the Center for Chinese Studies, Taipei, under the direction of the Ministry of Education of the Republic of China. A postdoctoral fellowship from the Center for Chinese Studies at the University of California, Berkeley, enabled me to bring this study to conclusion. I am also grateful to the Faculty of the Humanities at Tel Aviv University for a generous research grant.

Finally, and most deeply, I am grateful to my wife, Noga Zhang-Hui Shahar.

M.S.

Contents

Reference Matter

Table, Maps, and Figures

Table

Maps

Figures

Preface

"Crazy Ji" was a late twelfth- and early thirteenth-century Buddhist monk who lived near the city of Hangzhou (in Zhejiang province), then the capital of the Southern Song dynasty (1127–1279). His clerical name was Daoji, but the nickname his contemporaries gave him, "Crazy Ji" (Jidian), suggests that he was no ordinary Buddhist cleric. Disrespectful of Buddhist law and his fellow monks alike, Crazy Ji repeatedly transgressed monastic regulations. His eccentricity estranged him from the Buddhist establishment, but it did nothing to diminish his sanctity in the eyes of the laity. Crazy Ji was venerated by his lay contemporaries as a miracle worker, and following his death in 1209, he became the subject of an enormous body of popular literature. During the twentieth century, for example, no fewer than forty novels have been devoted to him. Simultaneously with the growth of this popular lore, Crazy Ji became the object of a religious cult, which, by the twentieth century, has spread from Beijing in north China to Malaysia in southeast Asia. This book examines Crazy Ji's life and posthumous career, focusing on the available information on the historical Daoji, works of fiction that celebrate him, and the spread of his religious cult. In it I interchangeably refer to the eccentric saint by his Buddhist name, Daoji, his popular nickname, Crazy Ji, or the title under which he is most commonly worshipped, "Sire Ji" (Jigong).

The book's division into three parts reflects the three areas of investigation. Part I concerns the historical Daoji and his religious background. Daoji was a Buddhist monk who violated the monastic regulations of his own faith. Such antinomian behavior is known in many religious traditions; however, rather than examine Daoji's craziness from a comparative or a theological perspective, I search for the origins of his eccentricity within the Chinese religious context. I suggest that he probably belonged to a class of miracle workers whose extraordinary powers were believed to be inextricably linked to extraordinary behavior. For the most part, these miracle workers were itinerant monks on the fringes of the monastic community. They transgressed monastic regulations and were frowned upon by the Buddhist establishment. And yet, perhaps because of their estrangement from that establishment, they were venerated by the laity.

Part II, which occupies the bulk of this book, examines the growth and spread of Daoji lore. In it I chart the development of vernacular fiction on this saint through the twentieth century. Different novels portray Daoji in different lights, reflecting the personal tastes and beliefs of individual authors, the gradual transformation of the Daoji cult, and, in some cases, developments inherent to the vernacular fiction itself. Thus, for example, the portrayal of Daoji as a fearless warrior in late nineteenth-century fiction was due not to a transformation in his cult but to the contemporaneous emergence of martial-arts fiction. I pay particular attention to the relation of oral and written fiction to the growth of Daoji lore. All novels on this crazy saint derive, directly or indirectly, from oral literature; at the same time, most of them have served as sources for further storytelling. The interplay of the oral and the written provides us with a key for understanding the geographical spread of Daoji lore and, ultimately, the spread of his religious cult as well. Oral literature in local dialects served as a source for written fiction in the standardized vernacular. The latter crossed regional and linguistic boundaries and served as a source for oral fiction in new regional dialects. I also examine, albeit briefly, the development of drama on Daoji not as theater but in terms of its relation to fiction on him. Similarly, I do not attempt to cover in any depth the enormous body of twentieth-century plays, television serials, and movies on this eccentric. Instead I focus on a few examples only.

Part III of this book is dedicated to the growth and spread of the religious cult of Daoji. It is based both on historical sources and on anthropological fieldwork I conducted in Taiwan in 1987–88. My survey of this cult highlights its heterogeneity. Over the centuries, the cult of the eccentric Daoji has assumed a variety of forms, ranging from temple worship and spirit possession to spirit writing and spirit painting. This multiplicity of forms is related to a multivocality of meanings, as diverse social and religious groups have variously interpreted Daoji's image to suit their own ideological agendas. Thus, for example, whereas rebels and outlaws have highlighted Daoji's rebellious traits, authors of "morality books" (*shanshu*) have used him as a mouthpiece for conservative values. I pay particular attention to Daoji's role in sectarian religion (the Unity Sect) and in monastic Buddhism. The latter is especially interesting, for it reveals a complex pattern of interaction between beliefs among the laity and monastic dogma. Under pressure from the lay believers, the Buddhist establishment, which granted Daoji neither title nor position in his own time, admitted him into its gallery of saints. The eccentric saint figures today in the pantheons of the amorphous popular religion and organized Chinese Buddhism alike.

My aim in this book is to shed light on the history of one Chinese deity. But, at the same time, I attempt to use Daoji's career to address four larger issues. The first is the relation between Chinese religion (which I also refer to as "Chinese popular religion") and Chinese Buddhism (defined here as Chinese monastic Buddhism). Daoji's posthumous career reveals a complex pattern of interaction between lay piety and monastic beliefs, between popular literature and canonical scriptures. Second, this study illustrates the role of popular literature (written and oral vernacular fiction) in the transmission of cults of deities. These were primarily vernacular novels and the surrounding body of oral literature and drama that spread the cult of Daoji and shaped his image. The posthumous career of Daoji suggests, then, that the body of religious beliefs and practices we now call Chinese religion (or Chinese popular religion) is inseparable from the works of fiction and drama that have served as vehicles for its transmission. Third, Daoji's image sheds an interesting light on the relationship between the Chinese supernatural and the Chinese social and political order. It has often been argued that the Chinese heavens and hells have been fashioned after the bureaucratic order of the Chinese state. And yet the carefree Daoji is anything but a bureaucrat. This eccentric and humorous deity suggests that the Chinese pantheon of divinities has done more than mirror the existing order; it has contested it, and has compensated for it as well. This third consideration leads directly to the fourth: the social impact of a deity who disregards accepted norms and hierarchies. Does such a deity serve as a model for people who question the existing order? Or, on the contrary, by relieving tensions created by the system does he ultimately serve to strengthen it? I will suggest that these possibilities are not necessarily mutually exclusive.

Before I proceed, a few questions of terminology need to be briefly addressed. First, most scholars use the terms "Chinese religion" and "Chinese popular religion" interchangeably—to describe the large, amorphous body of religious beliefs and practices shared by the overwhelming majority of the Chinese laity in late imperial and modern times. This religious tradition is also sometimes referred to, in the scholarly literature, as the "diffused" or "lay" Chinese religion, as distinct from the "institutional" or "clerical" religions of China, terms usually reserved for the Buddhist, Taoist, and sometimes the Confucian traditions. The diffused religion of the Chinese laity owes much to the institutional religions of China, but it has combined its borrowings from them with its own ancient traits to create a unique tradition that warrants the description of a religion unto itself. Among these quintessential traits are a rich, heterogeneous, and unique pantheon of deities; a reverence for ancestors coupled with a ubiquitous apprehension of ghosts; various divination techniques, including geomancy; widespread spirit-possession and spirit-writing cults; and a yearly calendar of holidays and religious festivals, many of them celebrations of deities' birthdays.

As for "popular literature," I use this term to refer to written fiction in the vernacular, as well as the oral narratives from which it often derives and for which it has often served as a source. Vernacular fiction was written in China as early as the eighth century, but this book is concerned with works in this genre, especially novels, written from approximately the fourteenth century on. In what sense is fiction in the vernacular "popular"? To be sure, this genre has not been limited to the lower classes (the written vernacular was by definition accessible to the educated elite only). Nor is the term meant to suggest that the genre lacks artistic refinement (some works in the vernacular are today considered masterpieces of world literature). "Popular" is meant to say, however, that, with some exceptions, vernacular fiction was by and large not considered a respectable art form in late imperial times. Respectable literary genres—such as poetry, history, and philosophy—were written in the classical language, and most works in the vernacular, despite, or perhaps because of, their great popularity, were not considered serious literature.[1] The oral vernacular did not enjoy a respectable position in late imperial culture. This point is familiar and need not be elaborated—suffice it to mention that oral literature was deemed unworthy of publication, and readers, as well as amateur performers, interested in narratives on Jigong had to satisfy themselves with handwritten manuscripts, which were usually carelessly copied. The case of the written vernacular is, however, more complicated. Recent scholarship has shown that some novels in the vernacular were greatly esteemed by members of the literati elite as early as the late Ming.[2] This was not, however, true of the bulk of works in this genre, and certainly not of the novels on Crazy Ji examined in this volume. Despite the enormous popularity of these novels, some are forever lost, others survive in a handful of copies, and the authors of almost all remain anonymous. This is true even of Republican period novels on Jigong, which, despite their popularity (and repeated pirating), usually survive in as few as one or two copies worldwide, and whose authors remain unknown.

Vernacular fiction is thus "popular" in the sense that despite its wide dissemination (in written form among the educated, in oral form throughout society), prior to the modern era it has seldom been deemed a respectable genre. It is largely in this sense, I believe, that the adjective "popular" is also applicable to Chinese religion. The body of religious beliefs and practices we now call "Chinese religion" or "Chinese popular religion" has by no means been limited to the peasantry or the lower echelons of urban society. At least some aspects of it have been prevalent throughout society, even though colored in different hues by different social groups. Jigong, for example, has been worshipped by peasants and members of the educated elite alike, but his cult has taken different shapes in diverse social strata: for example, whereas the crazy god manifested himself to peasants in the possessed bodies of mediums, he communicated with the educated through spirit writing.[3] Some members of the elite worshipped Crazy Ji, many others venerated other deities, and they experienced other aspects of the popular religion, such as divination and participation in religious holidays, as well. However, even as they partook of the popular religion, the literati were somewhat hesitant about their participation in it. This religious, or "superstitious," dimension of their lives was something private and was not paraded and displayed to the same degree as their cultural achievements. Just as they authored vernacular novels under pseudonyms, members of the educated classes were not keen on admitting the fervor with which they themselves, or members of their families, worshipped this or that popular deity. In some instances, they were hostile toward certain aspects of the popular religion, which they associated with the unruly masses. Thus, vernacular fiction enjoyed a position similar to that of the religion, for which, as I try to argue in this book, it has served as a vehicle. Both were widespread. Neither was very respected. It is probably because vernacular fiction did not enjoy an honored, let alone "sacred," position in Chinese culture that little attention has been paid to its significant impact on the Chinese religious mentality.

Three more terms need to be briefly addressed—"saint," "deity," and "god" are the titles by which I interchangeably describe the divinity of this book's protagonist, Crazy Ji. Chinese religion is polytheistic, and the Chinese laity has for centuries been venerating a great multitude of deities with diverse characteristics: old, young, male, female, martial, clownish. One characteristic is, however, common to almost all these gods: as Henri Maspero has pointed out, most Chinese deities were humans promoted posthumously to the ranks of the gods. Like Crazy Ji, most Chinese deities are historical figures, and even those modern scholarship has shown not to be are still presented as such. Unlike the infinitely remote god of the monotheistic religions, Chinese deities, who were all once human, share many characteristics as well as a close relationship with their devotees. Thus, in terms of their intimacy with the believer, Chinese deities resemble Catholic saints more than the monotheistic god, on behalf of whom they serve as intermediaries. However, even as the term "saint" captures the ease with which Chinese believers communicate with their gods, its application is in some ways misleading. First, "saint" implies notions of spirituality, renunciation of the world, and mortification of the flesh completely alien to Chinese popular religion. Crazy Ji delights in meat and wine, and many Chinese gods, far from being contemplative ascetics, are ruthless warriors whose martial skills earned them their divinity. Second, it is my impression that Chinese gods are seen as more powerful by believers than are Catholic saints. Indeed, unlike the latter, they do not function as intermediaries for an almighty creator; their divine powers are inherent in their persons. For these reasons I have opted to use "saint," "deity," and "god" interchangeably to highlight different facets of Jigong's personality. For example, in the case of novels on Crazy Ji, which are dedicated to his human career, I often found the title "saint" felicitous. However, for the description of Jigong's cult, the terms "deity" and "god" usually seemed more appropriate.

Crazy Ji

Chinese Religion and Popular Literature

INTRODUCTION

Religion and Vernacular Fiction in China

Unities and diversities coexist in the Chinese religious tradition. Even though each of China's diverse regions had its own religious tradition, certain features are shared throughout the vast Chinese state. Certain gods, for example, are worshipped only in specific localities: a given province, county, linguistic region, river basin, city, or even village. However, other gods—many of whom were originally worshipped in one locality only—figure today in religious cults throughout China, or at least in vast regions of it. To name just a few examples: the deities Guangong, Zhenwu (Xuantian shangdi), the Eight Immortals (Baxian), Nazha, Sun Wukong, Guanyin, and Mazu (Tianhou) are objects of worship in diverse regions. Evidently, in the case of the Chinese supernatural, regional diversity and a measure of cross-regional unity are not mutually exclusive.

The coexistence of local deities and cross-regional cults illustrates the complex interaction of regional identity and national culture in China. Local deities are the products of regional culture, whereas cross-regional cults evince the existence of a Chinese culture (and religion) that transcends regional boundaries. How do the two interact? What are the mechanisms that spread a national culture across regional (and linguistic) boundaries, and how do these processes of cultural equalization relate to regional cultures? To return to the example of cults of deities: Which processes transform a local deity into a nationwide one? How is a cult transmitted from one region to another, and how is the god's image shaped across regional (and linguistic) boundaries?

The question of the dissemination of cults devoted to particular gods is complex because Chinese religion has no unifying church or canonical body of sacred scriptures. Here a comparison between the amorphous Chinese religion and the so-called institutionalized religions of China might be helpful. Scholars sometimes refer to Chinese religion as a "diffused" religion. They distinguish it from the institutionalized religions of Taoism and Buddhism, each of which has a clergy conscious of its own religious identity. In the case of these institutionalized religions, the transmission of religious meaning is relatively easy to explain, since the Taoist and Buddhist establishments have been committed to the propagation of their respective ideologies. Thus, for example, Taoist and Buddhist clergy have spread the fame of the divinities they worshipped by building temples in their honor and by celebrating their supernatural powers in canonical scriptures. However, the amorphous popular religion has no such nationwide clerical organization, nor a universally respected body of scriptures. How, then, were the cults of its deities transmitted?

To be sure, the question of the transmission of cults to deities can be approached from diverse angles. Recent scholarship has suggested several avenues of research into the question of diversity and unity in the Chinese pantheon of divinities. One approach stresses the significance of the state in creating a unified, pan-Chinese image of the supernatural. The Chinese state bureaucracy somewhat resembled a church in function vis-à-vis the popular religion. The emperor granted titles of divinity to local deities, thereby transforming them into the objects of a nationwide official cult. Thus the state played an important role in spreading the fame of those deities whose cults it sanctioned.[1] Another approach emphasizes the role of travelers in transferring cults from one region to another. Scholars have pointed out the importance of various peripatetic groups—merchants, government officials, migrants, pilgrims—in proclaiming the efficacy of deities across regional boundaries.[2]

Another promising avenue of research concerns the role of diverse media—both performing and visual arts—in the shaping of deities' images. A large body of scholarship has pointed out the significance of drama in shaping Chinese social norms and religious beliefs. Traditional Chinese drama, like much of modern Chinese television and film production, is concerned with the supernatural. Whether performed by human actors or by puppets, traditional plays often narrated the divine careers of the gods. The theater did more, however, than just transmit myths about the gods; it also helped shape believers' conceptions of their appearance. Actors on stage were costumed consistently with the gods' temple iconography.[3] This leads us to the significance of the visual arts in shaping popular conceptions of the gods' appearance. Substantial research has been dedicated, for example, to the role of woodblock prints in propagating the gods' images. Cheap, usually colorful, prints brought such images into homes, where these visual representations served as objects of worship.[4]

Other media have helped transmit cults and mold their characteristics. For example, I allude below to Jigong's image in sectarian literature (known by the generic name *baojuan* or "precious scrolls") as well as in the edifying genre of "morality books" (*shanshu*). Ultimately, then, no one mechanism can explain the degree of unity that characterizes Chinese conceptions of the supernatural across regional boundaries. This is because various groups of people, ranging from government officials to migrants, and diverse media, including both performing and visual arts, have contributed equally to the dissemination of cults and the fashioning of the gods' images.

In this book I do not attempt to survey all the various agents and media that have contributed to the transmission of Chinese cults. Instead I focus on one medium, which, I will argue, has played a crucial role in bringing a measure of unity to Chinese conceptions of the supernatural in late imperial and modern times. This medium is vernacular fiction, both written and oral. As we will see below, a large body of vernacular fiction, especially novels, narrates the divine careers of the gods. A survey of the Chinese supernatural might well reveal that most deities whose cults transcend regional boundaries are the subject of vernacular fiction. I will suggest that during the late imperial and modern periods fiction has played a crucial role in the transmission of these deities' cults and the shaping of their divine personae.

The written vernacular has enjoyed a wide audience in late imperial and modern times. The reason lies in its relation to oral literature and drama. As the fiction on this book's protagonist, Jigong, demonstrates, many novels on the supernatural served as a source for oral literature and drama in local dialects. Thus, those who could not read the novels heard them narrated by storytellers or saw them performed on stage. Oral literature and drama, both of which were performed in local dialects, brought the novel to the unlettered masses in different regions. Thus vernacular fiction, through its wide reach, influenced conceptions of the supernatural in practically every segment of late imperial society.

The key to understanding written fiction's role as a mediator between national and regional cultures lies in its relation to oral literature (and drama) in local dialects. The medium of regional culture is the spoken dialect, and it is exactly this medium that creates barriers among China's diverse regional cultures. Because the oral literature and drama of any given region is performed in that region's local dialect, the contents are often incomprehensible to speakers of other dialects. This is what gives the standardized written vernacular its crucial significance as a bridge across the various spoken dialects. As evinced by the evolution of Jigong lore, written novels in the vernacular often derive from oral literature in one dialect, at the same time that they serve as a source for oral literature in others. Thus, one region's local culture becomes an integral part of other regional cultures as well. In this process, regional lore is transformed into what may be termed a "national" culture.

In this book I suggest the following paradigm: the myth of a given regional deity would usually be transmitted first orally in that region's local dialect. If, and when, this local lore was recorded in a novel, then the latter would transmit the story to other regions. The novel would then serve as a source for oral literature (and drama) in local dialects other than the original one. The god, whose myth had been transmitted originally in one dialect only, would be celebrated now in diverse forms of oral literature and drama, each in its own regional dialect. Often, though not always, the cult to this deity would follow a similar route of dispersal. At least in some cases, in any given region the first signs of the deity's cult would follow the emergence of regional lore on him there, which itself derives from novels.

Needless to say, this is only a paradigm, which like all others of its kind is the result of a process of abstraction. We would be hard-pressed to find actual cases that correspond precisely to it (even though the example of this book's divine protagonist, Jigong, does). In the majority of cases, the paradigm would have to be revised, or supplemented, in order to allow room for variation. To give just one example, many novels on the supernatural derive from, in addition to oral literature, sources ranging from official histories to Buddhist and Taoist scriptures to short tales in the classical language. Some novels may not derive from oral literature at all. However, I would suggest that, whatever their origins, the impact these novels exercised on the popular religion was largely related to their ability to penetrate local cultures. This ability was in turn due to the novels' role as a source for oral literature and drama in regional dialects.

We should note, further, that many cults had crossed regional boundaries long before their deities figured as the subject of the written vernacular. Evidently the veneration of these deities had spread for centuries by means other than the novel. However, even when a deity had enjoyed a long history of cross-regional veneration prior to its appearance in a novel, the latter could still influence its cult. The novel could amplify the cult, spread it further geographically, and contribute to its temporal dissemination to future generations. Whatever the novel's date of publication relative to the history of the cult, it could play an important role in shaping future adaptations of the deity's myth.

The novel's power to influence the later stages of a cult is related to its ability to transform the deity's image. Storytellers and novelists could alter the personality of a divine protagonist in ways that changed its appeal. A novel's portrayal of a deity could have direct impact, therefore, on that deity's clientele. We will see in the following chapters how a nineteenth-century novel's transformation of Jigong's image significantly increased his circle of worshippers. This novel, *The Storyteller's Jigong*, portrayed its divine protagonist as a martial artist and the champion of the poor in their struggle against abusive authority. Thus, it provided Jigong's cult with the symbolic resources that made it, for the first time, attractive to social bandits and rebels.

I have highlighted the significance of the local dialect as the linguistic medium that ultimately enables lore about the gods to penetrate the local culture of a given region and mentioned the importance of the written standardized vernacular (in which most novels were written) in bridging various local dialects. A similar interplay of written standardized idioms (both the vernacular and the classical) and local dialects may be evident in the case of liturgical texts. Chinfa Lien has compared Taoist texts collected in Taiwan with their antecedents in the Taoist canon and found in the Taiwanese texts evidence of linguistic adaptation to the Min dialect, in which they were performed in Taiwan. Thus an interplay of standardized written idioms and local dialects may have played a significant role not only in transmission of myth but also in the dissemination of ritual.[5]

Literati Observations

At least some Qing period literati, including several fiction writers, were aware of vernacular fiction's role in the transmission of cults to deities. Some even noted the mechanisms by which fiction influences the religious beliefs of the unlettered masses. They highlighted the relation between written novels in the vernacular and oral literature and drama, emphasizing that in it lies the key to fiction's widespread dissemination. Cao Xueqin (1715?–63), author of the *Dream of the Red Chamber*, voiced his recognition of fiction's religious impact through his protagonist Baoyu, who does not believe in the reality of popular gods precisely because fiction serves as the vehicle that spreads their cults. Baoyu explains:

> I hate the silly, senseless way in which vulgar people offer worship and build temples to gods they know nothing about. Ignorant old men and women with too much money to spend hear the name of some god or other—they've no idea who it is, but the mere fact that they've heard some unfounded tale or piece of fiction [*yeshi xiaoshuo*] seems to them incontrovertible proof of the god's existence—and go founding temples in which these fictitious deities can be worshipped.[6]

Cao Xueqin's protagonist employs the verb "to hear" in his description of fiction's impact on the dissemination of deities' cults. Evidently, in Baoyu's view, oral fiction influences the "ignorant old men and women" whom he holds in such contempt. Another eighteenth-century literatus, the prolific historian Qian Daxin (1728–1804), provides an even fuller explanation of fiction's impact on the religious beliefs of the masses. According to Qian, those who cannot read fiction hear it or see it performed. In other words, written fiction is capable of shaping beliefs because it is related both to oral literature and to drama. Interestingly, Qian saw fiction and religion as so inextricably linked that he chose to term the latter "fiction" (*xiaoshuo*). (The amorphous body of religious beliefs that scholars refer to nowadays as "Chinese religion" did not have a name in late imperial times.) He wrote:

Of old there were three religions (*jiao*): Confucianism, Buddhism, and Taoism.[7] Since Ming times [1368–1644] there has been one more, called *xiaoshuo* (fiction). Works of fiction and historical romances (*yanyi*) do not proclaim themselves a religion. Nevertheless, among literati (*shidafu*), peasants, workers, and merchants alike, there is no one who is not familiar with them. Even children, women, and illiterate persons have all heard [these stories] or seen them [performed]. This [i.e., fiction] is their religion, and compared with Confucianism, Buddhism and Taoism, it is more widespread.[8]

Qian discussed the relation between fiction and religion in general terms. Other authors singled out specific novels for their impact on religious life. Tao Chengzhang (d. 1911) attributed the success of the White Lotus sect in north China and that of the Heaven and Earth Society in the south to the influence of the novels *Enfeoffment of the Gods* (*Fengshen yanyi*) and *Water Margin* (*Shuihu zhuan*), respectively: "Throughout the area of Shandong, Shanxi, and Henan [i.e., the north] there is no one who does not believe (*zunxin*) in the *Enfeoffment of the Gods* story. Throughout the area of Jiangsu, Zhejiang, Fujian, and Guangzhou [the south], there is no one who does not venerate (*chongbai*) the book *Water Margin*."[9] Another late Qing literatus, Wu Yong (fl. 1900), traced the Boxer Uprising to the impact of these same novels (*Enfeoffment of the Gods* and *Water Margin*), as well as the *Journey to the West* (*Xiyou ji*), on the uneducated masses of north China. Interestingly, Wu Yong distinguished two types of vernacular fiction that shaped popular belief: novels on the supernatural (such as *Enfeoffment of the Gods* and *Journey to the West*) and novels on martial heroes (such as *Water Margin*).[10]

Aware of fiction's role in the shaping of the supernatural, some fiction writers even noted the possibility that the products of their imagination might unwittingly become the object of religious cults. They observed that once a fictional character caught the readers' fancy, it could—contrary to its creator's intentions—be worshipped as a deity. A character named Xu Sheng, in one of Pu Songling's (1640–1715) tales, arrives in Fujian province, where, to his astonishment, the local people worship the simian protagonist of the *Journey to the West*, Sun Wukong. Xu Sheng shares Baoyu's disdain for ignorant people who worship fictitious creations: "Sun Wukong is nothing but a parable (*yuyan*) invented by [the novelist] old Qiu," he protests. "How can people sincerely believe in him?"[11] The narrator points out in the tale's epilogue that fictitious characters, once created, are independent of their creator's will. Deities exist because people believe they do, and fictional characters can thus be transformed into *real* gods, once they are conceived of as such by readers. He proceeds to illustrate his point:

> A gentleman once passed by a temple and painted a mandolin on the wall. By the time he came to the spot again, the efficacy (*ling*) of this mandolin was renowned, and incense was being burned there nonstop. Certainly, it isn't necessary for someone [like Sun Wukong] to actually exist in this world: if people believe someone to be efficacious, then he will be efficacious for them.[12]

Fiction on the Supernatural

I have marshaled statements by some Qing period literati to suggest that vernacular fiction played an important role in the dissemination of cults. However, how wide is the body of vernacular fiction on the supernatural? How many novels are dedicated to deities' careers? Or, conversely, how many deities figure in novels? As early as 1952 Willem Grootaers noted the significance of the late Ming novel *Journey to the North* (*Beiyou ji*) in the dissemination of Zhenwu's cult,[13] and recent studies have revealed that such popular deities as Guangong, Huaguang, Guanyin, Mazu, the Eight Immortals (Baxian), and Zhong Kui figure prominently in vernacular fiction.[14] Chapters 3–6 of this book are dedicated to an examination of novels' role in the spread of Jigong's cult. These studies, however, are but a beginning; the overwhelming majority of novels concerned with the supernatural have not yet been studied. This vast literature, classified by Sun Kaidi as *lingguai xiaoshuo* (fiction on the supernatural), is as yet uncharted.[15] Some of the most important novels in question, such as the *Enfeoffment of the Gods* (early seventeenth century?), have not even been dated.[16] Future studies may well reveal that this literature features most of the gods whose late imperial and modern cults cross regional boundaries. (See Table 1 for a few examples of deities who figure in novels.)

The little we know about *lingguai* novels suggests that they can be divided into two types. The first consists of hagiographic novels, which focus primarily on one deity. They outline the deity's career (which often has a human stage followed by a divine one), describe his or her supernatural powers, and recount the miracles performed

TABLE I
Some Deities and Some of the Novels in Which They Figure

Deity	The Novel(s)
Guanyin	*Nanhai Guanyin quanzhuan* (Wanli period, 1573–1620) *Journey to the West* (1592)
Mazu	*Tianfei niangma zhuan* (Wanli period)
Guangong	*Romance of the Three Kingdoms* (late Yuan) and antecedents
Xuantian shangdi (Zhenwu)	*Journey to the North* (Wanli period)
Jiang ziya	*Enfeoffment of the Gods* (early 17th c.?)
Sun Wukong	*Journey to the West* (1592), antecedents and sequel
Nazha santaizi	*Enfeoffment of the Gods* *Journey to the West*
Huaguang tianwang	*Journey to the South* (Wanli period) *Journey to the North* (Wanli period)
The Eight Immortals (as a group or individually)	*Journey to the East* (Wanli period) *Feijian ji* (Wanli period) *Han Xianzi quanzhuan* (1623) *Lüzu quanzhuan* (1662) and sequels
Jigong	*The Recorded Sayings* (1569) and sequels
Zhong Kui	*Zhong Kui quanzhuan* (Wanli period) and sequels

by the god on behalf of humanity. During the Wanli period (1573–1620), a group of publishers in Jianyang, Fujian, published several novels that belong in this category. They portray such deities as Zhenwu, Huaguang, Guanyin, Mazu, Zhong Kui, Bodhidharma (Damo), and the Eight Immortals.[17] The Jianyang novels are closely interrelated; some deities that are the subject of one novel appear as secondary characters in others. Huaguang, for example, is the subject of a novel entitled *Journey to the South* (*Nanyou ji*), but he figures also in a novel dedicated to Zhenwu, *Journey to the North*.[18] Several deities have been the subject of an entire series of hagiographic novels, the study of which can help us unravel the deity's history.

Zhong Kui, the Eight Immortals, and this book's protagonist, Jigong, are three examples.

The second type of *lingguai* fiction consists of large-scale novels that portray an enormous cast of supernatural characters, even if they focus on only a few of them. The two prime examples are the *Journey to the West* (1592) and the *Enfeoffment of the Gods*, both of which were published, like the Jianyang novels, during the late Ming. The *Journey to the West* has a Buddhist bent, even though it features many deities of Taoist origin. Conversely, the *Enfeoffment of the Gods* is oriented to Taoism, but it also celebrates many Buddhist deities. Between them, the two novels describe almost every god in the interregional pantheon of late imperial China.[19] Thus these two enormously popular novels alone could have served as vehicles for the transmission of the cults of numerous deities. Many deities who are the subject of a hagiographic novel are also portrayed in one of these larger-scale works of mythology. Guanyin, for example, is the subject of a Jianyang novel, but her appearance as one of the primary protagonists of the *Journey to the West* probably played an even greater role in the spread of her cult.

Novels on the supernatural (*lingguai*) were not the only ones to spread gods' cults. A novelist did not have to portray his subjects as deities for his novel to serve as a vehicle for their veneration. As Henri Maspero has noted, in China "every god, great or small, is a man who, after death, was promoted for various reasons to the dignity of a god."[20] Thus, even if a novel portrays only the human stage of a deity's career, it could still contribute significantly to the promotion of that god's cult. Two notable examples are the novels *Romance of the Three Kingdoms* (*Sanguo yanyi*; probably late Yuan) and *Water Margin* (probably Yuan-Ming), neither of which is classified by bibliographers as *lingguai* fiction. By and large these two martial novels portray their heroic protagonists as humans, not as gods.[21] Nonetheless, these novels probably contributed to the transformation of their human protagonists (especially Guangong in the *Romance of the Three Kingdoms* and Song Jiang in the *Water Margin*) into gods, whose cults spread throughout China.

Vernacular Fiction and the Shaping of Gods' Images

A large number of late Ming and Qing novels celebrate the careers of the gods. I have suggested that because these novels are related to oral literature and drama in local dialects, they have played an important role in the dissemination of cults dedicated to their divine protagonists. If this is indeed the case, then the question arises of how the medium of vernacular fiction has influenced the images of the gods, whose veneration it has helped foster. Does vernacular fiction lend a special flavor to the deities it portrays? Do the gods, as depicted in vernacular fiction, share certain tendencies in terms of their personalities as well as in their social and cultural traits?

The question of the novels' portrayal of the gods needs to be discussed in relation to the multivocality that characterizes Chinese deities, each of which has often been understood differently by diverse social and religious groups.[22] One reason for the deities' multifarious meanings has been the process of mutual borrowings among the various Chinese religions. The popular religion, the state religion, Taoism, Buddhism, and a variety of sectarian religions have borrowed one another's gods, which they then have proceeded to conceive in their own fashion. Thus, one and the same deity may emerge in a completely different light in the imperial decree bestowing upon it a title of divinity (representing its position in the state religion), and in Taoist, Buddhist, and sectarian scriptures. How do novelistic portrayals of deities compare to those found in these genres? Does vernacular fiction highlight aspects of the gods that canonical scriptures tend to obscure?

To take this book's protagonist, Jigong, as a case study, we should note first the heterogeneity of the vernacular tradition itself. Different novels on Jigong portray him in various lights, reflecting the tastes and beliefs of individual authors, the growth of this eccentric saint's religious cult, and, in some cases, the development of the vernacular genre of fiction. One sixteenth-century novel on Jigong was even pieced together from two different texts, which present two disparate conceptions of his image (see Chapter 3). Nonetheless, I will suggest that the portrayals of Jigong in most works of vernacular fiction share certain traits. Exceptions notwithstanding, vernacular fiction tends to highlight Jigong's eccentric and rebellious traits more than do the other genres in which he figures.

All novels on Jigong describe him as an eccentric who defies authority and deviates from accepted norms of behavior. They do differ, however, in their choice of the authority he challenges as well as in the social norms he transgresses. Most novels highlight Jigong's disregard for the laws of the monastic community, to which he belongs. They describe his violation of the Buddhist dietary laws (he eats meat and drinks wine) and, in some novels, his transgression of the monastic vow of chastity (he dallies with courtesans). Other authors emphasize, in addition, Jigong's deviation from what may be described as the accepted norms of politeness. They depict his dirty and shabby appearance and describe his idiosyncrasies: for example, his habit of somersaulting in a manner that reveals his male member to the gaping spectators. Finally, nineteenth-century vernacular fiction added an element of social protest to Jigong's rebelliousness. It transformed Jigong into the skilled leader of a troop of social bandits, who regularly steal from and even murder corrupt officials. Thus, in some novels, the crazy saint becomes the champion of the poor in their struggle against the abusive state (see Chapter 5).

The eccentric and rebellious traits attributed to Jigong in the majority of these novels are usually mitigated in the scriptures (as well as the oral preachings) of those religious establishments that sanctioned his cult. For example, the Unity Sect (Yiguan dao), which adopted Jigong as one of the leading deities in its pantheon, transformed his image to make him adhere to its dietary rules. According to this sectarian religion, Jigong never ate meat or drank wine, and all novelistic accounts to the contrary are false. We find a similar transformation of Jigong's image in the genre of morality books (*shanshu*), which has experienced a recent revival in Taiwan. Morality books are the product of an automatic writing technique, in which one or more persons in a trance wield a writing implement said to be controlled by a deity. The writings thus produced are considered to be divine revelations on the part of the deity in question, and in Taiwan during the 1970s and 1980s this was often Jigong. The Taiwanese morality books advocate sexual prudishness and denounce violent crimes of all sorts. Thus, this literature employs Jigong to voice conservative values, which he himself transgresses in many of the novels dedicated to him.

The attempt to reform Jigong's personality so that it conforms to the ideology of a given religious establishment is also evident in the case of the Buddhist monastic community, which, like the Unity Sect (but much earlier in time), incorporated this crazy saint into its pantheon of divinities. Members of the Buddhist clergy, just as have their Unity Sect counterparts, usually argue that at least some of the antinomian traits attributed to Jigong in works of fiction are false. In the majority of cases, then, the novelistic treatments of Jigong's personality tend to be freer of ideological constraints than are his portrayals in the proselytizing scriptures of organized religious movements. Novelists allow their imagination to roam freer than do the clergy in their portrayal of this divine clown. The result is an image of Jigong in which, usually, his eccentricity and rebelliousness are accentuated. Further, if the sources permitted, a comparison of the written and oral vernacular fiction on Jigong might reveal that the oral versions highlight Jigong's defiance more than do the written. Most oral fiction on Jigong is, of course, forever lost. However, we do have some nineteenth-century handwritten transcriptions of oral narratives on Jigong, and the element of social protest in them tends to be more overt than in the novels, which we know to be derived from these oral narratives. Indeed the novels may represent a conscious effort to muffle the brazen animosity toward officials found in their oral sources.

The history of Jigong's cult suggests therefore that the eccentric and rebellious facets of a deity's personality would often be accentuated in vernacular works of fiction, both oral and written (usually more so in the former than in the latter). By contrast, proselytizing religious literature would usually try to mitigate at least some of the deity's antinomian traits. Canonical scriptures (Buddhist or other), sectarian writings, and morality books would often present a tamer image of the god, one that succumbs to the organized religion's ideological code. To be sure, this paradigm does not apply in every case. It is a mere generalization, which even in Jigong's case needs to be amended to allow for exceptions. For example, we know of at least one seventeenth-century novelist (Wang Mengji) who attempted to tone down the rebellious traits attributed to Jigong in other works of vernacular fiction. His own novel resembles sectarian writings in its attempts to reform its divine protagonist's personality.

The notion that the portrayal of deities in vernacular fiction tends to accentuate their rebellious traits more than does their portrayal in proselytizing and canonical religious literature ignores one important genre (which is irrelevant to the history of Jigong's cult): the classical tale. Some deities figure in prose pieces in the classical idiom (usually in the genre of *zhiguai*, or accounts of the strange), which occasionally highlight even darker aspects of their personalities than vernacular fiction does. Ursula-Angelika Cedzich has shown, for example, that the late Ming *Journey to the South* presents a much more respectable image of the Wutong deities (under their new incarnation, Huaguang) than did earlier classical tales. In the latter they are regularly portrayed as incubi who rape women in their sleep.[23]

Leaving aside the question of the classical tale, is the paradigm suggested by Jigong's cult accurate as far as the vernacular is concerned? Does vernacular fiction tend to highlight the defiant aspects of gods? Are the rebellious aspects characteristic of Jigong's portrayal in works of fiction evident also in the case of other deities? As I have noted above, the vast body of vernacular fiction on the supernatural is by and large uncharted. We have very few studies that examine the images of the gods as portrayed in works of fiction. Nonetheless, it is at least my suspicion that Jigong's case is far from unique, and future studies may well reveal that vernacular fiction tends to color its supernatural protagonists in a defiant tone. Vernacular fiction may well reveal an aspect of the Chinese supernatural that canonical scriptures are prone to conceal.

To give a few examples, as portrayed in vernacular fiction, the defiance, or deviance, of the gods could take a variety of forms. Some deities challenge the traditional family structure, with its hierarchies of age and gender. In the *Enfeoffment of the Gods* the infant Nazha tries consciously to murder his father, and in their respective hagiographic novels, the goddesses Guanyin and Mazu disobey their fathers' command that they wed.[24] Other deities call into question political authority, whether human or divine. Martial deities, such as the *Water Margin* protagonists, engage in social banditry, and the simian protagonist of the *Journey to the West*, Sun Wukong, rebels against the entire heavenly bureaucracy. Finally, some gods, like Jigong, deviate from what can be described as polite norms of behavior. The Eight Immortals, for example, are described, in a series of Ming and Qing novels, as lascivious drunkards.[25] I will suggest, therefore, that, whichever form it takes, a tendency to challenge authority and deviate from accepted social norms does characterize at least some deities as portrayed in vernacular fiction.

The tendency of novels to reveal an eccentric or rebellious facet of the Chinese supernatural could be understood both in terms of their authorship and, perhaps, in terms of certain characteristics of the genre of vernacular fiction. Novels on the supernatural were not written by clergymen. For the most part, they were authored by professional writers, who were often engaged in other forms of popular literature. For example, Guo Xiaoting (fl. 1900), who authored an extremely popular novel on Jigong (*The Storyteller's Jigong*), also published a martial-arts novel, and Tianhua Zang Zhuren (fl. 1650), who authored—or at least wrote the preface to—another Jigong novel (*Drunken Puti*), is known to us as a prolific author of "scholar and beauty" (*caizi jiaren*) romances. The fact that they did not belong to a religious establishment, nor indeed to the government bureaucracy, provided these authors with the freedom to explore various aspects of their divine protagonists' personae. For this reason, their portrayal of the gods could satisfy symbolic needs not met by the establishment's interpretations.

Beyond the relative freedom enjoyed by fiction writers, we may also note the ambiguous position occupied by vernacular fiction in late imperial culture. I mention in the Preface that despite, or perhaps because of, their enormous popularity, many novels were not considered significant literature (not to mention sacred). This is certainly true of fiction on this book's protagonist: the authors of most novels on Jigong remain anonymous, and the novels themselves were not deemed worthy of preservation—some are forever lost, and others survive in a handful of copies worldwide. This ambiguous attitude toward many novels was related both to their vernacular medium (respected genres were usually written in the classical language) and, perhaps, to a certain ideological bent that characterizes at least some of them. As Patrick Hanan has pointed out, vernacular fiction often treats aspects of Chinese society and culture that the classical tradition usually leaves obscure.[26] For example, physical heroism and sex figure in vernacular fiction much more prominently than in genres written in the classical language. I would suggest that an examination of vernacular fiction might reveal that, just as it highlighted aspects of Chinese social life largely ignored by the classical tradition, it throws significant new light on the Chinese supernatural.

Recent scholarship has made us increasingly aware of the complex relations between the Chinese supernatural and the Chinese sociopolitical order. We know now that the Chinese heavens did not simply mirror China's political system, nor did they merely reify its social hierarchy. Whereas many Chinese gods are often imagined as the heavenly counterparts of earthly bureaucrats, many others are not. Even though one facet of the Chinese supernatural has been fashioned after the bureaucratic order of the Chinese state, the Chinese pantheon of divinities has other facets as well.[27] A study of Chinese deities as portrayed in vernacular fiction may contribute to our understanding of the multivocality that characterizes the Chinese heavens. The eccentric and rebellious traits that vernacular fiction attributes to such deities as Jigong demonstrate that the Chinese supernatural does not merely reflect the existing order. It also contests it and compensates for it.

Deities and Social Order

As portrayed in vernacular fiction, Jigong reveals an upside-down dimension of the Chinese supernatural. Eccentric, rebellious, and clownish, he inhabits a world in which defiance and deviance are the norms. What impact have deities such as Jigong had on the social structure against which their cults have emerged? Does Jigong serve as a model to his devotees? Do they follow him in defying the system? Or, on the contrary, does this divine clown soothe the pains of their social existence in a manner that ultimately enables the latter to persist?

Historians of medieval Europe have asked a similar question regarding the functions of carnival in medieval society. Mikhail Bakhtin's description of the culture of carnival captures at least some characteristics of deities such as Jigong as portrayed in Chinese vernacular fiction: "A boundless world of humorous forms and manifestations opposed the official and serious tone of medieval ecclesiastical and feudal culture. . . . A second life, a second world of folk culture, is thus constructed; it is to a certain extent a parody of the extracarnival life, a 'world inside out.'"[28] How does this second world interact with the one it has turned "inside out"? Does the carnival function as a safety valve, allowing society to let off steam (and thereby ultimately strengthening the social order)? Or does it lead to the actual questioning of the existing system?

Historians such as Emmanuel Le Roy Ladurie have shown that the carnival could function both ways. On the one hand, the carnival coexisted with the hierarchical world against which it had emerged. It offered all members of society a temporary respite from this world without endangering it. On the other hand, given the right historical circumstances (as in Romans, France, in 1580), theater and reality merged as the carnival turned into a bloody revolt.[29] The following chapters reveal a similar complexity in the social and political circumstances of Jigong's cult. Whereas some devotees of this crazy god did follow his example and challenge the system, others did not. Rebels, outlaws, and bandits have chosen Jigong as their tutelary deity because they have perceived in his image a potential for resistance. Concurrently, the cult of this divine madman has been sanctioned by social groups who, far from challenging the system, are staunch supporters of it. Thus Jigong has been worshipped simultaneously by rebels, bandits, and members of the elite. Each of these groups has tried to manipulate Jigong's image for its own ideological purposes.

The history of Jigong's cult suggests that a deity's potential as a locus of resistance, even when exploited, can be variously directed. The example of Crazy Ji may be emulated in diverse contexts, ranging from the family to the political arena. Children may evoke the model of the scruffy Jigong to explain their refusal to wash, and disgruntled rebels may use him as a rallying point for social discontent. In some instances Jigong's image has been used by one and the same group as a symbol for one type of resistance and another type of acquiescence. Here the novels figuring Jigong provide us with interesting examples. *The Storyteller's Jigong*, for example, depicts Jigong as the champion of the poor in their struggle against abusive authority; at the same time it uses him as a mouthpiece for conservative family values. As portrayed in this novel, Jigong is a Robin Hood–type bandit, who cherishes the values of filial piety and sexual chastity. The eccentric Jigong could thus simultaneously challenge one set of hierarchies and validate another. In this instance he questions political authority, even as he endorses the traditional family hierarchy (see Chapter 5).

Comparative Notes

Vernacular fiction was not written by clergymen, and its multifarious meanings defy doctrinal purposes. And yet, this genre, as I hope to demonstrate in the following chapters, has played a crucial role in shaping Chinese conceptions of the supernatural. In this respect, vernacular fiction resembles another literary genre, which, in the context of other polytheistic religions, has played a similar role. This is epic poetry. Despite the fact that it was composed by poets, not clerics, epic poetry contributed enormously to the creation and the dissemination of both the Greek and the Hindu pantheons of divinities. Writing of the former case, Walter Burkert comments: "Religious texts in the narrow sense of sacred texts are scarcely to be found: there is no holy scripture and barely even fixed prayer formulae and liturgies. . . . [Rather], interweaving tales of the gods with heroic narratives, epic poetry, pre-eminently the Homeric *Iliad*, set its seal on the way the gods were imagined."[30] The similarities between vernacular fiction and epic poetry extend into the mechanisms that enabled them to influence large segments of society. Epic poetry, like vernacular fiction, has been intimately related both to oral literature and to drama, media that brought its narratives to the unlettered masses. Of course, many works of epic poetry were composed for oral performance. But, in addition, epic poetry has served as a source for storytellers performing in other oral genres, as well as for playwrights. Thus, for example, the sixteenth-century epic of Tulsidas, the *Rāmcaritmānas*, is continuously reinterpreted in northern India in a large variety of oral and dramatic genres.[31]

If the Chinese, Greek, and Hindu religious traditions resemble each other in that in all three a genre that cannot be narrowly construed as religious has played a crucial role in shaping conceptions of the supernatural, then they also resemble each other in another respect: originally none had a name. The body of religious beliefs and practices nowadays referred to by scholars as "Chinese religion" or "Chinese popular religion" had no name in late imperial times, just as the Greek and Hindu religious traditions lacked ones. (The term "Hinduism" was coined by British scholars.) In one respect, the role that vernacular fiction and epic poetry played in the shaping of these religious traditions may help us understand why it is that they lacked names—they were inseparable from the cultures within which they emerged. C. K. Yang has pointed out that the amorphous Chinese religion has no institutions independent of the building blocks of Chinese society: the family, the clan, the guild, the state.[32] We are now in a position to supplement his insight: in terms of its textual tradition, Chinese religion is inseparable from vernacular fiction and drama. It is exactly because Chinese religion did not exist as an entity independent of Chinese society and culture that it had no name in late imperial times.

Finally, a note that pertains to comparative literature. In this introductory chapter, I have followed the common practice of applying the Western term "novel" to lengthy narratives in vernacular Chinese (which are usually referred to in the original as *xiaoshuo*, or *changpian xiaoshuo* [lit., "lengthy *xiaoshuo*"]). And yet the religious dimension of these narratives alerts us that in one sense at least this application is misleading. The term "novel" has been applied in the West primarily to works whose subject matter is human experience.

Of course, many Chinese narratives are concerned with the human realm, but the subject of many others is the supernatural. Their protagonists are deities, whose religious powers are never questioned, even when they themselves are portrayed humorously. Whereas in the West, the human and the divine are strictly separated, in China they are not. Perhaps because most Chinese gods were originally humans the same literary genre can be applied to both.

PART I

Daoji the Man

ONE

Daoji the Man

Daoji (?–1209) did not occupy a prominent position in the monastic establishment of his time. In fact, his name is hardly mentioned in Song and Yuan Buddhist literature. "Transmission of the lamp" texts, which list the names of eminent masters in the Chan lineage, do not mention him; his name does not appear, for example, in the *Jiatai Period Record of the Universal Transmission of the Lamp* (*Jiatai Pu deng lu*; 1204) or the *Five Lamps' Compendium* (*Wudeng huiyuan*; 1253). Nor is he referred to in records of important monastic events such as the *Record of the Lineages of Buddhas and Patriarchs* (*Fozu tongji*; 1271) or the *Comprehensive Record of the Successive Generations of Buddhas and Patriarchs* (*Fozu lidai tongzai*; 1344). The only contemporary Buddhist source with a biography of him testifies to the eccentric monk's problematic position within the monastic community. This is *Beixian's Collected Prose Writings* (hereafter: *Collected Prose*; preface dated 1217) by the eminent Chan master Jujian (1164–1246).[1]

Jujian spent most of his religious career in various monasteries in Zhejiang province; his pen name "Beixian" (Northern Stream) reflects the period he resided in seclusion by the Northern Stream in the outskirts of Hangzhou. In his later years, he served as the abbot of the Jingci Monastery, also in the vicinity of Hangzhou.[2] Chapter 10 of Jujian's collected writings include his eulogies of eminent monks and officials. The eulogies were inscribed on the deceased's stūpa, or memorial tablet. In the case of Daoji, the eulogy was inscribed on the reliquary that contained his cremated remains (*sheli*; *śarīra*).[3] Each inscription is preceded in the text of Jujian's *Collected*

Prose by a brief biographical sketch of the deceased. Daoji's memorial inscription and biography read:

Inscription on the Śarīra Relics of the Recluse from the Lake, Elder Fangyuan (Square-Circle), Jidian (Crazy Ji)[4]

As for *śarīra* relics, whoever does even one good deed regularly has them. However, if the cremation (*zhewei; jhāpita*) method is not used, they cannot be seen.[5] Because of the sparkling *śarīra* relics of the Recluse from the Lake, Elder Fangyuan, the people of the capital [i.e., Hangzhou] became flustered, and the news was blown out of proportion. This is because they do not know this [i.e., that whoever does even one good deed regularly has such relics].

The elder was from Tiantai county in Linhai prefecture [in modern Zhejiang]. He was a descendant of Commandant Li Wenhe.[6] He was ordained at the Lingyin Monastery by the Chan Master Fohai.[7] He was wild and carefree yet upright and pure. He would not soften his critiques (*zhuyu*), which on the whole were not in line with the accepted norms. His achievements were in many respects outstanding. He had the same exquisite poetic skill as the famous monks of the Jin [265–420] and the [Liu] Song [420–79] periods.

He wandered over half the land;[8] for four decades he was a disillusioned vagabond. On Mount Tiantai and Mount Yandang[9] [both in Zhejiang], he adorned the walls of secluded huts and hidden cloisters[10] with exquisitely elegant writings. Hot or cold, he never had a whole garment to his body; whenever one was donated to him, he would immediately use it to pay the waiter in the wine shop. His bed and meals were never regularly provided. He devotedly prepared medicines[11] for old and sick monks. Yet when it came to visiting powerful households, he would not go if they tried to compel him for no good reason.

He was quite similar to the Sichuanese monk Zujue.[12] [However,] Zujue excelled him in his sense of humor. When Zujue died, the elder [Daoji] asked me to write a eulogy to be offered at his funeral. It reads:

> . . . The Master [Zujue] was not restrained either. Endowed with a love of jest and a sharp wit, he did not follow the common path to the other shore. Yet he never arbitrarily transgressed the rules. He walked alone barefooted and, in remote places, shed the dust of this world. Once he passed through the gates of enlightenment, one day equaled a thousand aeons. Employing humor, he far transcended the world of dust. The ignorant ones did not understand this.
>
> He followed the dharma and accorded with compassion. He took refuge in emptiness. Abandoning the cities, he discarded stately mansions[13] and paid no heed to the [welcoming] crowds [awaiting him in them]. He considered the changing and formless to be the true teaching. He rejected that which is fixed and clearly defined as mere

pleasantry. Thus he died while sitting in the meditation posture; he entered nirvāṇa while standing erect.[14]

As to the people who vainly boast and brag, the spread of their desires is the root of the false Buddha. Speaking with his lay followers, he made the following point: "This is not what we call the Way. If our spiritual teaching is to forge ahead, then inevitably it will offend these people. If it does not offend these people, it can not be considered the spiritual teaching. This is what we call the 'Way.' "

The elder [Daoji] said: "Wonderful! You can also offer this eulogy at my funeral." By the time he passed away, [I realized] that indeed he was not inferior to Zujue. I therefore read this piece as an offering to him. My promise was thus fulfilled.

The elder's name was Daoji. He was also called Huyin (The Recluse from the Lake) and Elder Fangyuan (Square-Circle). All these names were given to him by his contemporaries. He passed away at the Jingci Monastery on the fourteenth day of the fifth month, the second year of the Jiading period [June 17, 1209]. The local people sorted his *śarīra* remains and stored them below the Twin Peak.

The [*śarīra*] inscription [I wrote] reads:

The jade disc was not smashed;[15] who left these behind?
Sparse stars, dense stars, as bright as the sun.
The shark did not shed tears;[16] who stirred the waves?
Big pearls, small pearls, rushing together to a plate.[17]

Jujian's *Collected Prose* provides important data: for example, the names of the monasteries in which Daoji was ordained and passed away (see Map 1). Perhaps more significantly, his account brings to life the eccentric monk's personality. Daoji was sharp, witty, unrestrained, and wild. Yet he was also a man of integrity and compassion; "he devotedly prepared medicines for sick and old monks." By the time he passed away, Jujian was convinced of his worth and offered him the eulogy he had originally written for Zujue. However, even as he expressed respect for Daoji's religious integrity, Jujian left no doubt that Daoji was far from the mainstream of the monastic community of his time. Most of his life Daoji did not even reside in a monastery. "A disillusioned vagabond" for four decades, he led the life of a wandering monk. His travels covered Zhejiang province, demarcated by Mount Tiantai, Mount Yandang, and the West Lake, which earned him his alias The Recluse from the Lake. So poor was he that "his bed and meals were never regularly provided." Jujian does not mention that Daoji ever held a clerical post. The title—"elder" (*sou*)—by which Jujian refers to him also reflects Daoji's lack of standing within the monastic hierarchy. In contrast, Jujian refers to most other monks in his eulogies by terms denoting eminence within the monastic establishment: *chanshi* (Chan master), *fashi* (Vinaya master), or *dashi* (eminent master). The *Collected Prose* even hints of possible conflicts between Daoji and contemporary clerics: "If our spiritual teaching is to forge ahead," it quotes, "inevitably it will offend these people."

The schism between Daoji and the Buddhist establishment was certainly related to his disregard for the accepted norms of the monastic community, for which he received the nickname "Crazy Ji." "He was wild and carefree" writes Jujian; "he did not follow the common path to the other shore," he further elaborates in the eulogy. The hallmark of Daoji's eccentric behavior was his apparently habitual drinking: "whenever [a cassock] was donated to him, he would immediately use it to pay the waiter in the wine shop." Eccentric traits were perhaps characteristics of the Chan school as a whole, if not as a living tradition during the Song, then at least as a literary ideal. They are reflected in the shouting (*he*) and beating (*da*) practices described in the "Recorded Sayings" of famous Tang masters, such as Linji Yixuan (?–866). Yet Daoji's drinking sets him apart from any of his predecessors in the orthodox Chan school, since drinking is a breach of monastic law. The prohibition on wine is one of the "Ten Novice Precepts" (*shami jie*), accepted upon ordination by every Buddhist monk regardless of school.[18] Furthermore, it is one of the first five of the Ten Novice Precepts, collectively known as the Five Precepts (*wujie; pañca śīlāni*), that bind not only members of the clergy but also the lay devotee.[19] Daoji was thus a monk who regularly transgressed one of the primary laws of his own religious faith. The phenomenon of the crazy holy man is known in other religious traditions as well. Like Daoji, the Sufi masters drank wine in breach of Islamic law.[20] Shabtai Tsvi transgressed Jewish law, and the Pāśupatas, to name another example, violated Hindu laws of purity and pollution.[21] Generally speaking, such antinomian behavior implies a belief that truth lies outside society's accepted norms. In some cases, such religious transgressions betray the notion that magical powers are related to ritual pollution. The question of the specific origins of Daoji's antinomian behavior are discussed in the next chapter.

Daoji's antinomian behavior estranged him from the monastic establishment, but it did not diminish his sanctity in the eyes of the

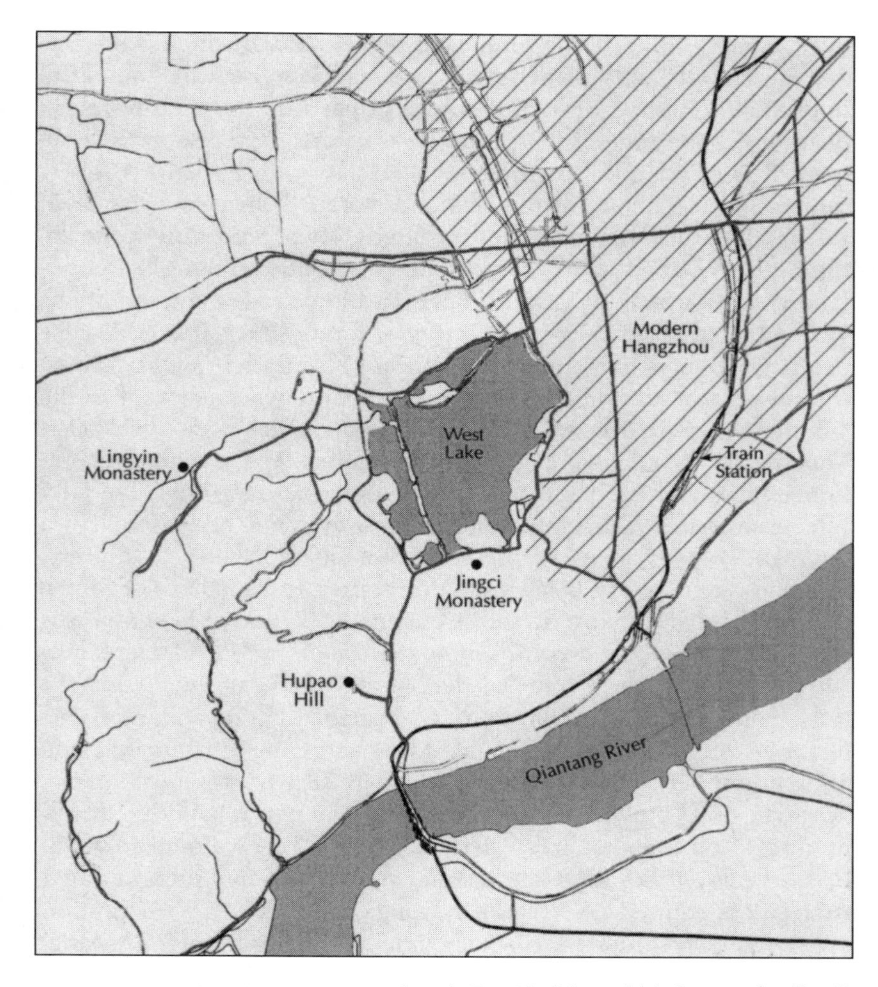

Map 1. Hangzhou sites associated with Daoji's life and his later cult. Daoji is worshipped today at the Lingyin Monastery (where he was ordained), at the Jingci Monastery (where he passed away), and on Hupao Hill (which, beginning in the sixteenth century, was pinpointed as the site of his burial stūpa). 0.5 inch = 1 mile.

laity. Jujian's *Collected Prose* indicates that already during his lifetime he was sought for his religious powers. Members of "powerful households" tried to procure his help, particularly, it appears, in healing. By the time of his death, he was already a celebrated holy man. It is striking that members of the laity rather than his fellow monks "sorted his *śarīra* remains and stored them below the Twin Peak" (the exact location is not specified). Then, according to Jujian, the news of Daoji's *śarīra* relics created a sensation among the population of the capital. Indeed it is not difficult to sense the reservations with which this cleric treats the popular fervor that followed Daoji's death. In Jujian's view, the news of Daoji's *śarīra* relics was "blown up out of proportion," exactly because people were ignorant of the fact that whoever does even one good deed regularly has such relics. This discrepancy between clerical reservations and popular veneration was to characterize Daoji's posthumous career. It was the laity who transformed Daoji into a literary and dramatic hero as well as a god, and only under lay pressure did the monastic community, centuries later, accept Daoji and admit him into its gallery of saints.

One point in Jujian's account remains to be noted: his emphasis upon Daoji's literary accomplishments. Daoji "had the same exquisite poetic skills," he wrote, "as the famous monks of the Jin and the [Liu] Song periods." Collections of Hangzhou lore and monastic histories published during the late Ming and Qing attribute to Daoji quite a number of literary pieces. Most are clearly spurious;[22] some, however, may be authentic.[23] One poem that can reliably be attributed to Daoji is found in an early collection, Meng Zongbao's *Collected Poems on the Dongxiao Monastery* (*Dongxiao shiji*; preface dated 1302).[24] It is entitled "A Voyage to Dongxiao" and was written upon a visit to a Taoist monastery, Dongxiao, in Yuhang county, Zhejiang, some twelve miles west of West Lake. Meng Zongbao gives its author as "The Recluse from the Lake, Daoji." The poem throws no light on Daoji the man, except to verify a literary inclination on his part; it reads:

> At dawn I set out[25] for Yuhang;
> The small boat rides up the clear stream.
> Climbing the bank and stretching for two or three miles,
> The narrow path winds through the wooded hills.
> Mysterious peaks soar above the Axis Mundi [Monastery];[26]
> Tranquil are the valleys and cliffs by the Nine Locks [Mountain].[27]
> On the clouds' root,[28] the immortals' abode—
> The fabulous place no man can envision.

Inside the gates an aura of splendor;
Gold and emerald dazzle the eyes.
Playing chess under the ancient pine tree,
The chirping birds accompany me from above.
The Taoist priest reads the [*Scripture*] *of the Yellow Court,*
The *Inner Effulgences*[29] is appropriate for self-cultivation.
Penglai and the distant Weak River,[30]
Through the "Nine Transformations"[31] can be reached.
The poem composed by Sire Po,[32]
Is engraved in stone, commemorating his visit of old.
It augments the valleys' and mountains' spectacular views,
Being transmitted for generations without interruption.
I came here to pay homage to [Su Dongpo's] memory.
But my mind seems empty; in awe I search in the dark.
Holding a torch, I enter the Dadi [cave].[33]
My collar and sleeves rustle in the cold air.
The milk dripping[34] on the hanging cliffs,
Has not been gathered in a thousand years.
The woodcutter points to the cave:
"From here one can reach the dragons' pool."
By the time I emerge from the eastern cave,
The red sun is rushing to the west.
As I leave the mountain, I linger,
The emptiness makes the gibbons and cranes[35] sound sad.

TWO

Madness and Power in Chinese Buddhism

Daoji was a wandering holy man who transgressed the rules of his own religious tradition. He was far removed from the monastic establishment of his time and yet was revered by the laity as a saint, particularly, it appears, because of his powers of healing. What is the historical background for his antinomian behavior? Why was he considered a saint even as he openly ignored primary articles of his own faith? Antinomian practices are not uncommon in human religious behavior. The belief that social conventions hinder the search for truth and that magical powers can be obtained through violations of moral codes appears under different guises in a variety of religious traditions. Hidden sages, holy fools, and eccentric miracle workers appear in traditions as different as the monotheistic religions of the West, polytheistic Hinduism, and Tantric Buddhism. In China we find—contrary to the Confucian concept of the sage—an almost bewildering variety of religious eccentrics. The Chinese holy fool crosses the boundaries between high and popular culture. He appears simultaneously in the organized religions (Taoism and Buddhism) and in popular lore. Furthermore, the notion that eccentricity is related to genius appears not only in Chinese religion but also in Chinese aesthetics, where the eccentric sage appears in the guise of the insouciant artist.

Paradoxically, the most ancient form of religious eccentricity in China is also the one most easily visible today. It appears in the form of the spirit medium, a residue of the "shamanistic substratum" of

Chinese religion.[1] Descriptions of the shaman in ancient China are limited, but his modern descendant, the "divining youth" (*tâng-ki* in Hokkien), is readily visible. In this case madness is the product of possession. In one sense the medium is the unfortunate victim of the god (in Taiwan this is often the deified Daoji) who has chosen the youth to be his oracle. The medium's position as mediator between humans and gods endows him with power, but at the same time it subjects him to the mortification of the flesh—a terrible spectacle that serves as proof of his authenticity to believers. The social position of the medium, as one subject to the capricious powers of the gods, is also ambiguous: he is both exalted and shunned.[2]

Religious Taoism owes much to the ancient shamanistic religion of China, and a rich gallery of Taoist holy fools manifests eccentric traits similar to those of the shaman. It includes such figures as Tao Hongjing's (456–536) humble disciple Huan Kai, who, though only a lowly menial, was believed to have attained immortality before his pompous and ambitious master.[3] Holy fools figure also in what is generally considered the philosophical dimension of Taoism. Hidden sages appear as early as the *Laozi* and the *Zhuangzi*. In the latter, the social marginality of the crazy sage is reflected in his physical deformity. Mutilated and crippled eccentrics are endowed with the wisdom necessary for ruling the empire, and hideous sages have the power to move heaven and earth. This is the case with Uglyface Tuo (Aitai Tuo), who was "ugly enough to give the whole world a fright . . . none the less wild creatures would couple where he stood. . . . This was obviously a man with something different about him."[4] The *Zhuangzi*'s image of the carefree sage deeply influenced a group of artistically inclined noblemen of the third century A.D. who later came to be known as the "Seven Worthies of the Bamboo Grove" (*Zhulin qixian*). The seven advocated naturalness, individual expression, and nonconformity. They were particularly renowned for their habitual drunkenness. One of them, the gifted poet Ruan Ji (210–63), is said to have violated the social code by eating meat and drinking wine during the mourning period for his mother. Nevertheless he was inwardly so grieved that he "wasted away for a long time."[5]

The nonconformity of the seven worthies had a political dimension. By feigning madness, scholars such as Ruan Ji were able "to escape the hate and envy of their contemporaries, the despotism of princes, and the follies committed by those in power."[6] (A different type of political madness is exemplified by the official and poet Qu Yuan [340?–278 B.C.E.], whose extreme commitment to moral government led to his downfall and eventual suicide.)[7] But the eccentricity of the seven worthies had an aesthetic dimension as well. These prominent poets and musicians felt that nonconformity is a precondition for individual expression and, ultimately, artistic creativity. Their conception of the artist as a carefree genius who dashes off poems in the heat of wine was further developed during the Tang. Its quintessential manifestation was the carefree poet Li Bai (701–62), whose persona is succinctly summarized in Du Fu's (712–70) poem "Eight Drinking Immortals": "A hundred poems per gallon of wine—that's Li Bai."[8] To the best of my knowledge, it was also among Li Bai's eccentric friends that Daoji's nickname, *dian* (crazy) first appeared. The famous calligrapher and drunkard Zhang Xu (fl. 750) would draw his masterpieces only in a state of drunkenness, for which reason he was nicknamed "Crazy Zhang" (Zhangdian).[9]

Holy fools, ranging from celebrated Chan masters to illiterate itinerant monks, also figure prominently in Chinese Buddhism, where they are depicted in a wide variety of literary and artistic genres. Eschatological literature, for example, mentions hidden sages, "sometimes . . . disguised as fools and sinners,"[10] who will assist the future messiah. Chan literature depicts even the sixth patriarch, Huineng (638–713), as an illiterate scullion, working in the monastery's threshing room.[11] Eccentric and even antinomian traits are apparent also in Chan pedagogical techniques, which favor the use of "strange words and extraordinary actions" (*qi yan ji xing*).[12] In an attempt to liberate their disciples from a false dualistic perception of reality, Chan masters would employ such radical techniques as shouting and beating. Mazu (707–86), for example, grabbed the nose of his disciple Baizhang (749–814) and twisted it until the latter attained enlightenment.[13] Yet even though Chan masters behaved in an eccentric manner, they rarely transgressed monastic regulations. A rich body of Buddhist lore, however, celebrates wandering miracle workers who did transgress specific monastic vows, such as those forbidding meat and wine. These itinerant monks were venerated by the laity for their magical powers, and as we will see below, they probably exercised a great influence on Daoji.

A perception of the saint as inherently eccentric is also apparent in many Chinese Buddhist works of art. Chinese artists often chose to portray their enlightened subjects as fools clad in rags. This is particularly the case with saints of foreign origins, such as Bodhidharma (Damo) or the arhats (*luohan*). Chinese artists endowed these saints, who were originally Indian or Central Asian, with an eccentric countenance by exaggerating their foreign features. They highlighted their bushy eyebrows, enlarged their protruding noses (and nostrils) to almost preposterous dimensions, and even pierced their earlobes with large earrings, reminiscent of pirates' accessories in Western folklore.[14] Damo and the arhats thus appear in Chinese visual representations as comical eccentrics whose features are decidedly otherworldly. Chinese-born eccentrics (historical and imaginary) further enlarged the gallery of holy fools celebrated in Chinese Buddhist art. Three eccentrics that became a particularly popular subject in Chinese (and Japanese) Buddhist painting are the Three Sages of Tiantai Mountain: Hanshan, Shide, and Fenggan. The historicity of the three is doubtful. Hanshan is said to have been an unconventional poet who led the life of a recluse among the cliffs and caverns of Tiantai Mountain. He would feed on leftovers from the Guoqing Monastery, which were provided to him by the scullion Shide. Fenggan was renowned for the meek tiger that followed him wherever he went. The three eccentrics and their lazy beast are often "shown huddled together in deep slumber."[15] In this relaxed posture they are known collectively as the Four Sleepers.

No survey, however brief, of the holy fool in Chinese Buddhism would be complete without mention of the possibility of foreign influences. Michel Strickmann's *Mantras et mandarins* has revealed to us the depth and the extent of Tantric influences on the religion of medieval China. Particularly pertinent to this discussion is his discovery that Tantric sexual rites—previously thought to be too outrageous for the sedate Chinese—actually figured in medieval Chinese Buddhism, at least in written form, if not in practice.[16] It is therefore not impossible that some of the antinomian aspects associated with Tantric saints contributed to the shaping of Chinese holy fools. The Mahāsiddha, or perfected person of the Tantric school, uses polluting substances to achieve spiritual purification. He resides in cemeteries and covers his body with ashes. He obtains the spiritual goal of monastic life—liberation—by leading the life of a layman, and accordingly he marries and establishes a family. Finally, in his attempt to gain enlightenment through humiliation, the Mahāsiddha often engages in the lowliest occupations. Celebrated Mahāsiddhas such as Dārika even served prostitutes.[17] Regarding the possibility of

Tantric influences on Chinese holy fools, it is noteworthy that the symbolism of excrement, which is prevalent in Tantric literature, appears in late Song hagiographies of eccentric Chinese monks such as Budai heshang (?–ca. 902).[18] In other words, even if the Mahāsiddha ideal did not influence eccentric Chinese monks of the medieval period, it might have influenced some of the literature that grew up around them in later periods.

Within this bewildering variety of eccentrics, where do the origins of Daoji lie? Here a distinction should be drawn between the image of Daoji as it developed in Ming and Qing popular literature and the historical Daoji. In the world of popular literature the distinctions between Buddhist, Taoist, and nonreligious eccentrics dissolve. The figure of Daoji in fiction and drama was thus influenced by a variety of Buddhist and non-Buddhist fools. We will see in Chapter 3, for example, that the sixteenth-century novel *Recorded Sayings* portrays Daoji simultaneously as an eccentric Chan master and as a carefree poet in the style of Li Bai. In the case of the historical Daoji, however, one category of fools is probably most relevant for understanding his figure—eccentric miracle workers. These were itinerant monks who, like Daoji, violated monastic regulations and were far removed from the Buddhist establishment of their time. At the same time they were venerated by the laity for their miraculous powers. Jujian, whose attitude toward Daoji was characterized by clerical reservation, did not explicitly attribute to him miraculous powers. Nonetheless, Jujian's biography of Daoji suggests that the laity sought him for his powers of healing.

The magic feats of Buddhist thaumaturges are the subject of a large body of literature. As John Kieschnick has shown, miracle workers' lives occupy an important position in hagiographic literature composed by the Buddhist clergy.[19] Since Huijiao's (497–554) celebrated *Biographies of Eminent Monks* (*Gaoseng zhuan*), hagiographic collections on Buddhist monks have generally been arranged according to the primary occupation of the monks in question. They have sections on translators, exegetes, self-immolators, meditators, and, among others, each has a section on miracle workers, who are referred to as *gantong seng* (monks of miraculous powers), *shenyi seng*, or *shen seng* (both the latter terms mean "saintly" or "divine monks").[20] Information on miracle workers is included also in the "transmission of the lamp" texts of the Chan school. This hagiographic literature is arranged genealogically; the biographies of a given master's disciples are grouped together in one chapter under his name. The biographies of miracle workers did not fit this genealogical scheme, since for the most part these were unordained, itinerant monks whose masters were unknown. Therefore their biographies are generally grouped together in one chapter, an arrangement that defies the chronological structure of the text as a whole. For example, the biographies of the Three Sages of Tiantai Mountain (Hanshan, Shide, and Fenggan) first appeared in the chapter on "unordained yet famous monks" of the *Jingde Period Record of the Transmission of the Lamp* (*Jingde chuandeng lu*) of 1004.[21]

The miracle worker's clientele consisted of lay persons, and it is therefore not surprising that much of the literature on wonder workers was written by members of the laity. Collections of popular lore such as Hong Mai's (1123–1202) *Yi Jian's Record* (*Yi Jian zhi*) include many anecdotes on itinerant miracle workers, and local gazetteers inform us of the fame these holy men enjoyed in specific localities.[22] In addition, literary anthologies such as the *Extensive Records Compiled During the Taiping Period* (*Taiping guangji*; 978) and encyclopedias such as the *Comprehensive Collection of Ancient and Modern Charts and Writings* (*Gujin tushu jicheng*; 1725) have special sections on Buddhist miracle workers.[23] Finally, biographies of wonder workers were written even by members of the ruling elite. The Yongle emperor (r. 1403–25) himself compiled a hagiographic collection on miracle workers, entitled *Biographies of Saintly Monks* (*Shenseng zhuan*) (preface dated 1417), and his father, the Ming founder Zhu Yuanzhang (r. 1368–98), left us a biography of an eccentric miracle worker, Zhoudian (Crazy Zhou), whom he personally consulted.[24]

A survey of the literature on miracle workers, whether written by the clergy or by the laity, reveals that many—though not all—of them were, like Daoji, eccentric monks who transgressed monastic regulations.[25] They feigned madness (*yangkuang*) and were often referred to as "crazy monks" (*dian seng*), "mad monks" (*feng heshang*), or "wild monks" (*ye heshang*). Like Daoji, most miracle workers were itinerant monks who occupied the fringes of the monastic establishment. They did not receive a Buddhist education, and many of them were not officially ordained. For this reason they were known as "half-clergy, half-lay" (*banseng bansu*). (Daoji, however, was ordained.) Far removed from the monastic establishment, the miracle workers belonged in that gray area where at least some of the distinctions between Buddhist, Taoist, and shamanistic religious practitioners dissolve.[26] The itinerant Buddhist performs on behalf of the laity the same miracles of healing and fortune-telling as the wandering Taoist and the shaman, and his craziness is similar to theirs as well. (Itinerant Buddhists and Taoists differ from shamans in that they are not subject to involuntary possession.)

Itinerant miracle workers transgressed monastic regulations, most notably the dietary rules; they ate meat and drank wine and were therefore known as "meat and wine monks" (*jiurou heshang*). Their antinomian behavior alienated them from the monastic establishment. In modern times "wild monks" were not permitted to lodge in Buddhist monasteries.[27] The paucity of concrete biographical information on miracle workers indicates their great distance from the ecclesiastical establishment. Hagiographic collections often fail to provide the miracle worker's exact dates. Nor can the monkish chronicler relate the miracle worker's birthplace or his eventual fate. He may not even know the miracle worker's real name, but only the nickname given him by the laity.

The monastic establishment's attitude toward itinerant miracle workers was ambivalent. Miracle workers operated among the laity and were by and large outsiders to the monastic community. Nevertheless, the ecclesiastical establishment was willing, at least posthumously, to accept the laity's verdict as to their sanctity. The inclusion of miracle workers' biographies in hagiographic collections itself evinces the establishment's acceptance of their path. Monastic communities in other Buddhist societies, Theravāda and Mahāyāna alike, similarly displayed tacit approval of charismatic monks who operated independently at the fringes. Both the "forest monks" of Southeast Asia and the *hijiri* of Japan were venerated by the laity even as they distanced themselves from the monastic community. Nevertheless, in both instances the ecclesiastical establishment accepted their path of self-cultivation as a viable alternative to its own monastic approach.[28] The legitimation of the independent ascetic dates back to some of the earliest Buddhist texts, which recognize two paths to salvation: the communal monastic path, and the path of the hermit, who dwells alone "like the solitary horn of the rhinoceros."[29]

Itinerant miracle workers were sought by the laity mainly for healing and fortune-telling. However, they were believed to possess other supernatural powers as well. Hagiographic collections attributed to their eccentric protagonists powers ranging from rainmaking to taming wild beasts.[30] Interestingly, the supernatural qualities attributed to them were closely linked to their itinerancy. The wandering saint's clientele saw him appear and disappear, but they did not know where he came from, or by what means of transportation he arrived. Legends attributed to miracle workers the abilities to travel at the speed of lightning, to reveal and conceal themselves at will, and to duplicate themselves and appear simultaneously in several places. The historical fact of itinerancy thus became an integral part of the miracle worker's mythology. In the eyes of his believers, the itinerant holy man was a messenger traveling between their locality and the divine realm.

Itinerant miracle workers occupied an important position in Chinese folk Buddhism from the introduction of the religion to China until modern times. It is probable, however, that a significant increase in their numbers occurred during Daoji's lifetime. The Song government's policy of selling ordination certificates (*dudie*) for exorbitant prices placed monastic life beyond the reach of many applicants and led to the rise of uncertified practitioners, who performed religious services outside of the claustral establishment.[31] Itinerant miracle workers were among these unlicensed practitioners. A complete survey of Buddhist miracle workers in Chinese history is beyond the scope of this study. In the following, I try to illustrate their eccentricity and its relevance to the understanding of Daoji by four examples selected from Buddhist as well as non-Buddhist sources. In each case I examine the eccentic saint's earliest biography only.

Beidu

Beidu's (?–426) biography is included in the miracle workers section of Huijiao's (497–554) *Biographies of Eminent Monks*.[32] Huijiao himself was a Buddhist monk, yet his description of Beidu leaves little doubt that the latter was far removed from the monastic establishment of the time. Huijiao cannot tell whether Beidu was ordained, nor does he know his original surname. He further notes that "nobody knew where Beidu had come from." Beidu did spend some time at a monastery in Jiangsu (the Yanxian si) yet for the most part he led the life of an itinerant monk in that province: "Sometimes wearing wooden shoes, he would climb mountains; at other times he would march on foot to the marketplace." He used to sojourn in the houses of lay devotees, some of whom were as influential as the regional inspector of Yanzhou (in Jiangsu), whereas others were impoverished peasants. Beidu's estrangement from the monastic community was certainly related to his eccentric and antinomian behavior. He wore tattered rags that barely covered his naked body, and he violated monastic dietary rules outright by drinking wine and eating meat; "even when it came to eating bitter minced fish, he was no different from the laity."

Beidu's antinomian behavior did not diminish his sanctity in the eyes of the laity, who venerated him for his supernatural powers. Indeed these were the miraculous powers that earned him his nickname "Beidu" (literally, "crossing by the cup"). The name derives from his practice of crossing rivers by means of a wooden cup, which he tossed into the water and rode to the other shore. "Without the aid of wind or oars, [he would cross the water] at such speed that he appeared to be flying." Beidu employed his supernatural powers to reward—handsomely—those members of the laity whose hospitality he enjoyed. Once he stayed for six months at the house of a lay devotee named Huang Xin who was so poor that he had nothing but barley to eat. Beidu repaid his kindness with 36 baskets filled with silver and silk. Huang Xin realized that these were alms that Beidu had obtained by duplicating himself and traveling simultaneously to other localities. The symbol of Beidu's supernatural powers—and possibly their source as well—was a reed basket, which he carried wherever he went. Whereas he lifted it with ease, other people, even in groups of ten or more, were unable to budge it. Once a child peeped into it and saw the Heavenly Kings of the Four Quarters (Si tianwang; Catur-mahārājas) sitting inside. They appeared as children clad in bright clothes and were only a few inches tall.

Beidu's supernatural powers were especially in demand for the purpose of healing. Occasionally he needed to recite only one charm (*zhou*) for a patient to recover. Interestingly, he continued to provide healing services even after his death. In fact he died and was buried twice. He passed away and was buried for the first time in Yanzhou, but a few days later he was seen carrying his reed basket in the direction of Pengcheng (in Jiangsu), whereupon people opened his coffin and found only his shoes.[33] He died the second time in 426 and was buried on Fuzhou Mountain (also in Jiangsu). However, even after this second and final burial, he responded to his followers' supplications and reappeared occasionally. In one instance he used a charm to cure a devotee, and "his speech was just as it had been [prior to his death]." According to Huijiao, he made his final appearance in 428, whereupon he bade farewell to his followers and disappeared.

Huijiao's account of Beidu's posthumous miracles reveals a difference between his monastic view of the eccentric saint and the laity's view. Whereas he was careful to put a temporal limit on Beidu's involvement in human affairs (the year 428), members of the laity continued to report having seen him as late as Huijiao's own days (497–554). This is evident from Huijiao's comment: "Recently there have been again rumors that people occasionally see Beidu." Huijiao hastens to deny the veracity of these rumors, yet his account of them gives us a glimpse into what must have been an ongoing veneration. Lay persons evidently conceived of Beidu as a deity some one hundred years after his death.

Budai (Cloth Bag)

The man who was to be worshipped posthumously as the potbellied incarnation of the Buddha Maitreya was in his day a little-known itinerant monk by the name of Qici (?–ca. 902). He was referred to more commonly by his humorous nicknames Budai (Cloth Bag) or Budai heshang (Cloth-Bag Monk). His earliest biography is included in the section on miracle workers of Zanning's (919–1001) sequel to Huijiao's *Biographies of Eminent Monks*, the *Biographies of Eminent Monks Compiled During the Song Period* (988).[34] Zanning, like Huijiao, was a Buddhist monk, yet his biography of Budai, like Huijiao's biography of Beidu, leaves no doubt that its subject was not a member of the monastic community. Cloth Bag was never ordained, and his origins were unknown. He never resided in a monastery. Instead, he led the life of an itinerant monk in Zhejiang, "sleeping wherever he happened to be," even outside in the snow or "with his knees upright" on the city's bridge. Perhaps the strongest indication of Budai's estrangement from the monastic community is the fact that he died outside the claustral establishment and was buried, like Daoji, by lay persons rather than by members of the clergy. (Interestingly, later Buddhist biographers insist that Budai died in a monastery, where he delivered his valedictory poem in proper Buddhist fashion.)[35]

Budai was an eccentric miracle worker, whose "speech was irregular." He used to violate monastic dietary rules by eating everything offered to him, including "pickled fish." His idiosyncrasies of character were mirrored by his idiosyncratic appearance; he was obese, with a large protruding belly. Nevertheless, he was venerated by the laity for his supernatural powers. He used to sleep outside in the snow, and yet the snow would not cover him; this was seen as an indication of his divine nature. Budai's miraculous powers were particularly apparent in the area of fortune-telling. His behavior and even his attire were seen as omens of things to come. For example, when Budai wore grass sandals softened by water, it was known that rain was imminent, whereas when he wore high wooden clogs, the weather would be dry. The symbol of his supernatural powers, like that of Beidu, was a mysterious bag that he carried wherever he went. The bag was made of cloth rather than reed, and it was this bag that earned him his nickname—Cloth Bag.

Budai, like Beidu, enjoyed posthumous veneration by the laity. Zanning notes that after his death and burial people in other provinces claimed to have seen him carrying his bag. He also quotes a line from a song that suggests an identification of Budai with Maitreya, the messianic Buddha of the future: "O Maitreya! True Maitreya! None of your contemporaries recognizes you." But the clearest evidence of a popular Budai cult was the spread of his icons. Zanning observes that after Budai's death, "many people in Jiangzhe [Jiangsu and Zhejiang] painted his icons." Judging by Zanning's account, in his own days the cult of Budai was still limited by and large to the laity. However, unlike Beidu's cult, it was later adopted by the monastic establishment as well. Under pressure from the laity, Budai was accepted by the monastic community as the incarnation of the Buddha Maitreya. An unordained miracle worker on the fringes of the Buddhist community thus became one of the most important deities in the pantheon of that community. His image—an obese jovial monk with a prominent belly button—became an omnipresent feature of Chinese Buddhist monasteries.

Jiuxian Yuxian

Eccentricity crossed the boundaries between religion and aesthetics in medieval China. The crazy sage appeared not only in religious garb but also in the guise of the lighthearted poet. The images of the religious and the artistic crazy man were often interrelated. The eccentric monk Yuxian (922–1009) illustrates the influence of the artistic madman on the religious one, since his nickname "Wine Immortal" (Jiuxian) derived from the sobriquet of the carefree poet Li Bai (Jiuxian weng). Yuxian, like Li Bai, used to compose songs in the heat of wine. His earliest biography is included in Zhengshou's *Jiatai Period Record of the Universal Transmission of the Lamp* (1204).[36] Zhengshou arranged his collection genealogically according to the various lineages of the Chan school. Yuxian's biography, however, is included in a chapter that defies the genealogical structure of the work and is dedicated to "incarnated saints" (*yinghua shengxian*). According to Zhengshou, Yuxian was ordained at the age of 30 (in Zhejiang), but to judge from his account, Yuxian never rose to a position of authority within the monastic establishment. Zhengshou makes no mention of any official post ever held by Yuxian or any official title bestowed upon him. He does not describe Yuxian as a Chan master, and refers to him simply as a monk (*heshang*).

Yuxian's eccentricity, like that of Beidu and Budai, was only a manifestation of his divine nature, which was evident even before his birth; his mother conceived after dreaming of swallowing a big pearl. Yuxian's supernatural traits were equally apparent after his death; his body remained firm in the meditation posture and even the color of his lips did not change. A series of miracles testified to Yuxian's supernatural powers during his lifetime. Once he was riding a boat when a storm threatened to capsize it. He took off his cassock and raised it as a sail, whereupon the storm subsided and the passengers were saved. On another occasion he subdued a tiger. In some cases it sufficed to invoke Yuxian's name for miracles to occur. A group of masons searching for stone pillars for a temple recited his name; thereupon the rocks of the mountain they were on crumbled into the necessary shapes. The laity was particularly interested in Yuxian's powers of healing. His amulets (*fu*) were reputed to cure all illnesses. Interestingly, Yuxian's therapeutic powers were intimately related to his antinomian behavior. Once when a plague raged through town, he vomited into a mortar, apparently drunk. He covered the vomit and let it ferment, and the potion thus produced cured all who drank it.

Huiji

Buddhist miracle workers were similar to shamans and Taoist priests both in terms of the services they provided—healing, exorcism, and fortune-telling—and in terms of the ritual tools they employed—amulets, charms, and incantations. A fine example of the similarities between Buddhist miracle workers and their Taoist and shamanistic counterparts is provided by a monk named Huiji

(?–1134), whose exploits were recorded by a member of the laity, Hong Mai, in his compendium on the supernatural, *Yi Jian's Record*.[37] According to Hong Mai, Huiji was originally a layman (surnamed Zhang) employed at the magistrate's office in Yugan county (in present-day Jiangxi). Once when he was chasing bandits in the mountains, a divine maiden riding a celestial chariot was revealed to him. She handed him a book and ordered him to become a monk; thereupon he left his wife and journeyed to Yihuang county (in the eastern part of present-day Jiangxi). He feigned madness (*yangkuang*), and no one was aware of his divine powers. The county was suffering from a prolonged drought and in their desperation the local people built an earth dragon and prayed to it for rain. Huiji suggested that he himself be sacrificed instead; he prophesied that either it would rain by noon the following day or they could burn him alive. The people constructed a pyre and tied him to it. The next day, just as they were about to light it, the rain started pouring down. Following this "the local people began to venerate him."

In 1121 Huiji traveled eastward to Taining county (in present-day Fujian), where a religious practitioner by the name of Huang Wenfu bought him an ordination certificate and established for him a small cloister (*an*) on a mountaintop. It is interesting that Huiji chose to reside in a cloister rather than in a monastery (*si* or *yuan*). Cloisters were smaller than monasteries and, unlike the latter, were neither recognized nor supervised by the central government. Leaders of sectarian rebellious movements such as the White Lotus sect tended to reside in cloisters; for this reason the government periodically ordered their destruction.[38] Thus, Huiji's residence in a cloister indicates his distance from government-sponsored mainstream Buddhism.

Huiji's supernatural powers earned him fame in Taining and neighboring counties. He demonstrated his magical skills by healing, exorcising ghosts, and telling fortunes. "[He] was able to cast a spell on water so that it would cure diseases, and pilgrims from hundreds of miles around lined up to see him." He was equally capable of "catching demons in broad daylight." In one instance, the local magistrate dreamed that a young woman set his official residence on fire. Huiji realized that an evil female spirit was the cause of the dream, and he proceeded to exorcise her. The blood of the injured spirit gushed forth, and she never bothered the magistrate again. The exorcist ritual performed by Huiji in this instance is indistinguishable from those of the Taoists or shamans. His other miraculous feats had no identifiable Buddhist characteristics either. For example, rainmaking by self-immolation (threatened or real) was performed by shamans, as well as by government officials, throughout Chinese history.[39] Even the mythology surrounding Huiji's magic was by no means Buddhist. The divine woman revealed to him was not a Buddhist goddess, but a Chinese one. Similar goddesses were encountered by scores of Taoist hermits, as well as by artists and poets of no religious affiliation whatever. Huiji was thus a Buddhist by his own testimony only. As Valerie Hansen has pointed out, his identification as such was probably significant for his unlettered clientele, to whom it suggested that he had access to the divine authority revealed in Buddhist scriptures.[40]

Huiji, like Beidu and Budai, was venerated posthumously by the laity. Hong Mai noted that "to this day the people of Taining paint icons of him." It is interesting to note the title by which he was worshiped. Hong Mai observed that "they don't call him by his name [i.e., Huiji], but only Zhanggong [Lord Zhang], or Zhang heshang (Monk Zhang)." Budai was also known to posterity primarily as "Budai heshang" (Monk Budai). But more important for this discussion is the appearance of the title *gong*, since it was under this title that Daoji was posthumously worshiped as "Jigong."

Conclusion

Daoji was not the only holy fool in the history of Chinese religion. Crazy shamans, eccentric Taoists, wild Buddhists, and carefree poets played an important role in the religion and art of China throughout its history. Within this bewildering variety of crazy saints, one group can be singled out as directly relevant to the understanding of Daoji's antinomian behavior—Buddhist miracle workers. In the case of many—though not all—Buddhist miracle workers, extraordinary powers were inextricably linked to extraordinary behavior. Many miracle workers were eccentric monks whose wild behavior and shabby dress distinguished them from clergy and laity alike. Like Daoji they violated the rules of their own religious faith, in particular the dietary laws forbidding ingestion of meat and wine. Their antinomian behavior distanced them from the monastic establishment. For the most part, they were itinerant monks who, like Daoji, occupied the fringes of the monastic community, and in some cases they were not even ordained. Nonetheless, they were venerated by the laity for their supernatural powers. Since many itinerant miracle workers did not receive a Buddhist education, they were not much different from uneducated Taoists or from village shamans. Buddhist miracle workers, Taoist wizards, and shamans shared similar supernatural powers and similar eccentric traits (even though Buddhist, and Taoist, miracle workers did differ from shamans in that they were not subject to involuntary possession).

Eccentric miracle workers resembled Daoji not only in terms of their human careers but also in terms of their posthumous ones. The veneration many miracle workers enjoyed during their lifetimes continued after death, when they were worshipped as deities by the laity. Daoji's cult was eventually adopted by the monastic community, and likewise the cults of some miracle workers, most notably that of Budai heshang, were eventually sanctioned by the Buddhist establishment, which in their own times had granted them neither position nor title. (Budai, however, came to occupy a much more prominent position than Daoji in the monastic pantheon.) Furthermore, like Daoji, many miracle workers became posthumously the subjects of plays, stories, and novels, which further spread their cults. Budai heshang, for example, is celebrated in a *zaju* play by the thirteenth-century playwright Zheng Tingyu.[41] Another crazy miracle worker, Baozhi (?–514), appears under the name of Zhigong, in the late Ming vernacular story "Emperor Wu Returns to Heaven."[42]

The gallery of historical Buddhist fools celebrated in vernacular fiction and drama was further enlarged by fictional characters. In some cases historical monks who had never displayed eccentric or antinomian behavior were transformed by storytellers and playwrights into holy fools. For example, Su Shi's friend Liaoyuan (better known by his alias Foyin) (1032–98) is depicted in a large body of Ming fiction as a carefree poet and drunkard, who dallies with courtesans.[43] Other crazy monks described in popular novels and plays are purely invented figures. Dong Jieyuan's (fl. 1200) medley version of the *Western Chamber Romance* features a jolly monk named Facong, who delights in eating meat-filled pastries. It is he who courageously saves the play's romantic protagonists when they are threatened by robbers.[44] Another beloved eccentric is Lu Zhishen of the Yuan or Ming novel *Water Margin*. This outrageous monk drinks wine and eats dog's meat inside the monastery itself. Nevertheless, "he has a corresponding star in heaven," and he passes away in the meditation posture, thereby indicating his saintly nature.[45]

In several novels itinerant mad monks serve as messengers between the human and the divine realms. Their appearance on stage therefore carries great significance as an omen of things to come. In the *Plum in the Golden Vase* (*Jin Ping Mei*; ca. 1590), a barbarian monk (*huseng*), who drinks wine and eats meat, gives Ximen Qing an aphrodisiac, which satisfies the latter's desires and yet will serve as the instrument of his doom.[46] In Cao Xueqin's *Dream of the Red Chamber* two mad monks, one Buddhist, the other Taoist, bring the novel's protagonist into the world in the form of a precious jade and take him back at the novel's conclusion.[47] Finally, just like historical Buddhist and Taoist eccentrics, their fictionalized representations bear a close resemblance. A group of semi-mythological Taoist eccentrics known collectively as the Eight Immortals figures prominently in both Yuan drama and late Ming fiction. Their images are clearly related to those of mad Buddhist monks in the fiction and drama of the same periods.[48]

Why were mad monks believed to possess miraculous powers? Why did the laity venerate them, celebrate them in fiction and drama, and posthumously worship them? This question can be approached from different angles. Here I will point out only that from a sociological perspective the laity's veneration of itinerant mad monks probably reflected a measure of resentment toward the organized Buddhist community. The same popular fiction and drama that celebrates the supernatural powers of itinerant mad monks also delights in ridiculing members of the monastic establishment. Monks are a frequent target of satire, mocked for their greed, lechery, and above all hypocrisy. In court-case (*gongan*) literature, for example, a large proportion of the criminals are monks, and their crimes are mostly of a sexual nature.[49] The veneration of itinerant eccentric monks occupying the fringes of the monastic establishment is thus closely related to the hostility felt for that establishment. Mad monks were venerated precisely because their antinomian behavior distinguished them so sharply from the monastic community. They were considered to possess miraculous powers because their charisma was untainted by membership in the Buddhist establishment.

PART II

Crazy Ji the Fictional Character

THREE

Monk and Magician

The earliest evidence of a popular body of Daoji lore dates to the sixteenth century. Its richness and variety suggest, however, a lengthy period of accumulation of legends on the eccentric holy man prior to the sixteenth century. In the short period between the 1530s and 1569, we can find evidence of Daoji's role in oral literature, a short vernacular story as well as a lengthier text (probably a novel), both lost, and finally and most significantly, the earliest known extant novel on Daoji. All four pieces of evidence originated in Hangzhou, the city in whose outskirts the historical Daoji was ordained and passed away. The oral story was told by Hangzhou storytellers, the short story and the extant novel were published there, and the information on the now-lost novel comes from a Hangzhou writer. All four are closely interrelated, and at the same time they are part of a large body of Hangzhou lore celebrating Buddhist monks, historical and fictional.

Evidence for Daoji as a character in oral fiction comes from one of the few sources on Ming storytelling, Tian Rucheng's (*jinshi* 1526) account of Hangzhou lore: *Supplement to the Guide to the West Lake* (*Xihu youlan zhiyu*). Tian Rucheng mentioned Crazy Ji as a subject of a form of chantefable with alternating verse and prose called *taozhen*:[1]

> Many of the blind men and women of Hangzhou learn to play the *pipa* [four-stringed guitar]. They sing old and new stories (*gujin xiaoshuo*) and popular tales (*pinghua*), thereby earning a living. This genre is called *taozhen*. For the most part. they narrate Song [period] affairs. . . . The stories "Honglian"

(Red Lotus), "Liu Cui," "Jidian" (Crazy Ji), "Leifeng ta" (Leifeng Pagoda), "Shuangyu shanzhui" (Twin-fish fan pendant), and similar ones all narrate miraculous events in Hangzhou.[2]

Tian Rucheng's description of the *taozhen* genre indicates that at least by the early sixteenth century Daoji was already a popular figure in Hangzhou lore. His name is listed as a topic for *taozhen* along with some of the most celebrated Hangzhou legends: the White Snake legend ("The Leifeng Pagoda") and the Honglian and Liu Cui story complex.[3] Tian Rucheng left no description of the contents of the Jidian *taozhen* story. Yet in another section of his *Supplement*, dedicated to famous Hangzhou monks, he includes a biography of Daoji that throws much light on the development of his figure in local lore. The biography, like the list of *taozhen* topics, refers to the eccentric monk by the name Crazy Ji (Jidian), indicating that this nickname had superseded the names Daoji and Elder Fangyuan in popular usage:

Crazy Ji's (Jidian) original name was Daoji. He was wild and did not pay attention to small details of conduct. He used to drink wine, eat meat, and drift about the marketplace. People thought he was mad, for which reason they called him "Crazy Ji." Originally he was ordained at the Lingyin Monastery. Yet the monks there disliked him; therefore he took up residence in the Jingci Monastery. He would recite sūtras and light funeral pyres for people, and in each case they would attain salvation. At the age of seventy-three, he sat down in the meditation posture and passed away. Someone composed a eulogy in his honor; it reads:

> "He was neither a layman nor a monk, neither mortal nor immortal.[4] He broke a path through the Forest of Thorns.[5] He leaped out of the Diamond Circle.[6] His eyebrows were intertwined, his nostrils reached heaven.[7] When he burned amulets, 'bits of paper would float like clouds and mists.'[8] At times he would build a thatched hut and sit in meditation on a remote mountain summit. At others, he 'would be found slumbering in the wineshops of Chang'an City.'[9] His spirit engulfed the entire land, yet in his sack there was not as much as a penny. When the time came, he left this world like a cicada casting off its skin.[10] He emanated *śarīras*: 84,000 in number.[11] His praises cannot here be exhausted; (therefore) we can only say this brief *gāthā*."

Alas! is not it for this that he is named Crazy Ji? His molded statue is still preserved in the monastery.[12]

The *Supplement* extends Crazy Ji's antinomian traits; whereas Jujian only had him drink wine, Tian Rucheng has him breach another monastic rule and eat meat, thereby bringing Crazy Ji into line with the emerging trope of the crazy holy man as wine drinker and meat eater. The conflict between Jidian and the monks of the Lingyin Monastery that leads to his move to the Jingci Monastery is also new. The eulogy quoted by Tian Rucheng illustrates the ease with which the image of the crazy sage could cross the boundaries between the secular and the religious realms and be applied to the uninhibited artist and the eccentric holy man alike. The eulogy quotes Du Fu's poem "Eight Drinking Immortals," in which the Tang poet describes his eccentric literary friends. The line "would be found slumbering in the wine shops of Chang'an" applies in Du Fu's poem to Li Bai. (The eulogy maintains the reference to Chang'an even though Daoji never visited it.) And the expression "would float like clouds and mists" describes the writing of the famous calligrapher and drunkard Zhang Xu (fl. 750), known to his contemporaries as "Crazy Zhang" (Zhangdian).[13]

The *Supplement* expands not only Jidian's antinomian traits but also his magical powers. It informs us that those for whom Jidian lit funeral pyres would "attain salvation." As discussed below, the earliest extant novel about Crazy Ji, the *Recorded Sayings* (1569), abounds in descriptions of miracles performed by Jidian during funerals. Jidian, we learn, was able to guarantee rebirth in favorable circumstances to those whose funerals he attended. The *Supplement* not only indicates a growing veneration of Jidian on the part of the laity but also gives a first glimpse into his reappropriation by the monastic establishment, which in his own days granted him neither title nor position. Tian Rucheng records that "[Jidian's] statue is still preserved in the monastery." He does not state so explicitly, but it is implied that the monastery in question is the Jingci, where Jidian resided. (This identification is confirmed by other sources, which are examined below.)

It is noteworthy that two of the other stories mentioned in Tian Rucheng's record of the *taozhen* genre, "Honglian" and "Liu Cui," feature eccentric monks. The title characters Honglian and Liu Cui are two courtesans who figure in a rich body of vernacular fiction and drama, in which their counterparts are Hangzhou monks.[14] In some stories the courtesan seduces the monk; in others she is led to salvation by him. In each case, however, their association places the monk in a risqué situation. The Honglian and Liu Cui monk and courtesan stories clearly influenced early Jidian lore, which in the case of the *taozhen* genre was narrated by the same storytellers. The Baowentang library catalogue (ca. 1560) lists a story now lost, whose title, "Red Beauty Tries Jidian" ("Hongqian nan Jidian"), suggests a similar theme.[15] The story was probably one of the *Sixty Stories* (*Liushijia xiaoshuo*) published in the mid-sixteenth century by the Hangzhou editor Hong Pian (fl. 1549).

Almost concurrently with the listing of the short story "Hongqian nan Jidian" in the Baowentang catalogue, a collection of miscellaneous writings by the Hangzhou author Lang Ying (b. 1487) informs us of a lengthier Jidian narrative as well. Lang's *Draft Notes on Seven Categories of Learning* (*Qixiu leigao*; ca. 1550)[16] quotes several short pieces by Hangzhou authors, including one—a fund-raising petition for the Dafo Monastery—attributed to Jidian. The piece is followed by a brief note by Lang Ying, which sheds much light on the figure of Jidian in sixteenth-century lore:

> Jidian was a saintly monk. During the Song he repeatedly manifested his holiness between the mountains and the lake of our Hangzhou. To this day the number of stories transmitted about him is very large. There is a biography of him that circulates in the world (*you zhuanji yiben liu yu shi*). In addition there is a small stone statue of him in the arhats hall (*luohan tang*) of the Jingci Monastery.[17]

Lang Ying thus confirms Tian Rucheng's account of a Jidian statue at the Jingci Monastery and provides further evidence of his co-optation by the Buddhist establishment. More important, he informs us of the existence of a biography of Jidian, which must have been substantial in length since it circulated as an independent volume. One can assume that this was a fictionalized biography, which incorporated elements from the growing body of popular lore surrounding its protagonist. It no longer survives, but it might well have influenced the earliest extant fictionalized biography of Jidian, the *Recorded Sayings*.

The "Recorded Sayings"

The earliest extant novel about Jidian, *The Recorded Sayings of the Recluse from Qiantang Lake, the Chan Master Crazy Ji* (*Qiantang hu yin Jidian Chanshi yulu*; hereafter *Recorded Sayings*), enjoyed considerable popularity during the late Ming and early Qing to judge from the number of surviving editions.[18] The first edition is dated 1569.[19] It is presented as narrated (*xushu*) by one Shen Mengpan of Renhe (in Hangzhou prefecture), and its publisher is given as Sixiang gaozhai

(Lofty Studio of Four Fragrances). An illustration of a barefooted monk, holding a gnarled wooden staff, appears on the front page (see Fig. 1). It is followed by the same eulogy in honor of Jidian quoted by Tian Rucheng in his *Supplement to the Guide to the West Lake*. It is an unpolished edition; there are errors in characters and mistakes in pagination. Evidently it was a popular publication. Two late Ming editions followed. One forms part of Feng Menglong's (1574–1646) tripartite collection *Chance Selection on the Three Doctrines* (*Sanjiao ounian*).[20] In addition to the novel about Jidian (representing Buddhism), the collection includes a novel about a Taoist figure (Xu Sun) written by Deng Zhimo (fl. 1603), and a novel about a Confucian figure (Wang Yangming) written by Feng Menglong himself. The two late Ming editions of the *Recorded Sayings* were followed by two Qing editions, one of which differs from previous ones in that it divides the novel into twelve *juan*.[21] Finally, evidence for the popularity of the *Recorded Sayings* comes also from two other novels that are closely based upon it, one entitled *The Complete Biography of Jigong* (*Jigong quanzhuan*), the other entitled *Drunken Puti* (*Zui puti*). Both were written during the seventeenth century and are discussed in the next chapter. (See Appendix A for a chronological and annotated list of all written fiction on Jigong.)

"Recorded sayings" (*yulu*) is an unusual term to be found in the title of a novel; it does not designate works of fiction but rather a Buddhist literary genre that evolved within the Chan school. Works in this genre typically record the sayings and sermons of Chan masters as transcribed by their immediate disciples. Of course, from the perspective of historical accuracy the *Recorded Sayings* is not a proper *yulu*. It was written no less than three hundred years after the death of Daoji.[22] But, more significantly, the *Recorded Sayings* does not even attempt to simulate the *yulu* form. Indeed it is a record not of sayings but primarily of deeds. It is an extended narrative biography of Jigong's life, spanning a period from before his birth until after his physical death, and it shares many motifs with other fictionalized biographies in Ming vernacular literature. The judgment that it should be classified as a work of fiction has been shared not only by twentieth-century scholars but also by seventeenth-century critics and writers such as Feng Menglong, who for this reason chose to include it in his novel-trilogy, *Chance Selection on the Three Doctrines*. (Interestingly, Feng Menglong omitted the term *yulu* from the novel's title.)[23]

The *Recorded Sayings* is thus by no means a Buddhist *yulu;* it is a work of fiction. Why, then, the name *yulu*? For one thing the *Recorded Sayings* narrative indeed contains a large number of literary pieces and sayings attributed to its protagonist. In this respect it resembles the only other work of vernacular literature known to me that contains the term *yulu, The Dialogues and Recorded Sayings of the Lay Devotee* [*Su*] *Dongpo and the Chan Master Foyin* (*Dongpo jushi Foyin Chanshi yulu wenda;* hereafter *Dongpo Foyin yulu*).[24] Ranging from popular songs to incantations and charms, the passages attributed to Jidian are a far cry from the sayings of orthodox Chan masters. Still, presented as his words, they certainly qualify for the term *yulu* in its literal meaning of "recorded sayings." Second, one section of the *Recorded Sayings,* referred to below as Text A, is imbued with Buddhist lore, and within it at least one passage is modeled after a classical *yulu.* As shown below, the scene of Jidian's enlightenment is strikingly similar to the enlightenment of the famous Chan master Linji Yixuan as described in his "recorded sayings." Third, unjustified as it is from a standard Buddhist perspective, the term *yulu* probably reflects the novel's perception of itself as a work of religious significance. A religious attitude is clearly borne by Jidian's characterization in the novel. He is described as a Buddhist saint, an arhat (*luohan*), who has been incarnated into the world in order to manifest his divinity to the people of Lin'an (Hangzhou). At crucial moments of his religious career, he displays his "Golden arhat body" (*jin shen luohan*), and throughout his life he amply demonstrates his supernatural powers in a series of miracles. Furthermore, the omniscient narrator insists that Jidian continues to display his supernatural powers after his physical death by responding favorably to the faithful. The implied author thus refers to Jidian as a saint, and his novel is in this respect not a biography but a hagiography.

As a novel that blurs the lines between fiction and proselytizing literature, the *Recorded Sayings* belongs to a genre of late Ming hagiographic literature. Similar novels were published during the Wanli period (1573–1619) by a group of publishers in Jianyang, Fujian.[25] They include novels on such prominent saints and deities as Bodhidharma (Damo), Zhong Kui, Mazu, Guanyin, Zhenwu (or Xuantian shangdi), and Huaguang.[26] In terms of their language and structure, as well as in the quality of the surviving editions, these novels are lowbrow publications. The novels' implied authors approach their protagonists without ironic distance and appear convinced of their divinity. There are clear parallels between some of the novels and other works in genres more commonly considered religious. Thus, for example, the Guanyin novel was influenced by a *baojuan* text,[27] and both the Guanyin and the Mazu novels are closely related to a late Ming collection of saints' lives, *The Great Compendium of All the Deities Throughout the History of the Three Religions* (*Sanjiao yuanliu soushen daquan*).[28] It is hard to tell whether a conscious proselytizing zeal underlies these novels. But at least one of these novels, that on Zhenwu, contains a ritual appendix prescribing "rules of worship,"[29] and some of the novels are still distributed in temples today.[30] Thus, while providing light entertainment, the novels also functioned as tools in the dissemination of cults. As such, they remind us that the application of the Western term "novel" to lengthy narratives in the *xiaoshuo* genre may occasionally be misleading. Whereas "novel" has been applied in the West primarily to works whose subject matter is human experience, these late Ming hagiographic narratives are concerned with the supernatural, and their protagonists are deities.

Although, as a hagiographic novel, the *Recorded Sayings* belongs in the same category as the Jianyang novels, it also differs considerably from them. For the most part the Jianyang novels are full-fledged works of mythology, and their action takes place in a fantastic world of gods and demons. The *Recorded Sayings*, in contrast, focuses on the life of its divine protagonist in his human incarnation. As such, its immediate antecedents are stories about monks, not gods. One such story is that of Lu Zhishen, whose portrayal in the *Water Margin* resonates with that of Jidian. Another is a "mad monk" (*feng*, or *fengmo*, *heshang*) who figures prominently in a series of novels and plays about the patriotic hero Yue Fei (1103–41). Tradition has it that Yue Fei was murdered by order of the treacherous Prime Minister Qin Gui (1090–1155), who conceived this cabal in the course of a conversation, by his mansion's eastern window, with his wife. After the murder, as Qin Gui and his wife worship at a Buddhist monastery, their Eastern Window Plot (*dong chuang shifan*) is exposed by a mad monk, who, like Jidian, is a deity in disguise residing at the Lingyin Monastery. This mad monk figured first in the Yuan period *zaju* play *The Eastern Window Plot*, and his character was further elaborated in a series of Ming period novels and plays about

Yue Fei.[31] He remained, like Jidian, a popular figure in Qing period fiction and drama and had a significant influence on Jidian's portrayal in nineteenth- and twentieth-century fiction.[32]

Thus, the *Recorded Sayings* is related to the Yue Fei story cycle, which features a mad saint from Hangzhou. Likewise, this novel shares common features with four interrelated short stories celebrating other eccentric Hangzhou monks: "The Chan Master Wujie Seduces Honglian" ("Wujie Chanshi si Honglian ji"), "Master Foyin Teases Qinniang Four Times" ("Foyin shi si tiao Qinniang"), "Monk Yueming Leads Liu Cui to Enlightenment" ("Yueming heshang du Liu Cui"), and "Chen Kechang Attains Immortality During the Duanyang Festival" ("Chen Kechang duanyang xianhua").[33] The stories were written between the late fourteenth and early sixteenth century, probably in Hangzhou. Their protagonists often reside in the same monasteries as Jidian and the eccentric saint of the Yue Fei story: the Lingyin and the Jingci. Poems by them are included in the stories. A sexual trial stands at the center of each story; the monk seduces, or is seduced by, a young girl. Out of shame or indignation, he then wills himself to death. The stories detail the funerary ceremonies that follow and record the eulogies offered him. The stories form part of a larger body of monkish lore, itself related to the *Recorded Sayings*. The protagonist of the first two is the historical monk Foyin (1032–98), whose friendship with Su Shi is the subject of the *Dongpo Foyin yulu*. The stories also figured in Hangzhou oral literature; the female heroines of the first and the third, Honglian and Liu Cui, are named, along with Jidian, in Tian Rucheng's list of *taozhen* topics. Finally, the stories are related to drama; the third story, "Monk Yueming Leads Liu Cui to Enlightenment," developed from a Yuan *zaju* play of the same title.[34] As discussed below, its saintly protagonist shares important characteristics with Jidian.

The *Recorded Sayings* thus has features in common both with a group of novels on gods and with a large body of lore concerning monks—particularly monks in Hangzhou. At the same time, in the creation of his novel the compiler of the *Recorded Sayings* had a large number of sources on Jidian himself to draw on. As noted above, by the second half of the sixteenth century, Jidian had figured in a short story, a fictionalized biography, and in oral literature. Indeed, the novel itself seems to reflect the influence of a few, often mutually inconsistent, sources. It strikes one not as a coherent narrative but as an uneasy medley of different traditions. The novel was probably sewn together from at least two texts, in such a rough manner that the stitches are still apparent. What I call Text A occupies the first quarter of the novel and seems to have been copied as a whole from one source. Text B constitutes the bulk of the novel; it is much less coherent in structure and seems itself to have been pieced together from a few sources. Both texts belong to the tradition of vernacular fiction, yet they differ from each other in everything from language to the characterization of the main protagonist, Jidian (the dividing line between the two texts falls on p. 5b).

Text A is a coherent narrative, describing Daoji's life in chronological order from his birth through his ordination and enlightenment until his master's death. It is written in a relatively elevated vernacular and draws heavily upon Buddhist lore. Its action takes place mainly within the confines of the cloister: the monasteries where omens of the saint's birth appeared, where young Daoji revealed his religious genius, and where he was finally ordained and attained enlightenment. Daoji is referred to either by this name or as Jidian. He is described as an eccentric, enlightened monk, and his figure is modeled at least partially on that of famous Chan masters. As mentioned above, the scene of his enlightenment is patterned after that of Linji, as described in the latter's "recorded sayings."

Text B is a medley of mostly unrelated episodes, only loosely connected through such expressions as "one day" or "next day." This episodic structure lends itself readily to the incorporation of incidents from different sources, and, indeed, at least one story in the second text can be shown to derive from a source at odds with the rest. The text is written in a decidedly spoken, occasionally vulgar, form of the vernacular, and it displays the marks of the Wu dialect of Zhejiang and Jiangsu through its use of the first-person pronoun *wonong*.[35] It draws heavily on oral literature or, at least, simulates it. Its action takes place outside the monastic establishment, in the marketplaces and houses of the laity. The name of the principal protagonist is changed from Jidian to Jigong, and he is transformed from an enlightened monk to a magician and miracle worker.

The *Recorded Sayings* was not the first vernacular narrative to draw on two distinct sources. The historical romances of the Yuan and early Ming known as *pinghua* (popular tales) were an uneasy hybrid of official histories on the one hand and popularized oral histories on the other.[36] In both cases, the sources differ not only in terms of language but also in terms of interpretation. In the case of the *pinghua* novels, this is historical interpretation of the rise and fall of dynasties, and in the case of the *Recorded Sayings* a religious interpretation of the novel's protagonist, Jidian. Whereas Text A sees Jidian as an enlightened monk in the Chan tradition, Text B depicts him as a miracle worker in the tradition of popular religion. The differences in the portrayals of Jidian in the two texts may well reflect the emergence of two distinct beliefs in him in sixteenth-century Hangzhou. We know that by the time the *Recorded Sayings* was compiled, the monastic establishment was beginning to recognize Jidian as a saint, since both Tian Rucheng and Lang Ying mention the presence of his statue in the Jingci Monastery's Arhats Hall. Text A, in its portrayal of Jidian as an enlightened monk, probably reflects a layer of belief close to that of the monastic establishment. I say "close," since both the eccentric traits the text attributes to Jidian and the religious significance it grants him are still much more pronounced than those attributed to him in any canonical source of the period. On the other hand, Text B, by bestowing upon Jidian the title *gong* and expatiating upon his miracles, probably represents the popular conception of Jidian and suggests the seeds of his incorporation as a god into the pantheon of popular religion.

The Buddhist Layer: Text A

Text A is, on the one hand, a fictionalized biography written in the vernacular, and as such it belongs to the world of the sixteenth-century novel. On the other hand, it is imbued with Buddhist lore and its portrayal of Jidian is at least partially modeled on those of famous Chan masters as described in their recorded sayings. We know little of the attitude of the Buddhist establishment toward Jidian in the sixteenth century, but what we do know seems to resonate with Text A. Even though it grants Jidian a religious significance much larger than that bestowed upon him in any sixteenth-century canonical text, it represents a layer of belief colored by Buddhist attitudes that was probably similar to the Buddhist interpretation of him.

By the mid-sixteenth century a statue of Jidian was displayed in the Arhats Hall of the Jingci Monastery. In like manner, Text A portrays Jidian as a "golden-bodied arhat from Mount Tiantai who was incarnated into the world and went to Lin'an county [Hangzhou] to reveal his divine presence" (p. 1a). Jidian's birth is perceived as an arhat's incarnation, and his divine origins are revealed in an event that occurs in the Guoqing Monastery on Mount Tiantai as he is being conceived; one stormy night a thunderclap is heard, and the statue of an arhat falls from its seat to the ground in the monastery's Arhats Hall.[37]

The term *arhat* originally denoted the perfected man of the "Hīnayāna" tradition. In China, however, the arhats, in groups of sixteen, eighteen, or five hundred, came to be worshipped as saints of the Mahāyāna branch of Buddhism.[38] They occupied a particularly important position in Chinese Buddhist art, where their eccentric foreign features—protruding noses, large eyes, and bushy eyebrows—were exaggerated, and their earlobes were occasionally even pierced with large earrings.[39] In the world of vernacular fiction and drama, holy men, particularly of the crazy variety, are often called arhats. For example, one of the Jianyang novels is a collection of hagiographies of 24 arhats.[40] A few of the protagonists of the Hangzhou short stories, as well as the wild monk of the play *Monk Yueming Leads Liu Cui to Enlightenment* and Lu Zhishen, are all referred to as arhats.[41] In the case of Jidian, however, his identification as an arhat goes beyond the common association of arhats with eccentric religiosity. The narrator skillfully weaves the birthplace of the historical Daoji, Tiantai county, into the common legend that the five hundred arhats reside on the most famous topographic feature of Tiantai county, Mount Tiantai.[42] Text A thus identifies Jidian as one of the five hundred venerated saints of Mount Tiantai.

The birth of a saint is by definition miraculous. Jidian's mother conceived after dreaming that she had swallowed the rays of the sun (p. 1a). Within the Buddhist tradition, miraculous conceptions revealed to the mother in a dream begin with the Buddha Śākyamuni himself, whose mother dreamed that a "white king elephant" entered her body.[43] In late Ming vernacular fiction, such miraculous births are attributed equally to deities of Buddhist and Taoist origin. As in the case of Jidian, most commonly the mother dreams that she swallows a ray of light, a star, or a sun.[44] The divine nature of Jidian's birth is indicated not only by a dream but also by its date. Jidian is born on the eighth day of the twelfth month, the date on which Śākyamuni is said to have attained enlightenment.

Already at the age of twelve, young Jidian (then Xiuyuan) triumphs over an elderly master in a quick exchange of Chan repartee. He dedicates his youth to the study of Buddhist scriptures, having firmly resolved to become a monk. Nonetheless, he delays his entry into the Buddhist order out of consideration for the Confucian virtue of filial piety. Only after both his parents have passed away, when he is already 29 years old, does he travel to Hangzhou, where he is ordained at the Lingyin Monastery. The monastery's guardian spirits inform the abbot, Huiyuan, that Daoji is in reality an arhat from Mount Tiantai, and the abbot pays special attention to the guidance of the young novice, whose enlightenment takes a typically Chan form:

> Daoji said: "Ever since this disciple made his obeisance to you as his teacher, you have not even once instructed him. How could he possibly attain the fruits of enlightenment?" The abbot said: "You are too impatient. Since this is the case, come forward." Daoji advanced and was firmly grasped by the abbot, who slapped him, declaring: "This man should be enlightened." Lo and behold Daoji rose to his feet, cast a glance at the abbot's chest, and bumped his head against it, knocking the abbot upside down off his meditation seat. Then he rushed straight out. The abbot shouted loudly: "Robber!" Hurriedly all the monks gathered. "What did he steal?" they asked. "The great treasure of Chan teaching," the abbot answered. (p. 4b)

Daoji's enlightenment scene is fashioned after descriptions of sudden enlightenment found in the recorded sayings of Chan masters in the Linji line, where master and disciple often grasp and beat each other. It is particularly reminiscent of the enlightenment scene of Linji (?–886) himself, described in the ninth-century *Recorded Sayings of the Chan Master Linji Huizhao from Zhenzhou* (*Zhenzhou Linji Huizhao Chanshi yulu*): "During these words, the master [Linji] had the great awakening. . . . Dayu grabbed him and said: 'You little devil, still wetting your bed! . . . What have you seen? Speak quickly, speak quickly!' The master, while Dayu was still grabbing him, gave him three punches in the ribs."[45]

The expression "robber" (*zei*), used by Huiyuan after Daoji has knocked him off his chair, appears frequently in Chan literature. It is used in Chan dialogues as a good-humored compliment to a quick-witted partner who grasps the essence of the question or *gongan* (*kōan*) at hand. Thus, for example, we find it again in Linji's recorded sayings: "One day Puhua was eating raw cabbage before the meditation hall. The master saw him and said: 'You have quite the air of an ass.' Puhua began to bray. The master said: 'This robber.' Puhua went away, shouting 'Robber, robber.'"[46]

The scene of Daoji's enlightenment also differs from those of orthodox Chan masters. The elements Text A borrows from classical

Chan literature are comically exaggerated. Thus Daoji strikes his master—not with his hand—but with his head, and his master falls "upside down off his meditation seat." Furthermore, Text A was addressed to a lay audience, and its author could not assume his readers' familiarity with such technical Chan usages as "robber." Therefore, he had to use concrete imagery to explain them: " 'What did he steal?' the monks asked. 'The great treasure of Chan teaching,' the abbot answered."

At the same time as Text A identifies Jidian as an arhat and depicts him as an enlightened monk in the style of the Linji school, it also attributes to him wildly illicit behavior. Jidian is described as an eccentric who drinks wine and eats meat. Here his image is modeled not on that of Chan masters in Buddhist literature, but on that of eccentric monks in vernacular fiction, most notably Lu Zhishen, who eats meat inside the monastery itself.[47] For example,

> Crazy Ji was getting wilder and wilder; often he would go to the Cool-Spring Pavilion (Lengquan ting)[48] and turn somersaults in it, falling flat on the ground. He would enter the Summoning-the-Monkey Cave (Huyuan dong) and invite the monkey to somersault with him;[49] or else, he would lead a group of children to the wine shop, where he would sing popular songs [*shan'ge*; literally "mountain songs"]. Sometimes, just when the monks were reading sūtras or receiving lay patrons in the hall, he would appear. Holding a plate of meat in one hand and beating the *yinqing* drum in the other,[50] he would play havoc in their midst. He would sing popular songs and, collapsing to the ground, eat the meat inside the Buddha Hall. (p. 5a)

The reference to the popular songs known as *shan'ge* is not accidental. Most of the Ming *shan'ge* preserved today are risqué, and it would have been just as inappropriate for a monk to sing them as it would have been for him to eat meat or drink wine. (Interestingly, one extant *shan'ge* humorously describes a monk who sings a *shan'ge*.)[51] Jidian's somersaults, often mentioned in the text, provide an etiological explanation for his nickname, Jidian, or "Upside-Down Ji," that is, Crazy Ji. Occasionally they reveal bodily parts not commonly displayed in a monastic setting:

> [The abbot] said: "Is there anyone in this assembly who remembers what happens at the moment [of enlightenment]?" Daoji happened to be washing in the bathhouse next door and he overheard the question. "I understand this," he said to himself. Hurriedly he fastened his bathrobe, threw on his cassock, and rushed into the Assembly Hall. Pressing his palms together in a salute to the master, he said: "I remember what happens at that moment."

The abbot said: "Since you know, why not reveal it in front of the whole assembly." Then and there Daoji somersaulted in front of the dharma seat, revealing that thing that he had in front. The monks covered their mouths and burst out laughing. (p. 5a)

The disrespectful and antinomian behavior of Jidian leads to recurring conflicts with the bureaucratic authorities in the monastery. The superintendent (*jiansi*), in particular, repeatedly complains about his behavior, to no avail. The abbot defends Jidian and eventually even designates him his spiritual heir by the symbolic act of bequeathing to him his cassock and alms bowl. Lu Zhishen, too, was persecuted by his fellow monks led by the head monk (*shouzuo*) and the superintendent.[52] This discrepancy between the abbot's recognition of the eccentric monk's religious potential and the superintendent's animosity toward him may be inherited from Chan literature. The superintendent or the head monk often appears in Chan literature "only as a foil for the Chan Master," and as a "symbol of someone who has become paralyzed and religiously impotent by his dependence on some pre-determined religious position."[53] And in the ninth-century *Platform Sūtra of the Sixth Patriarch* (*Liuzu tan jing*), Hongren (601–74) chooses the illiterate Huineng (638–713) as his spiritual heir over his head monk, Shenxiu (?–706).[54]

The overriding tone of Text A, like all later Jidian novels, is comical. Jidian's religious eccentricity is not of the polluting or dangerous type. The symbolism of excrement, blood, and bones of Tantric texts such as the *Hevajra Tantra* is completely absent. Jidian is not a terrifying ascetic but a benevolent clown, whose adventures are entertaining and humorous. The tenor of the narrative is lighthearted, as in the following description of Jidian's trials in meditation, which again makes much of his nickname *dian* (literally, "upside down"):

Daoji sat [in meditation] until the third watch, and his body was growing weary. Suddenly he fell upside down (*diandao*) from the meditation bench. He could not tell where he was, and a long wail escaped from his mouth. Before he knew it, a large bump emerged [on his head]. The superintendent said: "Daoji, how could you fall down? I will forgive you for now, but if this happens again, I will certainly discipline you with a beating." Daoji rose up and sat down again to meditate. Sweet drowsiness enveloped him, and it seemed as if the time would never pass. He fell a second time. The superintendent said: "This is already the second time you have fallen today. It's getting harder to forgive you." A moment had not gone by before Daoji fell again; this was his third fall, and his body was already covered with some seven or eight bumps. The superintendent said: "Daoji has only recently shaved his head, it is fitting that he now get a taste of the *zhubi* rod."[55] Daoji said: "I am already covered with bumps and you want to add another big one with the *zhubi*?! I am going to complain to the abbot." (p. 4a)

The Popular Layer: Text B

The clearest indication that the *Recorded Sayings* has been pieced together from more than one text is the sudden change in the protagonist's name and the accompanying transition in language. One-quarter of the way into the novel, the eccentric monk's name changes without warning from Jidian to Jigong—I maintain the name Jidian here for the sake of continuity—and simultaneously the language of the narrative shifts to a lower form of the vernacular, interspersed with the traits of the Wu dialect. The text marked by these changes (Text B) differs from the preceding Text A in other respects. It is episodic in structure and was probably itself pieced together from other sources. It is much closer to oral literature, or at least simulates it more closely. Its characterization of Jidian is also significantly different. Jidian is depicted not as an enlightened monk in the Chan tradition, but as a miracle worker in the tradition of popular religion—and also as a poet.

The appellation *gong* has several meanings; it is a polite term of address for men used in a variety of social circumstances. In late Ming vernacular fiction, it is most commonly applied to old men. The references to Jidian as *gong* might reflect an abrupt change in his depiction from that of a relatively young novice in Text A to that of an old man in Text B. However, the title *gong* also has religious connotations. As early as the sixth century, Buddhist miracle workers, many of whom shared Jidian's antinomian traits, were often called by this title.[56] Text B portrays Jidian as a miracle worker, and it is thus fitting that it titles him *gong*. Furthermore, at least some miracle workers were posthumously worshipped under this title as well. As noted above, Huiji was venerated as Zhanggong. Non-Buddhist deities were also sometimes worshipped as *gong*; for example, Guangong (the protagonist of the *Romance of the Three Kingdoms*), Leigong (the Duke of Thunder), and Zaogong (the kitchen god). From the early twentieth century on, we have clear evidence that Jidian himself has been worshipped under the title *gong*. The appearance of the name Jigong in Text B might suggest, therefore, that he was worshipped under this title as early as the sixteenth century.

In addition to the abrupt change in the protagonist's name and the simultaneous shift in language, Text B differs significantly from Text A in terms of narrative structure. Whereas Text A has a coherent narrative, Text B is a conglomeration of mostly unrelated episodes. Text B covers a much larger segment of Jidian's life than Text A does. Yet, unlike the latter, only its opening sequence is narrated in chronological order. The sequence opens with one of Jidian's drinking sprees, which leads to a major conflict with the monks of the Lingyin Monastery. The monks expel him from their monastery, and Jidian is obliged to transfer to the Jingci Monastery. (This story tallies with Tian Rucheng's biography, in which a conflict with the Lingyin monks led to Jidian's withdrawal to the Jingci Monastery. As noted above, there is no historical basis for the story.) Following this incident, the narrative of Text B dissolves into a series of unrelated episodes only tenuously connected through such expressions as "that day," "suddenly one day," or "the following day." For the most part, these episodes are arranged in no apparent order. They describe various miracles performed by Jidian or record occasions on which he composed poems and songs. Some are very short in length—only a few lines each. The following summary of two typical pages can serve to illustrate the highly episodic structure of Text B.

At the Jingci Monastery, Jidian is watching the progress of work on a mural for which he had raised the necessary funds. Suddenly he feels an urge for wine and leaves the monastery. On his way he passes a mansion under construction whose owner requests a protective charm for it. He consents, but not before drinking a large quantity of wine. Next he is treated by the proprietor of a nearby restaurant to a bowl of dumplings. He reciprocates with a brief tribute to the dumplings, which he writes on the wall. A man passing the restaurant's front door collapses dead on the ground. The proprietor is afraid of being implicated. Jidian solves the problem by means of a charm that orders the corpse to go elsewhere. Jidian heads back to the monastery and runs into a young man, burdened by the weight of evil karma accumulated in a previous life. Jidian leads him to the Jingci Monastery, where he uses a charm to absolve him of his sins. One day Jidian leaves the monastery and arrives at the Qianyang Nunnery. His fame has preceded him, and the nuns ask him to raise funds for a new iron bell for their nunnery. Jidian agrees on the condition that he is served a large quantity of wine. He writes a petition that on the face of it makes no sense, except that it mentions the first names of two persons who will happen to pass by the nunnery and donate the necessary sum. Jidian returns to the Jingci Monastery. An old man is looking for him. He begs Jidian to preside over the funeral ceremonies of his daughter, the famous prostitute Lan Yueying. A prostitute is a social outcast, yet Jidian agrees—again on that condition that he be served wine first. He offers Lan Yueying a eulogy that cleanses her of her sins (pp. 16a–17a).

The two pages include no less than six unrelated episodes. Moreover, the eulogy, the fund-raising petition, the literary tribute, and the charms that are written or recited by Jidian in the course of these episodes are all recorded in full. Such an episodic structure lends itself easily to the incorporation of stories from diverse sources, which occasionally are mutually inconsistent. In particular, the incident at the Qianyang Nunnery seems to derive from a literary tradition at odds with the rest of the narrative. First, Text B repeatedly mentions the conflicts between Jidian and the monks at the Lingyin Monastery that led to his decision to move to the Jingci. It has Jidian reside in the latter and perform most of his fund-raising miracles on its behalf. Nevertheless, the nunnery episode alludes to a fund-raising miracle performed by Jidian on behalf of the Lingyin Monastery, and it implies that he resides there. This inconsistency has been noted by later publishers of the novel, all of whom change this episode's reference from the Lingyin Monastery to Jingci Monastery.[57] Second, the miracle in question—Jidian drinks wine and vomits on the statues of the three Buddhas, thereby coating them with gold—is narrated in a manner that assumes readers' familiarity with the story. The nuns hear about it and are so impressed that they decide to ask Jidian to help them with their renovation project. However, contrary to the assumption underlying the nunnery episode, the reader who has seen only the *Recorded Sayings* would be unfamiliar with this miracle, for the simple reason that it is not narrated in the text. We know about the miracle from a later novel about Jidian (in which, of course, it occurs at the Jingci Monastery).[58] Third, despite the brevity of the nunnery episode, it refers to Jidian twice by a religious title not mentioned elsewhere in the text, *huofo* (Living Buddha).[59]

The fact that Text B is written in a pronouncedly vernacular language, occasionally even in a form of the Wu dialect, raises the possibility that at least some of its episodes were borrowed from oral literature. We know, of course, that Jidian did figure in oral storytelling, as a subject of the *taozhen* genre, and it is also interesting to note that the *Recorded Sayings* is presented as "narrated" (*xushu*) by Shen Mengpan. The term *xushu* may imply an oral medium. Other novels are generally presented by terms that denote writing or editing, such as *zhu* (to write or author) or *bian* (to compile or edit). It is also noteworthy that at least one seventeenth-century author considered Text B a product of oral literature. In his novel *Jigong quanzhuan*, Wang Mengji introduces the figure of a storyteller who narrates Jidian stories, and all these stories are borrowed verbatim from Text B.[60] As we shall see, the various poems and songs attributed to Jidian in Text B provide further evidence of the close connection between Text B and oral literature.

Jidian the Poet

To judge from Jujian's *Beixian wenji*, the historical Daoji was an accomplished writer. "His literary abilities were in every respect outstanding," Jujian exclaims. The lore that grew up around Daoji in later generations further highlighted his literary skills. The portrayal of Daoji as a poet enabled storytellers and writers to attribute to him a large number of poems, songs, and other literary pieces, thereby diversifying and spicing up their stories. Whereas the Song period *Beixian wenji* does not mention that Jidian held the monastic position as a writer, two Ming period hagiographic collections attribute to him the title "scribe" (*shuji*).[61] Text B, likewise, describes Jidian as the Jingci Monastery's scribe, and its narrative is interspersed with no less than 72 pieces attributed to "Scribe Jidian." The diversity of these literary pieces, ranging from poems and songs to eulogies and magical incantations, is itself testimony to the eclectic nature of Text B.

The portrayal of Jidian as a poet brings him into line with the monkish protagonists of the four Ming period Hangzhou stories, all of whom entertain their lay patrons by dashing off poems in the heat of wine. A slightly later Hangzhou novel, on the Taoist immortal Han Xiangzi, depicts its eccentric protagonist as a poetic genius as well.[62] The figure of Jidian the poet is particularly close to that of Foyin, the subject of two of the Hangzhou stories as well as the *Dongpo Foyin yulu*. Text B explicitly mentions Foyin twice, and some of the poems it attributes to Jidian are reminiscent of passages in the *Dongpo Foyin yulu*. A series of four epigrams in Text B (pp. 15b–16a) is strikingly similar to the witty riddles and wordplay of the *Dongpo Foyin yulu*. The four epigrams are attributed to Su Dongpo, Qin

Shaoyou, Huang Luzhi, and Foyin, respectively. All four figure prominently in the *Dongpo Foyin yulu,* and text B gives Foyin the punchline much as the *Dongpo Foyin yulu* does.

In their poetic inclinations both the Hangzhou monks (including Jidian) and the Taoist immortal Han Xiangzi are modeled not after the wild holy man but after the insouciant poet who "writes quickly and voluminously; . . . drinks heavily; . . . does as he pleases and shows a cheerful disregard for custom and authority."[63] Their portrayal is particularly influenced by the image of the quintessential carefree genius, Li Bai, whose persona is succinctly summarized in the line from Du Fu's poem "Eight Drinking Immortals" quoted earlier: "A hundred poems per gallon of wine—that's Li Bai."[64] In Text B, Jidian compares himself to Li Bai twice. When dead drunk, he writes a fund-raising petition for the Jingci Monastery, exclaiming: "I am Li Bai, the more wine the better" (p. 10b). And on another occasion he composes a poem, entreating one of his lay patrons to offer him wine:

> The other day I heard that the immortal Li
> would drink "a gallon of wine and produce a hundred poems."
> O, gracious patron!—give generously, don't be stingy.
> See how this poor monk waters at the mouth. (p. 7b)

Whereas Jidian is depicted in Text B as a poet-monk in the style of the Hangzhou stories, the poems attributed to him are for the most part different from those found in the latter (with the exception of the poems included in the *Dongpo Foyin yulu*). In the Hangzhou stories—and in Chinese fiction in general, for that matter—poems are generally written in the classical idiom, even though the surrounding text is written in the vernacular. However, the poems and literary pieces in Text B are, for the most part, written in a racy vernacular throughout. This difference between Text B and the Hangzhou stories is particularly apparent in the case of eulogies. The Hangzhou stories record the eulogies offered to their monkish protagonists following the latters' self-willed deaths. The *Water Margin* records the eulogy offered to Lu Zhishen in a similar way.[65] Probably fashioned after Ming period Buddhist eulogies, these tributes to the deceased follow a standard form: a few lines of elevated classical prose, followed by the interjection *yi* or *duo,* and a couplet in poetic idiom. The prose passage generally outlines the moral merits of the deceased, ponders the vacuity of human life, and celebrates liberation from the cycle of life and death. Text B records many such eulogies offered by Jidian to members of the laity. In form they are identical to those included in the Hangzhou stories, except that the language and content of the prose passages change dramatically. In racy vernacular, they describe not liberation from illusory existence but that illusory existence itself. The result is a parody of the standard eulogy form. A eulogy for a noodle vendor, for example, becomes an occasion for celebrating his cooking skills:

> Old Wang the dumpling master,
> What an easygoing character!
> He ground more than a hundred sacks of beans,
> He steamed more than a thousand baskets of dumplings.
> . . . .
> How hard it is to leave behind his regular customers! (p. 13b)[66]

If eulogies for chefs are uncommon in Chinese fiction, eulogies for insects and frogs are all the more so. Text B includes eulogies for lice, a toad, and an elaborate series of funerary addresses for an invincible fighting cricket. (Interestingly, early in the twentieth century a Western observer in Beijing saw a group of children who were "playing at funerals, burying crickets who died with the morning glories, and pretending to repeat Buddhist 'sūtras' over the graves.")[67] One of Jidian's cricket eulogies has a tragic tone and laments the human greed that forced upon the cricket the livelihood of a murderer. Another eulogy has a comical tone, though with a dash of sadness. It refers to the cricket by the nickname Wang Yanzhang, after the famous tenth-century general of that same name:

> Wang Yanzhang the cricket,
> One whisker short, the other long.
> Exactly because he won thirty-six complete victories,
> Everybody called him "Iron-Spear Wang."[68]
> Stop racking your brains, do not grieve!
> This world's myriad creatures are all impermanent.
> Last night suddenly severe frost descended,
> Just like the "dream of Nanke." (p. 19a)[69]

The lice funerary oration carries the parody of the eulogy form to its extreme. (Lice are also the subject of a humorous discussion in the *Dongpo Foyin yulu*.) The lice are still alive at the time the eulogy is offered to them. Removed by Jidian, they are about to be thrown into the fire (conceived of as the equivalent of a cremation pyre), when he offers this eulogy to them:

Lice, listen to my words:

. . . .

You only take up residence where there is blood and flesh.
You are not willing to take up a decent job.
Instead you come and make a living inside my pants.

. . . .

My own body cannot last,
How could you be imperishable?!
Now facing the stove fire
You shouldn't be afraid.
You will get rid of this wriggling body of yours,
And won't return to this worldly existence. (p. 13b)

The literary pieces attributed to Jidian in Text B are introduced by a variety of verbs: some he composes (*zuo*) or writes (*xie*); others he improvises (*kouzhan*), recites (*nian*), or chants (*yin*); still others he sings (*chang*). Written in free verse, some of the latter were probably popular songs in sixteenth-century Hangzhou that were incorporated into the novel. This was probably the case with the following wine song, sung by Jidian after a friend's wife accuses him of having a bad influence over her husband, whom he takes along on his drinking sprees:

Every day during the entire morning, I am as drunk as a log.
There hasn't been as yet one day on which I was sober.
My wife gets angry and curses me,
Saying: "You are just a useless drunkard!"
"Don't be a pain. [I retort]
Stop being stupid.
How long can a person live, anyway!" (p. 20a)

In terms of the possible influence of drama or oral literature on Text B, the most interesting compositions attributed to Jidian are those in which he describes himself. Text B includes no less than twelve literary pieces in which Jidian introduces himself to the reader. In some of these pieces Jidian reveals his divine identity or magical powers, and in all of them he elaborates upon his eccentric, carefree, or occasionally lascivious traits. Written in a dramatic style, these self-descriptive pieces simulate the position of the storyteller or the actor on stage. Some of them are written in the classical language and are imbued with Chan allusions that became common currency in Ming religious fiction. This is the case with the following poem, in which, in the tradition of Li Bai, Jidian confesses to indulge in two pleasures only—poetry and wine:

Since I shaved my head and wore black,[70] already a year has passed.
Wine and poetry only have I been destined to wed.
At leisure I watch Maitreya[71] sport in the emptiness.
And, when tired, I sleep on Vairocana's head.[72]
. . . .
In [this] vast world not one person knows me.
They still say: "[Look,] the mad monk is wandering in the marketplace." (p. 18a)

In one racy poem, however, Jidian professes to enjoy not only poetry and wine but also lovemaking. He portrays himself as a sexually promiscuous monk:

Every day he indulges in wine and sleeps with courtesans.
How can the libertine monk be like others?
His cassock is often stained with rouge.
His robes carry the fragrance of powder. (p. 7b)

Although some of the self-descriptive pieces attributed to Jidian are written in the classical idiom, most are written in the vernacular. The following quatrain, for example, is written in as simple and colloquial a language as one can possibly find in written Chinese (*dou* 都 instead of *jie* 皆, etc.). In it Jidian acknowledges, again, his vice of drunkenness:

In the past my parents did this thing [sex],
[And] gave birth to this stinking skin-bag of mine.
My heart is not like my parents.
My heart covets nothing but wine. (p. 8a)

昔我父娘作此態
生我這個臭皮袋
我心不比父娘心
我心除酒都不愛

The self-descriptive pieces in Text B are modeled after the introductory speeches by which an actor presents himself to the audience and a storyteller introduces a new character to his tale. Their pronouncedly vernacular language, like that of the text as a whole, is strong testimony to the impact of oral literature on Text B. Woven into the narrative of Text B, they serve an important function in the characterization of Jidian, who emerges from the text not as an enlightened monk but as an eccentric magician.

Jidian the Miracle Worker

Text B transfers Jidian from the confines of the monastic establishment into the world of the marketplaces and houses of the laity. Jidian spends weeks or even months at a time in the houses of his lay patrons, and when he returns to the monastery, the abbot invariably asks: "Where have you been all these days?" On one occasion, he tarries outside the monastery for such a lengthy period that the abbot is obliged to send a messenger to fetch him (p. 10a).

The narrator delights in describing Jidian's familiarity with his lay friends, whom he addresses in the most informal terms. He refers to his male acquaintances as *age* (brother) and the proprietress of a small tea shop who regularly treats him to tea as *apo* (auntie—an informal term of address for old women; p. 20b). In terms of social standing, Jidian's friends span the spectrum from petty vendors to high-ranking government officials. The former invite him to tea and dumplings in their little stalls; the latter treat him to lavish drinking sprees and sumptuous feasts in expensive restaurants and brothels. The implied author of Text B repeatedly emphasizes the great respect of the literati elite toward Jidian, an emphasis which suggests that in his eyes, and possibly in those of his audience as well, this respect itself is evidence of Jidian's religious significance. When Commander Chen is informed that Jidian is at the gate of his mansion, he goes in person to welcome him. And when Commander Wang spots Jidian in the street, he hurriedly descends from his sedanchair to inquire: "Why haven't I seen you for such a long time?" (p. 6b). This close friendship between Jidian and high-ranking officials differentiates Text B from nineteenth-century novels about Jidian, which transform him from the protégé of officials into the champion of the poor in their struggle for social justice.

Jidian entertains his lay friends, whether of humble or high social standing, with jokes, witty remarks, songs, and poems. Yet his primary function is not that of poet or entertainer but of miracle worker. Text B expatiates upon his miraculous powers, which are displayed in a wide range of performances, from healing to the administration of karmic retribution. One area where Jidian's supernatural powers are particularly in demand is funerary ritual. Buddhist clergymen have played an important role in Chinese funerary rites from the introduction of Buddhism to China until modern times.[73] The purpose of these rites was to guarantee the well-being of the deceased in the afterlife and thereby the safety and prosperity of the remaining kin. As early as Tian Rucheng's *Supplement,* there are suggestions that the lore surrounding Jidian attributed to him the ability to guide the deceased toward salvation: "He would recite sūtras and light funeral pyres for people, and in each case they would attain salvation."[74] Text B details Jidian's performances at six funerals. It records the eulogies Jidian offered to the deceased and describes the miracles that testified to the success of the funerary ceremonies. Jidian cleanses the deceased of a lifetime accumulation of evil karma and guarantees either his liberation from the cycle of life and death or his immediate rebirth into his own family. The attentiveness of Text B to issues of funerary ritual suggests the concerns of the sixteenth-century Hangzhou laity with the correct performance of funerary rites. A similar concern has been observed by historians and anthropologists alike in other periods of Chinese history.[75]

Supernatural revelations during the funeral ceremony itself inform the mourners that Jidian has indeed guided the deceased toward salvation or rebirth. This is the case when Jidian presides over the funerals not only of humans but also of insects and frogs. Both the toad and the cricket whom Jidian cremates appear in midair in the form of a "green-clad youth" (*qingyi tongzi*) to thank him for liberating them from the cycle of life and death (pp. 11a, 19b).[76] A particularly touching funeral miracle is performed by Jidian on behalf of two ill-fated lovers who commit suicide because their families will not allow them to marry. Jidian unites the lovers after their physical death. As he cremates their bodies, two shafts of red light emanate from them and unite in midair (p. 18b). In the case of the dumpling vendor Mr. Wang, Jidian specifically instructs the spirit to head not to the remote Western Paradise but to nearby Yuhang county. Sure enough, within minutes a messenger arrives from Yuhang and informs the astonished crowd that Mr. Wang's own daughter has just given birth to a son who bears a vermilion tattoo reading "Dumpling Master Wang" (p. 13b).

Jidian's funerary performances are characterized by an element of public spectacle. The astonished audience applauds when the cremated toad appears in midair, or when the messenger from Yuhang announces the rebirth of Mr. Wang. Jidian's religious services are thus the equivalent of a magician's show, a show not devoid of a certain humorous tone. As noted above, the eulogies offered by

Jidian parody the standard eulogy. Even more conspicuously, following the reincarnation of the dumpling master, Jidian responds to the crowd's applause by a somersault that reveals his penis (p. 13b). (Interestingly, it has been common in both north and south China to invite storytellers, actors, or acrobats to funeral ceremonies to provide entertainment during the wake.)[77] The humorous character of Jidian's religious performances does not, however, diminish their religious efficacy in the least. Indeed, these farcical eulogies lead the dumpling master and the cricket to rebirth and salvation. The association of humor with religious power has remained a primary characteristic of the god Jigong. Spirit-mediums of Jigong in present-day Taiwan entertain their followers with ribald jokes. Yet, even as they laugh, the followers are convinced of the medium's power and of the efficacy of the ritual.

Jidian employs his supernatural powers not only to guarantee the salvation of the deceased but also to benefit the living. Healing is one area where he amply demonstrates his magical powers. He heals a consumptive young woman (p. 17b), and in one case he both correctly prophesies a disease that will afflict one of his clients and offers in advance the prescription that will heal it (p. 8b). The administration of karmic retribution is another area for Jidian's supernatural powers. Under Jidian's guidance, one of his acquaintances finds a small bundle with ten ingots of silver in a public toilet booth. The following day a man commits suicide in that same booth. Jidian explains the karmic meaning of these events to his friend (and also to the reader): the ten ingots of silver belonged to Jidian's friend in his previous life. He was robbed of them and murdered by the very same man who in this incarnation committed suicide inside the toilet booth (p. 17a). The convoluted sequence of this miracle, in particular, might strike some readers as absurd or crude. Yet even Jidian's most fantastic magical feats are narrated in Text B with no apparent narrative irony. Text B resonates with the simplicity of folk beliefs, and its implied author appears convinced of the historical veracity of the events he records.

Charms and magical incantations play an important role in Jidian's performances. The image of him that emerges from Text B is closer to that of the popular religion specialist or the spirit medium than that of the educated monk. In one instance, Jidian instructs a young man to crouch under a table. He himself sits crossed-legged on top of it and recites a charm in rhyming verse that absolves the man of the burden of evil karma he has accumulated in a previous life (p. 16b). In another case described above, Jidian again uses a charm in rhyming verse to order a corpse to walk. (Ordering corpses around remains a common feature of Hongkong ghost movies, which are a curious combination of horror show and slapstick comedy.) Jidian's charm reads:

> Dead man, where did you originally live?
> What illness caused you to fall dead in the middle of the street?
> I will now point to you a road—
> Straight ahead, a quiet place, where you can rest in peace. (p. 16a)

Although most of Jidian's miracles benefit the laity, some are performed on behalf of his fellow monks. These are not the monks of the Lingyin Monastery, toward whom Jidian feels nothing but animosity, but most often monks from the Jingci Monastery, whose relations with Jidian are a mixture of mutual respect and bantering. The Jingci monks recognize Jidian's religious integrity and respect him. They also need him; his fund-raising abilities, his writing skills, and his contacts with high-ranking officials are of great use to them. (When the monastery's two superintendents are arrested on an unfounded charge, it is Jidian who intervenes with the authorities to release them.) They accept Jidian's eccentricity—the abbot even treats him to wine—but they also play pranks on him. On one occasion they offer him a sealed jug that contains water instead of wine. For his part Jidian comes and goes as he pleases. His one personal disciple is not a member of the monastic community but a former turnip vendor, now a devotee, who has followed him into the monastery. Jidian, as it were, resides in the monastery but is not of it. He readily assists his fellow monks, yet even as he does so, he cannot resist poking fun at them. When about to release the two helpless superintendents, their heads stuck in the cangue, he teases them: "Your two [bald] heads stick out from the cangues like lamps on a rack" (p. 14b).

The miracles Jidian performs on behalf of the clergy are related to fund-raising. As the official scribe of the Jingci Monastery, he writes fund-raising petitions. The petitions, like Jidian's other writings, are included in Text B. Most often they are effective not because of their literary brilliance or persuasive power but because of a prophetic insight hidden in them. As mentioned above, the fund-raising announcement Jidian writes for the Qianyang Nunnery appears to make no sense, except that it mentions the first names of two high-ranking officials who will happen to pass by the nunnery, be struck by the mention of their names in the petition, and donate the necessary sum (p. 16b). In some cases the petition itself does not suffice, and a supernatural revelation is necessary to accomplish the goal. The revelation takes place in the prospective donors' dreams. Jidian reveals to them his divine form as a "golden-bodied arhat" and persuades them to contribute the necessary funds. One of the fortunate donors is no less a figure than the empress dowager herself. Having witnessed his divine manifestation, she hurries to the Jingci Monastery and donates the astronomical sum of 3,000 strings of cash. Among the hundreds of clerics who gather to welcome her, she identifies the shabby-looking Jidian as the "golden-bodied arhat" revealed to her in her dream. In a manner typical of the eccentric monk, he responds by a somersault that reveals to the empress and her retinue "that thing that he has in front" (p. 11a).

Jidian's appearances in donors' dreams reflect a common belief in Chinese religion that gods can manifest themselves in their devotees' dreams. The narrator's assertion that it was Jidian's dream appearances that induced the believers to donate mirrors a religious environment in which donors and their beneficiaries alike attributed donations to the influence of divine revelations. Hong Mai's *Yi Jian's Record* as well as temple inscriptions show that as early as the Song period devotees attributed great importance to divine revelations in their dreams.[78] An inscription dated 1124 from a temple to Guanyin in Jiangsu tells of a man who donated a sandalwood arm for a Guanyin statue after the goddess was revealed to him in a dream.[79] Divine appearances were not restricted to Buddhist deities; according to Ding Baigui (1171–1237), an early temple to Mazu in Zhejiang was constructed after the goddess revealed herself in a collective dream to local residents and asked that a temple be built for her.[80] As in the case of Jidian himself, arhats, too, were revealed in dreams. Xie Yi (1069–1113) records a case in which "a military officer of Linchuan county contributed funds to a nearby temple after an arhat who had appeared to his daughter in a dream proved to be depicted in a painting, now in the family's possession, which had once belonged to the temple."[81] As late as the nineteenth century, dreams were considered a medium of communication with the divine. Dai Fengyi (fl. 1897) attests that his decision to write a biography of Guo Shengwang, possibly the most popular local deity in Fujian, followed the god's appearance in a dream.[82]

Jidian continued to perform fund-raising miracles on behalf of the Jingci Monastery after his physical death. (It is noteworthy that Jidian's death is modeled on that of the Buddha Śākyamuni; like the Buddha's it is preceded by severe diarrhea.)[83] The first manifestation of his immortal presence takes place right after his burial in the form of a miracle involving shoes that is a stock element in the hagiographies of Chinese Buddhist saints. Since Jidian never wears proper shoes, the Jingci abbot offers his own pair for Jidian's burial ceremony. Jidian is cremated—along with the shoes, naturally. Yet when the abbot returns from the cremation, he finds two wandering monks awaiting him at the monastery's gate. The two offer him his unburned shoes along with a letter from Jidian (p. 22b). This legend is clearly fashioned after a popular story about Bodhidharma, which was later appended in an almost identical form to the hagiography of Budai heshang. In the Bodhidharma legend, a diplomat returning from India to China runs into the saint—after the latter's death and burial—in Central Asia. Bodhidharma is returning to his homeland, India, and in his hands he carries a shoe. When the diplomat arrives in China, Bodhidharma's grave is opened and discovered to be empty, except for the one shoe Bodhidharma left behind.[84]

Text B's insistence that Jidian continued to manifest his supernatural powers even after his death attests to the implied author's conviction of his protagonist's divinity. Furthermore, Jidian's responsiveness to his devotees' requests may reflect his incorporation into the pantheon of popular religion, which is to say that the novel itself may provide us with evidence for the historical cult of its protagonist in sixteenth-century Hangzhou. The concluding sentence of Text B reads: "Jigong repeatedly revealed [his presence] and responded [to the believers' requests]. It is impossible to narrate all of these instances here" (*Jigong leilei xian ying, shu bu neng jin*) (p. 23a). Similar statements appear in Ming fiction in reference to other popular gods. Two late Ming hagiographic novels, *Journey to the North* and *The Biography of the Heavenly King Huaguang* (known also as the *Journey to the South*), on Zhenwu and Huaguang, respectively, include statements regarding the proven efficacy of worshipping their divine protagonists.[85] The *Romance of the Three Kingdoms* informs us that Guangong's spirit protected the common people, who responded by means of a temple built in his honor.[86] And the *Water Margin* concludes with an elaborate description of Song Jiang's responsiveness to people's supplications: "Those who prayed for wind received wind, and those who asked for rain received rain. . . . There was no one [who prayed for him and] did not get a [favorable] response (*wu you bu ying*)."[87] Like other Ming novels, Text B itself may thus provide us with evidence for its protagonist's cult.

A Holy Fool

[I have] eyebrows like a broom, and a huge mouth that cannot lie but can drink wine. Look at my white hair[88] and my often bare feet! I have physical form, but my mind is free. I have sex but am not attached. In my drunken stupor, I pay no heed to the waves of the worldly sea. My entire body covered with rags, I act like a madman. Under the bright moon in the fresh breeze, I laugh and sing. . . . Sitting backward on my donkey, I return to the heavenly ridges (p. 18b).[89]

This self-description is presented in text B as written by Jidian to accompany a portrait of him. Like Jidian's other poems and reflexive pieces, it describes him as a carefree eccentric, an outsider to both the monastic establishment and society at large. The insouciant monk Jidian is distinguished from ordinary clerics first of all by his shabby attire. Jidian's cassock is so worn that his "naked legs show through" (p. 8b). He often walks barefoot, and on one occasion he returns to the monastery "wearing on one leg a rush sandal and holding in one hand a straw sandal" (p. 5b). (This image is fashioned, again, after the common iconographic representation of Bodhidharma returning to the west, shoe in hand.) Jidian's shabby appearance prompts his patrons and friends to offer him new clothes, yet the modest monk generally declines. On one occasion Commander Chen offers Jidian two bolts of silk and two taels of silver for the express purpose of having a new set of clothes made. On his way back to the monastery, however, the generous Jidian donates the silk and the silver to a group of beggars trembling in the cold (p. 8b).

Not only his attire but his speech and demeanor distinguish Jidian from his fellow monks. Whether he addresses his lay friends as "brother" (*age*) or curses his fellow monks as "bald asses" (*tu lü*), the language Jidian uses is decidedly colloquial, a comic contrast to the formal or even pompous language that the reader would expect a cleric to use. Furthermore, Jidian enjoys foods that monks do not generally eat, and he consumes them at taverns and food stalls that monks are not supposed to frequent. Text B is seasoned by a kind of culinary interest. The narrator brings to life the night markets of Hangzhou with their abundance of restaurants and food stalls, and he describes in detail the exact dishes that Jidian enjoys there, all of which have the hearty flavor of home cooking: dumplings (*huntun*), fried dumplings (*guduo*), or *tofu* soup (*doufu tang*).

Jidian's mischievousness and even clownishness are reflected in his somersaults that all too often reveal "that thing in front." His playful and carefree characteristics are evident also in his fondness for children. Like Budai heshang, whose hagiography and iconography highlight his association with children,[90] Jidian occasionally prefers the company of urchins to that of adults. In one case he takes them in a boat to gather lotus flowers on the West Lake (p. 11a). Manipulating various points of view, the author often highlights Jidian's eccentricity by portraying him through another character's eyes and giving the other person's first impression of Jidian. A young man inquiring at the Jingci Monastery for Jidian is led to the kitchen, where he sees a seated monk (Jidian) delousing himself (p. 19b). Another visitor is directed to the Assembly Hall, where to his astonishment he discovers the holy fool comfortably asleep (p. 16b).

The specific monastic vow Jidian violates most often is that forbidding wine. As noted above, Jidian compares himself to Li Bai in that his poetic genius is inextricably linked to his drunkenness. Text B describes at great length Jidian's love of wine, his endless drinking sprees, and the huge quantities of liquor he consumes. Jidian consents to stay at an acquaintance's house only if wine is provided. When, for example, the master of the Upper Tianzhu Monastery (Shang Tianzhu si) reassures him that wine is available, he responds: "Since there is wine, I am willing to stay here one or two years, not to mention a month or two" (p. 12a). Wandering from one patron to another and accompanying them from one tavern to the next, Jidian goes on drinking sprees that can last days. In each sitting, he consumes fifteen or more bowls of wine, and in one case he hardly sits down before he "drinks right away more than twenty bowls" (p. 20a).

Jidian's drinking is similar to that of Lu Zhishen as described in the *Water Margin*. Both Jidian and Lu Zhishen drink so much that occasionally waiters suggest that they stop.[91] The two even use similar expressions when ordering wine. Jidian brushes off the waiter's warnings by declaring: "That's none of your business—just keep on pouring (*zhi gu shai lai*)" (p. 7b). And Lu Zhishen responds to a waiter's inquiry as to how much he wants by asserting: "Never mind how much—just see you keep pouring it in large bowls (*da wan zhi gu shai lai*)."[92] Jidian is further reminiscent of Lu Zhishen in terms of the rhythm that governs his drinking bouts. Both monks periodically attempt to control their craving for wine and remain at the monastery. However, a change of weather rekindles their desire, and off they go. For example, after Jidian has stayed in the monastery for some two months, "the snowstorms of winter's end arrive," and he feels cold (p. 6b). He thereupon sets out for a lengthy drinking spree in town. Similarly, Lu Zhishen remains at Wutai shan for four or five months, but "early winter arrives," and he leaves the monastery for a wild drinking bout.[93] The portrayals of Jidian and of Lu Zhishen thus share similar narrative patterns: a period of confinement followed by a change of weather and an unbridled drinking spree. These are not the only similarities between Text B and the *Water Margin*. The two novels also share a similar vocabulary as well as the same interest in the life of the urban lower classes. It may well be the case, therefore, that the *Water Margin* influenced Text B.[94]

The other cardinal monastic precept Jidian disregards is that forbidding sexual intercourse. Here, however, a distinction should be drawn between Jidian's self-descriptions and the text's prose narrative. In his many reflexive pieces, Jidian readily acknowledges that he engages in sex. "I have sex but am not attached," he declares on one occasion. And referring to himself in the third person, he further elaborates: "Everyday he indulges in wine and sleeps with courtesans. How can the libertine monk be like others?" (p. 7b). The prose narrative, on the other hand, has Jidian flirt with women but not make love to them. Jidian frequents brothels and composes bawdy songs, but he does not transgress his monastic vow. The prose narrative portrays Jidian as venturing into the dangerous realm of sexuality only to emerge from it pure.

The portrayal of Jidian as a flirtatious yet ultimately chaste monk is again reminiscent of the monkish protagonists of the four Ming period Hangzhou stories. The Hangzhou monks (including Foyin as depicted in the *Dongpo Foyin yulu*) associate with courtesans and even extol their beauty in poems, yet they often withstand the sexual trial involved. This is also the case with the monkish hero of the Yuan *zaju* play *Monk Yueming Leads Liu Cui to Enlightenment*, who has been sent into the world for the explicit purpose of leading to salvation a courtesan. (The eccentric protagonist of the *zaju* play resembles Jidian in other respects as well: he is an incarnated arhat who drinks wine and eats meat.)[95] One sexual trial in Text B is particularly reminiscent of those the Hangzhou monks endure. Jidian is led to a brothel by one of his lay patrons, who arranges for a prostitute to spend the night with him. Jidian emerges from his test with honor: whereas the prostitute spends the night in bed, he sleeps on the stove (p. 8a). This incident not only ties Text B to the Hangzhou stories, but also points to a link between the text and the lost sixteenth-century story "Red Beauty Tries Jidian," whose title indicates a similar theme.[96]

One of the finest examples of Jidian's dallying takes place at the house of a famous courtesan, named Wang. Jidian goes there in search of his patron Commander Chen. He does not find him, but the courtesan is there, sound asleep. Jidian climbs into her bed, removes the quilt, and places her shoe on her vulva. Of course, in the context of Chinese eroticism, the combined image of a woman's private parts and her little shoe is extremely powerful. Jidian explains his naughty behavior by means of a bawdy poem that uses religious terminology to describe the female private parts:

> Exhausted by love, the butterfly and the flowering branch
> Fall asleep, a spring dream from which it is hard to wake up.
> Her silk gown, discarded, is separated from her body.
> Her three souls journey to the immortals' abode.
> And her seven spirits encircle the islands of Peng and Ying.[97]
> Therefore, I used her silk shoe to cover the cave's entrance.
> If having awoken she is angry, then she ought to know:
> It isn't because Daoji has bad intentions
> That he blocked the road of life and death
> And shut the gate of being and nonbeing. (p. 7a)

Text B portrays Jidian on the one hand as an eccentric who transgresses the rules of his own monastic order and on the other hand as a miracle worker endowed with supernatural powers. The text makes it abundantly clear, however, that these two dimensions of Jidian's personality are inseparable. Indeed, it is exactly Jidian's misconduct that endows him with his miraculous powers. Since Jidian sees his poetic gift as inseparable from his drunkenness, wine becomes a precondition for his writing, whether secular or religious. When the Qianyang nuns ask him to write a fund-raising petition on their behalf, Jidian declares: "If you want me to do this, then I must first get drunk" (p. 16b). When asked by the Jingci monks to write an invitation letter for a new abbot, Jidian's unequivocal response is: "If you want him to come, you must first treat me to wine" (p. 14b).

Wine becomes a necessary provision not only for Jidian's writing but for all his other religious activities as well. Jidian cannot preside over funerary ceremonies unless wine is provided. Wine thus becomes the stuff that guarantees the deceased's salvation. It is also when drunk that Jidian's perception is at its sharpest. On one occasion Jidian is brought back to the monastery dead drunk. That same night a fire rages through the monastery, and Jidian saves his fellow monks' lives by waking them up (p. 14a).

In some cases drunkenness alone is not enough for the performance of a miracle, and other religious vows have to be transgressed as well. In order to heal a young consumptive woman, Jidian has to spend the whole night in her bedroom. He drinks a large quantity of wine and sits with his exposed back touching hers. The "meditation fire" (*sanmei huo*) gathered in his body is transferred to hers and cures her (p. 17b). Wine and an intimate association with a woman are thus the preconditions for healing. Salvation is born of sin.

Conclusion

Evidence points to the significance of Jidian in sixteenth-century Hangzhou lore. Jidian figured in oral literature and was the subject of both a written short story—now lost—and two novels, one of which, the *Recorded Sayings*, still survives. The oral and written stories as well as the two novels were probably interrelated, and at the same time they were part of a body of fiction and drama celebrating eccentric monks. Stories concerning Hangzhou monks, such as Foyin, exercised the greatest influence on the portrayal of Jidian. However, characteristics of other wild monks, such as Lu Zhishen, are also reflected in his image.

The most significant source for the study of Jidian in the sixteenth-century is the *Recorded Sayings*. This novel offers a unique vantage point on the history of Jidian, since it has probably been pieced together from two different texts, the first of which reflects a Buddhist-oriented understanding of Jidian, and the second his popular cult. The first text (Text A) is written in a relatively elevated form of the vernacular and draws heavily upon Buddhist sources. Its portrayal of Jidian is modeled at least partially on that of famous Chan masters. The second text (Text B) is written in a simple form of the vernacular, interspersed with evidence of the Wu dialect. It appears to owe much to oral literature. The eccentric monk's name is changed in it from Jidian to Jigong, and he is transformed from an enlightened monk to an arch-magician and a miracle worker. The two texts together thus indicate the existence of two types of belief in Jidian in sixteenth-century Hangzhou. One conceived of Jidian as an eccentric Chan master; the other saw him as an incarnate deity endowed with salvational powers. The former image of Jidian was probably prevalent in monastic circles or among the highly educated laity. The latter was probably particularly popular among the middle or lower echelons of urban society.

As a novel that draws on both Buddhist sources and popular lore the *Recorded Sayings* served as a bridge between high culture and popular culture, in this case monastic Buddhism and popular religion. It was through such novels that Chan stories and Buddhist legends became an integral part of popular lore. The exchange was not one-sided, however. The *Recorded Sayings* served not only as a channel through which Buddhist lore trickled down into popular religion but also as a vehicle for the incorporation of popular legends by the monastic establishment. During the Qing, legends from the *Recorded Sayings*, Text A and Text B alike, were gradually incorporated into the official histories of Hangzhou monasteries. Popular lore recorded in the *Recorded Sayings* received the approval of the Buddhist establishment and was included in the Buddhist hagiographies of Jidian. The final stage in the Buddhist canonization of the *Recorded Sayings* was its incorporation, early this century, into the Japanese Buddhist collection, *The Great Japanese Continuation of the Canon* (*Dai Nihon zokuzōkyō*). A text that originated in popular lore thus became part of the Buddhist canon.

The *Recorded Sayings* is an interesting novel not only as an example of dual origins—Buddhist literature and popular lore—but also as an example of a genre of hagiographic novels widespread during the late Ming. Typically, works in this genre lack narrative irony, and their implied authors appear convinced of their protagonists' divinity. The novels therefore blur the line between secular and religious literature. They remind us that the application of the Western term *novel* to works in the *xiaoshuo* genre may be misleading. Unlike Western novels whose primary subject matter is human experience, these late Ming narratives have as their subject matter the supernatural. Their protagonists are deities not humans. And even when these divine protagonists are humorous, their religious powers are never questioned.

FOUR

Clown and Moral Exemplar

Two novels, a play, and a short story testify to the growing popularity of Jidian in the seventeenth century. All four come from the Zhejiang-Jiangsu area, but not only, as in the sixteenth century, from Hangzhou. The playwright was from Suzhou, and the short story may have been written there as well. All four works derive from the sixteenth-century *Recorded Sayings*. The play and the novels draw on it directly, and the short story is based on one of the novels. The four works reflect different understandings of the eccentric saint Jidian. One novel, the story based on it, and the play reproduce the image of Jidian found in Text B of the *Recorded Sayings* and portray him, for the most part, as an eccentric miracle worker. By contrast, the other novel transforms him into a Buddhist teacher and moral exemplar.

The Novel "Drunken Puti"

Dating, Authorship, and Relation to the *Charming Stories*

Drunken Puti (*Zui puti*) was the most popular novel on Jidian until its eclipse, in the late nineteenth century, by the 240-chapter *Storyteller's Jigong* (see Appendix A). During the eighteenth and the nineteenth centuries, at least twenty editions of *Drunken Puti* were published.[1] *Drunken Puti* has the distinction of being the only novel on Jidian translated into a Western language, and it has received more scholarly attention than other works on him.[2] The title, *Drunken Puti*, captures the idiosyncratic nature of the novel's protagonist, whose personality combines eccentricity with sainthood. *Puti* is the Chinese transliteration of the Sanskrit *bodhi* (perfect wisdom or enlightenment). In the context of this novel, it is used not as an abstract noun but as a proper noun describing the enlightened nature of the drunken Jidian.

The earliest extant edition of the *Drunken Puti* dates from 1721,[3] and, like most later editions, it gives the author as Tianhua Zang Zhuren (Master of the Heavenly Flower Repository). Editions of the *Drunken Puti* are distributed by temples as proselytizing literature (see Appendix D), evincing the significance of novels in shaping the Jigong cult. One such edition, for example, is that published by the Buddhist Studies Publishing Company of Shanghai in 1932,[4] and another, published in Taiwan in 1983, is accompanied by a commentary attributed to Jigong himself, which was written using a planchette by the automatic spirit-writing technique. The title of this edition, *The Authoritative Biography of the Living Buddha, Jigong* (*Jigong huofo zhengzhuan*), is probably meant to distinguish it from the currently more popular *Storyteller's Jigong*.

When was the *Drunken Puti* written? A clue to this novel's date is provided, as Yves Robert has suggested, by its relation to a seventeenth-century collection of short stories, *Charming Stories of the West Lake* (*Xihu jiahua*; preface dated 1673), whose author is given as Molang Zi (Ink-Crazy Master).[5] This collection celebrates the religious and cultural lore of the West Lake. The subject of most of its stories are famous monks and poets who lived in reclusion on its shores. They include such figures as the fourth-century A.D. Taoist philosopher Ge Hong, the early Tang poet Luo Binwang, who was rumored to have become a monk following a failed coup against Empress Wu, and the Song official Shen Zhuhong, who renounced a brilliant career in order to join the Buddhist priesthood.[6] Reflecting the growing popularity of Jidian, one story, "Drunken Traces at Nanping" ("Nanping zuiji"; see Appendix A) narrates several famous legends associated with this saint. (Nanping is the name of the hill on which the Jingci Monastery is situated.) An examination of this story reveals that it is probably based on *Drunken Puti* and not vice versa. The story includes several episodes from the saint's life, all of them extracted almost verbatim from this novel and presented in the order of their appearance in *Drunken Puti*.[7] Some episodes are presented in slightly briefer versions than in the novel; allusions to episodes not included in the *Charming Stories*, as well as several poems, are omitted.[8]

Is it possible that the author of *Drunken Puti* borrowed episodes from the *Charming Stories*, enlarged them, and inserted material in between them to create his novel? This is unlikely for several reasons. First, it is generally more difficult to insert material between episodes, thereby lengthening a narrative, than it is to extract episodes and shorten it. Glen Dudbridge has shown, for instance, that the 100-chapter *Journey to the West* preceded two shorter versions of the same novel.[9] Second, other tales in the *Charming Stories* are also adaptations. For example, one story was adapted from Feng Menglong's *Common Words to Warn the World* (*Jingshi tongyan*), and another from the *Second Collection of West Lake Stories* (*Xihu erji*).[10] A lengthy legend included in yet another story was borrowed almost verbatim from a novel that preceded the *Charming Stories* by only five years.[11] It is thus in keeping with the composition of the *Charming Stories* that the Jidian story would be extracted from another source. Third and most significant, it is unlikely that *Drunken Puti* borrowed from the *Charming Stories*, because the former is based on another source, the *Recorded Sayings*. *Drunken Puti* seldom deviates from the story line of the *Recorded Sayings*. Most of the episodes included in the *Charming Stories* version of the Jidian legend are likewise present, in nuclear form, in the *Recorded Sayings*. It is highly unlikely that the authors of both *Drunken Puti* and the *Charming Stories* were adapting the *Recorded Sayings*, and that in specific instances the *Drunken Puti* author followed the *Charming Stories* adaptation. It is much more plausible that the *Drunken Puti* author adapted the *Recorded Sayings*, and that the *Charming Stories* author borrowed from his adaptation.

It is thus most likely that *Drunken Puti* preceded the *Charming Stories* and was written, therefore, before 1673. Who wrote it? As noted above, the earliest extant edition of the novel (dated 1721), as well as most later editions, attributes the novel to Tianhua Zang Zhuren. The latter is known to us as a prolific author. His name is associated—in the capacity of author, compiler, or writer of preface—with no less than fifteen other novels, thirteen of which belong in the category of "scholar and beauty romances" (*caizi jiaren xiaoshuo*).[12] However, the earliest written reference to the novel, in a Japanese list of imported books dated 1707, gives the author as Molang Zi, the same pseudonym that appears on the *Charming Stories* collection, and attributes only the novel's preface to Tianhua Zang Zhuren.[13] Furthermore, three of the novel's later editions give its author as Molang Zi.[14] Thus, it is impossible to conclude whether Tianhua Zang Zhuren did indeed author *Drunken Puti* or only its preface, or whether Molang Zi wrote both it and the *Charming Stories* collection. Another possibility is that both pseudonyms refer to the same person.[15]

Narrative Detail

The story line of *Drunken Puti* rarely deviates from that of the *Recorded Sayings*, and its portrayal of Jidian is similar to the latter's as well. The bulk of the *Recorded Sayings*, Text B, depicts Jidian as an eccentric arch-magician, and he emerges from *Drunken Puti* in much the same light. Nonetheless, the *Drunken Puti* differs significantly from its source. The differences are apparent first in the formal characteristics of *Drunken Puti* as a work of vernacular fiction. The *Recorded Sayings* presents itself as a record of Jidian's words, and it does not conform to the formal requirements of the late Ming and Qing novel. In contrast, *Drunken Puti* acknowledges itself as a novel. Thus, it divides the *Recorded Sayings* narrative into chapters, each of which concludes with the standard formula: "If you want to know what happened next, then listen to the following chapter." Another conspicuous difference between the two texts is the protagonist's name. The *Drunken Puti* smoothes over one of the most glaring inconsistencies of its source by referring to the eccentric saint, throughout most of the narrative, as Jidian, rather than, as in the *Recorded Sayings*, first as Jidian and then, without warning, as Jigong.[16]

The primary difference between *Drunken Puti* and its source is the amount of detailed description. Whereas the terse, almost synoptic, *Recorded Sayings* merely enumerates Jidian's miracles, *Drunken Puti* depicts its protagonists and their actions in minute detail. Conversations, which are merely summarized in the *Recorded Sayings*, are recorded in full in *Drunken Puti*. Even emotions, hardly mentioned in the *Yulu*, are described, albeit always in narrative speech. On the spectrum running from summary to scene, the *Recorded Sayings* is closer to the former, the *Drunken Puti* to the latter. What is told in the *Yulu* is shown in *Drunken Puti*. I will follow Ono Shihei's lead in choosing the episode of the empress dowager's visit to the Jingci Monastery to illustrate the difference between the two works. Jidian has appeared in the dowager's dream, and she hurries to the monastery to make a donation. The *Recorded Sayings* version reads:

> The [monastery's] gatekeeper reported that an imperial messenger had arrived. The latter announced that the empress dowager was coming to offer incense. The abbot hastily threw on his cassock and emerged from his

quarters. He led the monastery's monks, more than five hundred in all, to welcome her. When the imperial carriage of the empress dowager approached, the abbot and the others received her at the gate. The empress addressed the abbot saying: "Last night, during the third watch, I dreamt of a golden-bodied arhat, who asked that I donate three thousand strings of cash for the reconstruction of the [monastery's] Sūtra Hall. I have brought this sum now. I would like to meet this venerable arhat." The abbot followed her instructions. He picked up a censer and led the monastery's five-hundred monks. They entered the monastery's Buddha hall in groups and recited sūtras. Jigong was among them, and as he passed in front of her, the empress dowager pointed at him and said: "This is the monk." She was about to pay him homage when he instantly did a somersault. Since he was not wearing drawers, he revealed that thing that he had in front. He rose to his feet and then ran out. The abbot addressed the empress saying: "This monk has been suffering from some mental illness." The empress ordered Mao Junshi to take out of the coffer the three thousand strings of cash. The abbot received them. When the empress left, the abbot and all the monks accompanied her to the gate.[17]

The *Drunken Puti* version is almost three times longer:

The [monastery's] gatekeeper came flying to report that an imperial messenger was waiting outside. The latter announced that the empress dowager was coming to the monastery to offer incense. Her imperial carriage was already halfway there. The monks were in a state of panic. The abbot hastily threw on his cassock and donned his clerical cap. He led the monks outside the hall, where they all knelt down to greet her. Luckily it was at that very moment that the imperial carriage arrived. The empress was welcomed into the main hall. She first offered incense and then sat down.

Once the welcome ceremonies, led by the abbot, were completed, the empress dowager made the following statement: "Last night, during the third watch, I dreamt of a golden-bodied arhat, who asked that I donate three thousand strings of cash for the reconstruction of the [monastery's] Sūtra Hall. In my dream I have already promised him personally that I would do so. Today I came here for the express purpose of making this donation. The abbot himself can check and see." The abbot and all the monks kowtowed together and expressed their thanks for the donation. The empress dowager continued: "Even though I came here primarily to give alms, I would also like to meet this venerable arhat." The abbot again knelt down and said: "In this humble friar's monastery there are five-hundred monks. But they are all ordinary monks. I would not dare falsely claim that one of them is an arhat. I do not want to mislead the empress by being presumptuous." The empress dowager said: "Obviously an arhat who is incarnated into the world of mortals would not reveal his identity. Please summon these five-hundred monks. I would like to see them all. I will identify the arhat."

The abbot followed her imperial command. He ordered the monks to encircle the hall. One by one, carrying incense burners and reciting the Buddha's name, they passed in front of the empress. Jidian was among them, and when he passed in front of her, the empress immediately recognized him. She pointed at Jidian and said: "The arhat whom I saw in my dream is this monk. However, in my dream he had the color of precious gold and appeared very august. Why is it that he has chosen to assume this illusory form now?" Jidian said: "This humble friar is nothing but a mad, destitute monk. I am definitely not an arhat. The empress should not have any illusions about this." The empress dowager responded: "Since you are mingling with the ordinary inhabitants of this mortal world, it is but natural that you would not acknowledge your true identity. That's understandable. However, I have donated to you three thousand strings of cash. How do you intend to repay me?" Jidian said: "This humble friar is a destitute monk. The only way he can repay the empress is by doing a somersault. I hope that the empress will learn from this poor monk how to turn somersaults." As he was speaking he turned head over heels and performed a somersault. Since he was not wearing drawers, that thing that he had in front was completely exposed. The bevy of imperial consorts and palace ladies covered their mouths and burst into laughter. The court attendants and eunuchs, enraged by Jidian's impudence, rushed out of the Buddha Hall to catch him. However, he had already somersaulted away and nobody knew where he had gone to.

The abbot and his fellow monks were utterly horrified. They immediately knelt down, imploring: "This monk has been mentally sick for quite some time. Today he suffered from a seizure, for which reason he behaved impudently. Of course he deserves a thousand deaths for his crime. Nonetheless, we beg Your Highness to be merciful and forgive him." "This monk has never been mad," the empress dowager responded. "In fact he is an arhat. His exercise was intended to show me that I can be transformed from a woman into a man. This is a great Chan mystery, and I should really pay him homage for it. But he has already escaped, and I doubt that he would want to come back now. So we must leave it at that." She mounted her carriage and headed to the palace. The monks, led by the abbot, accompanied her to the gate.[18]

The actions summarized in the *Recorded Sayings* are brought to life in the *Drunken Puti* adaptation. The gatekeeper does not merely announce that the empress is on her way, he comes "flying" to make this announcement, which throws his fellow monks into a "panic." The *Drunken Puti* version also introduces several new characters: a bevy of palace ladies politely cover their mouths and burst into laughter upon seeing "that thing that Jidian had in front," and the court attendants, enraged by that same sight, attempt to seize the impudent saint. Even more noticeable is the elaboration of dialogue. The empress' discourse is as lengthy as that of a Chan master. It is she who reveals Jidian's divinity to the monks, and it is she who explains to them the symbolic significance of his supposedly crazy behavior. Thus the *Drunken Puti* author has succeeded in writing a livelier and more colorful narrative than can be found in his source. These qualities probably account for the significant popularity of this novel throughout the eighteenth and nineteenth centuries.

Even though the author of *Drunken Puti* followed the *Recorded Sayings* story line faithfully, he did insert five new episodes into the final chapters.[19] These episodes throw no new light on their protagonist Jidian, except, as Zhou Chunyi has noted, to highlight his magical powers.[20] All five narrate miracles performed by the eccentric saint. For instance, Jidian revives boiled snails and, on another occasion, uses his mantic powers to locate a box of rare incense misplaced inside the imperial palace. In another instance, Jidian devours two pigeons, which later fly, alive and well, out of his mouth, in a demonstration of the ability to vomit living animals, a power attributed to Buddhist miracle workers since at least the seventh century.[21]

At least two of the new episodes in *Drunken Puti* are not products of the author's imagination. They appear in other sources as well, and their inclusion in the novel reflects the growth of popular Jidian lore. In one episode, Jidian drinks a large quantity of wine and then vomits it on three statues of the Buddha, coating them with gold. This miracle is already mentioned, but not narrated, in the *Recorded Sayings*, where the author assumes the reader's familiarity with it.[22] Another lengthy episode tells how Jidian drinks a large quantity of wine and falls asleep for three days. In his sleep he travels to Sichuan, where he obtains several immense logs of wood, which are necessary for the reconstruction of the monastery. The logs travel by water to Hangzhou, where they emerge miraculously from the Jingci Monastery's well. This same miracle is narrated in Wang Mengji's contemporary novel *Jigong's Complete Biography* (1668).[23] The two versions are unrelated, and both probably derive from a third written source or from oral literature. The miracle of the logs remains one of Jidian's most celebrated. The legend has even been sanctioned by the monastic establishment. Today, visitors to the Jingci Monastery are shown the mysterious well from which Jidian's logs emerged (see Fig. 2).

Wang Mengji's "Jigong's Complete Biography"

Authorship and Relation to *Idle Talk*

Unlike the author of *Drunken Puti*, another seventeenth-century author, Wang Mengji (fl. 1668), substantially enlarged the *Recorded Sayings*, creating an original and sophisticated work of fiction. His novel, *Jigong's Complete Biography* (*Jigong quanzhuan*; hereafter *Complete Biography*), is about seven times the length of its source. It is written in an elevated form of the vernacular and is interspersed with literary allusions. Its plot is imaginative, and its narrative well structured. Furthermore, the novel makes a conscious effort to transform Jigong from a mere arch-magician to a moral exemplar. (As the title indicates, the novel refers to its protagonist for the most part as Jigong, which is the name I will use here.) The *Complete Biography* is significant in terms not only of the development of Jigong lore, but also of the history of Chinese fiction, as it adds several foreground narrators to the one background narrator characteristic of most vernacular fiction. This lengthy and sophisticated novel did not enjoy, however, the same popularity as its contemporary, *Drunken Puti*. Whereas the latter was repeatedly published, the *Complete Biography* survives in one edition only, whose preface is dated 1668 (see Appendix A).[24]

The *Complete Biography* is divided into 36 chapters in four volumes. The novel is given several names in addition to *Jigong's Complete Biography*, which is printed in large characters on its title page. The name *Qu toutuo zhuan* (The drunken ascetic) appears in each of the novel's four volumes as well as in small print on the title page. *Jidian dashi quanzhuan* (The complete biography of the eminent master Crazy Ji) appears on the first page of the text, and *Qu toutuo Jidian quanzhuan* (The complete biography of the drunken ascetic, Crazy Ji) is given in the table of contents. The author signed his preface with the pseudonym "the Buddhist Layman Xiangying" (*Xiangying jushi*; Xiangying is the name of an incense)[25] and added that the novel was written by West Lake. Likewise, the first page of the text gives the author as "the Buddhist Layman Xiangying, from West Lake."[26] The author is identifiable as Wang Mengji from his seal, which is affixed to the preface. An adjacent seal provides what is probably his style name, Changling. As yet, no information on Wang Mengji is available.

The *Complete Biography* edition is elegant. The table of contents is followed by twelve beautifully carved woodblock prints illustrating scenes from the novel. The prints are matched by brief poems, each of which is set in a different calligraphic style, ranging from "oracle bone" and "seal" scripts to the freer "grass" and "cursive" styles. Most of the poems are signed by fanciful, and occasionally playful, Buddhist-style sobriquets, such as "Foxin dushi" (Transcending the World by the Buddha-Mind) and "Yisi bugua" (a double entendre meaning both "carefree" and "stark naked"). At least some of the poems are by Wang Mengji himself. One is signed by his pseudonym, Xiangying, and one by his own name. Another poem uses a pseudonym similar to "Xiangying jushi"—"Aina jushi" 艾衲居士. *Aina* means a Buddhist cassock woven with artemisia. An attached seal writes *na* differently, with the silk radical 納. Written with this radical, Aina, like Xiangying, is the name of an incense.

An extensive commentary accompanies the text of the *Complete Biography*. It includes both elaborate critiques at the end of each chapter (*zongping*) and a running commentary in the form of notes in the upper margins. The first page of the text gives the commentator as "the Purple-Bearded Man of the [Buddhist] Way (Ziran daoren), from Yuanshui" [in Jiaxing county, Zhejiang]. It was not uncommon for seventeenth-century authors to write commentaries to their own novels. Li Yu (ca. 1610–80) probably authored most of the commentary to his *Carnal Prayer Mat*, as did Chen Chen (1614?–after 1666) for the *Later Water Margin* (*Shuihu houzhuan*; 1664) and Dong Yue (1620–86) for the *Supplement to the Journey to the West* (*Xiyou bu*).[27] The significant similarities in terms of content and diction in the text and commentary of the *Complete Biography* suggest that they, too, may have been written by a single author. As discussed below, the narrative and the end-of-chapter critiques alike laud the *Complete Biography* as the only accurate version of Jigong's life, even as they dismiss all other versions, oral and written, as factually wrong, morally misguided, and artistically vulgar.

The close relation between the narrative and its running commentary is particularly apparent in an episode, borrowed from the *Recorded Sayings*, that describes an argument between the abbot and the superintendent of the Lingyin Monastery. The latter demands that Jigong be punished for his behavior. The abbot retorts by means of a written epigram: "The Way of Chan is broad. Can't it encompass craziness?" (9.8b). The epigram is borrowed from the *Recorded Sayings*, where it is followed by the narrator's comment: "Crazy means sincere" (*dian zhe nai zhen zi ye*).[28] This comment, too, appears in the *Complete Biography*. However, unlike the *Recorded Sayings*, where it forms part of the narrative, in the *Complete Biography* it is included in the commentary, as a note in the upper margin above the abbot's epigram.[29] In this instance, then, one author appears to be dividing the *Recorded Sayings* material between the narrative and the commentary, both of which he himself probably authored. Thus it is likely that Wang Mengji wrote at least some of the commentary to his novel.

Two of the pseudonyms associated with the *Complete Biography*—the commentator's name, Purple-Bearded Man of the Way, and Buddhist Layman Aina (written with the cloth radical)—also appear on a seventeenth-century collection of stories, *Idle Talk Under the Bean Arbor* (*Doupeng xianhua*). The *Idle Talk*'s commentator is given as Purple-Bearded Madman (Ziran kuangke), and its author as the Buddhist Layman Aina. The commentator is said to be from Yuanhu (in Jiaxing county, Zhejiang), and the author from a place named Holy Water (*sheng shui*).[30] Likewise, the *Complete Biography*'s commentator is said to be from Yuanshui (another name for Yuanhu), and the name Holy Lake (*sheng hu*) is mentioned in the novel's preface in reference to West Lake. These similarities led Patrick Hanan to suggest that Wang Mengji also authored *Idle Talk*.[31] *Idle Talk* is undated, but Hanan has suggested that it probably appeared shortly after the *Complete Biography*, since, among other reasons, its frame story takes place a few decades after the fall of the Ming dynasty.[32]

Scholars have noted that *Idle Talk* occupies a unique position in the history of the vernacular story as the only collection in which the individual stories are embedded within a frame story. The stories—concerned to a large extent with questions of good, evil, and divine ordinance—are narrated by a group of villagers who gather under a bean arbor to weather the hot summer days. The frame is the story of the arbor, from its construction, meant to support newly planted beans, through its collapse following the villagers' final meeting. The villagers are the foreground narrators. The background narrator records their meetings and the history of the arbor under which they sit. In vernacular fiction, the narrator invariably simulates the storyteller. But only in *Idle Talk* is his audience described. The reactions of the villagers to the stories are recorded and vary according to age and temperament. Some believe the stories they hear, and others are skeptical. Still others challenge the narrators. In some cases the audience responds as one (*zhongdao*) to a given story.[33] It is characteristic of vernacular fiction that the narrator provides an authoritative interpretation of the events in comments interspersed through his narrative. In contrast, the background narrator of *Idle Talk* does not adjudicate the disputes between the foreground narrators and their audience. *Idle Talk* thus offers the reader a multiplicity of views on any given subject.[34]

An examination of the *Complete Biography* reveals similarities with *Idle Talk* that strengthen the case for Wang Mengji's authorship of the latter. At the most general level, the *Complete Biography* examines religious and moral questions. Like *Idle Talk*, it is thus concerned with the "fiction of ideas."[35] More specifically, an arbor as a social gathering place also figures in the *Complete Biography*. There it is located at the entrance to a small temple and is referred to as a "Tea Arbor" (*cha peng*), since tea is served in it (20.3a–4a).[36] The most striking similarities between the *Complete Biography* and *Idle Talk* are, however, to be found at the narratorial level. The multiplicity of narrative voices, which is characteristic of *Idle Talk*, is perceptible also in the *Complete Biography*, albeit in embryonic form. Admittedly the bulk of the *Complete Biography* is narrated by one background narrator, who frequently provides the reader with his unequivocal judgment of the personalities and events described. But the novel includes also several foreground narrators, the most conspicuous of whom is a monkish storyteller, whose yarn occupies all of Chapter 27. The author's interest in the storytelling situation is most visible in this chapter, but it is also apparent in several public debates recorded in the novel. The *Complete Biography* includes several instances in which a large group of people are chatting idly or arguing heatedly. Some of these discussions evolve into brief storytelling sessions in which the audience may or may not accept the storyteller's version of events. Two such sessions are notable.

In Chapter 18, Jigong, who has just been expelled from the Lingyin Monastery, arrives before dawn at the Qingpo city gate. A crowd of vendors and petty merchants are squatting on the ground there, waiting for the gates to open, and Jigong joins them. A certain fruit vendor vents his frustration: on a day when he has urgent business to accomplish, the gates are slow to open. "What business do you have that is so urgent?" somebody asks. The fruit vendor replies that a certain Mrs. Ma has asked him to deliver her fruit. "And what's so urgent about that?" inquires another. The fruit vendor spins an arresting tale in reply. Mrs. Ma, he explains, first married when she was 14 and at present is 30. In between she has married no less than ten times, and all her husbands died. The last one has just passed away, and the fruit is required for his funeral. One merchant is skeptical: "This [story] is just the kind of nonsense that Hangzhou people are capable of. I do not believe it." But another member of the group corroborates the fruit vendor's information. The other day he was invited to dinner at the house of Mrs. Ma's neighbors, and he overheard her singing a sad song—which he quotes—about the fate of her husbands. At this point, Jigong intervenes in the discussion, adding, as he usually does, a humorous touch: "This lady already has had no fewer than ten husbands. Do you think that she would agree to take a monk as the eleventh?" Like the *Idle Talk* villagers, the crowd responds as one (*zhongdao*): "No problem! If she wants to get married and a monk makes her an offer, she will gladly accept." (The fruit vendor's version of events is later confirmed, as Jigong employs his powers of meditation and exorcises the malignant insects that have infected Mrs. Ma and caused the deaths of her husbands.)

In Chapter 26, Jigong, mounted on horseback, accompanies a group of high-ranking officials on a hunting expedition. (State regulations prohibited monks from riding horses, but in the *Complete Biography*, as in the *Recorded Sayings*, government officials treat Jigong as their equal.) At one point Jigong strays from the company, dismounts, and enters a mysterious cave. Meanwhile the company chases, but fails to capture, a tiger. As the day draws to a close, they notice Jigong's absence and spot his straying horse. They worry lest the tiger has killed him. A page notes that Jigong was carrying a fund-raising petition, and he wonders aloud whether the tiger has devoured it as well. "Impossible," responds another person. "A tiger would never attack a monk carrying a petition." The answer arouses the curiosity of the entire group. "Why?" they all ask (*zhongdao*). The interlocutor is now briefly transformed into a storyteller as he spins in reply a long tale that, according to him, he once read in a book of jokes (*xiaohua ben*). Once upon a time, a tiger beseeched the spirits of the mountain and earth to send some human flesh his way. The earth spirit responded that a monk would come along, and the tiger might feast on him as he pleased. Sure enough, a monk arrived, and the tiger pounced. Terrified out of his wits, the cleric hurled at him his cymbal and button—he was a storytelling monk (*shuoshu heshang*)—which the tiger immediately devoured. The desperate monk was left only with his fund-raising petition, which he hurled at the beast. The tiger immediately withdrew. "Why didn't you eat him?" the earth spirit inquired later. "He said that I am a pious tiger," the beast responded. "Then he showed me a petition and asked for a donation. I felt so embarrassed that I had no choice but to run away." The story does not earn its teller the appreciation of the group's leader, Commander Chen, who finds it inopportune to joke under such urgent circumstances. Shortly after, as it is getting darker, the group disperses. (As for Jigong's whereabouts, this is disclosed to the reader in a later chapter.)

The wife anecdote, as well as the tiger and monk vignette, prefigure the exchanges between narrator and audience that characterize *Idle Talk*. A professional storytelling session in Chapter 27 of the *Complete Biography* is further reminiscent of *Idle Talk*. In this episode, the storyteller, his performance, and his audience are described in detail. The storyteller is a monk who, like the cleric of the tiger vignette, accompanies his performance with the cymbal (*naoba*). The background narrator compliments his professional skills, noting that his stories are truly entertaining. The performance takes place in the Deva-Kings Hall of the Zhaoqing Monastery on the bank of West Lake. It is interrupted midstream when the storyteller asks the audience for donations. "What I have told you so far are but a few episodes," he explains to his audience. "There are many more wonderful things to come. If each of you lay devotees (*jushi*) will search his pockets and donate some change, I will continue." The audience, like the storyteller, is minutely portrayed. It is a large crowd squeezed into a tight circle; latecomers have to elbow their way in in order to find a seat. One member of the crowd is described in particular detail. He is a 70-year-old lay devotee who lives in seclusion on the hills above West Lake. His surname is Mo, and his style Taixu (Great Emptiness) has been chosen for its religious connotations. He is deeply interested in the teachings of the Chan school, and for this reason he attends the public lectures of famous monks visiting the West Lake monasteries.

The subject of the storyteller's performance is Jigong. Introducing a storyteller's version of Jigong's career into a narrative set during

Jigong's lifetime posed a problem in narrative time for the author. Wang Mengji circumvented this by an abrupt turn in the plot. Jigong, who entered a mysterious cave in the previous chapter, disappears for a period of time, and his fate is unknown. Legends about him mushroom, and those narrated by the storyteller are presented as an example. The source of the legends is Text B of the *Recorded Sayings*.[37] Of course, the *Complete Biography* as a whole is based upon the former novel. Throughout most of the narrative, however, Wang Mengji significantly alters passages borrowed from the *Recorded Sayings* to suit his own artistic and religious agenda. The only lengthy section in the *Complete Biography* quoted almost verbatim from the *Recorded Sayings* is the storyteller's narrative in Chapter 27. Interestingly, it is also the only section of the novel in which Wang Mengji keeps almost all the songs and poems found in his source text. These would be essential, of course, for a storyteller's performance, which, in the case of most Chinese oral genres, is interspersed with sung sequences. Wang Mengji's decision to employ Text B in a storyteller's narrative illuminates not only his own writing technique but also the former text. Wang Mengji obviously considered Text B to be reflective of oral literature. Indeed, he chose to introduce it, hardly altered, as a storyteller's tale.

The monkish storyteller narrates some ten episodes from Text B of the *Recorded Sayings*. His audience does not approve of them. Once the performance is over, the lay devotee Mo Taixu raises objections to almost every episode, accusing the storyteller of distorting Jigong's image. Mo Taixu argues that Jigong was a moral teacher and a saint, not a mere playboy and drunk. He does not believe, for example, that Jigong ever visited a brothel or that he ever exposed in public "that thing that he has in front." His concerns are not only that Jigong's image is being distorted but also that it might serve as a bad example. He worries lest evil monks use such anecdotes as a pretext for their own dissolute behavior. His apprehensions are thus primarily ethical and doctrinal. Nonetheless, some of his criticisms may be characterized as literary or aesthetic. Some stories he simply finds too trivial or boring to be included in a Jigong narrative. Layman Mo concludes his diatribe with a vow to write a popular narrative (*pinghua*) of Jigong's life, which, unlike the one he has just heard, will present an accurate picture of this saint, thereby preventing future generations from being led astray.

Layman Mo's criticism of the monkish storyteller is as severe as that leveled against some of the foreground narrators in *Idle Talk*. There is, however, a significant difference between the *Complete Biography* and that work. In *Idle Talk*, the background narrator never adjudicates the disputes between the narrators and their audience. In the *Complete Biography* he does. The abbot of the Zhaoqing Monastery approves of Mo Taixu's criticism, and even the monkish storyteller himself thanks the lay devotee for enlightening him. Most significant, in the novel's final chapter the reader is informed that Mo Taixu did indeed compile a biography of Jigong, which is lauded by the background narrator as reliable (36.4b–5a). Thus the implied author leaves no doubt that he shares Mo Taixu's objections to the monkish storyteller's narrative and approves of the layman's own version of Jigong's life.

The storyteller episode is interesting for the light it throws on seventeenth-century oral literature. It may reflect Buddhist storytelling of that period. For the purpose of the present discussion, this episode is significant because, like the unfortunate husbands anecdote and the tiger and monk vignette, it points to a link between the *Complete Biography* and *Idle Talk*. The multiplicity of narrative voices and the dialogue between storyteller and audience that characterize the latter work are already present in the former. The case for Wang Mengji's authorship of *Idle Talk* is thus strengthened. A comparison of the two works' narrative structure could possibly help determine their relative dates as well. From the perspective of Wang Mengji's development as an artist, it would seem likely that the *Complete Biography* was the earlier work. Wang Mengji appears to be experimenting in it with the narrative innovations that he would develop further in *Idle Talk*.

Narrative Structure

Wang Mengji introduced a significant number of new episodes into his adaptation of the *Recorded Sayings*.[38] Most of these are not found in contemporary sources. Thus they are the product of Wang Mengji's creative imagination and, unlike the new episodes in *Drunken Puti*, do not mirror the growth of popular Jigong lore. The new episodes in Wang Mengji's novel serve a variety of functions. They provide an intricate and imaginative plot. They enrich the cast of characters with new protagonists, and they add color to others, transforming some from mere names to active participants in the story line. The new episodes also reflect a sustained effort to add moral substance to Jigong's displays of magical prowess. But even as the new material provides for a narrative much more complex than that found in the *Recorded Sayings*, it also remedies the latter's structural deficiencies. The *Recorded Sayings* was haphazardly pieced together from several different sources, and, as has been pointed out, it is lacking in overall structure. The new episodes in Wang Mengji's *Complete Biography* give the novel structural coherence.

The origins of the *Recorded Sayings* in Text A and Text B caused a discontinuity in the narrative. Episodes related to Jigong's family background, his supernatural birth, childhood, and early religious training found in the first part of the novel are hardly referred to in the second. Wang Mengji solved this structural deficiency by introducing new characters and subplots in the first part of his novel, which are then further developed in the second. The gap between what were previously Texts A and B is thus bridged. For instance, in the *Recorded Sayings* Jigong's birth is preceded by a supernatural omen in the Guoqing Monastery on Mount Tiantai. Wang Mengji identifies the arhat who falls from his seat in the monastery's Arhat Hall, thereby indicating that he is about to be incarnated into the world of mortals, as Arhat no. 188, Jiepona Guangfan (4.1b). This pseudo-Sanskrit name is Wang Mengji's own fanciful invention. It does not appear in lists of the Five-Hundred Arhats, nor is it mentioned in any previous source, Buddhist or other, in reference to Jigong. Jiepona Guangfan, thus introduced in one of the novel's early chapters, reappears in its conclusion. Chapter 34 describes a major renovation project of the Arhat Hall at the Jingci Monastery. As the artisans approach the statue of Arhat no. 188, Jigong's stomach begins to give way. His loose bowels, suggesting the Śākyamuni's diarrhea, indicate his approaching death. Several days later, it is announced that the newly renovated image of Jiepona Guangfan is about to be dedicated. Thereupon, Jigong, surrounded by his disciples and lay devotees, composes his valedictory poem and passes away in the meditation posture. The story line begun some thirty chapters earlier is brought to a conclusion as Arhat no. 188, Jiepona Guangfan, returns to the supernatural realm.

In some cases structural unity is provided by a character whose biography spans both sections of the novel. One is the Buddhist recluse Yin Biefeng, who, in the *Recorded Sayings*, is mentioned by name only.[39] Wang Mengji furnishes Yin Biefeng with a complex biography. He first appears in Chapter 6 as an eminent literatus who, having been saved at sea by the Goddess Guanyin, donates lavishly to Buddhist monasteries. Yin Biefeng meets the twelve-year-old Jigong and is so moved by the boy's religious insight that he resolves to become a monk himself rather than subsidize others' search for enlightenment. He reappears in Chapter 28 as a Buddhist recluse in seclusion on Mount Jingshan, where he is attended by four animal disciples: two monkeys and two tigers. His one human disciple, Shen Fanhua, wishes to be officially ordained, but Yin Biefeng refuses to grant this request himself. "You belong in the dharma-line (*fasi*) of a Hangzhou monk named Jigong. One day he will come here and ordain you." Sure enough, forty years after they first met, Jigong arrives at Jingshan and renews his friendship with Yin Biefeng. He accepts Shen Fanhua as his personal disciple and takes him back to Hangzhou on his return. The two friends meet once more shortly before Jigong sheds his earthly body (Chapter 34). Yin Biefeng arrives at the Jingci Monastery to bid his friend farewell. A sudden gust of wind presages his arrival mounted on a tiger, and he marches into the hall supported by his two simian disciples.

Sacred objects, like people, provide structural unity to Wang Mengji's narrative. In Chapter 3 a mysterious sandalwood block emerges from the sea. The retired emperor Gaozong is instructed in a dream that the block should be carved into a Buddha image and placed on Mount Tiantai. Jigong's father, Li Maochun, who has expressed his desire to retire from office and lead the life of a recluse, is given the task. He transfers the statue to the sacred mountain, where he and his wife take care of the small temple built for the statue and pray for an offspring. Sixty years later, the statue is revealed simultaneously in the dreams of Jigong and the empress dowager (Chapter 32). Jigong interprets both dreams: the statue, which has been neglected ever since Jigong's parents passed away, needs to be transferred to the Jingci Monastery. A government expedition headed by Jigong's disciple Shen Fanhua and a high-ranking palace eunuch arrives at Tiantai mountain. Two hundred people attempt to move the statue, but it will not budge. Only after it is presented with the empress dowager's edict does the statue consent to be moved. After a speedy journey, it arrives at the Jingci Monastery, where it is placed at the center of the Arhat Hall.

One character, introduced in the novel's opening chapters, plays a particularly significant role in providing overall unity to the text. This is a monk named Fanguang, who is presented as Li Maochun's alter ego, having been born in the same minute as he. Fanguang is a bright and politically savvy cleric. He rises to the top of the monastic establishment of his day and is appointed abbot of the Jingci Monastery. He also enjoys the favor of the imperial court, which he serves as consultant on matters both religious and secular. For example, he supervises the design and construction of the imperial Gathered Views Gardens. Unfortunately, Fanguang's enormous success blinds him to the Buddhist truth. He becomes arrogant, and he divulges divine secrets. Furthermore, led astray by his greed, he commits an error for which he will be punished. The retired emperor Gaozong rewards each member of the construction crew of the Gathered Views Gardens with a small sum for wine and meat. Fanguang, though vegetarian, receives the significant sum of 300 taels of silver. It would have been appropriate for him to decline this financial reward, but Fanguang chooses to keep it. As ill luck would have it, the money is stolen by two evil monks. Two innocent eunuchs, who have been appointed to accompany Fanguang, are accused of negligence and executed by order of the imperial court.

Fanguang's hubris leads to his demise, as the monastery's guardian spirit (*qielan*) assumes the form of a lay devotee (*jushi*) and tests him by posing a series of doctrinal questions. Asked to list the patriarchs of the Chan school, the conceited abbot lists himself as the seventh; the god Weituo appears in midair and hits Fanguang with his pestle, killing him. Next he appears in the form of a hungry ghost to Jigong's father, Li Maochun, who is praying for offspring on Mount Tiantai. Wang Mengji describes his grotesque image in detail. He is chained in a cangue and is repeatedly consumed by flames, which die out only to burst forth again. As he entreats Li Maochun to save him, he is so burdened by the weight of the cangue that he leans it against the door frame. (A minute description of a grotesque ghost is also included in *Idle Talk*.)[40] Fanguang presents Li Maochun with specific guidelines, which, if followed, will redeem him from his ghostly state. Sūtras should be read in front of the sandalwood statue of the Buddha, and offerings made there for 120 days. In addition, Fanguang's entire writings should be burned. Li Maochun and his wife do as requested, and when the ceremonies are complete, they are blessed with a son, Jigong, who is the reincarnation of Fanguang's redeemed spirit. (Evidently the narrator does not perceive a contradiction between Jigong as the reincarnation of Fanguang and his being an embodied arhat.)

Fanguang's biography, narrated in the novel's first four chapters, has repercussions that resonate throughout the narrative. For instance, the two monks who steal Fanguang's reward in the first chapter suffer retribution in the thirteenth. They die after drinking poisonous wine unwittingly served to them by Jigong, who is none other than Fanguang's own reincarnation.[41] More significantly, Fanguang's faults provide a karmic explanation for Jigong's transgressions. Jigong is predestined to eat the meat and drink the wine that could have been bought with the reward that Fanguang received from Gaozong. Jigong's behavior is thus not the result of a frivolous nature but divinely ordained. Indeed, the exact amount of wine and meat Jigong has to consume is predetermined, and once he has digested this amount, Jigong no longer transgresses the Buddhist dietary rules. The significance of Fanguang's biography for the overall structure of the novel is noted by the commentator, who points out to the reader narrative threads that will be developed later. As the evil monks steal Fanguang's reward, the running commentary explains "It will be told in later [chapters] how the murderous monks suffered retribution for their crime" (1.8a). And, as the god Weituo punishes Fanguang for accepting the reward in the first place, the commentator notes: "This is the [origin] of Jigong's wine and meat" (3.1a).

Extended subplots, such as those concerning Fanguang and Yin Biefeng, bridge the gap between the Text A and the Text B narratives. But Wang Mengji's novel addresses yet another structural deficiency apparent in the *Recorded Sayings.* Text B itself reflects several narrative traditions concerning Jigong, and it therefore lacks overall coherence. The text is a conglomerate of unrelated, and often extremely brief, episodes that, for the most part, are arranged in no apparent narrative order. These brief episodes are replaced in Wang Mengji's novel by larger narrative units. Some of these introduce new characters and subplots. Others emerge from the elaboration and consolidation of episodes from Text B. For instance, a certain Zhanggong figures in two unrelated episodes in Text B, each only several lines in length. One episode is included in the text's opening segment, the other toward its conclusion.[42] In the first, Zhanggong treats Jigong to a drinking spree; in the second, he is the beneficiary of Jigong's magical powers. Wang Mengji combines the two episodes into one, and this one episode, now further embellished, occupies almost an entire chapter (15.1a–6a).

In his adaptation of Text B, Wang Mengji not only substitutes large narrative units for brief episodes, but also introduces linear development. In order to achieve it, he does not shy from deleting characters and episodes central to his source. Text B narrates several fund-raising miracles performed by Jigong. The funds raised are channeled to two different construction projects at the Jingci Monastery. The first, supervised by the abbot Dehui, is the reconstruction of a hall that fell into disuse prior to Jigong's arrival at the monastery. The second, supervised by the abbot Shaolin, is the reconstruction of the entire monastery, which burned down in a fire several months later. (Abbot Dehui disappeared in the fire, and Shaolin was named his successor.)[43] Wang Mengji alters significantly this story line. The entire monastery has burned down in a fire prior to Jigong's arrival, and the figure of Shaolin is dispensed with, as Dehui remains abbot throughout Jigong's tenure in the monastery. The various fund-raising miracles of Text B are strung together as part of a continuous effort to reconstruct the Jingci Monastery. This effort culminates, shortly before Jigong's death, in the arrival of the sandalwood Buddha at the monastery. Thus, the reconstruction of the Jingci Monastery, extending through much of the narrative, becomes one of the threads that unify Wang Mengji's novel.

The *Complete Biography* and Lay Buddhism

In his preface to the *Complete Biography*, the author claims that his version of Jigong's life is no mere fiction. Rather, it is historically accurate. He writes: "I have studied [Jigong's] entire life, and I have compiled an authoritative biography (*zheng zhuan*)" (preface, 6a). A similar claim for the historical veracity of the narrative is made, within the text itself, by the background narrator. In the first chapter, the narrator compares his narrative to the four Wanli period mythological novels *Journey to the West*, *Journey to the East*, *Journey to the North*, and *Journey to the South*. The contents of these fantastic journeys, he argues, cannot be verified. In contrast, Jigong revealed his divine presence in the capital of China, and therefore the *Complete Biography*'s account of his life can be substantiated:

> The story I am about to tell is not a groundless and deceitful fabrication such as "The Journey to the West," "The Eastern Continent," "The Northern Hell," or "The Southern Heaven," which are unfounded and unsubstantiated lies. This arhat [Jigong] was incarnated and revealed on Mount Tiantai. The story of his previous deeds and their later fruition is truly

divine. It cannot be compared to these strange tales of the obscure wilderness. Indeed, it is a beautiful story of a plentiful time and a prosperous age. (1.3b)

The narrator's claim that his version of Jigong's life is historically accurate is related to his dismissal of all other fiction on Jigong, written or oral, as misleading. After Jigong's death, the narrative goes, Emperor Ningzong commissioned a biography of the eccentric saint. A scholar from the Hanlin Academy was assigned to the task, and he sent a dispatch to the metropolitan governor of Hangzhou requesting information about Jigong. No sooner was his request made public than he was flooded with conflicting biographies of the saint. The background narrator criticizes these biographies at great length as historically inaccurate, morally dubious, and artistically vulgar. The narrator's dismissal of the biographies submitted to Emperor Ningzong can be interpreted as the implied author's veiled criticism of contemporary Jigong literature. His emphasis that the biographies were many and diverse probably reflects the significant popularity of Jigong in seventeenth-century Hangzhou lore:

Some writers erred by omission, and others wrote superfluously. The accounts of some were wrong and of others vulgar. All in all, there were many who wrote unpolished records, and only a few who wrote elegant biographies. There were many whose tales were preposterous, and only a few who gathered reliable information. . . . Originally there was only one Jigong, but in later times there were thousands and myriads of Jigongs. All were fabricated by vulgar people of the marketplace, male peddlers and female vendors. (36.4a–b)

In one instance, the narrator singles out for criticism the legend of Jigong goldplating three statues of the Buddha with his vomit that we know was popular in the Jigong lore of his time, for it is mentioned in the sixteenth-century *Recorded Sayings* and narrated in detail in the seventeenth-century *Drunken Puti*.[44] The *Complete Biography*'s narrator dismisses it as absurd:

Pious people everywhere claim that after he had drunk wine, Jigong vomited gold, thereby adding luster to a Buddha statue. This is the result of meddlesome people spreading too much gossip. Whoever heard of a wine-drinking and meat-eating monk who vomited gold? If this were the case, then parasitic monks everywhere would use this as an excuse and spend their entire days drinking wine and eating meat. One would only have to offer them their fill and wait for them to vomit gold. Would not this just make it easier for this villainous lot? The reader ought to consider carefully. Could there possibly be such a thing? (32.10a)

The narrator finds fault with the story on pedagogical as well as logical grounds. He is concerned lest evil monks use this legend as an excuse for drinking, and he finds the legend itself absurd. The fantastic figures prominently in the *Complete Biography*, but this legend strikes the narrator as inane. Interestingly, he is not satisfied only to dismiss it. Rather, he offers his own version of the historical event that, in his view, is misrepresented in this legend. He suggests that Jigong used saliva as an ingredient in a solution to moisten the Buddha statue—in his version it is the sandalwood Buddha brought from Tiantai Mountain—resulting in the gold coating (32.9b–10a).

The implied author voices his criticism of contemporary Jigong lore not only through the background narrator but also through one of the novel's protagonists. This is the Buddhist layman Mo Taixu, whose scathing criticism of an oral Jigong narrative performed by a monk was discussed briefly above. Mo Taixu's criticism, endorsed by the background narrator, is remarkable, for it is directed in effect against the very source of the *Complete Biography*—the *Recorded Sayings*. (As noted above, all the episodes in the storyteller's performance were borrowed from the latter novel.) Mo Taixu, like the background narrator, dismisses specific episodes in his criticism of the storyteller's narrative. He does not believe, for example, that Jigong ever visited a brothel, or that he ever deloused himself (for this act involves the killing of living beings). Like the background narrator, he is concerned both with the historical veracity of the stories in question and with their moral impact on the monastic community.

The *Complete Biography*'s commentator, like the background narrator and Mo Taixu, disparages contemporary Jigong fiction. Like them, he is concerned with the distortion of Jigong's image in this literature, and he worries lest it corrupt monastic values. He lauds the *Complete Biography* as the only accurate account of Jigong, and he commends it for highlighting the moral and pedagogical dimensions of the eccentric saint's life. He even expresses the hope that this novel will lead its readers to the other shore and assist them in attaining sainthood (36:9a). The commentator's endorsement of the *Complete Biography* as accurate, as well as his scathing criticism of other fiction for distorting the saint's image, are similar, in content and diction alike, to comments made in the body of the text. For instance, the critique of Chapter 27 echoes the criticism made by Mo Taixu within that chapter itself:

> The fundamental purpose of this revised, short biography of Jigong is expressed in this chapter. In the lives of the Buddhas, patriarchs, sages, and worthies, the things that need be transmitted [from generation to generation] are those pertaining to body and mind, nature and ordinance, morality and the five human relations. If there was nothing to these worthies but wine drinking, meat eating, pointless chatter, aimless wandering, and the random compilation of bad poetry. . . then, everywhere, villainous bald asses would justify [their own wanton behavior] using these worthies' names. The monastic institution would be transformed into a den of rogues and criminals. This would cause the Buddhist school to fall into disarray, and it might even lead to its destruction. How could [such biographies of Jigong] be accepted as standard? When they read fiction or watch plays, the people of the world consider only flowery and erotic pieces to be noteworthy, and they praise [such pieces] as magnificent. They do not care at all whether these pieces have any moral content. Therefore, they would do better to spend three pennies, grab a stool, sit in a circle and listen to a storyteller narrate the *Water Margin* or the *Journey to the West*. Why should they bother to read this *Drunken Ascetic* [i.e., the *Complete Biography*]? (27.11b–12a)

The *Complete Biography*'s implied author (as voiced through the background narrator and Mo Taixu) and commentator criticize contemporary Jigong lore for distorting the eccentric saint's image. To what extent does Jigong's portrayal in the *Complete Biography* itself differ from that found in other Jigong novels? An examination of Wang Mengji's novel reveals a sustained effort to mitigate the saint's antinomian behavior and even absolve him altogether of some of his more outrageous traits. This effort is most apparent in respect to Jigong's sexual behavior. In the *Complete Biography*, the eccentric saint abstains from sexual intercourse. Wang Mengji omits the *Recorded Sayings*' self-descriptive pieces, in which Jigong readily acknowledges his dalliances. Furthermore, the Jigong of Wang Mengji's novel does not even flirt with women. In late Ming lore, Jigong often dallies with courtesans without actually making love to them. He undergoes sexual trials, but emerges from them with honor. In contrast, the Jigong of the *Complete Biography* carefully avoids such trials in the first place. Thus, for example, the episode in the *Recorded Sayings* in which the eccentric saint covers a courtesan's vulva with her tiny shoe is omitted from Wang Mengji's narrative.

Jigong's wine drinking—his most conspicuous antinomian trait—is retained in the *Complete Biography*. However, a karmic explanation for it is provided. Jigong's breach of monastic dietary laws is a punishment inflicted upon this holy man for a misdeed committed in a previous incarnation. Shortly before his death, Jigong reveals this secret to his disciple Shen Fanhua: "In this life I have been consuming large quantities of meat and wine on behalf of another person [i.e., his previous incarnation, Fanguang]. The filth in my heart has been a debt from a previous life. Worldly people do not understand this and think instead that I have been drinking for my own pleasure. In fact, this has not been my intention" (34.2a–b). Once Jigong has consumed the amount of meat and alcohol for which he was predestined, he abstains from these foodstuffs. In one instance, three ruffians, who bear a grudge against the eccentric saint for interfering with a previous ruse of theirs, attempt to force him into breaching his newly observed dietary vows. Jigong warns the three that it will cost them much to feed him, but they insist. Whereupon Jigong drinks the restaurant's entire wine supply and consumes all its meat. Terrified out of their wits, the rascals beg Jigong to pardon them. He responds to their pleas, and he spits out barrels of unspoiled wine, and the game he has devoured—deer, hares, pigeons, mynah birds, egrets—emerges from his mouth alive. Thus the ruffians need not pay for the meal, and Jigong remains true to his monastic vow (31.1a–7b). As noted above, in the contemporary novel *Drunken Puti* Jidian vomits living animals as well. But whereas the *Complete Biography*'s implied author uses Jigong's ability to vomit living animals as an apologia for his breach of the monastic dietary laws, in the *Drunken Puti* the epicurean saint delights in eating meat, and the instance in which pigeons fly out of his mouth serves only to demonstrate his magic powers.[45]

Even as Wang Mengji's narrative mitigates Jigong's antinomian behavior, it also adds a moral dimension to his miracles. The Jigong of the *Complete Biography* is not merely an arch-magician. He is a moral exemplar who is deeply concerned with both the social and the spiritual welfare of the lay population. His achievements are due as much to his persuasive abilities as a teacher as they are to his supernatural powers. In Chapter 31, the empress dowager commissions Dehui to have made a painting of the monastery's central hall, whose renovation she has funded. Jigong instructs the artist instead to draw the hungry masses who are suffering from a drought. The picture is presented to the alarmed emperor, who has been kept ignorant of the drought by ingratiating officials. Food is immediately distributed, and the population is saved. The court's respect for Dehui increases, since they consider him responsible for the painting. Jigong's role in the affair, itself unknown to Dehui, remains hidden (31.9b–10a).

The *Complete Biography* highlights the pedagogical dimension of the saint's activities. Jigong not only benefits the laity materially, but, more significantly, he leads them toward enlightenment. The beneficiaries of Jigong's miracles, as well as his friends and acquaintances, become firm Buddhist devotees. Some of them take up residence in hermitages (*jingshi*). Others go so far as to join the ranks of the monastic community. A devotee named Zhanggong is informed by Jigong that in a previous life he had been a butcher. In order to atone for this sin, he decides to retreat to a hermitage, where he and his wife lead the lives of recluses (15.5b–6b). Even a literatus friend of Jigong, the official Shen, chooses in old age to become a monk (15.13a). Deeply influenced by his moral example, Jigong's disciples help him help others. In one instance, a courtesan who has contracted syphilis is left to die in an open field by her heartless procuress. Jigong's literati disciple, Shen, carries the courtesan on his back to the Zhangs' hermitage. Jigong takes a bath there, and the water is used to wash the courtesan, who is instantly cured. (Jigong himself does not touch her.) Deeply moved, the courtesan decides to shave her head and become a nun. Later all four—the courtesan, the Zhang couple, and the official Shen—pass away in the meditation posture, as Buddhist saints (15.6b–13b).

The moral dimension of Jigong's miracles is highlighted by his willingness to help even those who have hurt him. An evil rich man schemes to have Jigong arrested. Nonetheless, Jigong warns him of an imminent fire that will burn his home down (20.1a–8a). Similarly, Jigong repays kindness for evil in his relations with the superintendent of the Jingci Monastery. In the *Complete Biography*, the superintendent's animosity toward Jigong is so intense that he attempts to murder the saint by drowning him in a pond. Inadvertently, however, he himself falls into the water and is rescued by his intended victim (16.5a–17.1b). Interestingly, even though Jigong is willing to forgive such adversaries as the superintendent, the narrator is not. The superintendent is eventually devoured by a tiger, and the rich man ignores Jigong's warnings and perishes in the fire, which consumes his residence (21.9b–10a and 20.7b).

The doctrinal significance of Jigong's miracles is pointed out by the commentary, which interprets some of them allegorically. In Chapter 11 Wang Mengji elaborates upon a monkey legend incorporated into his source, the *Recorded Sayings*. According to this legend, the abbot of the Lingyin Monastery, Huiyuan, had a monkey disciple (*yuanxing*). In the *Recorded Sayings* this monkey watches the abbot playing chess with a visiting official and, when the abbot passes away, wills himself to death. In the *Complete Biography* it is the monkey himself who plays, and wins, the chess match against the visiting literatus. The monkey does not will himself to death. Instead, Jigong touches him, and he is instantly petrified (11.3a–7a).[46] The commentator explains that the monkey stands for the unbridled mind, which needs to be tamed if enlightenment is to occur. This allegorical interpretation is borrowed from the *Journey to the West* tradition, which conceives of its monkey protagonist, Sun Wukong, as the "monkey of the mind" (*xinyuan*).[47] Elsewhere the commentator doubts the significance of the *Journey to the West* story cycle. Here he acknowledges his debt to it: "The book *Journey to the West* is good only for one word—'mind.' The [monkey] disciple stirs up heaven and earth. This is exactly what happens here. Jigong kills in one blow the black monkey, and simultaneously the mind attains emptiness" (11:7b).

The commentary itself uses allegory to elucidate the narrative's religious meaning. In one instance, the commentator applies the sixth-century parable of the "craziness spring" (*kuangquan*) to the conflict between Jigong and his fellow monks at the Lingyin Monastery:

> In a certain country there was a craziness spring. Whoever drank from it became crazy. Only the king did not drink [its water]. He was the only sober person. Everyone in the country considered him to be mad. They used medicines, acupuncture, and various painful methods that he could not bear to heal him. When he drank from the spring, he immediately became crazy. Ruler and subjects were now in harmony. They were mutually mad, and there was no disagreement between them. . . . Jigong was sober in his drunkenness. The monks were drunk in their sobriety. (14.8a).[48]

Thus the *Complete Biography* reflects a conscious effort to transform Jigong's image. The narrative and the commentary alike censure the characterization of Jigong in contemporary fiction. They labor, instead, to portray what they consider to be his true image. The Jigong of Wang Mengji's novel does not violate as many monastic vows as he does in other novels. His antinomian behavior has been mitigated. Furthermore, he is not merely an arch-magician. Rather, he is a Buddhist saint who leads his devotees to enlightenment. Nonetheless, Wang Mengji's novel does not mirror a monastic understanding of the eccentric saint. Like *Idle Talk*, the *Complete Biography* includes savage criticisms of the Buddhist establishment, which the latter would not have tolerated.[49] Whereas in contemporary lore Jigong's fellow monks are for the most part merely muddleheaded, in this novel some of them are criminals. Two monks are thieves; they steal Fanguang's imperial award. Another, the superintendent, attempts to commit murder. Even Fanguang himself is not free of faults. He is arrogant, he divulges divine secrets, and, most significantly, he accepts a financial award that he should have declined. The novel's criticism of the monastic establishment is not limited to the narrative's intradiegetic level. The narrator and commentator alike censure severely the monastic community of their own time. According to their testimony, they struggle to draw an accurate portrait of Jigong in order to prevent evil monks from using his distorted image as a pretext for crime.

Whereas most criminals in the *Complete Biography* are monks, most sages are outsiders to the Buddhist establishment. Jigong himself is of course an outsider vis-à-vis this establishment, and most other enlightened figures are not monks at all. Rather, like the implied author, Xiangying jushi, they tend to be lay devotees, *jushi*. Jigong's father, the recluse Yin Biefeng, and the recluse Mo Taixu are three examples. Even the deity Weituo assumes the figure of a lay devotee when he examines Fanguang. Interestingly, according to the background narrator, this was a lay devotee, Mo Taixu, who wrote an accurate biography of Jigong, whereas the storyteller who distorted the saint's image was a monk.

Thus, even though Wang Mengji's novel portrays Jigong as a Buddhist saint, it mirrors a lay, rather than monastic, understanding of him. It is noteworthy in this respect that the novel does not display influence of Buddhist literature. Rather, the author draws on vernacular fiction, primarily the *Recorded Sayings*. Whether he compares Jigong to the wronged poet-official Qu Yuan (14.8a) or applies the "craziness spring" parable to his religious career, the author's sphere of reference is primarily secular. I am not aware of any passage in the novel that draws directly on Buddhist scripture. What Buddhist terms are included in the novel were common currency by the time of its compilation, and their inclusion in the novel does not indicate familiarity with Buddhist literature. The term "monkey of the mind," for example, had appeared in vernacular fiction and drama, often in a nonreligious context, for centuries.[50] Likewise any lay devotee would have been familiar with the term *arhat* or the deity Weituo.

The Buddhist saint Jigong emerges from certain episodes of the *Complete Biography* as an ordinary human. In some cases he is even sentimental. In old age he bursts into tears as he recalls the sandalwood statue of the Buddha, formerly cared for by his father (32.6b). The saint's human dimension is revealed most clearly in his dreams, some of which he himself cannot interpret.[51] One dream provides a particularly revealing insight of Jigong the man, for in it his wish is frustrated. It is a dream visit to hell, and the narrator records it in detail. As he arrives at hell's lowest level, Jigong asks: "What is there beyond this place?" A ghost officer answers:

> "Beyond this place there is only a black path. Bordering the path on its other side is paradise. Currently the ghosts are unable to cross this path. Up to now there has been only the venerable Mulian who came here, recited the *Heart Sūtra*, and then crossed in broad daylight to the other side." Jigong said to the *jushi* [the lay devotee who was guiding him]: "If one needs only recite the *Heart Sūtra* in order to cross to the other side, then what's so difficult about that?" He approached the path, and just as he was about to recite, there was a sudden gust of wind from high above. . . . The mountains trembled, and the earth shook. The *jushi* waved his hand and shouted: "Hurry back, quickly. . . .You cannot as yet go to paradise." He had not finished his sentence when flames rose to heaven and a gust of wind swept the earth. A wave of dust hit Jigong's face, and he jumped up alarmed. And there he was, lying as before on the large boulder on top of the "Teahouse Peak," still mumbling: "*Jushi*, come quick, *jushi*, come quick." It was nothing but a dream! (21.8a–9a)

Throughout most of the *Complete Biography*, Jigong is depicted as a Buddhist saint, and the implied author appears convinced of his divinity. However, in this instance, the implied author approaches his protagonist with ironic distance. The comparison to Mulian highlights Jigong's limitations. According to a large body of fiction and drama, this saintly monk rescued his mother from the tortures of hell and transferred her to heaven. In contrast, Jigong is incapable of crossing the border between these two realms. Episodes such as this distinguish between Wang Mengji's novel and all other fiction on the crazy saint. Here Jigong is portrayed as a mere human, and the implied author appears to be interested in his psyche more than in the benefits of worshipping him.

The Play "Drunken Puti"

The earliest extant play on Jidian, *Drunken Puti* (see Appendix C), will be discussed here briefly, and only in its relation to novels on the eccentric saint.[52] The play's author, Zhang Dafu (fl. 1645), was a prolific dramatist from Suzhou. He authored more than twenty *chuanqi* plays, eleven of which survive, as well as six *zaju* plays.[53] Since Zhang Dafu spent some time at the Hanshan Monastery in Jiangsu, he chose the style Hanshanzi. His Buddhist inclinations are apparent in several of his plays.[54] His *chuanqi* play *Drunken Puti* derives from the *Recorded Sayings*. Most acts develop episodes from this novel, such as Jidian's trials in meditation, the eulogies he offered to a fighting cricket, his appearance in the empress dowager's dream, and the empress' subsequent visit to the Jingci Monastery. There are also textual borrowings. The play includes a eulogy and a poem that appear only in the *Recorded Sayings* and were omitted in later novels.[55] Zhang Dafu is thus borrowing directly from that work.

Even so, the play significantly alters the *Recorded Sayings*' story line. Zhou Chunyi has pointed out that many of the *Recorded Sayings*' episodes are transformed in this play and that new ones are added.[56] Thus, for example, in the play Jidian does not arrive at the Lingyin Monastery with the express purpose of becoming a monk. Rather, he happens to arrive with his cousin Commander Mao, a newly introduced character, who has been sent there as the empress's messenger to make a donation. Once in the monastery, Jidian reveals his understanding of Buddhist doctrine. The empress's gift, an ordination certificate, is bestowed upon him, and he is ordained as a monk. The episode of Jidian's visit to a brothel is similarly transformed. In the *Recorded Sayings* Jidian emerges from this sexual trial true to his monastic vow. In the play, he further leads the prostitutes to enlightenment. Several of the play's acts are entirely new. In one, Jidian's cousin, who has been dangerously ill, is dragged to hell by a ghost. Jidian arrives in the nick of time. He rescues his relative and restores him to the world of the living. It is noteworthy that the new episodes in Zhang Dafu's play are not included in the two seventeenth-century novels about Jidian.

The play is also textually related to the novel of the same title. In the play, the empress dowager, who is visiting the Jingci Monastery, proclaims: "This monk [Jidian] is truly an arhat. His exercise [i.e., his somersault] was intended to show me that I can be transformed from a woman into a man. This is a great Chan mystery." These same sentences appear in the novel *Drunken Puti*, but not in the *Recorded Sayings*.[57] In another instance, Zhang Dafu quotes a eulogy that is included in both the *Recorded Sayings* and, in an altered version, in the novel *Drunken Puti*. Zhang Dafu's version is almost identical to the latter.[58] Thus the play and the novel of the same title are clearly related. Which came first, the play or the novel? Is the novel borrowing from the play, or is Zhang Dafu quoting the novel? This question cannot be answered with certainty since neither the exact date of the novel nor that of the play is known. As noted above, the novel was probably written before 1673. As for the play, it is undated, and even its author's dates are unclear. It is known only that Zhang Dafu was active during the 1640s and the 1650s. But he may have been writing during the 1660s as well.[59]

Even though the question of antecedence cannot be answered with certainty, it is probable that the play followed the novel for several reasons. First, the novel follows closely the *Recorded Sayings* and abounds with textual borrowings. It is unlikely that in two isolated instances its author would have favored the play's text over his regular source, the *Recorded Sayings*. This is all the more likely, since the novel was not influenced by the play's new story line. Second, unlike the novel, the play does not follow the *Recorded Sayings* plot closely, and there are only two instances of textual borrowing from the *Recorded Sayings* in it.[60] What episodes the play borrows from the *Recorded Sayings* could have also been borrowed from the novel *Drunken Puti*, since they appear in it as well. It is therefore likely, though by no means certain, that the play followed the novel. If this is the case, then both the *Recorded Sayings* and the novel *Drunken Puti* were available to Zhang Dafu when he compiled his play. The two prose works share approximately the same story line, which he freely adapted. As for textual borrowings, in some cases he quoted the *Recorded Sayings*, in others the novel *Drunken Puti*.

Conclusion

Seventeenth-century fiction on Jidian reflects a significant diversity in the understanding of this eccentric saint. Whereas the novel *Drunken Puti* and the short story based on it depict him as a jolly miracle worker, Wang Mengji transforms him into a Buddhist teacher and moral exemplar. Nonetheless, even Wang's novel does not mirror a monastic understanding of Jidian, since its narrator severely censures the monastic community of his time. According to his testimony, he struggles to draw an accurate portrait of Jidian in order to prevent evil monks from using a distorted image of this saint as a pretext for their crimes. Thus, Wang Mengji's novel mirrors the Buddhist devotion of the laity, and its saintly protagonist serves as an inspiring model for lay devotees, not monks.

Seventeenth-century novels on Jidian also differ in terms of narrative technique. Wang Mengji's novel is the only one that offers an inside view of its protagonist. Its narrator records Jidian's dreams and tells of his frustrations, thereby demythologizing him. In some episodes, the eccentric saint is even approached with ironic distance. However, this sophisticated portrayal of Jidian did not shape the popular understanding of the saint. During the next two centuries, the novel *Drunken Puti* enjoyed immense popularity and was repeatedly reprinted, but Wang Mengji's novel was forgotten.

FIVE

Martial Artist and Champion of the Poor

The "Storyteller's Jigong"

No new novel on the eccentric saint Jigong appeared during the two centuries following publication of *Drunken Puti* and *Jigong's Complete Biography*.[1] However, this situation changed abruptly, in the late 1890s, when a Tianjin publisher issued a large-scale novel, entitled *The Storyteller's Life of Jigong* (*Pingyan Jigong zhuan*; hereafter: *Storyteller's Jigong*), in two installments.[2] This 240-chapter novel enjoyed enormous and immediate popularity—at least twenty late Qing and Republican period editions of it, most by Shanghai publishers, survive, and it is repeatedly published today.[3] But probably the most compelling evidence of this novel's success is the avalanche of sequels it precipitated—in rapid succession, between 1900 and 1926, no fewer than 38 sequels to the *Storyteller's Jigong*, totaling 1,515 chapters, were published.[4] These have been followed in recent years by several additional novels.[5] This enormous literary body inspired numerous dramatic representations—both as opera and as puppet theater in a variety of regional styles—of the Jigong story cycle, as well as in recent years a large number of television serials and movies in the mainland, Hong Kong, and Taiwan alike.

The *Storyteller's Jigong* and the sequels it inspired deviate significantly from the narrative line of earlier Jigong novels and represent a new stage in the development of Jigong fiction and the spread of this saint's religious cult. The *Storyteller's Jigong* shares not one episode with earlier Jigong novels. Indeed, it transforms its divine protagonist from a jolly miracle worker to the accomplished leader of skilled martial artists, and owes more to late nineteenth-century martial-arts fiction (*wuxia xiaoshuo*) than to any previous novel on Jigong. Whereas all earlier novels on this eccentric saint were written in Zhejiang and were influenced directly or indirectly by the oral literature of Hangzhou, the *Storyteller's Jigong* was written in north China and derives directly from Beijing storytelling. Thus this novel reflects the growth of indigenous Jigong lore in Beijing and signals the transformation of Jigong from a local saint in Zhejiang to a prominent figure in the popular culture—and popular religion—of China at large. As we shall see below, the publication of this novel coincided with the first signs of a cult of Jigong in north China (see the summary of information on the *Storyteller's Jigong* in Appendix A, and on its sequels in Appendix B).

Dating, Authorship, and Relation to Oral Literature

The *Storyteller's Jigong* was originally published in two parts of 120 chapters each. The earliest known edition of the first dates from 1898, that of the sequel from 1900. Both these editions are now lost, but their prefaces, appended to later editions of the novel, survive.[6] The earliest extant edition of the entire novel dates from 1906.[7] The prefaces to the earlier editions of the novel that are no longer extant ascribe its authorship to Guo Xiaoting, who, as argued below, should probably be identified with Guo Guangrui, known to us as the author of the slightly earlier novel *Everlasting Blessings and Peace* (*Yongqing shengping*; 1892). These prefaces identify the novel's first publisher as the Zhuzi shanfang (Professional writer's studio) of Tianjin[8] and note that it was originally printed by the imported technique of lithography (first employed in Shanghai in the late 1870s).[9]

From the perspective of the development of Jigong lore, the most conspicuous feature of the *Storyteller's Jigong* is the gap between it and the earlier narrative tradition. With the exception of its opening chapter, the *Storyteller's Jigong* has nothing in common with earlier fiction on Jigong. Indeed its plot contradicts the fundamental narrative line of earlier novels. Earlier novels make much of the conflict between Jigong and the narrow-minded Lingyin monks, who expelled him from their monastery. In these novels Jigong resettles at the Jingci Monastery and conducts all of his fund-raising miracles on behalf of the latter establishment. By contrast, in the *Storyteller's Jigong* this divine eccentric resides throughout at the Lingyin Monastery and is even occasionally referred to as the Lingyin Monastery's abbot (*zhanglao*). The very term "abbot" contradicts the spirit of earlier novels, in which Jigong seldom lives harmoniously with monastic authorities.

The narrative gap between the *Storyteller's Jigong* and earlier novels is related to a linguistic discrepancy. All the earlier novels on this divine clown were written in Hangzhou, and at least one, the *Recorded Sayings*, displays the marks of the Wu dialect prevalent in Zhejiang and Jiangsu. By contrast, the *Storyteller's Jigong*'s abundant use of Beijing dialect suggests that it was written in north China. The quintessential Beijing vocabulary evident in the novel includes such terms as *youda* 由打 (since), *yuan* 冤 (to cheat), and *duozan* 多咱 ("when"; a contracted form of *duo zaowan* 多咱晚). Similarly, the narrative alludes to typical Beijing edibles, such as the sweetened hawthorn fruit (usually sold on skewers), *hongguo* 紅果, and structures, such as the enclosed Beijing courtyard, the *sihefang* 四合房. Furthermore, even though the action of the novel takes place in Hangzhou, the narrator consistently refers to all addresses by the typical Beijing term for a street—*hutong* 衚衕.[10]

Since the *Storyteller's Jigong* is not related to earlier novels on this saint, it would seem likely that it derives from a local oral tradition, and since its vocabulary betrays a Beijing provenance, this local tradition would appear to be northern. Indeed, the novel's title and preface alike suggest a relation between it and northern forms of storytelling. The word *pingyan* (which I render "storyteller") literally means "oral performance." It is related to two other terms: *pinghua*, which is a general term for storytelling, and *pingshu*, denoting a specific genre of northern storytelling. The novel's original (1898) preface likewise indicates a relation to oral literature:

> My friend the provincial graduate Zhang Wenhai is a renowned scholar from Qiantang [i.e., Hangzhou]. For the purpose of his studies, he traveled to the capital [Beijing], where once, during a spare hour, he arrived at a place filled with a huge crowd. They were all listening to a storyteller narrating episodes from this novel. The stories were so captivating that the audience did not grow weary of listening to them. [My friend] searched the bookstores but could not find this novel. Just then, his friend Yan Huaxuan brought him [a version of] this novel written by Mr. Guo Xiaoting. Zhang leafed through it once. He found the portrayal of both monks and laymen so

vivid that he felt he was going through the experience himself and seeing the characters with his own eyes. Moreover, [Guo Xiaoting's novel] chastises the bad and upholds the righteous. It narrates marvelous tales and strange occurrences, and it describes out-of-the-ordinary creatures. This novel is rich and varied, and its contribution to the improvement of the current mores is by no means slight.

Thus Zhang was very much impressed with Guo Xiaoting's novel, and he realized that he could not possibly keep it a secret to himself. Therefore he discussed this matter with Wei Daipo, owner of the Tianjin publishing house Zhuzi shanfang. He spared no expense and prepared a lithographic edition of this novel, asking me to write the preface for it. I reckon that once this novel is published, people in every corner and neighborhood of the city will delight in reading it. Furthermore, I believe that to a certain extant this novel will serve as a vehicle for inculcating moral values and awakening people's minds.[11]

To judge from this preface, the popularity in Beijing of oral literature on Jigong created a demand in that city for written fiction on him. The preface suggests that Guo Xiaoting authored the novel in response to this demand, and even though this is not stated explicitly, we are led to believe that the novel derives from Beijing storytelling. Further evidence is provided by hints strewn in the body of the novel itself. Thus, for example, at one point the narrator introduces a martial character nicknamed the Red-Haired Plague God (Chifa wenshen), explaining that "according to the storyteller's romance" (*an shuoshu yanyi*), this character is "such and such" (165.224). Here the author uses the narrator's voice to explicitly acknowledge his indebtedness to professional storytelling. As we shall see below, we know enough about the figure of Jigong in nineteenth-century oral literature to pinpoint two northern genres of storytelling, *pingshu* and *guci* (drum-songs), from which the *Storyteller's Jigong* derives.

Pingshu

Pingshu, literally "annotating books," is a genre of oral literature that flourished in Beijing during the second half of the nineteenth century and the first half of the twentieth. From Beijing, it spread to the city of Tianjin and the northern provinces of Hebei, Liaoning, Jilin, and Heilongjiang. *Pingshu* is a prose genre—it has neither sung parts nor musical accompaniment. Instead, the storyteller punctuates his performance by hitting a small wooden block, about one cubic inch in size, against a table. The noise thus produced is also used to alert the audience to the beginning of the performance, and for this reason this wooden instrument is known as the "wake-up wood" (*xingmu*). The storyteller also wields a handkerchief, which can be used to represent a letter or a book, and a small fan, which may stand for such diverse objects as a sword, a bridge, or a ceiling.[12]

In nineteenth-century Beijing, most *pingshu* performances took place in the open air, under temporary awnings. By the 1910s, however, they usually took place in "storytelling teashops" (*pingshu chaguan*), which offered their customers both tea and entertainment by storytellers. In the 1930s there were some 70 or 80 storytelling teashops in Beijing, the largest of which could accommodate an audience of 300 people. Most storytelling teashops were located in the Tianqiao entertainment district in the southern part of the city, near the Temple of Heaven (Tiantan).[13] None survives, but the *pingshu* genre—which adapted to modern media—does. In north China, television and radio regularly feature *pingshu* shows.

Most *pingshu* stories are concerned with historical themes, martial valor, or the supernatural. Romantic love is a rare topic in this genre, which celebrates righteous officials such as Baogong, martial heroes such as Yue Fei, and mischievous deities such as Sun Wukong. Episodes from the historical novels *Romance of the Three Kingdoms* and *Tale of Utmost Loyalty* (*Jingzhong zhuan*), the martial-arts story cycles *Water Margin* and *Seven Heroes and Five Gallants* (*Qixia wuyi*), and the fantastic narratives *Enfeoffment of the Gods* and *Journey to the West* are popular subjects for *pingshu*. Most of these *pingshu* narratives are very long; in 1920s Beijing the performance of an average *pingshu* story cycle lasted two months; the audience returned each day to hear the story unfold.

Memoirs of the Tianqiao entertainment district in Beijing testify that from the late Qing through the Republican period Jigong was a popular topic in the *pingshu* genre. One such memoir, Yun Youke's *Collected Talks on the Itinerant Life* (*Jianghu congtan*; ca. 1932), provides us with the nickname by which *pingshu* storytellers referred to the performance of Jigong stories—"acting the Smallpox [Scarred Beggar]" (*chuan hua*).[14] This nickname alludes, of course, to Jigong's shabby appearance, which resembles that of a beggar. Other memoirs give the names of at least seven *pingshu* artists active during the last decades of the Qing who specialized in narrating the Jigong cycle. They included such renowned storytellers as Chen Shengfang,

Hai Wenquan, Shi Diancheng, and the "Great King of the *Pingshu* genre," Shuang Houping (fl. 1890–1920). In Yun Youke's judgment, Shuang surpassed all other *pingshu* storytellers in his ability to embody Jigong's sense of humor, and thus to keep his audiences in stitches.[15]

Late Qing *pingshu* performers of the Jigong cycle were followed by Republican period disciples. One of these, Li Zhiqing, impersonated the holy madman's spirit so convincingly that he was nicknamed Jigong Li. But, in Yun Youke's judgment, the best *pingshu* storyteller of the Jigong cycle was Liu Jiye, who, in the late 1920s and early 1930s, regularly performed it, during the eleventh and twelfth months of each year, at the Cuckold's [Storytelling] Teashop (Wangba chaguan). Yun Youke reminisces in loving detail upon a performance by Liu Jiye, which took place when Liu was still working for the Benevolence and Righteousness Teashop (Renyi xuan):[16]

Sometime ago, I, Old Yun, had some business to attend to in the eastern part of the city. As I was strolling through the Dongan market [on Wangfu jing street], I noticed on the Benevolence and Righteousness Teashop a placard announcing a "Jigong zhuan" performance by Liu Jiye (stage name: Liu Haibao). Luckily, I had nothing more to do that afternoon, so I could listen to some *pingshu*. It was about three in the afternoon when Liu climbed the stage. I looked at him: he was a small, thin man, and his face was pockmarked; the kind of face nicknamed "Plum Blossom Plate." He appeared to be a little over thirty years old. . . . Originally I intended to stay only a short while and then leave. I did not expect him to have the artistic ability to speak so compellingly. He repeatedly "shook the cloth wrapper" (*dou baofu*) (Itinerant artists refer to making the audience laugh as "shaking the cloth wrapper"), . . . and the audience roared with laughter. No wonder the place was jam-packed. Really Liu Jiye is endowed with dexterous skills, his artistic ability is very high, and he surpasses common performers. It was only when evening fell that the performance was over, and I returned home.[17]

Another native-resident of Beijing, H. Y. Lowe (Lu Xingyuan), describes how deeply impressed he was, as a child, by *pingshu* performances of Jigong stories:

Of the stories he heard, those which appealed to him the most were from the *Jigong zhuan*, or the "Life of Abbot Jigong." . . . The stories made such an impression on the young mind that he was noticed to refer to them on many an occasion at home and abroad. It was also discovered that one of the reasons behind his industry during his first school days later was that some day he might be able to read the *Jigong zhuan* in the original.[18]

The popularity of the Jigong story cycle in Beijing *pingshu* during the last decades of the Qing suggests that this genre may be the source of the *Storyteller's Jigong,* which was written during the same period and betrays the marks of Beijing patois. This hypothesis is supported by external and internal evidence alike. At least one observer of the *pingshu* world, Yun Youke, has argued explicitly that the *Storyteller's Jigong* derives from *pingshu* narratives,[19] and the novel itself includes several hints of its reliance upon this genre. First, there is the word *pingyan* ("oral performance") in the novel's title, which, as noted above, is related to *pingshu*. Then there is a curious homily on the virtues of *pingshu* storytelling in the body of the novel. The context is a familiar one in the vernacular tradition—a cautionary dream in which a character is exposed to the punishments awaiting sinners in hell. The character in question, here named Zhang Shifang, visits the familiar highlights of every netherworld tour—the mountain of knife blades, the blood pool, the burning pillar. But his horrifying tour ends abruptly, when he finds himself in front of two gorgeous bridges, one made of gold, the other of silver:

> And there he saw an elderly gentleman of a dignified and benevolent mien accompanied by a golden acolyte and a silvery acolyte. Each of these two was carrying a fan and a tray, in which was a folding fan and a 'wake-up wood' (*xingmu*) [i.e., the *pingshu* storyteller's paraphernalia]. Zhang Shifang asked: "How come this gentleman appears so leisurely?" The ghost warden replied: "In the world of light this man was a *pingshu* storyteller. He talked about things old and new, lectured about morality, and discussed benevolence and righteousness. He led the ignorant masses to the shores of enlightenment and convinced people to act morally. Therefore following his death, the golden acolyte and the silvery acolyte lead him across the golden bridge and the silver bridge. He will be reborn into a rich and noble household." (150.150)

The praise for *pingshu* storytelling in this passage suggests a close link between the *Storyteller's Jigong* and this genre. The novel's author, Guo Xiaoting, must have been greatly indebted to *pingshu* storytellers in order for him to incorporate this homily into his narrative. As we will see below, the little we know of Guo's other writings suggests that *pingshu* performances served as the regular source for his novels.

Guo Xiaoting and the Novel *Everlasting Blessings and Peace*

In addition to the *Storyteller's Jigong*, we know of at least one other late nineteenth-century novel that evinces close association with the *pingshu* genre. Interestingly enough, this novel, too, was probably written by Guo Xiaoting. The novel in question is *Everlasting Blessings and Peace*, which was issued in 1892 by the Baowen tang publishing house in Beijing.[20] The author's preface to this novel is signed by Guo Guangrui, whose style name (*zi*), Xiaoting, is also provided.[21] It thus seems highly likely that *Everlasting Blessings and Peace* and the *Storyteller's Jigong*—both of which were published during the last decade of the nineteenth century and, as discussed below, have significant similarities—were written by the same author: Guo Guangrui, to whom I refer by his style name, (Guo) Xiaoting.

Everlasting Blessings and Peace concerns the struggle, which supposedly occurred during the reign of the Kangxi emperor (r. 1662–1722), between the government and the rebellious Heaven and Earth Society and the Eight Trigrams Sect. This struggle is largely described in the novel as a magic contest, in which holy men with superior powers working for the government eventually crush the two sects' sorcerers. The novel concludes with the complete victory of the imperial forces, which ushers in an era of "everlasting blessings and peace." In terms of its ideological bent, the novel stands firmly on the side of the imperial government, causing some discomfort to critics in communist China, who would have preferred it to support the just cause of the rebellious masses.[22]

Everlasting Blessings and Peace shares significant similarities with the *Storyteller's Jigong*. At the most general level, both novels belong to the new genre of martial-arts fiction that emerged during the nineteenth century. More specifically, in both novels martial skills are intimately related to magic powers, and magic techniques of invulnerability figure prominently in both novels. Then, there is the reliance upon the *pingshu* genre of oral literature, which, in the case of *Everlasting Blessings and Peace*, is acknowledged by the author in the preface:

> In my youth I traveled all over the land, and once, in the capital [i.e., Beijing], I overheard a *pingshu* performance of *Everlasting Blessings and Peace*. This narrative offers a true account of the rewarding of loyalty and the condemnation of hypocrisy under our great Qing government, as well as this dynasty's destruction of rebels and heterodox sects. Its protagonists

include righteous and chivalric persons as well as selflessly heroic scholars. These heroes devotedly defended the state and single-mindedly protected the common folk. The story's logic is straightforward, and there is historical evidence to substantiate it. Nothing like the groundless histories (*yeshi*) common in *guci* [performances].[23]

This true story has been circulating ever since the founding of our dynasty. During the Xianfeng reign period [1851–61], there was a Mr. Jiang Zhenming, who used to talk of things old and new, and who once performed it. However, no one published it and transmitted it to the world. I once heard Mr. Hafuyuan perform this story. I carefully memorized it in my heart and, in my free time, recorded it in the form of four booklets (*juan*), in order to relieve my boredom. Now, my friend, the owner of the Baowen tang publishing company has read this book and was impressed by its straightforward message. He made up his mind to publish it and transmit it to the world—not because he is scheming for profit, but rather because he wishes to relieve the boredom of like-minded friends. I happily accorded with his plan. Revising and amending the manuscript, I recorded this true story in 100 chapters (*hui*). This way the names of loyal officials and righteous scholars will be passed on to future generations, and the punishments that treacherous cliques and evil bandits met with won't be forgotten either!

Written reverently by the retired scholar of Yannan, Guo Guangrui, [zi] Xiaoting, on the second month of the Xinmao year, in the Guangxu reign [1891].

Guo Xiaoting specifies the names of two *pingshu* masters whose oral narratives served as the source for his novel: Hafuyuan and Jiang Zhenming, whose performances influenced those of Hafuyuan. Both of these artists are mentioned in memoirs of the Tianqiao entertainment district. Yun Youke, who argued that the *Storyteller's Jigong* derives from *pingshu* narratives, attributed the origins of *Everlasting Blessings and Peace* to Hafuyuan and Jiang Zhenming and provides touching biographical data about the former. Hafuyuan, a Mongolian bannerman by descent, liked dogs. In fact he and his wife reared a dog whom they loved as if it were their only child (they were childless). Like many other Beijing residents, Hafuyuan and his wife used to sleep on the *kang*—an elevated platform with a stove underneath. One night, on the eve of the Lunar New Year, a blanket fell under the *kang*. In the ensuing fire, Hafuyuan, his wife, and their dog perished together. "*Pingshu* aficionados," concludes Yun Youke, "are still overcome with emotion whenever they think of Hafuyuan."[24]

The *pingshu* origins of *Everlasting Blessings and Peace* strengthen the case for the *Storyteller's Jigong*'s reliance upon this genre. Guo Xiaoting, the author of both novels, appears to have been a professional writer who specialized in the adaptation of *pingshu* narratives as novels. It is noteworthy that the interplay of *pingshu* and written fiction in the transmission of Jigong lore continued into the 1980s, when the Performing Arts Publishing House issued yet another novel on Jigong, based on contemporary performances by the *pingshu* masters Yang Zhimin and his disciple Guo Tianen (see Appendix A).[25]

Guci

Even though *pingshu* performances served as the immediate source of the novel *Storyteller's Jigong*, *pingshu* was neither the only, nor the first, genre of Beijing storytelling to celebrate the eccentric saint. By the mid-nineteenth century at the latest, Jigong was a popular topic in another genre of Beijing oral literature—*guci* (drum-songs). Unlike the *pingshu* genre, which is a genre of prose storytelling, the *guci* (also known as *shuochang guci*, "telling and singing drum-songs") is a chantefable; that is, it includes alternating sung and prose sections. The sung parts are characterized by alternating seven- and ten-character lines (the latter divided into three- and seven-character segments). The songs are accompanied by percussion instruments (usually a small drum and clappers) as well as string instruments such as the three-stringed guitar (*sanxian*).[26] One *guci* performer described his trade as follows:

> There are many professions in this world,
> But the hardest is the storyteller's:
> Hitting the drums and striking the clappers is not easy.
> And, you need memorize a thousand words and ten thousand phrases.
> First, your voice must be resonant.
> Second, your feet should stamp the beat.
> Enacting officials, playing warriors, I alone—
> Am the equal of an entire opera troupe.[27]

Most scholars trace the origins of the *guci* genre to the late Ming or early Qing. By the eighteenth century, this genre had spread throughout north China, and in nineteenth-century Beijing it enjoyed a reading audience. This is evidenced by a large number of handwritten transcriptions, or near transcriptions, of *guci* narratives, still extant today. These hand-copied manuscripts of *guci* narratives were either sold or rented to interested readers in Beijing. Like the *pingshu* stories that followed them, these *guci* narratives for the most part concern either martial heroism or the supernatural, and like *pingshu* they tend to be extremely long. *Guci* manuscripts come in the form of 25–30-page volumes, and many manuscripts, including, for example, the *Three Kingdoms* and the *Enfeoffment of the Gods*, are over a hundred volumes in length. By the turn of the twentieth century, *guci* had been eclipsed by the related genre of *dagu*, with which it is often confused (both genres are rendered in English as "drum-songs" or "drum-singing"). Even though the two genres are closely related, there are several significant differences between them: whereas the *guci* is a chantefable, *dagu* is sung only and includes no prose; *guci* narratives are very long, *dagu* songs are much shorter. Finally, unlike the *guci* genre, which features courageous warriors and invincible deities only, *dagu* songs celebrate romantic love as well.[28]

But, before we turn to examine a *guci* narrative on Jigong and its relation to the *Storyteller's Jigong*, a few words on the circumstances under which *guci* manuscripts were produced in nineteenth-century Beijing are in order. The *guci* genre, like most forms of oral literature, did not enjoy the position of respectable art form in late imperial times, and prior to the twentieth-century *guci* narratives were never published.[29] Instead, they were available to interested readers and amateur performers (*piaoyou*) in the form of hand-copied manuscripts. These could be purchased or rented from special shops, which hired copyists to transcribe new performances and to copy existing texts. Manuscript vendors and manuscript rental shops are identifiable by the seals on these copies. These provide the shop's name, address, and, in the case of rental shops, warnings to the readers not to doodle, scribble, or otherwise deface borrowed manuscripts. Shops that sold manuscripts carried a large variety of performance literature and drama, ranging from Beijing opera to *guci* and *dagu* oral narratives. In nineteenth-century Beijing, the most successful of these shops was the Baiben Zhang (Hundred-volumes Zhang), which sold its merchandise both from portable stands at temple fairs, and from a regular storefront in the northwestern section of the city.[30] By contrast most rental shops carried *guci* narratives only, and—in much the same way that American video stores sell popcorn and soft drinks—they also sold steamed dumplings.[31]

Both the rental shops and the shops that sold manuscripts vied to obtain accurate transcriptions of the most recent hits in the Beijing entertainment world. This is, for example, how one store, which specialized in a genre closely related to *guci*—*zidishu*—advertised itself: [32]

This concern copies Zidi Ballads, and also Shi-style drum-songs [This is a reference to the renowned *zidishu* artist Shi Yukun (ca. 1810–ca. 1871)] with accompanying paeans. They have been corrected by persons of consequence, the plots are sensible, and the ideas excellently done: they are not your run-of-the-mill [*sic*]. Other shops may have some, but they are thin [imitations] and only tack on that label to make their profit; the lines are mostly different from Shi-style tales. This concern, in the past few years, has searched out [texts] diligently and acquired some base texts, which, luckily, match the Shi-style tales exactly. Our customers need only compare [them] to realize that this claim is a true one.[33]

Two extant manuscript copies of the same *guci* narrative on Jigong testify that by the 1850s Jigong was a popular topic in the genre. The complete manuscript is in 110 volumes; only 20 volumes (numbered 34 through 53) of the other manuscript survive. With minor differences, these 20 volumes are identical to the corresponding chapters in the 110-volume manuscript, suggesting that these are two different manuscripts of the same text, which I will hereafter call the *Jigong Drum-Song* (the original titles appearing on these manuscripts are *Jigong zhuan* and *Jigong an*; see Appendix A). This text is itself a more-or-less accurate transcription of an oral narrative. The 110-volume manuscript was part of the so-called Prince Che's Residence (Chewang Fu) collection. This enormous collection of some 1,600 nineteenth-century manuscripts of drama and oral literature was purchased in the early 1920s by Ma Yuqing and Shen Yinmo from book vendors in Beijing, according to whom it came from "Prince Che's Residence."[34] The bulk of this collection is now located in two Beijing libraries: the Capital Library (Shoudu tushuguan), which holds the 110-volume *Jigong Drum-Song*, and the Beijing University Library.[35] Most manuscripts in the Prince Che's Residence collection bear no seals, leading some scholars to speculate that they were originally collected—or copied directly—from actors' scripts and storytellers' promptbooks. In the case of the *Jigong Drum-Song*, however, it is clear that the manuscript was purchased from a vendor. A seal on the last page of volume 32 identifies this vendor as a Mr. Pi Zan (Pi Zan *gong*), whose "old store" is located "at an angle across from the pawnshop." An accompanying, highly blurred, seal suggests that Pi Zan was also a pharmacist (see Fig. 3).

Whereas the complete *Jigong Drum-Song* manuscript in 110 volumes was purchased, the fragmentary manuscript in 20 volumes (numbered 34 through 53) was rented. This manuscript is preserved in the "popular performance literature" (*suqu*) collection of the Academia Sinica in Taiwan. It was itself put together from three different manuscripts, which were rented out by three different stores, identifiable by their seals. Fourteen of the extant twenty volumes were rented by the Everlasting Harmony Studio (Yonghe zhai), three by the Everlasting Abundance Studio (Yonglong zhai), and three by the Abundant Blessings Studio (Longfu zhai).[36] The exact locations in Beijing of all three stores are provided by their seals (see Map 2), which also furnish a wealth of information about rental procedures. Thus, for example, we learn that readers were allowed to borrow one volume (of a multivolume *guci* narrative) per day and were expected to exchange it the following day for the next volume. If a reader kept a volume for more than five days, the rental fee doubled, and if he failed to return it within two weeks, he lost his deposit. The shops also used seals and inscriptions to advertise other products they sold (such as steamed buns) and, more significantly, to warn their readers lest they damage the borrowed texts. The Everlasting Harmony Studio, for example, advises its readers unequivocally that "men who tear or burn books, add writings, or change characters are robbers, and women [who do the same] are prostitutes." These harsh words did not prevent readers from doodling and scribbling—mostly in Chinese but occasionally in Manchu—all over the borrowed manuscripts, sometimes right on top of the seals exhorting them not to do so (see Fig. 4). These marginalia consist primarily of ditties, riddles, and jokes (usually of a sexual nature), but there are also complaints about the quality of the rented volumes and their prices. One such complaint offers us, as Zhou Chunyi pointed out, a clue for dating the *Jigong Drum-Song*: "This book," one reader grumbles, "is poorly copied. [I,] Minggong, didn't like it. I wasted no less than forty coins on it." This is followed by the date: "the ninth year of the Xianfeng reign" or 1859.[37] The *Jigong Drum-Song* must therefore have been written prior to 1859. Since this written *guci* narrative was rented out by no less than three stores, and sold in an identical form by a fourth store, the oral narrative it transcribes

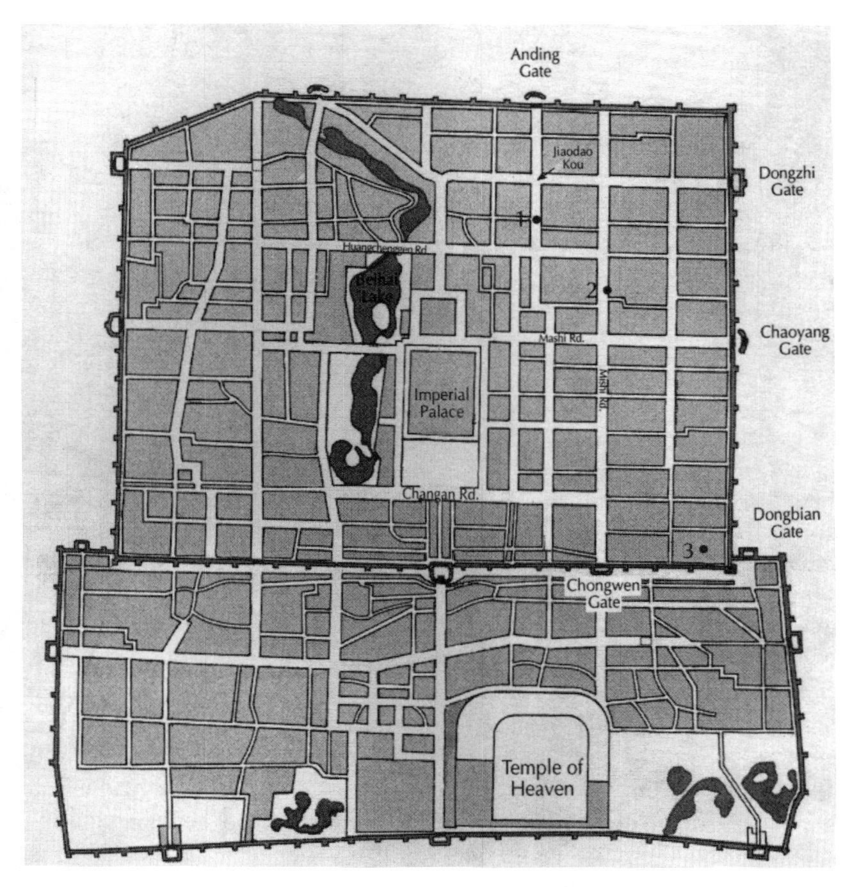

Map 2. Location of nineteenth-century Beijing stores that rented out the *Jigong Drum-Song* manuscripts: (1) Everlasting Abundance Studio (Yonglong zhai), on Jiaodao Kou South Road; (2) Everlasting Harmony Studio (Yonghe zhai), on the west end of Batiao Alley; (3) Abundant Blessings Studio (Longfu zhai), on Shenlu Street.

likely enjoyed considerable popularity for some time prior to that date.

The rich Beijing patois in which the *Jigong Drum-Song* is written leaves no doubt not only that this text was rented out in Beijing (as evidenced by the shops' seals) but also that the oral narrative it represents was originally performed there as well. First, there is the ubiquity of the Beijing retroflex ending *er* 兒, attached to an endless variety of words ranging from *shi'r* 事兒 (matter) and *cha'r* 茶兒 (tea) to *xiao dongxi'r* 小東西兒 (little thingy [derogatory]), *tou'r* 頭兒 (boss), and *qing'r* 情兒 (sentiment or favor). Second, there is a large variety of Beijing dialect words, which would be hard for anyone but a Beijing native resident to understand; for example: *deng* 登 (suddenly), *huzhou* 胡週 (nonsense), *jielie* 節(結)咧 (all right), *xiaoting* 孝(消)亭 (to rest; to relax), *xia dala* 瞎達拉 (to chat aimlessly), and *Zhang bachang, Li baduan* 張八長李八短 ("Zhang is such and such, and Li is so and so"—to gossip). Third, there are quintessential Beijing edibles, such as *miancha* 面茶 (a sesame porridge) and *douzhi'r* 豆汁兒 (a sourish drink made of green beans).[38] The rich dialect in which the *Jigong Drum-Song* is steeped reveals to us the difference between a transcribed oral narrative and a written vernacular novel, even when the latter derives from oral literature. The *Storyteller's Jigong* derives from Beijing oral literature, and it betrays its origins by the appearance of such Beijing words as *duozan* (when), and *hutong* (street). Nonetheless, by and large this novel is written in a standardized form of the vernacular, which would be understandable to any Chinese reader. By contrast the *Jigong Drum-Song* is written in a local patois, much of it incomprehensible to anyone but a native of Beijing.

Another obstacle for the modern reader is the large number of orthographic errors found in all manuscript versions of the text. These errors consist primarily of the homophonic substitution of one character for another of the same or similar pronunciation. Practically every line of the manuscripts contains such mistakes, proof of the copyists' low level of literacy. Some of the more common errors are *jin* 近 for *jin* 進, *zai* 在 for *zai* 再, *chu* 出 for *chu* 初, *jing* 京 for *jing* 驚, *er* 尔 (written in this simplified form) for *er* 而, and *jiu* 旧 (again in the simplified form) for jiu 就. The names of various historical figures are likewise misspelled: Qin Gui 秦貴 instead of Qin Gui 秦檜 for the infamous Southern-Song premier, and Qin Xi 秦喜 instead of Qin Xi 秦熹 for his son. The copyists'—and original performers'—low level of education is also evidenced by the large number of anachronisms in the text. Thus, for example, one character smokes, even though tobacco was introduced to China, by the Spaniards, some four hundred years after the period described.[39] The rented manuscripts of the *Jigong Drum-Song*, which are covered with readers' comments, reveal that the latter were no more educated that the copyists who produced the manuscripts. The same type of orthographic errors found in the text are prevalent in the readers' comments upon it. Thus, the manuscript versions of the *Jigong Drum-Song* offer us a glimpse of what may be defined as the lowest reading—and writing—public in late imperial Chinese cities. The people who rented the *Jigong Drum-Song* could not afford to purchase expensive printed books. Instead they rented handwritten transcriptions of the same drum-songs narratives they enjoyed listening to.[40] These readers, and the copyists who produced the texts they read, were able to read, and write, by using a limited number of characters to express a large number of homophones.

As noted above, the *Jigong Drum-Song* is a transcription, or near transcription, of *guci* narratives performed in Beijing. The *pingshu* stories about Jigong were likewise performed in that city, and the novel, *Storyteller's Jigong*, was written there as well. The similarities between the *Jigong Drum-Song* and the *Storyteller's Jigong* are striking. At the most general level, the *Jigong Drum-Song* and the novel alike are martial-arts narratives. Both texts depict Jigong as the invincible leader of fierce warriors, whose superior martial and magical skills enable them to subdue merciless bandits and crafty sorcerers alike. More specifically, much of the *Storyteller's Jigong*'s plot, especially the novel's first half, is prefigured in the written version of the drum-song. The bulk of the *Storyteller's Jigong*'s first half concerns Jigong's struggle against a bandit leader from western Sichuan, Hua Yunlong, nicknamed the "Heaven and Earth Bandit Rat," and this entire narrative line can be found in the *Jigong Drum-Song*. In both the drum-song and the novel, Hua Yunlong audaciously breaks into the premier's residence and steals a pearl-studded crown and a priceless jade bracelet. He murders a waiter who insults him as well as a chaste widow who refuses to submit to his desires. He fights a series of pitched battles against Jigong's disciples, and is finally subdued by Jigong's superior magic skills, brought to justice, and decapitated by imperial command. Other narrative lines in the novel are likewise found in the drum-song.

These include the unsuccessful attempt of several monks in the Lingyin Monastery to burn the hall where Jigong sleeps, as well as the equally unsuccessful attempt by the evil premier Qin Xi to destroy one of the monastery's towers. In all, about half the plot of the *Storyteller's Jigong* is narrated in the *Jigong Drum-Song*.

These similarities suggest that the novel derives, at least in part, from oral *guci* narratives. Since the *guci* narratives on Jigong preceded both the *pingshu* stories about him and the *Storyteller's Jigong*, by several decades, these *guci* narratives could have influenced the *pingshu* stories as well as the novel, but not vice versa. There are, however, significant differences in the plots of the *Jigong Drum-Song* and the *Storyteller's Jigong*. Some of the novel's more important subplots cannot be found in the drum-song. These include the prolonged magic campaigns launched by Jigong against, first, the Taoist master-sorcerer Hua Qingfeng (chaps. 91–94) and then Hua's colleague Shao Huafeng (this expedition occupies the bulk of the novel's second half). Likewise, much of the drum-song narrative is not in the novel, most notably, the lengthy affair between the lecherous Sun Guopei and the prostitute Saizhu'er. This complex narrative, which involves betrayal, suicide (by Sun's wife), murder (of Sun, by a jealous husband), and the rebirth of the principal heroes, is interesting for the sympathy shown toward the prostitute, whose love to the faithless Sun is true.[41]

Even when the *Storyteller's Jigong* follows the *Jigong Drum-Song*'s narrative, the two texts usually differ. In some cases the plot is almost identical, but the names—of characters, objects, and places—vary. For example, in both texts Jigong orders a disciple to steal a potent amulet from the premier's residence and return it to its rightful owners. In the drum-song this amulet is a painting of a netherworld judge; its owner is a Mr. Fan, and Jigong's disciple is Yang Meng. In the novel this amulet is the Five Thunders and Eight Trigrams Heavenly Masters' Charm; it belongs to one Li, and Jigong's disciple is Zhao Bin.[42] In some cases a narrative element is borrowed from the drum-song but placed in a completely different context in the novel. In the *Jigong Drum-Song*, for example, Jigong gazes through the window of the Myriad Treasures Restaurant at his martial disciples, who are fighting with Hua Yunlong's associates. In the novel he gazes through that same window at a different battle, which has nothing to do with Hua Yunlong.[43] Numerous other episodes reveal analogous differences between the drum-song and the novel; two examples will suffice. In the drum-song, the lecherous premier kidnaps a beautiful woman and her father; in the novel his lecherous son imprisons a beautiful lady and her husband. In the drum-song and the novel alike a place called the Zhao Family Tower (Zhaojia lou) serves as a battleground for Hua Yunlong and Jigong's disciples. In the drum-song the Zhao Family Tower is a teahouse and a brothel; in the novel it is part of a rich man's private residence.[44]

The differences between the *Storyteller's Jigong* and the *Jigong Drum-Song* suggest that the latter could not have been the former's immediate source. Those narrative units, characters, and themes that the novel borrowed from *guci* narratives were filtered through a third medium, and this medium was, as we have seen above, the *pingshu* genre. This conclusion is supported by the fact that the *Storyteller's Jigong* includes no songs in the *guci* meter. Thus, this novel's immediate sources were probably *pingshu* oral stories; these in turn were most likely influenced by oral stories in the *guci* genre. (Interestingly, according to some eyewitnesses of the Beijing entertainment world, *guci* served as a source for *pingshu* narratives.)[45] We may conclude that oral narratives in the *guci* genre influenced *pingshu* oral literature, and the latter served as the *Storyteller's Jigong*'s immediate source. One element is still missing, however, from this picture. As we will see below, some *guci* stories on Jigong were also a favorite topic of Beijing opera, and, probably, both genres influenced the *pingshu* stories that served as the *Storyteller's Jigong*'s source.

One final point needs to be made regarding the relation between *guci* stories on Jigong and the earlier narrative tradition. Whereas the *Storyteller's Jigong* is not related at all to the earlier novels on Jigong, the *Jigong Drum-Song* is. Several episodes in this drum-song derive directly from *Drunken Puti*, the most popular novel on Jigong throughout the eighteenth and the nineteenth centuries. These include three miracles performed by Jigong: his reviving of boiled snails, the coating of the statues with gold, and the transporting of the logs from Sichuan to the monastery's well.[46] These episodes testify that *guci* oral narratives on Jigong did derive, at least in part, from earlier novels on him. However, *pingshu* storytellers and/or the novelist Guo Xiaoting omitted those episodes. Thus, in the transformation of *guci* narratives into *pingshu* stories into a novel, the ties to the earlier narrative tradition were lost, and the *Storyteller's Jigong* shows no connection to the earlier novels.

We are now in a position to evaluate the respective roles of oral and written fiction in the spread of Jigong lore. Oral literature in Zhejiang inspired several written novels on this eccentric saint. These novels spread throughout China, and in at least one case—nineteenth-century Beijing—they served as a source for oral literature in the local dialect. This oral literature transformed the image of the eccentric saint into a martial artist, and it inspired a written novel (*Storyteller's Jigong*). The novel spread throughout China, precipitated numerous sequels (which were published for the most part in Shanghai), and inspired an enormous body of oral literature and drama in a variety of local dialects. Throughout this process, written and oral fiction mutually shaped each other. The significance of the written texts lies in their capacity to cross regional and linguistic boundaries. The special strength of oral genres is their ability to reach all members of society in any given locality.

The *Storyteller's Jigong* and Martial-Arts Fiction

The most striking difference between the *Storyteller's Jigong* and earlier fiction on this eccentric saint is its martial tone. The bulk of the narrative is dedicated to minute descriptions of his battles with a wide array of adversaries ranging from bandits and outlaws to Taoist sorcerers and fox-spirits. As a novel concerned primarily with physical heroism, the *Storyteller's Jigong* belongs to a large group of nineteenth-century novels that represent a new development in the history of Chinese fiction. These are martial-arts novels that celebrate the physical prowess of individual warriors bent upon the protection of the poor and the helpless against local bullies, corrupt officials, and supernatural monsters. Some notable examples are the novels: *The Cases of Lord Shi* (*Shigong an*; 1820?), *Three Heroes and Five Altruists* (*Sanxia wuyi*; 1879), *The Patriotic Junior Five Altruists* (*Zhonglie xiao wuyi zhuan*; 1890), *The Cases of Lord Peng* (*Penggong an*; 1892), and Guo Xiaoting's other novel, *Everlasting Blessings and Peace* (1892). This new genre of martial-arts fiction (*wuxia xiaoshuo*) continues to enjoy great popularity to this day in the works of such widely read authors as Huanzhulou zhu (1902–62) and, more recently, Gulong (1937–1985) and Jin Yong (b. 1924).[47]

Nineteenth- and twentieth-century martial-arts novels differ from the earlier "military romance" in the type of warfare described.[48] Whether they narrate historical or fantastic warfare, military romances such as the *Three Kingdoms* and the *Enffeofment of the Gods* are concerned with the deployment of large-scale armies. They describe the tactical ordering of battle arrays (*zhen*) as well as the strategic maneuvering of the army. By contrast, nineteenth-century martial-arts novels are concerned with the martial skills of individual warriors, who sneak over high walls into heavily guarded palaces and overwhelm their adversaries with their superior swordsmanship and pugilistic skills. (Thus, martial-arts novels are reminiscent of the *Water Margin*'s early chapters, which are dedicated to the protagonists' individual adventures. But these novels differ from the *Water Margin*'s later chapters, where the bandits fight as a unified army first against, and then for, the government.) Differences in military strategy are related to differences in weaponry: whereas much of the warfare in military romances is conducted from horseback, with spears, lances, and arrows, the protagonists of martial-arts novels are rarely mounted, they specialize in boxing, and their weapon of choice is the short sword. Finally, martial-arts novels differ from the military romance in warfare's ultimate purpose. The protagonists of the military romance lead their armies to gain the throne or to defend the nation. Martial heroes in nineteenth-century fiction are concerned with local issues. They battle this or that bully, treacherous official, or monster, and only rarely lead an army against foreign aggressors, as in Qian Cai's military romance, *The Complete Yue Fei Story* (*Shuo Yue quanzhuan*).[49]

In the *Storyteller's Jigong*, the martial artists are presented as Jigong's disciples. In several other martial-arts novels, they work in the service of a righteous official. This is the case, for example, with the novel *Three Heroes and Five Altruists*, which features the celebrated Judge Bao (Baogong). The latter was the subject of a large body of Ming and early Qing court-case fiction (*gongan xiaoshuo*)—the Chinese equivalent of Western detective literature. His appearance in *Three Heroes* has led some scholars to classify this, and other martial-arts novels, as court-case literature as well. However, martial-arts novels, unlike court-case literature, emphasize military, rather than judicial, skills, and in most of these novels the judge is a mere pretense for the heroic deeds of his disciples. Thus whereas Yuan court-case drama and Qing court-case fiction celebrate Judge Bao's detective skills, in the *Three Heroes* he is completely overshadowed by his followers' martial prowess.[50]

In addition to a common subject matter and a similar ideological bent, nineteenth-century martial-arts novels share other common traits as well. Many of these novels (unlike their twentieth-century successors) derive, as did the *Storyteller's Jigong*, from northern forms of oral literature. *Three Heroes*, for example, is based upon the oral narratives of the *zidishu* artist Shi Yukun, and, as noted above, Guo Xiaoting's *Everlasting Blessings and Peace* derives from *pingshu*.[51] This reliance on oral sources is related to another characteristic shared by many of these novels—their open-ended and episodic structure, which, for its part, facilitated the addition of sequels. Many martial-arts novels, including *The Cases of Lord Shi*, *The Cases of Lord Peng*, and *Three Heroes*, have been followed, as was the *Storyteller's Jigong*, by several sequels. In the following I will not attempt to cover this entire new genre of martial-arts fiction, but will focus on some martial aspects of the *Storyteller's Jigong*.

Martial Artists

Whereas in the earlier novels Jigong rescues his devotees by himself, in the *Storyteller's Jigong* he is assisted in his fight against evil by a devoted group of fearless warriors. These martial artists fight on Jigong's behalf against a wide array of adversaries, ranging from corrupt officials and bandits to local bullies and licentious monks. They usually operate in small task forces of one, two, or three warriors each, and they receive specific and detailed operational instructions from their saintly leader. For example, Jigong may order one disciple to break into the premier's residence, steal a priceless amulet, and return it to its rightful owner, and simultaneously order several other disciples to accompany and protect a lone and defenseless traveler, who would otherwise be attacked by robbers. The close co-operation between Jigong and his martial disciples is based on his prognostication skills. Jigong knows where and when a crime will be committed, and he sends his devotees to capture the culprits in the act. Occasionally he also assigns them the task of punishing sinners—and the punishments may be severe. In one case Jigong allocates the death penalty to a young man who tried to kidnap and sell his young cousin on route to her wedding (73.357–60). Jigong's martial disciples, most of whom became his devotees after he saved their lives, treat him with great respect and obey his orders to the letter. They kneel in front of him, address him as "master," and refer to him—just as the narrator does—as an arhat (*luohan*) or a "living Buddha" (*huofo*). (The second term was first applied to Jigong in the

Recorded Sayings, but it gained currency only in the *Storyteller's Jigong*.)[52]

With the exception of one disciple, who is a fruit vendor by day and martial artist by night, Jigong's martial devotees are professional warriors, who earn a living by their martial skills. Some serve as armed escorts (*baobiao*); others "sell their art" (*maiyi*) in public displays of martial skills. Interestingly, both types of livelihood were common among nineteenth-century martial artists. During the late Qing, insurance companies, known as *biaoju*, hired armed guards to escort goods in transit.[53] As for public displays of martial arts, according to one turn-of-the-century observer, "in every market and every temple fair there are martial artists who demonstrate their skills."[54] Some of these martial artists combined boxing or displays of swordsmanship with acrobatics. Many others also sold medicines, especially ointments.

The descriptions in the *Storyteller's Jigong* of martial-arts demonstrations are similar to those found in contemporary nonfictional sources. The narrator emphasizes that, like all other street performers, martial artists must be endowed with oral skills or else they will not be able to attract an audience. In order to succeed in public performances, martial artists, like fortune-tellers and other performers, need to master the language of the itinerant world (*jianghu hua*) (163.212). Yun Youke's memoir of the Beijing entertainment world, the *Jianghu congtan*, includes a chapter on martial-arts performances. Yun, like the narrator of the *Storyteller's Jigong*, emphasizes that martial artists "must be endowed with both oral skills and physical dexterity, or else they cannot make a living. Physical dexterity is the real art that earns them their livelihood. Oral skills, namely eloquence, enable them to 'tie the horse to the stake' [i.e., attract an audience that will watch the show]."[55] Yun Youke illustrates this point by quoting a typical speech of a martial artist *cum* medicine seller:

"Today I will perform a special exercise." Saying this, [the martial artist] places a porcelain teapot on his table. On its spout he balances a large copper coin, on which he puts a clay ball. In front he places, upside down, a teacup, on which he puts another clay ball. He points with his hand at these things, and declares: "Today I will perform the following exercise: I will use this slingshot to shoot this pellet. The pellet will fly in one straight line. First, it will hit the clay ball of top of the teacup, without breaking the teacup. It will make the ball fly, and this ball will hit the other ball, of top of the teapot, causing it to fly. But the teapot won't break. Moreover the large copper coin on its spout won't fall. This trick has a name: it is called 'hitting a pellet with a pellet,' and it is also nicknamed 'hitting a ball with a ball.' On ordinary days I don't perform this trick. But since you are all here today I will perform it, so that you will all spread my name." . . . Saying this, he holds the slingshot in his left hand and takes the ball in his right. . . . He gives the impression that he is about to shoot. . . . But, in fact, he will not. . . . This is what is called "tying the horse to the stake."

He now addresses his audience again: "I am about to perform this exercise of 'hitting a pellet with a pellet,' 'hitting a ball with a ball.' The teacup won't smash, the spout won't break. You should all clap your hands and cheer me on—yes, yes, clap your hands with all your might and cheer me loudly. . . . Now, you probably think that I am doing all of this to get some money from you. Well, you need not worry—had I wanted money I would have asked my ancestors to give me some! I don't want even a penny. I want no money whatsoever. All I want is that you spread my name. In fact you need not even spread the wonders of my 'hitting the ball with a ball' exercise. Instead you may want to spread the wonders of this"—he reaches with his hand to the table and lifts a large box of ointment—"You should spread my name saying that my ointment is the best!"[56]

The familiarity of the *Storyteller's Jigong*'s author with the world of professional martial arts is not surprising. Guo Xiaoting recorded in this novel (more or less accurately) oral narratives performed by *pingshu* storytellers, who belonged to the same community of itinerant performers as martial artists. Storytellers performed in the same markets and temple fairs where martial artists touted their military skills, and they must have been familiar with their performances. It is therefore not inconceivable that, as Wang Hailin has suggested, the emergence of martial-arts fiction during the late Qing was related to the rapid spread of martial-arts performances during the same period.[57]

Whereas some of Jigong's martial disciples are armed escorts or public performers, others make a living as roving bandits. One disciple leaves his mountain manor each year and briefly tours distant provinces. There he robs and steals—albeit "from wealthy households of officials or big merchant families only"—enough to last him the entire year (60.293). Another does not hesitate to murder a fellow bandit in order to obtain a powerful sedative, which he needs for his robbery expeditions. This disciple even tries, on several occasions, to murder Jigong himself, and it is only after Jigong overpowers him and later saves his life that he becomes an ardent follower.[58] Finally, even Jigong himself does not always follow the letter of the law scrupulously. He may not murder or steal, but he often makes a point of leaving restaurants without paying, especially if he has been treated rudely by a waiter, who, mislead by this crazy saint's outer appearance, mistook him for a mere beggar.[59]

Even those disciples of Jigong who do not themselves transgress the law are still closely associated with outlaws. Jigong's martial disciples exercise with, eat with, drink with, and make merry with the same criminals they fight. They belong, like their opponents, to the outlaw community, referred to in this, as in other nineteenth-century martial-arts novels, as the "greenwood world." (Greenwood, or Lülin, is the name of a mountain in present-day Hubei province that served as a rebel-army base during the first century C.E. By Tang times this term came to denote any group of armed rebels or robbers hiding in mountains or forests).[60] Jigong's martial disciples share the same social and professional background as their criminal adversaries. Thus, for example, before they head into battle they disguise their faces, so as not to "lose face" having to fight their close friends (96.467). Indeed, even Jigong's archenemy—the bandit leader from western Sichuan, Hua Yunlong—was originally a sworn brother of Jigong's disciples, who regularly extend their hospitality to him. This affinity between martial heroes and their criminal adversaries is characteristic of many nineteenth-century martial-arts novels, and it can be traced as far back as the *Water Margin*, whose rebellious heroes are, after all, bandits. In the *Water Margin* and its successors alike, martial heroes differ little from criminals, for they help themselves liberally to the ill-gotten spoils of the corrupt officials they fight.[61]

The similarity between martial heroes and their criminal adversaries raises the question of difference. What distinguishes a disciple of Jigong from his opponent? What is the difference, in a martial-arts novel, between the good and the bad guys? In the *Storyteller's Jigong* the dividing line is sharp, and it is drawn by sexual crimes. Jigong persecutes those bandits who seduce other people's wives and, especially, rapists. He battles Hua Yunlong not because of the latter's countless robberies (which include an audacious looting of the premier's residence), but, as he himself explains, because Hua Yunlong murdered a chaste widow, who refused him.[62] Jigong's disciples likewise terminate their association with another former colleague because he tried to seduce a sworn brother's wife.[63] Whereas social banditry, if not approved of, is certainly not condemned in the *Storyteller's Jigong*, the novel vehemently denounces sexual license.

The narrator describes in minute detail the outlaw world shared by his good and bad characters alike. One characteristic of all martial artists in this novel—Jigong's disciples and their opponents alike—is their fanciful heroic nicknames. Jigong's followers are known by such martial sobriquets as Mountain-Climbing Leopard, Cloud-Chasing Swallow, Star-Plucking Constellation Pacer, Eight Directions Awe-Exerting, and Incarnated Plague God. Their adversaries' appellations are no less awe-inspiring. Hua Yunlong (literally Cloud Dragon) and his gang are known as the Five Ghosts and One Dragon from Western Sichuan. The Five Ghosts are the Clouds-Midst Ghost, Wind-Arousing Ghost, Black Wind Ghost, Crowing-Cock Ghost, and Disheveled-Hair Ghost.[64] These nicknames are similar to those found in other nineteenth-century martial-arts novels. In the *Storyteller's Jigong* Hua Yunlong is styled the Heaven and Earth Bandit Rat, and similarly the *Three Heroes'* martial protagonists are known as the Five Rats: the Heaven-Piercing Rat, the Earth-Penetrating Rat, the Mountain-Boring Rat, the River-Churning Rat, and the Beautiful-Furred Rat.[65] Hua Yunlong's name Cloud Dragon is reminiscent of the protagonists' names in Guo Xiaoting's *Everlasting Blessings and Peace*. There the martial heroes are named Blessing Dragon, Responding Dragon, and Becoming Dragon.

The narrator pays detailed attention to the language of the outlaw community. With quite some fanfare, he congratulates himself on disclosing to his readers what he describes as the "secret language of the itinerant greenwoods" (*Jianghu lülin zhong de heihua* 江湖綠林中的黑話). In this secret argot martial artists are called *gua* 掛; those among them who guard buildings are "internal *gua*" (*neigua* 内掛); those who serve as armed escorts, "external *gua*" (*waigua* 外掛); and those who earn their living as public performers, "star *gua*" (*xinggua* 星掛).[66] Martial artists use a "centipede ladder" (*wugong tizi* 蜈蚣梯子) to climb over tall walls, and before breaking into a building, they throw a "testing-the-road stone" (*wenlu shi* 問路石) to check its inhabitants' alertness.[67] These terms are similar to those found in other nineteenth-century martial-arts novels. Thus, for example, the protagonists in both the *Storyteller's Jigong* and the *Three Heroes* wear the same Ninja-type outfit of buttoned body-tights with a large waistband called "night-work gear" (*yexing yi* 夜行衣).[68] Interestingly, some of the terms found in these novels were probably used by nineteenth-century martial artists, at least in north China. The *Jianghu congtan*, like the *Storyteller's Jigong*, refers to martial artists as *gua* or *guazi* 掛子, and it distinguishes different types. Its terminology is slightly different, however: guards are called *zhigua* 支掛, those who serve as armed escorts are *lagua* 拉掛, and those who give public performances are *diangua* 點掛.[69]

The descriptions in the *Storyteller's Jigong* of a secret martial artists' argot reflect, if not historical fact, at least a common nineteenth-century perception that such a language did exist. Again, Yun Youke's *Jianghu congtan* provides us with evidence: "All those who study martial arts, once they mastered the martial techniques—and no matter whether they intend to work as armed escorts or guards—must in addition study anew the jargon of professional itinerants. . . . In whatever situation they encounter, they rely on both their martial techniques and the secret argot of the itinerant world. Only then can they wander all over the land."[70] Yun Youke proceeds to give an example of the way armed escorts use this secret argot: Itinerant martial-artists, he explains, are called *laohe* 老合; therefore once they are on the road, armed escorts repeatedly shout *hewu* 合吾, meaning: "I am a *laohe*." This way they inform fellow warriors that they belong to the same community, and they warn potential adversaries that it would be a mistake to mess with them.[71] Interestingly, a term very similar to *hewu*—*hezi* 合字, appears in an identical context in the *Storyteller's Jigong*. A bandit, attacked by two of Jigong's disciples, begs for mercy, crying: "Sirs, don't do this! We are all *hezi*" (57.282).[72]

The narrator of the *Storyteller's Jigong* describes in minute detail not only his protagonists' argot but also their weaponry. Most of the martial artists in this novel use a short sword or a dagger (which they sometimes hide inside their boots). Some use more elaborate weapons such as the "bamboo-joint whip" or the poisoned-tipped "faster than wind, brighter than light" lance. Semi-magical weapons, such as the "mind-blurring sand bag," are also employed. The latter is a small pouch of noxious vapor that knocks out the enemy.[73] These various weapons are used in accordance with fixed techniques, whose names, sometimes fanciful, are provided by the narrator. Jigong's disciples, for example, practice the "36 positions of the left gate club," the "48 positions of the right gate club," and the "six maneuvers of the *zhuang* style club," and they wield their swords in the fixed tactics of "weeding the grass in search of the snake" and "fishing for the moon at the sea bottom."[74] Another weapon frequently used in the *Storyteller's Jigong*, especially by the bad guys, is sedatives. Bandits disguise sedatives as medicines, which they offer to their trusting victims, or they slip a mickey into their adversaries' wine. Some of these sedatives resemble modern chemical weapons; these are special gases that render those who inhale them unconscious. This is, for example, how Hua Yunlong and two of his associates try to rape several women, who are sleeping, together with their maids, in the women's quarters of a rich merchant household: "Hua Yunlong took six pieces of cloth, and the three bandits sealed well their nostrils. He took the incense box, lit [the incense], and pulled the 'immortal crane spout.' He made a small hole in the paper window. Then he pushed the spout through the hole. He pulled the [crane's] tail, and stirred its wings once. Those fumes emerged from the spout and filled the room" (70.345). In this instance Hua Yunlong was unable to carry out his evil designs, for Jigong' disciples arrived in the nick of time and saved the already unconscious girls.

The use of sedatives, especially by the bad guys, is common in late Qing martial-arts fiction, and it may be traced as far back as a famous robbery in the *Water Margin*, in which the armed escorts guarding the convoy carrying the premier's gifts are paralyzed by a mickey.[75] Of course, this is not the only element that martial-arts fiction borrowed from the *Water Margin*. The *Storyteller's Jigong* inherited several of its narrative patterns from that novel. In both narratives, heroes meet in the wilderness, fight, and, in the course of the duel, come to realize that their adversary is the famous master they have been longing to meet. In both novels they run into each other in taverns, eat, drink—or fight—and, when necessary, escape through open windows. More specifically, one of the *Water Margin*'s protagonists, the fighting monk Lu Zhishen, influenced no fewer than three martial monks in the *Storyteller's Jigong*: the first is nicknamed like him the Tattooed Monk (Hua Heshang); the second uses the same Shaansi dialect first-person pronoun that he uses—*sajia* (in the *Water Margin* only Lu Zhishen uses this quaint word, which comes to characterize him); and the third is Jigong himself, whose antinomian behavior was influenced by Lu Zhishen's as early as the sixteenth-century *Recorded Sayings*.[76] One episode in the *Storyteller's Jigong* derives directly from a famous Lu Zhishen story: a corrupt scion of a high-ranking military official uses illegal means to take another man's wife as his own. To his great dismay, he discovers that the person emerging from the bridal sedan-chair is not the woman he coveted but the ugly-looking Jigong! This scion's disappointment is surely similar to that of the *Water Margin*'s bandit, who coerces an old man into giving him his beautiful daughter in marriage. None other than Lu Zhishen awaits this bandit in his bridal bed and beats the hell out of him.[77]

Like their *Water Margin* predecessors, the martial heroes of the *Storyteller's Jigong*—good and bad guys alike—are outstanding warriors, who "fly over eaves and walk on walls."[78] Their military skills are matched by their fearless spirits. Hua Yunlong, for example, is not intimidated by scores of police officers who surround him. "Those who stand in my way will die," his voice roars. "Those who let me by will live." And tracing a bloody trail with his sword, he manages to escape. On another occasion, when several yamen runners order him to follow them for an investigation, Hua Yunlong displays similar courage—and panache: "It's fine with me to accompany you," he says "but I have a friend, who doesn't approve." "Where is he?" ask the yamen runners. "As far away as a thousand miles, and as near as your face!" answers Hua Yunlong as he unsheathes his sword.[79] Hua Yunlong's adversaries display the same courage and contempt for death: when stabbed in the back by Hua Yunlong's poisonous spear, Jigong's disciple Yang Ming laughs scornfully: "It was I who taught you how to use this spear." Awaiting their death at the hands of the Taoist sorcerer Hua Qingfeng, two of Jigong's disciples address a third one, saying: "It's not a big matter if we two die. Above—we are not bound to parents; below—we have no wife or children to take care of. . . . But you, our elder brother, shouldn't die! At home you have a white-haired mother, a beautiful wife, and a son who hasn't reached adulthood. If you die, who would take care of your old mother, lonely wife, and young child?!"[80] (It goes without saying that all these disciples are eventually saved by their master—Jigong.)

The *Storyteller's Jigong* is a suspense novel, in which the narrator maintains a sense of uncertainty as to the outcome of most battles. To use Tzvetan Todorov's terms, this novel is a *thriller* rather than a *whodunit* story, for the criminal's identity is known throughout, and the reader is motivated by suspense (what will happen next?) rather than curiosity (who did it?).[81] In this lengthy thriller, two narrative patterns are discernible. First, Jigong's disciples repeatedly forgive their rival Hua Yunlong and allow him to go free, even though all of them have been victims of his machinations.[82] This forgiveness strains the novel's psychological credibility, but it serves an important narrative function—it keeps the arch-enemy alive, thus allowing further confrontations. Here the difference between the novel and its oral sources is evident. In the latter, the storyteller could get rid of his evil protagonist after any given episode. By contrast, the novelist was obliged to keep him alive as long as possible so as to string together several different episodes about him. Indeed Hua Yunlong is kept alive throughout the bulk of the novel's first part, and is executed as late as Chapter 117. Second, Jigong is repeatedly obliged to rescue his disciples from situations he himself had warned them about.[83] Endowed with prophetic powers, Jigong often advises his martial followers to avoid a given place at a given time. But because of forgetfulness or unexpected circumstances, they ignore his warnings and find themselves in grave danger. In order to save them, Jigong relies on a power that, for the most part, they do not possess—magic.

Sorcerers, Monsters, and Magical Warfare

At the Merciful-Clouds Temple, there was a Taoist priest called the Red-Haired Spiritual Official Shao Huafeng. He was planning to capture 500 *yin* souls, in order to build a "*yin* souls battle array" (*yinhun zhen*). He sent five Taoist priests to summon 500 souls. The five priests were the Perfected One of the Front Hall, Zhang Letian, and the Perfected One of the Rear Hall, Lileshan; then there were the Perfected One of the Left Hall, Zheng Huachuan, and the Perfected One of the Right Hall, Li Huashan; finally there was the Perfected One of the Seventh Star, Liu Yuansu. Each one went his way to summon 100 souls. Liu Yuansu went to Little-Moon Village, at the western outskirts of which there was a Three-Emperors Temple. He stationed himself at that temple. At a communal burial mound, he dug up 100 bones of dead people and placed them together in one spot. Then he gave them orders using charms. This way he created a Hundred-Bones Human Monster (*Baigu renmo*). Every evening after the first watch [around 9:00 P.M.] the Taoist priest would lay out a table of offerings in his temple. He would also prepare a gourd. Then he would give the Hundred-Bones Human Monster a summoning-the-soul tablet and order him to head to Little-Moon Village and bring him a soul. The Taoist would imprison the soul and place it in his gourd. He was planning to spend 100 days there in order to summon the necessary number of souls. (123.12)

Shao Huafeng and his fellow Taoists possess what Philip Kuhn has defined as biodynamic powers: the ability to "manipulate [the] life-force by extracting it from living beings or instilling it into inanimate matter."[84] These and their other magic powers make Taoist sorcerers much more powerful than Jigong's disciples. In order to contend with such formidable enemies, martial skills do not suffice—magic powers are necessary. Therefore in the *Storyteller's Jigong,* it is the eccentric saint himself—not his military disciples—who battles with sorcerers (which, following Kuhn, I define as those seeking to enhance their personal power by manipulating the spirit world). Jigong also relies on his supernatural powers to combat two other types of noxious beings: evil female spirits (vixens and other female animal-spirits, who, disguised as sexy women, suck the male vital force) and monsters (hideous creatures born of the copulation of supernatural beings with animals). Jigong's ongoing battle with these supernatural creatures adds an important dimension to the depiction of warfare in the *Storyteller's Jigong.* Victory in battle depends not merely on swordsmanship and pugilistic skills but also on the mastery of magic techniques, the recitation of charms, and the possession of magic weapons. Martial skills give way before magic warfare.

Shao Huafeng relies on his biodynamic powers to create an army of ghosts who obey his commands. Other Taoist sorcerers steal the souls of specific individuals they have been commissioned to hurt. For this purpose they inscribe the victim's astrological signs on a peachwood idol, which is placed under the victim's bed. (The use of idols in sorcery is familiar from earlier novels such as the *Dream of the Red Chamber*.)[85] Then, in a nearby temple, the sorcerers conduct a series of elaborate rituals, involving the writing of amulets, the incantation of charms, and the brandishing of a "precious sword" (*baojian*). These enable them to steal parts of the victim's soul and imprison them in a bottle; consequently the victim dies (140.97). In other cases, souls are stolen in order to forge invincible weapons, such as the "five ghosts *yin* wind sword" (*wugui yinfeng-jian*). As its name suggests, the smelting of this sword requires the souls of five victims, who are ritually murdered and their *yin* souls extracted from their hearts. Here, too, the stolen souls are placed temporarily in bottles (92.448–50).

The notion that the preparation of a dangerous weapon requires human sacrifice is as ancient as the legend of the Spring and

Autumn–period blacksmith Gan Jiang, who tried unsuccessfully to smelt an invincible sword. Finally his wife jumped into the molten steel, thereby giving it the necessary potency.[86] However, contrary to Gan Jiang's wife, who sacrificed herself voluntarily, in the *Storyteller's Jigong* Taoist sorcerers look for innocent victims for the preparation of their weaponry. One of the most horrendous weapons introduced in this novel is the "child and mother *yin* soul rope" (*zimu yinhun sheng*). This lasso-type weapon is prepared by soaking a rope in the blood of a mother and her unborn male fetus (153.162). It appears that the more dangerous the weapon, the more hideous its method of preparation.

Despite their horrendous weaponry, the Taoist sorcerers are no match for Jigong. The reason lies probably in the difference between their magical and his supernatural powers. Taoist sorcerers obtain their powers through the mastery of learned techniques. Their soul-stealing operations are conducted according to rigid ritual recipes, which involve offerings to supernatural beings, amulets, and charms. By contrast Jigong has no need to follow a ritual program or lay out an offering table; his powers are innate to his divine being. Admittedly Jigong, like his adversaries, does use charms, and he does have one magic weapon—his hat. However, one gets the impression that he does not need them and could have done just as well without them (indeed in the course of one battle Jigong lends his hat to one of his followers [134.68]). This impression of Jigong's innate divinity is borne out by the effortlessness with which he overcomes his adversaries; what is for them an all-consuming effort, is for him not much more than an entertaining pastime. Here is an example:

Hua Qingfeng addressed Jigong, saying: "Aren't you a moth flying straight into the fire, searching for his own death! If you understand the situation, you better kneel down, kowtow to me, and address me three times as the Grand Patriarch. Then, since I am virtuous and life-loving, I may spare you your life." The monk [Jigong] laughed heartily: "You, Taoist priest, are full of lies. Even if you kneel down, kowtow to *me*, and address *me* three times as the Grand Patriarch, I will not spare you." When Hua Qingfeng heard this, anger arose in his heart and madness in his gall. He lifted his precious sword and struck, aiming straight at the monk's head. The monk dodged the blow, slipped around the priest, and pinched him in the back. The Taoist turned his head, pointed his sword at the monk, concentrated, and stabbed. The monk dodged and evaded him again. Faking a left, Jigong aimed with his right hand, and—smack—punched the Taoist in the face. The Taoist got really nervous. . . . He recited a charm, pointed with his sword, and lo and behold!—a herd of poisonous snakes and hideous pythons attacked the monk. The monk laughed heartily. He pointed with his hand, recited the Six-Characters Charm, and a ray of yellow light hit these poisonous snakes and hideous pythons, which instantly evaporated.

The Taoist got really nervous! He decided to use an underhanded method. . . . He uttered a charm, and the flames of his True Fire of Meditation leaped to the sky and encircled the monk. . . . Who would have thought that Jigong would utter the Six-Characters Charm, *oṃ maṇi padme hūṃ*, point with his hand, and the circle of fire would leap on the Taoist. The Taoist's clothes were instantly burned. Seeing that the situation did not look too good, he hurriedly squeezed his body and leaped into the Mist-and-Clouds Pagoda. The monk recited a charm, and the fire, getting bigger and brighter, engulfed the Mist-and-Clouds Pagoda. Hua Qingfeng's beard and hair were burned [eventually, as he usually does, Jigong spares this Taoist's life]. (93: 456–58)

The battle escalates in a manner typical of most military engagements in this novel. In his desperation, Hua Qingfeng, like other Taoist sorcerers in the *Storyteller's Jigong*, uses progressively more dangerous weapons and magical techniques, all of which prove equally ineffective against the crazy saint. The most powerful weapons of these Taoist sorcerers are their gourds. These have an ancient history in Chinese magic. A rich body of lore dating back to the first centuries C.E. describes tiny gourds, whose size can magically be transformed so that they contain the entire world. Visual works of art associate Taoist immortals and seekers of medicinal herbs with such gourds.[87] In the following passage, Jigong battles the Ancient [Taoist] Immortal, Son-of-Kunlun (Kunlun Zi), who possesses the Heaven and Earth Mysterious Great Gourd. Kunlun Zi, unlike most Taoists in this novel, is not an evil person, and Jigong engages in a lighthearted magical contest with him, rather than a life-or-death battle. (The narrator is careful not to attack the Taoist faith wholesale; he portrays the truly accomplished Taoist masters, unlike their juniors, as positive figures):

The ancient immortal addressed Jigong, saying: "This gourd of mine has a history of four sexagenarian cycles. No matter which spirit is imprisoned inside, within a short while it is transformed into pus and blood. Don't be mislead by its small size. This gourd can encompass the Three Mountains and Five Peaks, the Ten Thousand States and Nine Continents." The monk

[Jigong] said: "Anything else wonderful?" The ancient immortal said: "I'll put you inside and after twelve hours you will turn into pus and blood." The monk said: ". . . If I find it hard to bear inside, and I say: 'Master, please forgive me.' Will you, the moment I say this, release me?" The ancient immortal said: "All right. If you realize how powerful I am and submit to me, I will forgive you." The monk said: "Well then put me inside, as you please."

The ancient immortal promptly pulled out the gourd's cork, recited a charm, and—lo and behold—a whirlwind of rosy and golden rays of light . . . encircled the monk. In the twinkling of an eye these rosy and golden rays engulfed him, and he was seen no more. The ancient immortal retrieved the rays of rosy light and sealed his gourd. He called: "Crazy Monk?" Indeed the monk responded from inside the gourd: "Yes!" The ancient immortal said: "How are you doing in there?" And the answer came from inside the gourd: "Actually very good. I have a place to live. This is not bad at all." The ancient immortal said: "Crazy Monk, if you do not beg me, I will shortly transform you."

At that time the Night-Pacer Ghost—Little Kunlun—Guo Shun, as well as Sun Daoquan, Lei Ming, Chen Liang, and even the Little Enlightened Master [these are all Jigong's disciples] all knelt down in front of the ancient immortal, and said: "Grand Patriarch! Have mercy on his life! Our master is a little bit crazy. You shouldn't take him as seriously as you take other people." . . . The ancient immortal was just about to release Crazy Ji, but—"click-a-clack"—there they saw Jigong walking outside and approaching them. Everybody was dumbfounded!

The ancient immortal gasped: "Crazy Monk, I sealed you inside this gourd. How did you manage to escape?" The monk said: "I was very bored inside, so I squeezed my way out." The ancient immortal checked and saw that the gourd was still sealed—how could this monk have squeezed his way out? Moreover, the gourd still felt heavy. He proceeded to uncork it and turned it upside-down—*Bang*—nothing else but Jigong's shabby monk hat fell from it. The ancient immortal said: "So all along it was this shabby monk hat [that was in my gourd]?!" The monk said: "Don't belittle this shabby monk hat, you are no match to this old hat of mine." The ancient immortal contemplated: "Gazing upward, I understand the stars; looking down, I know the earth. Why should I be afraid of that monk hat of his." Having thus concluded, he said: "Monk, what great deeds did this hat of yours accomplish?" "Actually no great deeds," the monk responded, "but it is quite powerful." The ancient immortal said: "I don't believe this. Let me see how powerful this hat is." "All right," said the monk. He threw the hat upward and uttered the Six Characters Mantra. The ancient immortal looked: This hat rose in midair. It emanated ten thousand rays of sunlight and a thousand columns of auspicious clouds. It was surrounded by a whirlwind of golden light. As big as Mount Tai, it aimed at the Taoist and started to descend on him. . . . Had Jigong actually used this hat, it would have cost the ancient immortal 500 years of religious practice [i.e., his powers would have diminished by 500 years of practice]. (154.166–67)

Some magic weapons in the *Storyteller's Jigong* are familiar from pre-nineteenth-century military novels. One such weapon is the True Fire of Meditation (*sanmei zhenhuo*) with which Hua Qingfeng attempts to burn Jigong. The True Fire of Meditation has a Buddhist provenance: *sanmei* is a transliteration of the Sanskrit word *samādhi*—meditation. The term originally denoted the flames that consumed the Buddha's body when he entered nirvana. But in the context of Chinese popular religion, this fire was transformed into a magic weapon. Skilled adepts, in fantastic novels such as the late Ming *Enffeofment of the Gods* (*Fengshen yanyi*), produce blazing flames that engulf their adversaries.[88] The True Fire of Meditation is also used in some novels for therapeutic ends. In the sixteenth-century *Recorded Sayings*, for example, Jigong uses it to heal a consumptive woman.[89] Other weapons in the *Storyteller's Jigong*—even if prefigured in earlier fiction—became prevalent only in nineteenth-century novels. This is especially the case with the deadly rays with which Jigong destroys his enemies. The early military romances usually required physical contact between the weapon (sword, arrow, fire) and the enemy. Sun Wukong, of the sixteenth-century *Journey to the West*, is capable of multiplying himself into 84,000 monkeys that fight on his behalf. But these simians must engage in hand-to-hand combat with their adversaries. By contrast, in nineteenth-century fiction we find a large variety of deadly rays and transparent snares that destroy the enemy from a distance. As Chen Pingyuan has suggested, the prevalence of these long-range weapons in late-Qing martial-arts fiction may reflect the impact of modern Western firearms on the Chinese popular imagination.[90]

In addition to magic weaponry, the fight between Jigong and his Taoist adversaries involves the use of charms. In the *Storyteller's Jigong*, battles take the form of incantation contests in which the combatants hurl mantras at each other. Jigong relies on one charm only: the Six-Characters Mantra (*liuzi zhenyan*): *an mani bami hong* (from Sanskrit: *oṃ maṇi padme hūṃ*). His adversaries, likewise, have only one charm at their disposal: *jiji rulü lingchi* (act promptly, as ordered by the law), to which they sometimes add the name of the Taoist deity Taishang laojun (Ancient Lord on High). Both spells have an ancient history. The Chinese transliteration of the Sanskrit mantra *oṃ maṇi padme hūṃ* illustrates the influence of Tantric ritual on Medieval Chinese Buddhism, and prior to its adoption by the Taoist clergy, the formula "act promptly, as ordered by the law" was used in Han period government documents.[91] But here these charms' ancient pedigrees are less significant than their widespread dissemination. By late imperial times both spells were commonly used in works of fiction and drama, such as the *Journey to the West* and *Peony Pavilion* (both sixteenth-century).[92] In other words, the appearance of these incantations in the *Storyteller's Jigong* does not testify to arcane knowledge on the author's part. These charms were introduced into the *Storyteller's Jigong* because they were prevalent at the time of its composition. The author displays no familiarity with classical religious texts (Buddhist or Taoist), and the appearance of these spells in his novel is no exception.

Jigong combats two other types of magically potent beings: malignant female spirits (usually vixens, but sometimes female spirits of other animals such as wolves or deer) and monsters (born, for example, of the unnatural copulation of dragons with horses or donkeys). Both types of creatures achieve their supernatural powers through aeons of practice. But if hit by Jigong, they lose their powers. This loss of potency is measured in years of practice; one blow by the eccentric saint usually costs them several hundred years of training. Once subdued by Jigong, female spirits and monsters often turn into his ardent followers and work in his service. As is common in Chinese lore, female animal-spirits assume the form of bewitching young women (husbands and even parents-in-law sometimes refuse to accept that a charming wife is a vixen). But when overcome by Jigong, they resume their original form, which is described in realistic, hence eerie, detail. One vixen proves to be "about the size of a dog," and another leaves behind "traces of blood and yellow fur" (66.324; 95.462). At least one female vixen is actually good-hearted and well-meaning (and is indeed spared by Jigong). Following aeons of practice, she assumes a human form and, being deeply devout, becomes a nun. As ill-luck would have it, a young man falls in love with her and, contrary to her wishes, convinces the abbess to give her to him in marriage (147.132).

Among the monsters Jigong fights, perhaps the most hideous is the "Crocodile" monstrosity, spawn of a dragon and a pheasant. This freak of nature settles in White-Water Lake and coerces the villagers on its shores into sacrificing one boy and one girl to him per day. (The *Journey to the West* features a monster who consumes the same diet, albeit on a yearly, rather than a daily, basis.)[93] The hapless villagers organize a lottery, and each day, by rotation, one unlucky family makes the sacrifice. The monster emerges from the lake in the form of "yin-yang vapor" and consumes his meal—until Jigong comes to the rescue. The divine clown uses peals of thunder to attack the monster, who, in self-defense, covers his head with a cloth soaked in a woman's "polluting stuff" (i.e., menstrual blood). This device proves effective, and Jigong is forced to remove this headgear from the ogre's head before he can finish him off (132.57–134.68).

The crocodile-monster's usage of female "pollution" for self-defense is reminiscent of the Taoists' soul-stealing: both types of black magic were practiced, or thought to have been practiced, at the period in which the novel was written. The belief that women's menstrual blood is polluting and yet powerful was widespread in late imperial times, and remained prevalent in agricultural communities as late as, at least, the 1970s.[94] Menstruating women were forbidden, for example, to enter temples. But because of its power, menstrual blood—and by association women (who produce it)—were used in magic warfare. During the Wang Lun rebellion of 1774, the government forces placed prostitutes on the walls of a besieged city and encouraged them to take off their underclothing and urinate across the wall, thus protecting the defenders from bullets. Dogs and chickens were slaughtered and their blood poured over the wall in simulation of menstrual blood.[95] The fear of soul-stealing was extremely common throughout the eighteenth and nineteenth centuries, and resulted in several famous cases of mass hysteria, the latest of which occurred in 1876.[96] In the soul-stealing scare of 1768, for instance, sorcerers were thought to steal people's souls and cause their deaths by "enchanting either the written name of the victim or a piece of his hair or clothing."[97] Usually the soul-stealers were believed to work, as Philip Kuhn has shown, in the service of a master sorcerer, who used the stolen souls for his own private ends. This belief in a soul-stealers' network is echoed in the *Storyteller's Jigong*'s description, quoted above, of the master sorcerer Shao Huafeng, who assigned five Taoist priests the task of obtaining for him 100 souls each.

Another technique of magic warfare in the novel that was actually practiced at the time is the armor of the golden bell (*jinzhong zhao*). (Interestingly, this invulnerability technique is also elaborated upon in Guo Xiaoting's other novel, *Everlasting Blessings and Peace*.)[98] The armor of the golden bell had been practiced in north China since at least the late eighteenth century, and in the mid-1890s it occupied a central place in the martial training of the Big Sword Society, precursor of the Boxers United in Righteousness.[99] Practitioners combined physical exercises, such as beating their bodies with bricks, with the incantation of spells and the drinking of charms (burned and mixed in water) to achieve invulnerability to swords and even bullets. A contemporary observer left this description of the armor of the golden bell ritual as practiced by members of the Big Sword Society:

> In the middle of the night, they kneel and receive instruction. They light lamps and burn incense, draw fresh water from a well and make offerings of it. They write charms on white cloth. The words of the charms are vulgar and improper. There are such phrases as "Patriarch, Duke of Zhou; Immortals of the Peach Blossom; Golden Bell, iron armor protect my body." Those who spread the art can neither read nor write. They have others write for them. They also teach spells. While chanting spells they burn charms, mixing [the ashes] in water and instructing [the initiate] to kneel and drink. Then [the teacher] breathes in from above the lantern, and blows out over [the initiate's] entire body. Then he beats him with a brick and staff. After chanting the spell for three nights, one can withstand swords. It is said that after chanting for a long time, even firearms can not harm one.[100]

In the *Storyteller's Jigong* a warrior monk, whose nickname, The Tattooed-Faced, resonates with that of the *Water Margin*'s tattooed monk, Lu Zhishen, teaches the armor of the golden bell technique to one of Jigong's disciples. According to the novel, this technique makes one invulnerable to swords and spears, except for three spots: the eyes, the throat, and the navel.[101] This is not the only point of contact between the *Storyteller's Jigong* and late nineteenth-century martial arts. One character in the novel carries the martial sobriquet "Spirit Boxer" (*shenquan*)—the very name by which, in the late 1890s, the Boxers of northwest Shantung were known. (This name had been used by various martial-arts groups since the mid-eighteenth century.)[102]

Thus, three types of magic described in the novel: soul stealing, manipulation of female pollution, and the armor of the golden bell were actually practiced, or believed to have been practiced, in late imperial times. In terms of the temporal and geographical proximity to the novel, the armor of the golden bell is the most striking. This invulnerability technique was the hallmark of the Big Sword Society during the period immediately preceding the novel's publication, in the same geographic region—north China. Elements of the golden bell magic were even adopted by the Boxers, who swept across north China in 1899–1900—exactly the period in which the *Storyteller's Jigong* was written. Thus, the *Storyteller's Jigong* mirrors beliefs and practices popular at the time of its conception. But this relation between magic warfare in fiction and in history has yet another dimension. Novels may have shaped beliefs in magic. Joseph Esherick has pointed out that the Boxers were possessed by the protagonists of vernacular fiction and drama.[103] It is also possible that novels contributed to the Boxers' understanding of magic. The Boxers, like members of the Big Sword Society before them, could not have read the *Storyteller's Jigong* (which was published too late for that), but they may have heard the oral narratives from which this novel derives. Listening to a storyteller's description of Jigong's magic powers, the Boxers' may have been reassured as to the efficacy of their own similar magic. Thus, novels such as the *Storyteller's Jigong* mirrored magic practices, even as they reinforced the belief in these practices' efficacy. The key to these novels' impact on society's lower echelon was their intimate relation with oral literature.

Social Protest and Moral Conservatism

"Avenging the Wronged" (*ping bu ping*) is the motto underlying the heroic deeds of military heroes in martial-arts novels. These fearless warriors fight on behalf of the poor and the helpless against local bullies and corrupt officials. Judge Bao's disciples in the novel *Three Heroes*, for instance, are locked in a life-or-death struggle with treacherous officials, who, in their insatiable search for power, attempt to murder the infant emperor himself. Martial-arts novels are thus characterized by an element of social protest, and this entailed a significant transformation of Jigong's image in the *Storyteller's Jigong*. In the earlier novels, Jigong is closely associated with high-ranking officials, suggesting that—in the authors' eyes—the respect Jigong is shown by officials is an indication of his religious significance. By contrast, in the *Storyteller's Jigong* this crazy saint becomes the champion of the poor in their struggle against abusive authority (although Jigong maintains amicable relations with some righteous officials).

Abuse of power in martial-arts novels is often of a sexual nature. A lengthy literary tradition dating back to the *Water Margin* attributes to high-ranking officials and their scions the forceful abduction of other people's wives and daughters. In the *Storyteller's Jigong,* Premier Qin Xi's relatives engage in such crimes. The premier's younger brother owns an entire harem of kidnapped women. His favorite pastime is to stroll by West Lake in the outskirts of Hangzhou and abduct young maidens. Indeed his outrageous behavior results in the collapse of the West Lake tourist industry, since people are afraid that their womenfolk will be abducted if they visit this scenic spot (12.56; 160.197). The premier's son, Qin Da, is no better. When a vegetable vendor's wife attracts his fancy, he attempts first to bribe the husband into giving him his wife, and having failed, he has both husband and wife beaten mercilessly. In the latter case, it is Jigong himself, rather than one of his disciples, who saves the couple and punishes the lecherous scion. He employs his magic powers to make Qin Da's head swell like yeast whenever the latter behaves immorally (Chapters 20–24). This form of moral control is reminiscent of the metal band by which Xuanzang of the *Journey to the West* subdues the impish Sun Wukong. Whenever Sun Wukong disobeys his religious master, the metal band attached to his skull causes him intolerable headaches.

Financial extortion, like sexual coercion, is a common form of the abuse of power in the *Storyteller's Jigong.* A restaurant owner nicknamed the Pock-Marked Tiger relies on his connections in high places to bully his neighbors. In one case his general manager lends money at high interest to a beancurd vendor. When the vendor is late in his payments, Pock-Marked Tiger has his tough guys smash the beancurd shop—utensils and all—to pieces (162.207–163.210). The narrator's minute description of the vendor's financial worries is typical of the *Storyteller's Jigong*'s concern with the daily toil of the lower echelons of urban society. The novel elaborates upon the troubles of petty clerks who lost their jobs, as well as the anxiety of loyal servants who were carrying their masters' money when it was stolen. In one instance lost bolts of satin are found, and the implied author has one of his characters comment that "if they were lost by an owner who could afford it, that's not so grave, but if they were lost by a servant who was carrying them on behalf of his master, this is a matter of life and death" (29.141).

Even Premier Qin Xi himself abuses his authority. He orders the dismantling of a splendid tower at the Lingyin Monastery because he wants to use its building materials in the construction of his own palace. This sacrilegious act brings the premier into direct confrontation with Jigong, and it is only after the latter employs moral persuasion, intellectual wit, and, above all, magic powers that the premier relents (Chapters 16–24). The confrontation between Jigong and the premier and, in particular, the latter's surname—Qin—point to a link between nineteenth-century fiction on Jigong and stories of yet another mad monk who figures in a body of legends surrounding the patriotic hero Yue Fei. Tradition has it that Yue Fei was murdered by order of Premier Qin Gui, whose crime was exposed by a "mad" monk (*feng heshang*), who, like Jigong, is a deity in disguise and, like him, resides at the Lingyin Monastery. The legend of this defiant saint evolved through a series of Yuan and Ming period plays and novels and crystallized in Qian Cai's early Qing novel *The Complete Story of Yue Fei* (*Shuo Yue quanzhuan*), which enjoyed extensive popularity throughout the eighteenth and nineteenth centuries.[104] The similarities between the crazy saint Jigong and the mad monk of the Yue Fei cycle suggest that as early as Ming times their legends may have been related.[105] But it was only in the nineteenth century that the figure of a treacherous premier surnamed Qin was borrowed from the mad monk lore and incorporated into fiction on Jigong. In a transparent effort to distinguish the Premier Qin challenged by Jigong from his predecessor of the Yue Fei cycle, the *Storyteller's Jigong* presents the former as the latter's son; the narrator explains that Qin Gui's son, Qin Xi, succeeded his father, and it was he who ordered the destruction of the Lingyin Monastery's tower, thereby incurring the crazy saint's wrath (19.92–93).[106] Still most readers would be hard-pressed to distinguish the premier of the *Storyteller's Jigong* from that of the Yue Fei cycle, for throughout the bulk of the novel the premier is referred to not by his full name, Qin Xi, but, as in the Yue Fei cycle, simply as "Premier Qin."

The figure of Premier Qin was incorporated into the oral narratives that served as the source for the *Storyteller's Jigong*. Premier Qin's attempt to destroy the Lingyin Monastery's tower is narrated in detail in the *guci* narrative, the *Jigong Drum-Song*, which in turn was probably influenced by an oral, rather than a written, version of the mad monk legend. The Yue Fei cycle and, in particular, its mad monk episode were widely popular in nineteenth-century Beijing oral literature and drama (the title of most such pieces is *The Mad Monk Sweeps Away [Premier] Qin* [*Fengseng sao Qin*]).[107] It is therefore most likely that the storytellers who composed the *Jigong Drum-Song* relied on an oral version of the mad monk legend, and it is even possible that the same performers specialized in narrating both stories. The *Jigong Drum-Song* and the novel it inspired differ, however, in their attitude toward the premier: in the *Storyteller's Jigong* he is respectfully called "Premier Qin"; in the *Jigong Drum-Song* he is referred to by such abusive terms as "criminal premier" (*zeixiang*) and "son of a bitch" (*gouzi*). The oral narrative is thus more acrimonious than the novel in its attitude toward officialdom. Social discontent is more pronounced in the *Jigong Drum-Song* than in the *Storyteller's Jigong*, which may represent a conscious effort to muffle the animosity toward officials so brazen in its oral source.

The similarities between the mad monk of the Yue Fei cycle and Jigong—both hide their divine nature behind a facade of madness, both reside at the Lingyin Monastery, and both defy an evil prime minister surnamed Qin—are so striking that it is surprising they did not merge into one figure. Actors who specialize in enacting one of these eccentrics often play the other role as well, and at least one Taiwanese puppeteer uses the same puppet for both.[108] The two crazy holy men are also worshipped side by side in Buddhist temples. The monastic establishment adopted both saints from the realm of popular lore, and their images are often placed together in the arhat halls of Buddhist monasteries, where they are usually referred to as the "crazy monk" (*dianseng*) and the "mad monk" (*fengseng*). The former (Jigong) sometimes carries the emblems of a fan and a gourd; the latter's icons include a broom (with which he "sweeps away traitors" such as Qin Gui) and a pipe for fanning the fire (with which he stirs the nation for action) (see Figs. 5 and 6).

Since officials from the premier down regularly abuse their authority, the *Storyteller's Jigong* is clearly marked by a tone of social protest. It is therefore not surprising that social banditry is not condemned in this novel. As noted earlier, several of Jigong's martial disciples make a living as roving bandits, although, as the narrator is quick to emphasize, they steal from "wealthy households of officials or big merchant families only" (60.293). Even as the narrator sanctions social banditry, however, he is in matters of family propriety and sex strictly conservative. Illicit relations with unwed or married women are a grave crime in the *Storyteller's Jigong,* and the implied author's prudishness extends even to the realm of widow chastity. In one episode, a young woman, whose fiancé has passed away prior to the wedding, demands that his coffin be opened so that she can bid him farewell. Having done so, she cuts her hair and announces her desire to become a nun. The novel extols her conduct (46.229).

The implied author's conservative moral outlook is most conspicuous in the realm of filial piety. The narrator is at pains to highlight the filial behavior of Jigong's disciples. One martial devotee arranges for a loyal friend to look after his elderly mother whenever he heads off on his roving expeditions (61.300). Another disciple refuses to participate in a military operation ordered by Jigong until he obtains his mother's permission (10.50). Filial piety in the *Storyteller's Jigong* extends even to the animal kingdom. A dog butcher, who is in the habit of treating his mother rudely, is moved by a puppy's desperate attempts to shield his canine mother from his knife. The puppy's filial behavior causes the butcher to mend his ways, as well as to renounce his filthy occupation (14.67–15.69).

Even the crazy saint himself is depicted as a paragon of filial piety in the *Storyteller's Jigong*. Being a dutiful son, Jigong enters the monastic order only after both his parents have passed away, and after his ordination he continues to display filial devotion to his one remaining elder relative, his uncle. "Your nephew is paying his respects to his uncle," Jigong addresses his elder kin as he kneels before him (148.137–38). Even more significant than this ritual homage, on several occasions Jigong employs his magical powers to save his uncle and his cousin's lives. As befits a hidden saint, he rescues his relatives without their knowledge. In one instance Jigong retrieves his uncle's soul, which was stolen by black magic (Chapters 139–45), and in another he saves his cousin from the murderous designs of the crew of a boat he is riding in (Chapter 137). Jigong's reliance on his magical powers to protect his kin addresses an ancient dilemma in the history of Chinese Buddhism: how to balance the virtues of celibacy and filial piety. Chinese critics of the Buddhist faith have argued that by abandoning their families, monks violate the cardinal virtue of filial piety. The answer given in the *Storyteller's Jigong,* like that of the Mulian legend, is that a monk can apply the powers acquired by his virtue to benefit his kin. Mulian uses his powers to save his mother from the torments of hell, and Jigong employs his magic to protect his relatives. Rather than being a hindrance to filial behavior, celibacy is transformed into a tool for its perfection.

The values propagated by the *Storyteller's Jigong* are thus by and large Confucian. The narrator highlights the importance of filial piety and sexual propriety, rather than typical Buddhist virtues such as nonviolence, compassion, or vegetarianism. It is noteworthy in this respect that despite its protagonist's Buddhist affiliation, the *Storyteller's Jigong* does not include as much as one quotation from, or allusion to, a Buddhist source. As far as I am aware, the novel contains only one quotation from a canonical scripture, and that is from a Confucian text. A petty clerk, falling on hard times and forced to earn a living by pulling boats, recites the appropriate statement from the *Doctrine of the Mean*: "The superior man does what is proper to the station in which he is; he does not desire to go beyond this" (28.138).[109] It is perhaps not surprising that the novel's author, Guo Xiaoting, alludes only to this Confucian classic rather than to any Buddhist scripture. Guo, whose novels derive from oral narratives, was probably unfamiliar with Buddhist literature. But like any Chinese who received a modicum of education, he must have memorized the Confucian Four Books in his childhood. It is interesting that unlike members of the literati elite, who would have assumed their readers' familiarity with an elementary text such as the *Doctrine of the Mean* and would not have thought it necessary to identify the source, Guo Xiaoting does.

The *Storyteller's Jigong*'s mixture of social protest with Confucian moral values is interesting from a historical perspective. This novel derives from popular oral narratives, and its blend of animosity toward officialdom with traditional family values may reflect sentiments that were widespread among the lower urban classes at the turn of the century. The *Storyteller's Jigong*'s mélange of social rebelliousness and conservative morality reveals the diverse, and even contradictory, uses to which the irreverent personality of Jigong has been put. European medievalists have shown that the upside-down world of the carnival could both strengthen accepted norms (by allowing society to let off steam) and, given the right historical circumstances, lead to the questioning of the existing order.[110] The *Storyteller's Jigong*'s portrayal of its clownish protagonist suggests that, somewhat like the carnival, Jigong could both validate and call into question accepted norms. In this instance the eccentric saint strengthens conservative family values at the same time that he serves as a rallying symbol for social discontent.

A Saint in Disguise

According to an old Beijing tradition, on the night of the eighteenth day of the first lunar month, the Taoist Immortal Perfect descends to his residence in the capital, the Temple of the White Clouds (Baiyun guan). Those who are lucky enough to gain a glimpse of him thereby "ward off illness and prolong their years."[111] But the Immortal Perfect is hard to recognize; legend has it that he hides his divine identity, transforming himself into a lowly pilgrim or beggar. In this he resembles Jigong, who has always assumed the persona of a down-and-out bum. In sixteenth- and seventeenth-century novels, Jigong reveals his true form—that of a "golden-bodied arhat"—only in his devotees' dreams. Otherwise he appears as a scruffy monk covered in rags. He walks barefoot, and in front of such important dignitaries as the empress dowager he somersaults, thereby revealing "that thing that he has in front."[112] Jigong and the Immortal Perfect are not the only saints who hide their divinity. Disguise is an important characteristic of crazy saints worldwide. Whether the Cynics in ancient Greece or the Indian Pāśupatas, gods on earthly tours often hide their divinity behind the persona of the socially outcast and psychologically mad.

In the *Storyteller's Jigong*, disguise has both a social and a magical dimension. Socially Jigong assumes the guise of a panhandling monk. Restaurant owners and bartenders, misled by his external appearance, try to ward him off with such excuses as "Ours is a respectable establishment" and "We give alms only at the New Year and the Lantern Festival" (55.270; 3.17). Because his magical powers contribute to his masquerade, even deities fail to recognize Crazy Ji's divinity. The narrator explains that supernatural beings emanate divine light visible to their peers, but Jigong knows how to turn off his divine aura, thereby misleading his supernatural adversaries into underestimating his powers:

> Jigong touched the top of his head and turned off the three lights: the Buddha light (*foguang*), the spiritual light (*lingguang*), and the golden light (*jinguang*). . . . Hua Qingfeng examined him with his eyes: the monk's body was short and his stature small. His face was greasy with dirt, and on his head was a bristle of hair some two inches thick. He was wearing a

sleeveless, collarless, worn monk robe, tied at the waist with a hemp rope full of knots and bumps. His appearance, shabby beyond words, suggested that he was a begging monk.

Hua Qingfeng thought: "Hearing of someone's fame is not as good as seeing him face to face. Seeing someone's face is better than hearing of his fame. I have heard that Crazy Ji is an arhat. But had he been an arhat, his head would have emanated a golden light. Had he been a guiding golden immortal, his head would have emanated a white light. Had he been a noxious spirit, there would have been a black vapor. Since he has neither golden light nor white light nor vapor, he must be an ordinary mortal." (93.455–56)

The readers, unlike Hua Qingfeng, are aware all along of Jigong's supernatural powers, and they anticipate with pleasure the moment in which the crazy saint will display his divinity and crush the Taoist sorcerer. The temporary disguise of Jigong's powers sets the stage for the comic effect produced by their revelation. But the significance of a hidden divine identity goes beyond the pleasure produced by revealing it. In 1989 I interviewed the Taiwanese opera playwright Chen Shengguo, who authored more than thirty *gezaixi* opera plays on Jigong. I asked him why people in Taiwan love Jigong so much. His answer elucidates the significance of Jigong's disguised identity, as a primary reason for his popularity: "Jigong is an ordinary person (*xiao renwu*)," he said, "and most Taiwanese people are ordinary people too; therefore they like him." This answer offers us a key to the crazy saint's hiding of his divinity. Masking his supernatural powers under the facade of a pauper, Jigong becomes Everyman, and therefore everybody likes him. Masquerading as a scruffy beggar, Crazy Ji is as powerless as anyone can be, and yet he has power. His victories over haughty officials and Taoist sorcerers are therefore Everyman's triumphs. Disguised as a common person, Jigong becomes the latter's supernatural ally, and it is for this reason that he is loved and venerated.

Jigong in Nineteenth- and Twentieth-Century Drama

As discussed above, the immediate sources of the *Storyteller's Jigong* were *pingshu* oral narratives, which derived from another genre of oral literature—*guci*. However, this picture is incomplete. During the nineteenth century, the eccentric saint was also the subject of at least three Beijing opera plays: *The Zhao Family's Mansion* (*Zhaojia lou*), *The Ma Family's Lake* (*Majia hu*), and *The Dabei Tower* (*Dabei lou*) (see Appendix C). *The Zhao Family's Mansion* was probably the most popular of these plays; it survives in three manuscripts, and advertisements for it can be found in nineteenth-century manuscript-vendors' catalogues.[113] The other two plays survive in one manuscript each; the manuscript of *The Dabei Tower* is dated 1898.[114] Assuming that the other manuscripts were not transcribed much earlier (and this is by no means certain), this would mean that Jigong was celebrated on the Beijing opera stage during the same period in which he became a popular topic of the *pingshu* genre—the last three decades or so of the nineteenth century. This would also mean that his appearance in Beijing opera probably postdated the *guci* oral narratives about him. In any event, it is clear that the plays *Zhao Family's Mansion* and *Ma Family's Lake* were popular at the time the *Storyteller's Jigong* was being written: "Theatrical troupes adopt episodes from this story for the stage," reads the novel's preface, "for example, the plays *Zhao Family's Mansion* and *Ma Family's Lake* and similar pieces. However, audiences always feel that these plays omit too much and are not detailed enough."[115]

All three plays narrate episodes familiar from both the written novel *Storyteller's Jigong* and its predecessor, the *guci* narrative *Jigong Drum-Song*. *The Zhao Family's Mansion* and *The Ma Family's Lake* elaborate upon decisive battles between Jigong's martial disciples and their bandit adversaries, and *The Dabei Tower* depicts Hua Yunlong's unsuccessful attempt to burn Jigong inside the tower of that name. A comparison of the novel, the *guci* narrative, and the plays reveals that the novel's version of the Dabei Tower episode is closer to the *Jigong Drum-Song* version than to that of the play.[116] By contrast the novel's versions of the Zhao Family's Mansion and Ma Family's Lake episodes are much closer to those found in the plays than in the *guci* narrative. In the novel and the play alike, the Zhao Family's Mansion is not merely—as in the *Jigong Drum-Song*—the site of a decisive battle between Jigong's disciples and Hua Yunlong, but the place where Hua Yunlong and his associates attempt to rape the Zhao daughters as they sleep.[117] And, in the novel and the play alike, the battle at the Ma Family's Lake is launched against the "Disheveled-Hair Ghost," Yun Fang, rather than, as in the *Jigong Drum-Song*, against Hua Yunlong.[118] We need therefore to supplement our picture of the origins of the *Storyteller's Jigong*. The *pingshu* narratives on which this novel is based derive not only from *guci* but in at least two instances were probably influenced by Beijing opera as well (even though borrowings were probably mutual, and the plays themselves might have been influenced by *pingshu* narratives).

Even though it was probably influenced by Beijing opera, the *Storyteller's Jigong* itself served as a source for a significant number of plays in this genre. During the twentieth century, Jigong was the subject of at least six Beijing opera plays, in addition to the three plays for which nineteenth-century manuscripts survive. These six plays correspond to specific episodes in the novel. All of them concentrate on major battles between Jigong's disciples and their bandit adversaries or on the magic warfare between Jigong and his supernatural enemies. One play re-enacts the battle between the crazy saint and the "Crocodile monster." Another play depicts a sorcerer's attempt to murder five disciples of Jigong, whose stolen souls he intends to use to smelt an invincible sword.[119] Like their nineteenth-century predecessors, these are martial plays (*wuxi*), whose performance requires acrobatic skills and swordsmanship. Actors who specialized in martial roles (*wusheng*) performed these plays, and the Binqingshe opera school (fl. 1917–30s), which emphasized martial training and acrobatics, staged three of them.[120] It could be argued that some of these plays might have been performed prior to publication of the *Storyteller's Jigong*'s (even though we have no such evidence). However, this is certainly not the case with another type of Beijing opera inspired by this novel—serialized plays (*liantai benxi*). These plays, whose performance could last several months or more, follow the novel's plot closely and enact it episode by episode. One such Beijing opera play was performed in Shanghai during the early 1920s, and the manuscript of another is preserved at the Beijing Municipal Institute of Performing Arts.[121]

The impact of the *Storyteller's Jigong* on Chinese regional drama has been felt in areas far remote from Beijing. In the Taiwanese handpuppet theater (*budaixi*), Jigong has been one of the most popular subjects, and renowned twentieth-century Taiwanese puppeteers—Huang Haidai (1900–), Li Tianlu (1910–), and Xu Wang (1936–) to name a few—have performed numerous plays about him.[122] Following the decline of traditional handpuppetry in the 1980s, the eccentric saint made the transition into the rejuvenated form of this genre—televised serials using puppets. Huang Haidai's son, Huang Junxiong (1933–), who played an important role in the adaptation of handpuppetry to modern media, created two televised puppet-serials on Jigong, in 1973 and 1985–86, respectively (see Fig.

7). He was followed by Hong Liansheng, who composed a 60-chapter serial on this saint in 1983.[123] In the summer of 1989, I conducted interviews with Xu Wang, Huang Haidai, and Huang Junxiong, and asked them about the origins of the Jigong figure in the Taiwanese handpuppet theater.[124] According to Xu Wang, Jigong was not part of the handpuppet repertoire when this genre was brought to Taiwan from Fujian in the mid-nineteenth century, and even during Xu Wang's own childhood (in the 1940s) puppet-plays on this saint were still rare. He said that his father, Xu Tianfu (1892–1955), was probably the first to have performed puppet plays on Jigong.[125] Huang Haidai and his son agreed that as late as the 1940s Jigong plays were rarely performed. But according to the elder Huang, it was not Xu Tianfu but "Opium Xian" (Yapian Xian) who was the first to perform Jigong plays, in the 1920s. Huang Haidai reminisced how Opium Xian and he had competed in a public performance of Jigong plays. Opium Xian's voice was already coarse due to opium smoking, and Huang Haidai won. Still he complimented his rival's artistic skills. Despite the disagreement over the identity of the puppeteer who first performed Jigong plays, the three interviews alike suggest that Jigong did not figure in the Taiwanese handpuppet theater prior to the 1920s—some twenty years after publication of the *Storyteller's Jigong*. This information tallies well with Jiang Wuchang's findings that martial-arts novels were first adapted to the handpuppet stage in the 1920s, but did not gain currency before the late 1930s and early 1940s.[126]

Taiwanese handpuppet plays on Jigong are based on the *Storyteller's Jigong*. According to Lü Lizheng, Li Tianlu created his cycle of Jigong plays in the 1940s on the basis of the *Storyteller's Jigong*,[127] and Huang Haidai gave me the same explanation regarding the origins of his plays. Xu Wang told me that he had read the novel, outlined the passages he liked, and adapted them to the stage. Those plays that he inherited from his father, he said, also derived from the novel.[128] (I suspect, however, that two of his father's plays might have been influenced by Beijing opera.)[129] In the summer of 1989, I attended Xu Wang's performance of his play *Jigong Subdues the Precocious Child* (*Jigong shou shentong*), which is based on the *Storyteller's Jigong*. As is usually the case with traditional Taiwanese handpuppetry, the occasion for the play was religious—it was the birthday of the Jade Emperor's brother, the Purple Mysterious Great Emperor (Ziwei dadi), and the play was staged in a small temple dedicated to this god in the Longshan neighborhood of Taipei. Attesting to the gradual decline of traditional handpuppetry, the audience consisted mostly of elderly men, even though some children occupied the front rows. Sitting on motorbike seats, some passersby watched the play from behind the back rows. The play describes the magic battle between Jigong and the Taoist adept Chu Daoyuan, nicknamed the Precocious Child. In one scene, which follows closely the novel's text, the Precocious Child kneels in front of his Taoist master and is deeply humiliated to discover that the latter is in fact Jigong, who has magically assumed his master's form. When, shortly thereafter, the Precocious Child runs into his real master, he beats him up on the mistaken assumption that he is Jigong.[130] Like other martial-arts puppet plays (known in Taiwan as "swordsmanship plays" [*jianxiaxi*]), the *Storyteller's Jigong* gives the puppeteer ample opportunity to display his dexterity—his martial puppets fly through windows in the backdrop and attack each other with delicately made swords and spears.

Of course, Taiwanese handpuppet theater is not the only genre of regional drama influenced by the *Storyteller's Jigong*. Jigong became a popular figure in Cantonese opera (*yueju*) in the 1920s, suggesting that it was this novel that induced interest in his figure, and, as discussed below, the *Storyteller's Jigong* exerted a significant impact on Taiwanese *gezaixi* opera as well.[131] Famous battle scenes from this novel were also celebrated during the twentieth century in Hebei *bangzi* (clapper) opera, Anhui *huiju* opera, and Hunan *xiangju* opera.[132] However, the impact of the *Storyteller's Jigong* on regional drama does not necessarily mean that no plays on the eccentric saint existed before this novel's publication. The title of one Hubei *hanju* opera on Jigong, *Subduing the Consumption Insect* (*Shou laochong*), evokes a scene from the sixteenth-century *Recorded Sayings*, in which Jigong uses his fire of meditation to suck a consumption-causing insect out of a woman's body, thereby curing her.[133] It is possible then that this play has been performed for centuries. Future research on Hubei *hanju* opera and other regional dramatic styles may reveal that Jigong was the subject of regional drama before publication of the *Storyteller's Jigong*.

No account of the impact of the *Storyteller's Jigong* on drama would be complete without mention of the modern media—film and television. During the 1970s and 1980s Jigong was celebrated in several commercial movies, which enjoyed significant popularity throughout the Chinese-speaking world, including the Overseas Chinese community in Malaysia.[134] Television did not lag behind. In addition to the televised puppet-serials discussed above, Jigong has been the subject of at least five television serials, in the mainland, Hong Kong, Singapore, and Taiwan (where two serials were produced: one in Mandarin, the other in Taiwanese) (see Fig. 8).[135] The Taiwanese-language series, entitled *Big and Little Jigong* (*Da xiao Jigong*), does not follow the novel's plot closely, but it does elaborate upon the martial-arts and magical warfare themes, which were first introduced into Jigong lore in the *Storyteller's Jigong*. Jigong's Buddhist sandal is transformed in *Big and Little Jigong* into a kind of flying carpet, enabling him to attack his various Taoist adversaries from midair. The creators of this series could not resist adding a dash of sexual comedy. Jigong is aided throughout his battles by two attractive young women of supernatural powers, who are both enamored of him and try to seduce him. As the title suggests, *Big and Little Jigong* introduces yet another newcomer to the novel's original cast of characters—"Little Jigong." Presented as Big Jigong's disciple, Little Jigong is a child, who, dressed like his elder and furnished with the same magic weapons, participates in all of the latter's pranks. Shortly after the series was aired, Taiwanese *gezaixi* operas began featuring a "Little Jigong" as well.[136] The theme song of the mainland television serial enjoyed great popularity during the late 1980s and early 1990s, and for some reason, it has even been adopted by soccer fans, who sing it to encourage their teams. The song captures the tone of social protest characteristic of the *Storyteller's Jigong*:

> Torn sandals, worn hat, shabby monk's robe . . .
> Wherever there is injustice, there I am.
> (*nali you bu ping, na you wo* 哪里有不平,哪有我).

"*The Living Buddha Jigong*"

It is impossible to cover at any depth here the large body of regional dramas, puppet-theater plays, movies, and television serials inspired by the *Storyteller's Jigong*. Instead, I will briefly examine one play: the opera, *The Living Buddha Jigong* (*Jigong huofo*), performed by the Minghuayuan Company of Pingdong, Taiwan. Scholars trace the origins of the *gezaixi* opera genre to the *jin'ge* songs, which the Chinese settlers from southern Fujian brought to Taiwan during the late Ming and early Qing. However, as a distinct genre with its own unique features, *gezaixi* opera emerged in Taiwan during the mid-Qing. During the early Republican period, this genre was deeply influenced by Beijing opera, especially in its depiction of martial scenes and its use of acrobatics. Like most forms of regional drama, *gezaixi* operas are usually performed in temples on the occasion of religious festivals, such as a god's birthday. For this reason, because the third lunar month contains the birthdays of such prominent deities as Mazu, Xuantian shangdi, Baosheng dadi, and the God of the Eastern Peak (Dongyuedi), it is the busiest month for *gezaixi* performers.[137] On the eve of World War II and during the immediate postwar years, *gezaixi* also enjoyed great popularity in theater halls (*neitai*). But in recent decades this genre has been eclipsed by Western theatrical forms as well as the modern media—television and films—and most *gezaixi* troupes have been forced out of theater halls and into the traditional setting of temple and street performances (*yetai*).[138]

The Minghuayuan Company, which performs the play *Living Buddha Jigong*, is one of the most renowned *gezaixi* troupes in Taiwan. It was established in the 1930s by Chen Mingji (b. 1911), and since his retirement, it has been managed by his children and grandchildren. The lead clown role is performed by Chen Mingji's son, Chen Shengzai, and the lead martial roles by Shengzai's brothers Chen Shengfa and Chen Shengshun. Another brother, Chen Shengfu, is the company's general manager, and his wife, Sun Cuifeng, plays the lead female roles. Members of the next generation of the family have already joined the company as well. The Minghuayuan is thus, by and large, a family enterprise. During busy seasons, the company—in all some fifty actors, set designers, costume makers, and stagehands—is divided into two or three troupes, which offer simultaneous or alternating performances. This way, during the Donglong Temple festival in Donggang, for example, the Minghuayuan can provide seven days of continuous entertainment, 24 hours a day.[139] These performances are intended to entertain both human and divine audiences. The stage faces the temple's main hall, and the gods watch the performance from their seats inside. In recent years *gezaixi* opera and Taiwanese culture in general have been the subject of growing academic interest in Taiwan, which is itself related to political changes. Native Taiwanese have been asserting their cultural identity vis-à-vis the Mandarin-speaking minority, which has ruled the island since 1945. This growing self-confidence on the part of the Taiwanese majority has elevated *gezaixi* opera to the realm of nationally sponsored culture. Thus the Minghuayuan Company was the first *gezaixi* troupe to perform (in 1983) at the prestigious Sun Yat-sen Memorial Hall in Taipei.[140]

The Minghuayuan repertoire includes thirty-odd plays on the divine clown Jigong, all of them written by Chen Mingji's son, Chen Shengguo. In the summer of 1989, I watched a performance of one of these plays, *The Living Buddha Jigong*, at the Tianfu Gong Temple in Gaoxiong in southern Taiwan.[141] A crowd of several hundred people, each carrying his or her own stool, filled the area between the temple and the makeshift stage. The performance was magnificent: superb acrobatics combined with gorgeous costumes and colorful special effects transformed the show into a spectacular visual experience, and the lead clown, Chen Shengzai, enacted the divine clown's role perfectly (see Fig. 9). The children in the audience were drawn to the stage and even climbed on it, forcing the Minghuayuan manager to come on stage several times and ask them to withdraw. Following the performance, I interviewed Chen Shengguo, who has himself a small role in the play. I asked him the same question that I had posed to Taiwanese puppeteers—When did Jigong first figure in Taiwanese local drama? Chen answered that plays on this saint used to be extremely rare, and only after their success in the handpuppet theater were they adopted into the *gezaixi* repertoire. The Minghuayuan first performed a play on Jigong in 1981, he said, and this play might well be the first *gezaixi* opera on this saint. Chen Shengguo's answers may be slightly biased in favor of his own troupe, but the interview, whose results were confirmed in conversations with his brother Chen Shengfu, does suggest that Jigong did not figure in *gezaixi* before the second half of this century—at least fifty years after publication of the *Storyteller's Jigong*.

In *The Living Buddha Jigong*, a fox spirit cultivates its magic powers for a thousand years until it is finally able to assume human form at will, at which point it transforms itself into a man—fox spirits usually assume the form of women—and heads to the world of mortals. This fox-man, who calls itself Hu Weiguan, meets and falls madly in love with Ge Caixia, the beautiful daughter of a high-ranking official. She reciprocates his love, and—given by her father the option of choosing a husband from among the kingdom's martial heroes—chooses Hu. Lü Dongbin, the great Taoist divinity, is outraged by this amorous relation between a woman and a fox, and he assigns the latter several difficult trials as conditions for the marriage. First, Hu has to peel off his own fur (which entails the loss of his magic powers) and offer it to his loved one as a shawl. Second, he has to steal Jigong's torn cassock and offer it to Lü (Lü assigns Hu this task knowing that—since Jigong is all-powerful—it will be impossible to accomplish). However, contrary to Lü's expectations, Jigong is so moved by Hu's true love for Ge Caixia that he helps him peel off his fur (whereupon Hu is transformed into a *real* human) and willingly hands him his cassock. Lü, now greatly annoyed, confronts Jigong: "He is a beast; he would cause misfortune to any human he marries." "A beast with feelings (*qing*)," answers Jigong, "is superior to a human with none." "Do you think that just because you are a golden-bodied arhat you can behave like a madman?" shouts Lü, who has by now completely lost his patience. "And do you think that just because you are the Protecting Great Emperor, you can behave like an evil tyrant," retorts Jigong, whereupon the two deities engage in a fierce battle, which provides some of the play's best acrobatics. The battle rages from the deepest hell to the highest heavens, throwing them all into complete confusion, until the exhausted combatants realize that Hu Weiguan and Ge Caixia have in the meantime married, and the play reaches its happy ending.[142]

This brief summary suffices to show that the plot of *The Living Buddha Jigong* differs significantly from that of the *Storyteller's Jigong*. The figures of the fox-man and his beloved human maiden are products of Chen Shengguo's imagination. Furthermore, the very theme of romantic love, which was later developed in the Taiwanese television serial *Big and Little Jigong*, is absent in the novel and is new to Jigong lore. Chen Shengguo's play is a lighthearted romantic comedy, in which, to the audience's great delight, Jigong helps the young lovers fulfill their romantic dreams. By contrast, the Taoist deity Lü Dongbin assumes the role of the bad guy who does everything in his power to obstruct the young lovers' search for happiness. The assignment of this role to Lü is not surprising in light of this deity's image in Taiwanese folklore, which portrays him as a lecherous old man, constantly jealous of young couples' happiness. Legend has it that ever since Lü failed to seduce the goddess Guanyin, he has been meddling in other peoples' relationships. Fearful of his envy, young people in Taiwan are careful not to bring their boyfriend or girlfriend along when they worship at Lü Dongbin's temples. The origins of this Taiwanese view of Lü can be traced back to the late Ming novels *Record of the Flying Sword* (*Feijian ji*), and *Journey to the East* (*Dongyouji*), which elaborate upon the lecherous deity's romantic misadventures.[143]

Nonetheless, the differences between *The Living Buddha Jigong* and the *Storyteller's Jigong* notwithstanding, the play does borrow significant elements from the novel. Foremost among these are martial arts, which have a crucial role in the play. Like most other twentieth-century dramatic representations of the Jigong cycle, *The Living Buddha Jigong* is a martial-play (*wuxi*), and in this respect it derives from Guo Xiaoting's novel. Other motifs in Chen Shengguo's play were likewise borrowed from the *Storyteller's Jigong*: supernatural creatures who cultivate their magic powers through aeons of practice, the network of Taoist masters, and the repeated pattern of junior Taoists seeking the protection of their seniors upon being overcome by Jigong. (In the play one of Lü Dongbin's disciples calls him to the rescue, upon discovering that Jigong is helping the young lovers.) Thus, even though *The Living Buddha Jigong*'s plot differs from the novel, this play still belongs to the narrative tradition established by that work. Chen Shengguo himself confirms this conclusion. He explained to me that he had read the novel and had borrowed the figure of Jigong from it, but he had relied on his own imagination for the creation of his plays' plots.[144]

Conclusion

The turn of the twentieth century represents a watershed in the growth and spread of fiction on Jigong. Until the eighteenth century Jigong was celebrated primarily in Hangzhou lore, but during the nineteenth and twentieth centuries he became a prominent figure in the popular culture of China at large. At the center of this development stands Guo Xiaoting's novel, the *Storyteller's Jigong*. Unlike earlier novels on the eccentric saint, all of which were written in Zhejiang and derived, directly or indirectly, from Hangzhou oral literature, this novel originated from Beijing traditions of storytelling. Mirroring the emergence of indigenous Jigong lore in north China, the *Storyteller's Jigong* played a crucial role in furthering the geographic spread of fiction and drama on this saint. It precipitated a great many sequels (published for the most part in Shanghai), and it served as a source for an enormous body of dramatic adaptations ranging from Taiwanese puppet theater and Cantonese opera to television serials and movies. Moreover, as we shall see below, the publication of the *Storyteller's Jigong* coincided with and fostered the spread of the Jigong cult. Beginning in the late nineteenth century and continuing through the twentieth, Jigong was gradually transformed from a local Hangzhou saint into the object of a nationwide cult.

The rapid spread of Jigong lore during the late nineteenth and early twentieth centuries was related to a significant change in his image. From an easygoing clown, Jigong was transformed in the *Storyteller's Jigong* into a skilled leader of fearless martial artists. His assistants fight local bullies and corrupt officials, and he relies on his magic powers to battle Taoist sorcerers and noxious animal-spirits. This change in Jigong's image arose not from religious developments but from the stylistic constraints of the literary genre that transmitted this story. The *Storyteller's Jigong* and its sequels belong to a new genre of martial-arts fiction, which emerged during the second half of the nineteenth century. The tone of social protest characteristic of this genre entailed yet another change in Jigong's image. In the *Storyteller's Jigong*, the crazy saint becomes the champion of the poor in their struggle against abusive authority. The transformation of Jigong into a martial-arts rebel has had a significant impact on the development of his cult and paved the way for martial-artists, bandits, and rebels to choose him as their tutelary deity.

PART III

Jigong the God

SIX

From Spirit-Possession to Monastic Appropriation

The evolution of the Jigong cult paralleled and followed the growth of fiction devoted to him. Two stages are apparent in this history. In the first, beginning shortly after the historical Daoji's death and lasting through the early nineteenth century, this eccentric saint was the object of a local cult primarily (but not only) in Zhejiang. In the second, from the turn of the twentieth century through the present, the Jigong cult grew rapidly, as it spread to diverse areas such as the north China plains, Taiwan, Thailand, and Malaysia. The first stage paralleled the lengthy period in which oral and written fiction on Jigong was produced in Zhejiang. The second stage was signaled by the emergence of indigenous oral literature on Jigong in Beijing, and it followed the *Storyteller's Jigong*'s enormous impact on the growth of regional Jigong lore throughout the Chinese cultural realm. Thus, the transformation of Jigong into the object of a cult that spread throughout the Chinese cultural sphere followed close upon the emergence of regional fiction and drama on him, which themselves derived from the novels—especially the *Storyteller's Jigong*—celebrating him.

The turn of the twentieth century represents a watershed not only in terms of the geographic spread of the Jigong cult but also in terms of the diversification of its forms. The earliest records of Jigong's role in spirit-possession and spirit-writing cults, in a sectarian movement (the Unity Sect) and in a religious uprising (the Boxers), date from the turn of the century or, more often, later. Even in terms of iconography, the crazy god's cult did not achieve maturity prior to the twentieth century. Only in the first decades of this century did Jigong acquire what are now his standard iconographic traits. At least some of these developments were due not only to the popularity of the *Storyteller's Jigong* (and its oral and dramatic adaptations), but also to this novel's portrayal of its divine protagonist. Only in the *Storyteller's Jigong*—and its oral antecedents—did the eccentric god acquire the qualities of a martial-arts rebel that made him an attractive object of worship to groups as diverse as the Boxers in north China and Chinese gangsters in Malaysia.

Early Signs of Jigong's Veneration in Zhejiang

Whereas an abundance of sources attest to Jigong's popularity in twentieth-century Chinese religion, evidence of this saint's veneration through the eighteenth century is limited both in volume and in geographical scope. The little evidence we do have comes from Zhejiang province, where the historical Daoji lived, and where, following his death, he became the subject of oral and written fiction. As is the case with many Chinese deities, Jigong's veneration in Zhejiang centered upon his birthplace and his tomb. The first hint of it appears in Jujian's biographical sketch of Daoji, written shortly after the eccentric monk's death. According to Jujian, it was not Daoji's fellow monks but rather "the local people [of Hangzhou] [who] sorted Daoji's *śarīra* remains, and stored them below the Twin Peak (Shuangyan)." Jujian further comments, unfavorably, on the popular fervor that followed Daoji's death. In his view the news of Daoji's *śarīra* relics was "blown up out of proportion" by the people of Hangzhou, who were ignorant of the fact that "whoever does even one good deed regularly has [such] relics."[1] Thus, even though he found the popular fervor that accompanied Daoji's death distasteful, Jujian's account does indicate that Daoji was venerated by the Hangzhou laity shortly after his death.

The apparent enshrinement of Jigong's remains outside a monastic compound is also indicative of his veneration by the laity. According to Jujian, they were kept below the "Twin Peak" (whose location is unspecified). Sixteenth- and seventeenth-century novels about Jigong point to Hupao (Running Tiger) Hill, southwest of West Lake, as the site of Jigong's burial stūpa.[2] Hupao is located several miles from the two monasteries in which the historical Daoji resided, the Lingyin and the Jingci (see Map 1, p. 27).[3] By the early twentieth century, a temple dedicated to Jigong was located there. By that time, Hupao was considered not only the site of Jigong's burial but also the place where he had originally lived, and Jigong's original bedroom, located inside the temple, was shown to pilgrims. Spirit-writing séances, in which Jigong communicated with his devotees through the planchette, were conducted there, and the beddings in the saint's private room were kept fresh in anticipation of his imminent return.[4]

Jigong's temple on Hupao Hill still exists, and his private residence on the temple's second floor can be visited. In recent years the temple has been renovated by the Hangzhou Department of Tourism, and its walls have been decorated with scenes from the eccentric saint's life. The temple was designated a memorial museum, but devoted pilgrims transformed it from a tourist attraction into a place of worship. Pilgrims kneel and pray in front of an enlarged photograph of Jigong, taken from the 1980s television serial, and nearby, where Jigong's burial stūpa once stood, they make offerings to him. The religious revival at Hupao testifies to the impact of Taiwanese tourists on religious life in the mainland. In 1993 a Taiwanese pilgrim donated a statue of Jigong to the Hupao temple, said by local informants to have cost $U.S.3,000.[5]

Jigong's veneration in Hangzhou is also indicated by late Ming and Qing gazetteers of that city, most of which include biographical entries on him.[6] The same type of geographical sources also reveal that by the late sixteenth century Jigong's fame had spread from Hangzhou back to his birthplace in Tiantai county, in southern Zhejiang. The earliest Tiantai gazetteer to include a biography of the eccentric saint is Chuandeng's *Gazetteer of the Spiritual World of Tiantai Mountain* (*Tiantai shan fangwai zhi*; 1601).[7] As the title suggests, this gazetteer surveys the religious lore surrounding the sacred Mount Tiantai, which gave its name both to the surrounding county and to the Tiantai school of Buddhism. Legend has it that the 500 hidden saints, the arhats, reside in seclusion atop this mountain. Although the historical Daoji never lived on Tiantai Mountain, Chuandeng justified the inclusion of the eccentric monk's biography in his gazetteer on the grounds that Daoji was born in Tiantai county and that Daoji is one of the 500 hidden arhats. After his physical death, writes Chuandeng, Jigong rejoined these saints on top of the mountain.

This legend first appeared in the sixteenth-century novel *Recorded Sayings*, which Chuandeng acknowledged served as his source. Chuandeng was a Buddhist monk, and his reliance on a novel reveals the intimate connection between popular literature and canonical Buddhist scriptures that characterizes Jigong's posthumous career. As discussed below, all of this saint's monastic hagiographies derive, directly or indirectly, from the novels on him.

The inclusion of Jigong's biography in Tiantai gazetteers indicates that he was venerated there. However, none of these geographical sources mention a specific location associated with his cult. The earliest evidence we have of temples dedicated to Jigong in Tiantai county dates from the early twentieth century, and it concerns two temples, both still active. Reflecting the growing popularity of Jigong in recent years, both temples have even been mentioned in the Chinese-language press in America. They were featured in an article published by the New York–based *Shijie ribao* (World daily).[8] The first temple is located on the outskirts of Tiantai city, where Daoji was supposedly born.[9] The second temple, called the Jigong Hall (Jigong yuan), is perched on the slopes of the Chicheng (Red Wall) Peak of Mount Tiantai, where, according to local tradition, Jigong attended school. This temple was founded in the 1920s, but it was renovated and enlarged during the late 1980s.[10] It was reconstructed under the supervision of the Association of Elderly People of Tiantai County, which raised funds among the local population and secured financial support from the county government as well. Like the Hupao Temple in Hangzhou, the Jigong Hall enjoys the patronage of Taiwanese pilgrims. In recent years, several Taiwanese temples have designated the Jigong Hall the founding temple of the Jigong cult, and they conduct the customary "division of incense" (*fenxiang*) pilgrimages there. The purpose of these pilgrimages, which occupy an important role in any Chinese deity's cult, is to impart something of the deity's presence, most tangible at his birthplace, to the cult's branch-temples.[11]

Geographical sources indicate that by late Ming times Jigong was the subject of religious veneration both in Hangzhou and in his native Tiantai county. Another source for the study of the Jigong cult in Zhejiang is the Zhejiang novels that celebrate him. Sixteenth- and seventeenth-century novels on Jigong emphasize that following his physical death, he continued to display his supernatural powers and reward his devotees. For example, the *Recorded Sayings* concludes with the statement: "Jigong has repeatedly revealed [his presence] and responded [to the believers' requests]. It is impossible to narrate all of these instances here."[12] These novels were written in Zhejiang, and their insistence that Jigong responded to his devotees' requests may reflect the historical reality of his worship by the laity there. Other Ming novels on popular gods also describe posthumous miracles performed by their divine protagonists. Novels such as *Journey to the North*, *Journey to the South*, and *Romance of the Three Kingdoms* elaborate upon the proven efficacy of worshipping their protagonists (Zhenwu, Huaguang, and Guangong, respectively).[13] Thus the same novels that, I argue, served as vehicles for their protagonists' cults can also provide evidence of these cults' existence.

Of course, it is hard to know whether an implied author's claim for his protagonist's divinity reflects popular opinion or is meant to shape it. However, the Zhejiang novels on Jigong contain also what might be a specific hint of their protagonist's cult; they repeatedly refer to icons of Jigong in the houses of the laity. In the *Recorded Sayings*, Jigong appends two of his poems to such an icon, thereby increasing its religious potency.[14] In another instance in the same novel, he bequeaths an icon of himself to the proprietress of a small teashop in gratitude for the tea she frequently offered him free of charge. The proprietress, Mrs. Chen, is unimpressed with this painting of a sickly and emaciated monk and does not even hang it up. Nonetheless, Jigong's bequest proves to be of great value. High-ranking officials vie for icons of the crazy saint, and one of them pays Mrs. Chen no less than 3,000 strings of cash for the painting in her possession.[15] In the novel *Jigong's Complete Biography*, even the empress dowager pays homage to an icon of Jigong, which she places next to a Guanyin icon inside the imperial palace.[16] We do not know whether high-ranking officials of the late Ming placed icons of Jigong in their homes, and it seems highly unlikely that the empress dowager did. However, the novels' repeated references to Jigong icons may indicate that they could be found in the houses of the urban middle and lower classes in Zhejiang. Indeed, it is possible that icons of Jigong were popular with Hangzhou teashop owners such as Mrs. Chen.

The available information suggests that through the eighteenth century Jigong's religious following was limited both in scope and in geographical distribution. However, the paucity of information on the Jigong cult through the mid-Qing is probably due not only to the cult's circumscribed nature but also to its protagonist's eccentric personality. Jigong belongs to a class of eccentric and rebellious deities—Sun Wukong and Nazha are two examples—who figure primarily in spirit-medium cults. Large temples are rarely built in honor of such defiant gods. Instead, they appear as ancillary deities in other gods' temples, and more commonly, they are worshipped in small shrines (*tan*), which are often located inside spirit-mediums' homes. Such shrines are not mentioned in gazetteers or other official sources, and the historian must rely on the anecdotal literature to learn of their existence. In other words, the mediumistic aspect of the Jigong cult might have prevented it from appearing in official records. The cult, which through the eighteenth century was indeed limited, might have enjoyed slightly larger popularity than the available sources suggest.

Growth and Spread in the Nineteenth and Twentieth Centuries

The limited information on the Jigong cult through the early nineteenth century is replaced by a plethora of sources attesting to its growth during the twentieth. These sources illustrate both the geographic spread of the cult and the diversification of its forms. The earliest extant data on Jigong's role in spirit-possession, spirit-writing, and spirit-painting cults, in sectarian religion and in religious rebellion, date from the twentieth century. In the following I briefly survey these forms, beginning with the most ubiquitous: spirit-possession.

Spirit-Possession

Jigong may have figured in spirit-possession cults prior to the twentieth century. The tendency of official sources to ignore this form of religious activity might account for our ignorance of Jigong's early role in it. In any event, the earliest extant record of a mediumistic cult involving Jigong dates from 1900, and it concerns the Boxer uprising. The Boxers, who swept through the provinces of Shandong and Zhili, believed they went into battle possessed by deities who guaranteed them invulnerability. One frequently invoked deity was the eccentric Jigong. The evidence for Jigong's role in the Boxers' invulnerability rituals is followed by a wealth of twentieth-century data on spirit-possession cults involving him in other regions of China. During the twentieth century, Jigong figured in mediumistic cults in such geographically diverse regions as the provinces of Liaoning, Zhejiang, and Taiwan. Furthermore, his spirit-possession cult has become widespread among overseas Chinese in Malaysia and Thailand alike.[17]

In 1986–87 I conducted fieldwork on the Jigong cult in Pingdong county, in southern Taiwan, and I also visited temples dedicated to Jigong in other parts of the island. During that year I witnessed at least twenty mediums possessed by Jigong and interviewed nine. Those whom I interviewed belonged to the lower echelons of the native Taiwanese society (at least one was illiterate).[18] For the most part they were in their thirties or forties, but at least one was over eighty and was first possessed by the crazy god in 1945. Most mediums were male, but one was female, and, in her case, spirit-possession contributed to gender empowerment. Once she began earning a living as the god's spokeswoman, her husband quit his job and became her assistant. Interestingly, this woman was the daughter of a Christian convert and missionary and had been brought up a Christian.[19]

Mediums for Jigong share many characteristics with the spokespersons for other deities in Taiwan. Like other mediums, they are known as "divining youth" (Hokkien: *tâng-ki*), and, like others again, they usually provide religious services in small shrines located inside their own residences (even though they occasionally conduct séances in their clients' homes as well).[20] Most notably, like mediums for other gods, Jigong's living spokespersons invariably insist that they did not choose their vocation, but were coerced by the god into serving him. Sometimes the crazy god employs financial extortion: several mediums explained that Jigong forced them into bankruptcy before they surrendered to his powers. More commonly, however, Jigong, like other deities, inflicts an illness upon the medium, and the medium will not recover unless he complies with the god's order to serve him. One Jigong medium told me he acquiesced to the god's request after his son got sick. Another explained that he had been clinically dead for six days, and was even placed in a coffin, before he was brought back to life as the god's instrument. This same medium also told me that he used to suffer from periodic fits of blindness. But once revived as the deity's mouthpiece, he regained not only his mortal vision but also the "yin-yang eye," which enables him to see ghosts. The mediums' unanimous insistence that the god coerced them into becoming his messengers accords well with the popular explanation for the very term "divining youth" (*tâng-ki*) by which they are known. Informants usually explain that mediums are people fated to die young whom the god keeps alive only so long as they comply and serve as his spokespersons.[21]

The mediums' assertion that they were forced into their vocation suggests an interesting similarity between them and the biblical prophets. Spirit-mediums and prophets serve, of course, different functions. The former cater to the human needs of their clientele, the latter pronounce god's moral message. But prophets, like mediums, do not choose to serve as the god's messengers, and the Hebrew Bible expatiates upon their futile attempts to avoid their ordained vocation. Amos and Moses tried to excuse themselves as being inarticulate, even speech-impaired, and Jonah boarded a ship and ended in the leviathan's belly in his attempt to escape his lord. From a sociological perspective, the prophets' and mediums' claim that they were chosen is meant to convince their clientele that they are genuine. They do not feign being the god's mediums; indeed, the god forced them into serving him, and they are but his helpless instruments.

There are also differences between Jigong's spokespersons and mediums for other deities in Taiwan. First, mediums for Jigong differ from others in their dress. During their performances, most mediums wear a small apron with the symbols of the yin, yang, and eight trigrams. By contrast spirit-mediums for Jigong bear his iconic emblems. Once in a trance, they are helped by their assistants into a clown-like outfit, as befitting a clownish god. Their costume includes a long gown (black or yellow) covered with colorful patches, a small hat inscribed with the character *fo* (Buddha), and a tattered fan (see Fig. 10). I discuss the iconographic import of this outfit below. Here suffice it to mention that the patched garb alludes to the tattered robe described in novels on Jigong, except that in the present version it is covered with colorful patches, which add a touch of gaiety and humor to the clownish saint.

In addition to wearing a comedian's outfit, Jigong mediums act clownish. Embodying the spirit of a comic god, they crack jokes and act silly during the séance. They engage in humorous dialogues with their clientele, and they may demand that a devout patron who is reverently kneeling laugh with them. They also enact the crazy saint's most conspicuous trait—his drunkenness. All mediums for

Jigong carry a gourd filled with wine, and once in trance they drink, sometimes inviting their clients to drink along. Many mediums claim that they drink only when possessed, and many more argue that no matter how much they drink, once out of trance they are no longer intoxicated. Their performance of the crazy saint exemplifies the intimate relation between drama and ritual in Taiwan. Professional actors in Taiwanese opera and television serials enact Jigong exactly as do his possessed mediums, and they wear the exact same costume (compare Figs. 8–10). As noted above, the publication of the *Storyteller's Jigong* in 1900 inspired a large body of Taiwanese opera, puppet plays, and television serials, and it is likely that Jigong's portrayal in these genres influenced his spirit-medium cult. However, the mediums themselves are usually offended by the suggestion that their trance-performances have been influenced by entertainment drama. When I asked whether they watch Jigong television serials, their answer was invariably negative; "We do not need to learn to enact Jigong," they protested, "we are possessed by him."

The similarity between Jigong's character as manifested by possessed mediums and his persona as enacted by professional actors raises the question of the latter's religious attitude. Do actors who perform Jigong's role on the commercial stage believe in his divinity? And what is—in their minds—the relation between the Jigong who figures in entertainment shows and the one who is the object of a religious cult? To be sure, the answer to this question varies from one performer to another. Nonetheless, it is perhaps noteworthy that at least one actor specialized in the role of Jigong became an ardent follower of the crazy saint. This is You Benchang, who starred as Jigong in the immensely popular mainland television serial aired during the 1980s. Following his experience in playing Jigong, You Benchang became the principal sponsor of a large Jigong temple in Changping county some twenty miles north of Beijing.[22]

Jigong's clownish personality creates a difference between his mediums and his devotees. The mediums are uninhibited and silly, as befitting the god by whom they are possessed. By contrast, the lay participants in the séances are grave and respectful. Even as the medium offers them wine and forces them to laugh, they consider him an incarnated deity, in whom they confide matters of great personal urgency. Thus, whereas he is carefree and jocular, they approach him with awe and treat him with great respect. One medium showed me a photograph, taken some time before, that crystallized this inherent tension. Clad in the clownish god's costume, he was seated on a chair, with a large grin on his face. Some forty devotees, silent, serious, and reverential, surrounded him. The photograph brought to mind pictures of the adoration of the baby Jesus by the Three Wise Men, paying homage to the just-born lord. A god can be a baby or a clown, and as such he may act uninhibitedly, but his devotees may not. In this respect the difference between god and devotees is similar to that between master and servant. Whereas the former may behave like a foolish clown, the latter must remain grave and deferential.

Like other mediums in Taiwan, spirit-mediums for Jigong function primarily as oracles and answer questions on a wide range of topics—marriage, family, education, business.[23] They also serve as healers. In one séance I witnessed, the Jigong medium shut his eyes and employed his spiritual vision to examine the devotees' internal organs. Others claimed familiarity with various branches of Chinese medicine, such as herbal pharmaceutics. In addition to their primary functions as oracles and healers, Jigong mediums offer a variety of other services: they change people's luck (*gaiyun*), and they soothe anxious babies (*shoujing*; babies who cry too much are brought to the medium, who chants charms and waves his fan to pacify them). Some mediums offer channels for communication with the dead, and many write amulets (*hushenfu*), which, burned and mixed with water, are sometimes taken as medicine. One medium, whom I have seen writing amulets, acknowledged being illiterate. Her eyes were closed when she wrote, and, indeed, the signs she drew—being mere simulations of real Chinese characters—made no sense. Nonetheless, as is often the case with religious phenomena, the abstruseness of her writings was taken as proof of their efficacy.

The same services are provided by every Taiwanese medium, no matter which deity he or she speaks for. But there are certain requests that only Jigong's spokespersons grant. Only mediums for a god who is himself disrespectful of the law would be willing to help people who engage in semi-legal or even illegal activities. For example, during the mid-1980s, mediums for Jigong benefited from an illegal gambling craze, known by the wishful euphemism Everybody's Happy (Dajiale), that swept the island. Everybody's Happy is a system of shadow gambling, which originally depended on the national lottery. In order to win the national lottery, the successful bettor had to select the three winning numbers between 1 and 99 (a one in a million chance). Everybody's Happy gamblers would try to guess any one of these three numbers only (increasing their chances to three in a hundred, since their one bet was applicable to all three numbers). Boxes numbered from 00 to 99 would be drawn on a sheet of paper, and the bettor would place a bet on one of these. The successful bettor would sweep the entire board, less 10 percent for the pool organizer.[24] A surplus of ready money in Taiwan, combined with few avenues for productive investment (due to rising labor costs in the 1980s), pushed a significant percentage of the population into Everybody's Happy gambling. A 1987 police report estimated that three million people were involved in Everybody's Happy, and one pool organizer was caught with over NT$17 million (over half a million U.S. dollars) on hand. The government unsuccessfully tried various means to stop this wave of illegal gambling and, in desperation, finally canceled the national lottery; the resourceful Everybody's Happy gamblers then turned to the Hong Kong lottery for the winning numbers.[25]

At the height of the Everybody's Happy craze, bettors turned to Crazy Ji for help. A god obsessed with wine and meat, they thought, would be sympathetic to *their* obsession and help them win. As many bettors explained, no respectable deity would deign to get involved in gambling. August gods such as Guangong or Guanyin are bound by moral principles. They reward the righteous and punish the wicked, but they would never help one obtain something that is not rightfully his or hers. By contrast, the carefree Jigong did not mind blessing his devotees with that extra little luck needed for sweeping a board of other people's money. The main beneficiaries of this belief were Jigong spirit-mediums, whose clientele rose sharply. These mediums helped gamblers in one of two ways. First, in a trance the medium would produce paintings and writings believed to contain hints as to the lottery's results. For example, if he drew a monkey, pronounced *gao* in Taiwanese, this could mean that the digit 9, also pronounced *gao*, albeit in a different tone, would appear in the winning number. These drawings and writings were made available to gamblers for an appropriate fee. Second, the medium, again in a state of trance, would provide written or oral hints to individual clients. Advertisements for both types of services were widely distributed (see Fig. 11).

In the spring of 1987, I participated in two Jigong gambling séances, one in Taizhong city (where Everybody's Happy originated) and one in Pingdong. Both séances took place on the day before the national lottery, and each had at least a hundred participants. The demand for the Taizhong medium's services was so great that he was obliged to conduct two séances that day (one during the day, the other at night), and the Pingdong medium's popularity was attested by food stalls and game booths that mushroomed on the temple grounds. The procedure, in both séances, was identical: at the appointed time the medium went into trance and, with his assistants' help, donned the Jigong costume. The believers lined up outside the shrine and after paying a fee (in the Taizhong case NT$200, or approximately U.S.$6), entered one by one. Laughing, waving his tattered fan, and drinking from his gourd, the medium scribbled several characters, digits, or a drawing for each bettor (see Fig. 12). His suggestions were invariably ambiguous: a 9 could be turned upside down and read as a 6. In the cases I witnessed, this ambiguity prevented the gamblers from accusing the medium of failing to provide accurate information. Nonetheless, according to one Pingdong informant, frustrated bettors sometimes beat mediums up, and a Taizhong newspaper reported a case of disappointed bettors angrily smashing a statue of Jigong.[26]

The Everybody's Happy craze contributed to the growth of the Jigong spirit-medium cult in Taiwan during the 1980s. This growth is hard to measure accurately, because spirit-mediums usually operate in unregistered shrines. There are, however, several indications of it. Hu Taili, who conducted a detailed study of the impact of Everybody's Happy on religious activities in Taizhong, noted that at the height of this gambling craze three new registered temples for Jigong were built in that city. She also points out that all the shrines that joined the craze and served bettors, regardless of the main deity worshipped there, added a Jigong statue to the main altar. Indeed, the unprecedented demand for Jigong statues in the spring of 1986 pushed their prices up a hundred percent. Perhaps most significantly, Hu notes that several shrines dedicated to deities other than Jigong started featuring mediums for this crazy deity during the Everybody's Happy craze. Three of the Jigong mediums I interviewed were engaged in Everybody's Happy, and two of these had originally served deities other than Jigong; they changed divine patrons and started serving as Crazy Ji's spokespersons when the gambling fad erupted. Furthermore, because of Everybody's Happy gambling, all three mediums were able to abandon their previous occupations as taxi drivers and construction workers and to earn a living as full-time religious practitioners.

By contrast, many of this deity's long-time devotees rejected the view that he is involved in gambling. Most of the Jigong mediums I interviewed refuse to help gamblers, and one went to great pains to emphasize that he helps neither gamblers nor immoral nor unfilial people generally. The managers of one Jigong temple told me that they had decided not to hire any of the crazy god's mediums, for fear they might advise gamblers. Even the crazy god himself descended to earth to defend his reputation. In 1986–87, a poem attributed to Jigong and written by automatic spirit-writing was distributed by numerous temples in Taiwan:

> "Crazy, crazy," some people say I'm crazy,
> Claiming that I, Jigong, like to handle gambling.
> Are you aware that if I'm crazy, you are crazy,
> For instead of choosing a proper job, you ask about gambling.
> . . . .
> Beseeching the gods, praying to Buddhas, out of greed,
> Causes all the deities and sages to feel aggrieved.
> If the god doesn't respond to your requests, he suffers calamity.
> It is you who forcefully demand, not he who causes injury.
> How could you pass on the blame to the god,
> Saying that if I'm not efficacious (*ling*), you won't invoke [me].
> Drowning [the deity's statue] in ditches full of water,
> Some crazed disciples go to this extreme,
> Sharp knife in hand, they slash the god's image.
> . . . .
> If you continue to loiter idly
> The punishments for your crimes won't be tardy.
> Pray! Don't shorten your lives for "Everybody's Happy,"
> Under heaven there is always retribution.
> . . . .
> Save people from the ocean of misery!
> Then, in the Western paradise, on the Lotus Platform, you will
> receive your reward.[27]

The poem is interesting, for in it Jigong does not deny helping gamblers. He only claims that he does so because they—despite his warnings—leave him no choice. He himself would rather not assist bettors, for their own sake. Some of the crazy saint's devotees find other methods of defending his reputation, without denying the bettors' claim that they are being helped. One informant told me that there are two deities with identical external appearances, and both are named Jigong: one is "Righteous Jigong" (Zhengde Jigong), the other is "Devilish Jigong" (Xiede Jigong). It is the latter who helps the gamblers. Another informant disagreed: there is only one Jigong, and it is he who is involved in gambling, he told me. "Indeed he has been imprisoned by the Jade Emperor for his crimes." A Taizhong newspaper reported a similar version: according to some bettors, Jigong had been recalled to heaven to be admonished. For this reason he was no longer available for séances, and his mediums' efficacy had declined.[28]

Jigong is not the only eccentric god who helps gamblers. Bettors supplicate other rebellious deities as well. One is The Third Prince, Nazha, who, according to the legend narrated in the novel *Enfeoffment of the Gods*, deliberately tried to kill his father. Another category of beings who help gamblers are hungry ghosts. These unfortunate, and dangerous, beings suffered untimely and tragic deaths and left no descendants behind to conduct ancestor worship on their behalf. Because no one provides for them, these ghosts are obliged to pester the living for sustenance, sometimes by violent means. From the bettors' perspective, ghosts have one advantage over gods: they are not motivated by moral considerations, and they will reciprocate any help given to them. Several temples in Taiwan are dedicated to ghosts. One such temple, for instance, is dedicated to seventeen fishermen and their dog who died at sea and whose bodies were washed ashore.[29] The clientele of this and other similar temples rose sharply during the Everybody's Happy craze. Ghosts have no mediums; instead, gamblers would divine the lottery's winning numbers by deciphering patterns in the smoke rising in front of their altars or by throwing divination blocks. Reportedly, some bettors sought prophetic dreams from ghosts by sleeping in their temples or even in cemeteries.[30]

Jigong's role in Everybody's Happy gambling reveals the potential for resistance embodied in his figure. A god who disregards authority and strays from accepted norms of behavior can offer the symbolic resources necessary for economic, cultural, or political defiance. This rebellious potential has been perceived by both the Boxers in north China and members of secret societies overseas, and in both instances Jigong's spirit-possession cult has played an important role. The case of secret societies among Overseas Chinese has been studied by Jean DeBernardi, who conducted fieldwork in Penang, Malaysia, during the late 1970s. Secret societies in Malaysia are known as "black societies," and their membership usually consists of lower-class youths, who practice martial arts. Even though they do not necessarily engage in crime, members of black societies are commonly perceived as gangsters. According to DeBernardi, mediums for Jigong provide black societies with the symbolic resources necessary for the construction of their identity as a subculture within the larger society. Just as Crazy Ji defies the rules, the black society's illegal activities are justified. "In the process of the trance performance," she writes, "structure is inverted to create an antistructural world in which a Buddha is impure, the government is evil, and the socially marginal activities of the group are deemed good. In so doing, antistructure is for a time transformed into structure."[31]

The black societies' choice of Jigong as a religious symbol was probably due not only to his ancient antinomian traits but also, more specifically, to his portrayal in Guo Xiaoting's martial-arts novel, the *Storyteller's Jigong,* which was the first novel on Jigong in which he acquired the martial traits as well as the overtones of social protest necessary to attract lower-class martial-artists. One of DeBernardi's informants described Jigong to her as a "Robin Hood."[32] This analogy, which captures both Jigong's martial accomplishments and his social role of leader of the poor, could have been based only on Jigong's image in the *Storyteller's Jigong*. This novel—or, more accurately, the oral narratives from which it derives—probably also accounts for Jigong's role in the Boxer Uprising. The eccentric and rebellious deities, by which, when heading for battle, the Boxers were possessed, were invariably martial heroes. Some figured in martial novels such as the *Water Margin* and *Three Kingdoms*; others are to be found in narratives of fantastic warfare such as *Enfeoffment of the Gods* and *Journey to the West*.[33] It was only in the *Storyteller's Jigong* that the eccentric Jigong acquired the military qualifications necessary for joining this heroic group. Of course, the Boxers did not read the *Storyteller's Jigong,* which was written during the very years (1898–1900) in which their revolt broke, but they probably did hear the northern forms of oral literature from which this novel derives.

Several eyewitness accounts list Jigong as one of the deities by whom the Boxers were most commonly possessed. One Boxer leader was even known as "Abbot Jigong,"[34] and one of the incantations used by the Boxers before heading for battle reads: "Heaven is powerful, Earth is powerful; we call on our patriarchs to display their power. First, we invite the Tang monk and Zhu Bajie (Pigsy); second, we invite Sha Monk (Sha Seng; Sandy), and Sun Wukong (Monkey); third, we invite Erlang to display his divinity; fourth, we invite Ma Chao and Huang Hansheng; fifth, we invite Crazy Ji, our Buddhist Patriarch, . . . to lead the heavenly army of 100,000 spirits."[35] One source records a lengthy poem dictated by Jigong in a Boxer spirit-writing séance. Its anti-Christian content is the same as that found in other Boxer writings, but Jigong's quintessential laughter distinguishes it from documents attributed to other deities:

> In the year of *gengzi* [1900]
> The ocean will turn upside down,
> The mountain will tumble, and the earth will shake.
> The gods and spirits will emerge,
> Coming to this world,
> Transmitting to the people feats of fighting.
> If only you have a pious heart,
> Why would you be afraid of not becoming an immortal?
> Ha, ha, ha,
> Hi, hi, hi,
> . . . .
>
> There are many Christian converts in the world.
> They speak unreasonably.
> They deceive the emperor,
> Destroy the gods and Buddhas,
> Pull down temples and altars,
> Permit neither incense sticks nor candles,
> And cast away morality tracts (*shanshu*).
> Completely unreasonable:
> Their goal is to destroy the state.
> I am asking you: Did you know that that's their purpose?
> . . . .
>
> Bring your own provisions,
> Come and do away with the scourge of the country![36]

The Boxer Uprising provides us not only with the first recorded case of Jigong spirit-possession but also with the earliest indication of his popular veneration in north China. Prior to 1900, we have no evidence of a Jigong cult north of Jiangsu. It is striking that the earliest indication of such piety—provided by the Boxers—followed so closely the emergence of indigenous Jigong lore in north China. As we have earlier seen, it was in the mid-nineteenth century that Jigong became the subject of oral literature in Beijing, which for its part derived from the earlier Hangzhou novels on him. The Beijing oral narratives on the crazy god, which were first performed in the *guci* and then in the *pingshu* genres, served as the source for the martial-arts *Storyteller's Jigong*, and they probably also prompted the Boxers' choice of Jigong as a tutelary deity. The Boxers' pantheon thus provides clear evidence of the role vernacular fiction, oral and written, played in the spread of the Jigong cult.

Finally, does Jigong figure in spirit-medium cults on the mainland? The fieldwork, especially in agricultural areas, necessary to answer this question has not been conducted as yet. Nonetheless, during a three-day visit in December 1994 to Tiantai city, Zhejiang—the putative birthplace of the historical Daoji—I did locate one medium for Crazy Ji. Mediums in Zhejiang are known, like their Taiwanese counterparts, as "divining youths" (Mandarin: *jitong*) or by the similar term "youth hearts" (Mandarin: *tongxin*). The medium I met provided the same type of services—primarily fortune-telling and healing—offered by his Taiwanese counterparts. More significantly, he enacted the crazy god's role in much the same way they do: drinking wine, waving his tattered fan, laughing, and joking. According to this medium, there are many other mediums for Jigong in the agricultural area surrounding Tiantai city. Whether Jigong's spirit-medium cult is indeed widespread in Zhejiang and whether it has been revitalized in other regions of China as well can only be determined by future field research.

Spirit-Writing

In late imperial and modern times, spirit-medium cults have been found primarily among the peasantry. They were widespread in agricultural, not urban, areas, and in present-day Taiwan, they are to be found mostly in villages or among the lower echelons of urban society, usually in small towns. However, during the twentieth century, another form of possession by Jigong has enjoyed great popularity and has been common among at least some segments of the learned elite: namely, spirit-writing, variously referred to in Chinese as *fuji* (wielding a divination instrument) or *fuluan* (wielding the phoenix). These terms denote automatic writing techniques, in which one or more persons in a trance wield a writing implement said to be controlled by a deity. The writings thus produced are considered to be divine revelations. Spirit-writing has been widespread in China since at least the Song period, and it has been used for a variety of purposes, from divination and the writing of charms to the compilation of lengthy books on morality, salvation, and the supernatural. During the Song period, the goddess of the privy, the Purple Lady (Zigu), figured frequently in spirit-writing séances, providing anxious literati with the questions awaiting them in the examinations. Another god who, in the early stages of spirit-writing, often possessed the writing brush is the god of literature, Wenchang. In 1181 he dictated to his devotees a detailed autobiography, which is the earliest extant book-length document explicitly revealed by spirit-writing.[37]

Two literary genres in which spirit-writing has played an important role are morality books (*shanshu*) and sectarian writings. The term "morality books" designates texts that exhort people to do good and to desist from bad deeds. Such texts have been distributed in temples and have enjoyed a considerable readership since at least the sixteenth century. Some were considered divine revelations and were composed through spirit-writing; many others were not. (The earliest spirit-written morality book described by David Jordan and Daniel Overmyer in their survey of the genre was composed in 1622.)[38] Most morality books combine Confucian values with Buddhist ideas of karmic retribution.[39] They highlight the virtues of filial piety, frugality, self-restraint, acceptance of hierarchical social relationships, and charitable works.[40] At the same time they feature rewards and punishments largely borrowed from the Buddhist tradition of heavens, hells, and karmic retribution in a future life. "Sectarian writings" refers to the scriptures of sects whose eschatological hopes center on the Eternal Mother (Wusheng laomu). Sometimes referred to by the generic name "White Lotus religion" (Bailian jiao), such sects worship a goddess who is believed to have created the universe and is beseeched to redeem its inhabitants.[41] The scriptures of these sects are usually called *baojuan* (precious scrolls). By and large, before the nineteenth century these sectarian scriptures were not composed through spirit-writing. Automatic writing began occupying a significant role in the composition of *baojuan* only in the late nineteenth century.[42]

The earliest modern indication of Jigong's role in spirit-writing is the poem quoted above that Jigong dictated in a Boxer spirit-writing séance, which took place in Beijing in 1900. The content of this revelation was vehemently anti-Christian, and yet the next time Jigong appears in spirit-writing, he collaborates closely with Jesus Christ himself. In *Researches into the Spirit-Writing Superstition*, Xu Dishan describes a séance in Dalian, Manchuria, sometime in the 1920s. Several Christian converts were present at this séance, and they called on Jesus to possess the brush. To their disappointment, god's son discoursed in English (not Hebrew, as Xu Dishan notes), and Jigong was called in to the rescue. He grasped the spirit-brush and translated Jesus's message into Chinese.[43]

Several years after this séance took place, Clarence Day visited the Jigong temple on Hupao Hill, Hangzhou. He reported that spirit-writing séances, in which Jigong communicated with his devotees through the planchette, were regularly conducted there.[44] At that same period, the 1930s and 1940s, we also witness for the first time the publication of full-length books attributed to the crazy saint. This important development took place within a sectarian movement, the Unity Sect (Yiguan dao). Like "motherist" religion in general, the Unity Sect preaches universal salvation and return to the paradise-lost of the Heavenly Mother. Within this general framework, the sect's ethical and metaphysical teachings combine elements from the Confucian, Taoist, and Buddhist traditions. The Unity Sect derives from a sectarian tradition that dates back to the late Ming period, but it was probably established as an independent organization only during the late nineteenth century. Jigong became one of this sect's most prominent deities during the 1920s, when the then leader of the Unity Sect, Zhang Guangbi, better known by the name of Zhang Tianran (?–1947), declared himself an incarnation of Jigong. During Zhang Tianran's lifetime, numerous Unity Sect's publications were considered divine revelations from Jigong. Following his death, Zhang himself began possessing the spirit-brush, and since the literature he thus wrote carried the crazy saint's signature, the overall number of texts attributed to Jigong increased.

Jigong's role in the Unity Sect's literature represents an important development in the history of his cult. This is the first time that this eccentric god was incorporated into the pantheon of Chinese sectarian religion, and for this reason I discuss the sect's scriptures attributed to him separately below. Here, I will mention only that following the establishment of the People's Republic, the Unity Sect became active in Taiwan, and it was there that, some thirty years later, Jigong's role in spirit-writing underwent yet another significant development: the genre of morality books was revived in Taiwan, and Crazy Ji contributed significantly to this renaissance. During the late 1970s and early 1980s, at least eighteen new morality books, composed by the automatic spirit-writing technique, were attributed to him wholly or in part (see Appendix D). These works were distributed free of charge, as an act of piety, in temples, and some enjoyed enormous popularity. Three million copies of one book, dictated by Jigong, were distributed within five years of its initial publication (in 1978),[45] and this same book, *Journey to Purgatory* (*Diyu youji*), was still being disseminated through Taiwanese temples during the early 1990s.

The Taiwanese morality books attributed to Jigong mirror the same Confucian values that have always been characteristic of this genre. They employ the Confucian moral vocabulary of righteousness, benevolence, and filiality, and they base their arguments on quotations from the Four Books. At the same time, these spirit-written texts address problems specific to the rapidly modernizing Taiwanese society. In a society undergoing fast economic growth, this edifying literature denounces those who because of their newly gained riches forget benevolence (*wei fu bu ren*). People who ostentatiously display their wealth by wearing imported fashions only but give nothing to the poor are vehemently denounced. Cautionary tales are told about rich business executives who neglect their wives for the sake of kept women, as well as about female singers, who, once they become rich and famous, are no longer satisfied with their husbands. Prostitution (not uncommon in Taiwan) and especially trafficking in women for prostitution are considered sins in this literature, and abortion is criticized both for what is considered to be the taking of life and for leading to sexual promiscuity.[46] Placed against the backdrop of a rapidly changing society, this literature thus mirrors a conscious effort to restore traditional morality. Relying on the divine authority of the revealed gods, morality books attempt to revive traditional values.[47] For our purpose here, however, this literature is less interesting for what it tells us about religious revival in Taiwan than it is as a revelation of a new dimension of Jigong's personality. The same Jigong who helps gamblers is portrayed here as a staunch supporter of conservative moral values. I will try to illustrate this point with references to two of these morality books: the *Journey to Purgatory* and its sequel, *Journey to Paradise* (*Tiantang youji*; see Appendix D).

Journey to Purgatory (1978) and *Journey to Paradise* (1981) are two of the earliest and most successful Taiwanese morality books "written" by Jigong. Their popularity has been such that it prompted the compilers of sixteen subsequent morality books (ten of which are attributed to this saint) to include the word "journey" in their works' title.[48] Indeed, it could be argued that Jigong has become a prominent figure in the morality books genre because of the success of these two works. Both journeys were published by the Hall of Saints and Worthies (Shengxian tang) in Taizhong, and the same persons were responsible for their compilation. The principal wielder of the *fuji* was a Mr. Yang, whose first name, Zanru (literally "praising Confucianism"), certainly befits the traditional orientation of his compositions. At least forty other people assisted Mr. Yang in the séances that led to the two works' publication, and their names are listed in both. Indeed, most spirit-written morality books are not the product of one person's labor, but are produced by small groups of believers who channel their religious sentiments into the publication of these works. Such groups gather regularly for religious rituals, in the course of which the spirit-writing takes place. Usually these religious congregations are known as *bailuan* (worshipping the [spirit-writing] phoenix), or, due to the Confucian bent of their teachings, as "Confucian spirit religion" (*Ruzong shen jiao*). Sometimes they are referred to briefly as "Confucian religion" (*Rujiao*).[49]

The revelations recorded in the *Journey to Purgatory* and *Journey to Paradise* took place over several years, and they were originally published, in serialized form, in a spirit-writing magazine published by the Hall of Saints and Worthies. Usually each revelation tells of a journey to one or another department of purgatory, or paradise, during which the *fuji* wielder, Mr. Yang, is shown the sufferings and blessings awaiting sinners and saints in the afterlife. The terrifying, or blissful, sights are accompanied by moral exhortations from Jigong. Chinese religion envisions the netherworld not as hell, where sinners are condemned to eternal sufferings, but as purgatory, from which, after being suitably punished, sinful souls are released for rebirth in a life form determined by their past moral behavior. Heaven is usually imagined as a more permanent address, even though, according to some Buddhist conceptions, it is possible to achieve enlightened existence, which is superior to paradisiacal life.

Purgatory is divided into numerous wards, in each of which the hapless sinners are punished for their previous crimes. For example, those who spread malicious gossip are punished in the Cutting Mouths Purgatory, whereas careless drivers learn their lesson in the Wheel Instruction Purgatory. As Jigong and the *fuji* wielder, Mr. Yang, tour each of these torture chambers, the crazy god usually calls on one of the inmates to tell the story of his past deeds and current retribution for the benefit of Mr. Yang and the future readers of his book. This is, for example, the crime-and-punishment tale of one wretched soul tormented by merciless rats in the Kidney-Cutting, Rat-Biting Purgatory:

When I started going to high school, I was enticed by some evil friends. They took me to the red-light district, where we patronized brothels. Thereafter whenever I had some money, I would go and have fun there. Moreover, on numerous occasions, I brought classmates along to have them taste the experience as well. Thus it happened that as a young kid in high school I had already lost my chastity, and, moreover, I had contracted a sexually transmitted disease. Because I had committed these sexual transgressions in my youth, after I died I was sentenced to suffer punishment here. Can anyone understand the sufferings I am enduring? When I was in the world of the living I loitered about, but having died it is torturous to endure the passage of time here. When I think about it, I feel endless remorse.[50]

The inmate's story is followed by the warden's lecture on the dangers of sexual license. The reader learns that a wide range of sexual offenses bring sinners under this warden's jurisdiction:

This purgatory receives each day a thousand new sinful souls. Many types of sins are under this hell's jurisdiction: all those who recklessly indulge themselves in brothels and the roots of whose debauchery have not yet been cleansed; those who prior to getting married went to brothels and lost their chastity there; those who take sexual advantage of women; those who are already married (men and women alike) yet engage in illicit relations; those who have joined the Buddhist faith or the sages' faith and still behave dissolutely; those who engage in incestuous relations; and those who commit gang rape. The roots of these people's debauchery are too poisonous. Under one law, they are all sentenced to this hell to receive severe punishment![51]

Jigong summarizes the visit to the Kidney-Cutting, Rat-Biting Purgatory, by warning the *fuji* wielder and his readers against sexual promiscuity. To those who have already sinned, Jigong offers a gleam of hope, which interestingly centers on the very book *Journey to Purgatory*. Those who carefully read this book, help disseminate it, and reform their ways will be forgiven for their past transgressions:

I am urging the people of the world: don't be licentious. It is an extremely serious crime. Especially in the case of those who cultivate the way and need be more vigilant than others. There is no forgiveness for debauchery. . . . However, Heaven does care for living beings, and it offers them an avenue of redemption. If having read the *Journey to Purgatory*, you set your heart on repentance and mending your ways, if you print many copies of the *Journey to Purgatory* to exhort the people of the world, and if you commit no more of these crimes, then the Jade Emperor will issue a decree annulling your previous sins.[52]

The *Journey to Purgatory*'s sexual prudishness is revealed by the wide range of offenses for which people are punished in the Kidney-Cutting, Rat-Biting Purgatory. People are tortured by biting rats not only for participating in gang rape but also for having sex with prostitutes prior to marriage. As the reader follows Jigong and Mr. Yang to other departments of the netherworld, he comes to realize that even minor sexual offenses—such as watching striptease shows, or pornographic movies—entail a terrible price in the afterlife. This is, for example, the story of one inmate in the Gouging-the-Eyes Purgatory:

In my previous incarnation I was addicted to carnal pleasures. In today's society there is nothing you can't get. In addition to peeping at my neighbors' daughters and wives take showers, once, some friends of mine took me to a filthy theater to watch pornographic movies. Thereafter I never got tired of such movies, and I also tried to find, myself, new means of stimulation. Recently some friends took me again, this time to a certain hotel. Girls were lined up there, you could choose the one you wanted, and she would perform a striptease. About a year ago I was involved in a car accident, and I died. My soul flew to the netherworld. . . . I was sentenced by the king of the underworld to the Gouging-the-Eyes Purgatory. Each day I endure the torture of eye gouging. My descendants in the world of the living are unaware of my tragic situation, and my remorse is now useless. I hope that after he returns to the world of the living, this virtuous gentleman here [alluding to the *fuji* wielder, Mr. Yang] will tell my story to the people so that they know it.[53]

Having one's eyes gouged out as a punishment for voyeurism or for watching striptease and pornographic movies is perhaps somewhat harsh. But when the next inmate informs his visitors that he is enduring this punishment for cheating, as a schoolboy, on his exams, even Mr. Yang loses his composure: "This is too frightening! When I was a student, I also copied other students' answers during exams." Here Jigong is forced to mitigate his disciple's fears: "You need not worry," he consoles him, "Heaven doesn't punish those who repent and mend their ways!"[54]

Of course, sexual indecencies and cheating on exams are not the only offenses punishable in purgatory. People are tormented for a variety of other sins as well: murder, theft, pickpocketing, and membership in violent street gangs. Also severely punished are white-color criminals who deal in junk bonds, government officials who take bribes, producers of fake medicines, and vegetable vendors who use inaccurate scales. Particular attention is paid in the *Journey to Purgatory* to unethical behavior within the family: husbands who neglect their wives, wives who are disrespectful of their husbands, and, of course, unfilial children. One Christian convert is tortured in the Heart-Stabbing Purgatory for having smashed the ancestral tablets in his parents' home. (The warden is quick to explain that all religions are good, but one should never betray one's "roots," meaning the ancestors.)[55] This emphasis on filial piety also runs through the *Journey to Paradise*. In the tradition of the *Classic of Filial Piety*, it includes a special hall where the paragons of filial virtue are rewarded. As Jigong and Mr. Yang enter this hall, Jigong explains that "loyalty and filial piety are the foundation of ethical behavior."[56]

The *Journeys*' conservative values, especially in matters of sex, contradict the image of Jigong found in early novels such as the *Recorded Sayings*. In that novel, Jigong describes himself as a cleric "whose cassock is often stained with rouge, whose robes carry the fragrance of powder."[57] On a visit to a brothel, he himself playfully covers a woman's vulva with her tiny shoe. However, the Confucian conservatism of these morality books does accord with some aspects of the *Storyteller's Jigong*, which, I have been trying to argue, was the major influence in the twentieth-century spread of the Jigong cult. The implied author in Guo Xiaoting's novel is keen on promoting the virtues of sexual propriety and filial piety. In the *Storyteller's Jigong*, Crazy Ji's martial disciples may rob and murder, but they never indulge in sexual license, and all of them are filial. Indeed the moral conservatism of the *Storyteller's Jigong* extends even to the realm of widow chastity. The narrator extols a young woman who, after her fiancé died, cut her hair and joined the monastic order.[58]

Of course, the scope of the *Journeys*' moral conservatism is much broader than that of the *Storyteller's Jigong*. In Guo Xiaoting's novel, the eccentric saint promotes traditional family values even as he serves as a rallying symbol for social discontent. His martial disciples belong to the outlaws' world of "rivers and lakes" (*jianghu*). True, they are all filial, but they do not hesitate to steal, rob, or even murder. By contrast, the *Journeys* condemn all forms of criminal activity. Membership in street gangs, not to mention theft, robbery, and murder, entails severe punishment in purgatory. Indeed even minor criminal offenses, such as gambling, are vehemently denounced. During their tour of the netherworld Jigong and Mr. Yang meet several wretched souls who endure harsh punishments for nothing worse than betting. Jigong pronounces the following warning regarding their transgression:

> The idlers and good-for-nothing types don't want to do productive work or choose a decent job. Instead, they rely entirely on gambling for their livelihood. Quite a few good-hearted persons were enticed and fell into this trap, thereby gradually exhausting their families' fortunes. This is truly revolting. Recently, in the central region [i.e., Taizhong] there have also been several cases of robbery that were due to gambling. Gambling creditors are ruthless, leading people to acts of desperation. This is how gambling leads to criminal cases of theft and robbery. Gambling hurts people, and its poisonous impact is very deep. People should never get involved in gambling, or else they will regret it for the rest of their lives.[59]

The *Journeys*' attitude toward gambling contrasts sharply with Jigong's role in the Everybody's Happy craze. Even though the popularity of the Jigong cult in Taiwan increased, in part, because of the help he was believed to give Everybody's Happy gamblers, the two *Journeys* were published in the same city where Everybody's Happy originated (Taizhong) and were widely distributed during the height of this gambling craze. Here we have an example of the diverse and even contradictory uses to which Jigong's image has been put. In the very same locality, the eccentric god has served simultaneously as a rallying symbol for those upholding the law and those transgressing it.

The multivocality that characterizes Jigong's cult in Taiwan is also evident in other localities to which his veneration has spread. As noted above, Jigong figures prominently in the mediumistic cults of the Malaysian black societies, which are made up of lower-class members of the Chinese community. These black societies employ Jigong's rebellious traits to justify their socially marginal activities. And yet, Jigong is simultaneously a prominent object of worship among the business leaders of the Chinese community in Malaysia. Tan Chee-beng has pointed out the centrality of Jigong in the pantheon of the "morality-teaching associations" (*dejiaohui*), which are led by prominent members of the Chinese community, especially Teochiu groups. As suggested by their generic name, these associations are dedicated to the promotion of traditional Confucian values, such as filial piety. As in the Taiwanese case, their conservative ideology is often promulgated through scriptures revealed in spirit-writing séances.[60]

Jigong is believed to communicate with his devotees not only through spirit-writing but also through spirit-painting. In 1987 I participated in two séances of the Association of the Orthodox Religion's Writing and Painting (Zhengzong shuhua she) in Taipei. Somewhat unique among religious groups in Taiwan, this congregation channels its piety not into automatic writing but into automatic painting. At the time, the group was led by a dignified 80-year-old gentleman called Li Shouqi. Mr. Li had been a medical doctor in Chiang Kai-shek's army and arrived in Taiwan with the Nationalists. When possessed by the gods, Mr. Li paints, and he signs the works by the name of the deity that is supposed to have painted them. In the overwhelming majority of the cases, it is Jigong, who signs the paintings "The Crazy One drew [this]" (*Dian xie*). Mr. Li's paintings—or, as the members of his sect see it, the gods' paintings—have a divinatory value. On fixed dates of the lunar calendar, the believers gather to consult the painting oracle. The questioners kneel in front of an offering table, which serves as Mr. Li's drawing board. Each devotee, in his turn, makes offerings to the gods and contemplates his question in silence. The painting Mr. Li draws at this time is considered an answer (see Figs. 13 and 14). Since only the devotee knows the question (he does not utter it out loud), only he can interpret the answer. This oracular service costs each participant NT$500 (or approximately U.S.$15); according to the pamphlets published by the association, the fees are distributed for charity.

Li Shouqi insists that he has never studied painting, and that he creates his art only when in a trance. Nonetheless, some of his paintings are of considerable artistic value. One of the more interesting works I have seen is a painting of Jigong, signed by this eccentric deity (see Fig. 15). This painting addresses an ancient problem in Chinese religion: How can one ascertain that a statue or painting of a god is indeed a true likeness? Legends dating back to the ninth century, if not earlier, tell of deities who go to considerable trouble to verify that their images, to which people pay homage, are accurate. A Dunhuang manuscript entitled "The Record of a Returned Soul" ("Huanhun ji"), tells of a monk named Daoming, who, due to a bureaucratic error, is summoned prematurely to purgatory. When it is discovered that his death is not yet ordained, it is decided to send him back to the world of the living. The Bodhisattva Dizang takes advantage of this rare opportunity and entrusts Daoming with the following task: "You must observe closely the appearance [of my demeanor and comportment], noting clearly my proportions one by one, so that you can transmit them to the world."[61] After his return to earth, Daoming follows the god's instructions and paints his image. Li Shouqi, unlike Daoming, did not have to rely on memory to capture Jigong's likeness. His painting was drawn by the god himself. Being, as it were, a self-portrait, it is as accurate an image of the god as can be.

The spirit-painting séances of the Association of the Orthodox Religion's Writing and Painting reveal the socioeconomic diversity of the Jigong cult in Taiwan. Spirit-possession cults practice primarily in villages and in small towns, and most of the Everybody's Happy bettors who consult with mediums belong to the lower echelons of urban society (usually in Taizhong, or smaller cities). By contrast, Mr. Li Shouqi's painting séances take place in Taipei, and his clientele consists largely of the urban middle class. The association's offices are located across from the prestigious National Taiwan University, and some of the sect's members are students. Mr. Li is a medical doctor, trained in Western medicine, and during his spirit-painting trances, he is careful to wear a Western suit (see Fig. 14). The difference between his spirit-painting cult and spirit-possession cults reflects the Mandarin/Taiwanese dichotomy that runs through the island's society. Most of the spirit-mediums I interviewed were native Taiwanese, and their mother tongue was Hokkien. By contrast, Mr. Li is a mainlander and he speaks Mandarin. (He started serving as Jigong's medium-painter in 1945, when he was stationed with Chiang Kai-shek's army in Chongqing.) The political orientations of the Association of the Orthodox Religion are also unmistakable. The office walls are covered with photographs of Sun Yat-sen and Chiang Kai-shek. The group's Guomindang leanings are evinced even by Mr. Li's trance-performances. Even though the god who usually possesses his brush is Jigong, a few of Mr. Li's paintings are signed "Father of the Nation" (i.e., Sun Yat-sen), revealing that Sun is not merely the object of a modern state-cult, but, at least in this instance, has been incorporated into the pantheon of the amorphous popular religion as well.[62] The urban middle-class background of the association's devotees, as well as something of their pro-Guomindang politics, is also shared by the Unity Sect, to which I now turn.

The Unity Sect

Various avenues for the expression of religious piety were open to the laity during the late imperial period. One was joining a sectarian movement. Lay sects, which had their own temples, rituals, and sense of religious identity, have existed in China since the Yuan period. Usually they also had their own scriptures, often written in the vernacular, which were known by the generic name *baojuan*.[63] By the sixteenth century, many of these sects were "characterized by a belief in a female deity known as the Eternal Mother (Wusheng laomu), creator of mankind, and by the conviction that personal salvation could be found only through adherence to the teachings transmitted by her emissaries."[64] These sects—sometimes referred to in the scholarly literature as the "White Lotus religion," or "Motherist sectarianism"[65]—usually did not engage in military activities. But, given the right historical circumstances, their millenarian tendencies did lead to armed revolts, such as the Wang Lun uprising of 1774.[66] In addition to the Eternal Mother, White Lotus–type sects venerated also other deities, most notably the messianic Buddha of the future, Maitreya, who is to usher in the new millennium. One indication that Jigong did not occupy a prominent position in Chinese religion before the twentieth century is that—to the best of my knowledge—he was not adopted into the sectarian pantheon. It was only in the twentieth century, some twenty years after the publication of the *Storyteller's Jigong*, that the crazy god was incorporated into sectarian mythology, when the Unity Sect leader Zhang Guangbi declared himself an incarnation of Jigong, thereby making Jigong one of the sect's most prominent objects of worship. Zhang's choice of Jigong as his divine alter-ego not only reflects Jigong's growing popularity during the 1910s and 1920s but also contributed to it. In the Taiwanese case, for example, it is highly likely that the Unity Sect's proselytizing efforts augmented Jigong's popularity in spirit-possession and spirit-writing cults, even among those cults not directly related to this sect.

As noted above, the Unity Sect is a modern manifestation of a White Lotus / Motherist sectarian tradition, which dates back to the late Ming. The Unity Sect itself, however, claims a much more ancient pedigree. The creators of human civilization in remote antiquity Shennong and Fuxi, the great philosophers Confucius and Laozi, the propagators of the Buddhist faith Bodhidharma and Huineng, and a host of other cultural heroes are seen as precursors of the Unity Sect, sent by the Eternal Mother to save humanity. Within the more recent past, the Unity Sect singles out eighteen patriarchs, who are supposed to have transmitted the faith from the Tang period through the early twentieth century. An examination of the Qing period patriarchs reveals that some of them are indeed historical figures, who were involved in White Lotus–type sectarian activity.[67] The question is which one of these patriarchs was the first to have preached a faith similar, in name and content, to the Unity Sect as we know it in the twentieth century. In this regard, the Fifteenth Patriarch, Wang Jueyi, said to have been active during the second half of the nineteenth century, appears to be of great significance. Ma Xisha and Han Bingfang have recently unearthed Qing government documents from the 1880s in which reference is made to a Wang Jueyi who propagated a religion called "Unity Religion" (Yiguan jiao). Moreover, this Wang Jueyi is said to have authored a book called *Yiguan tanyuantu shuo* (Explicating the diagram of the exhaustive common origins).[68] A book with a very similar title, *Yiguan tanyuan* (An exhaustive exploration of the common origins), along with others attributed to Wang Jueyi, was distributed by Unity Sect's members during the 1940s, when Li Shiyu collected them.[69] For this reason, Ma Xisha and Han Binfang have concluded that the Unity Sect's foundations were laid by Wang Jueyi during the second half of the nineteenth century.[70] However, for the subject of this book, the 1920s are a date of greater significance, for it was then that the Eighteenth Patriarch, Zhang Guangbi, incorporated Jigong into the Unity Sect's mythology.[71] The following comments are intended to highlight the significance of Jigong in the Unity Sect's dogma and practice since the 1920s. They certainly do not do justice either to the complexities of the Unity Sect's theology or to its intricate history.

The Unity Religion propagated by Wang Jueyi during the 1870s and 1880s had a limited following, and it was the incarnated Jigong, Zhang Guangbi, who transformed it into a nationwide sect. Zhang assumed the official post of the Unity Sect's eighteenth patriarch in 1928, whereupon he set in motion an ambitious proselytizing plan. Under his leadership, branch temples of the Unity Sect were established in Beijing, Tianjin, Ji'nan (in Shandong), Shanghai, Nanjing, Anhui, and Sichuan.[72] His importance in the spread of the sect is acknowledged by Unity Sect followers, who worship him as the "Venerable Teacher" (*shizun*) and, out of respect for his divinity, treat his surname Zhang 張 as a taboo word, usually splitting it into two characters: *gong* 弓 and *chang* 長. Zhang passed away in 1947, and his young wife, Sun Suzhen (?–1975), who had been involved in the sect's activities during her husband's life, inherited control of the sect.[73] Today she is venerated as the sect's "mistress" (*shimu*) by most Unity Sect's members, alongside her husband, and is considered an incarnation of the Moon-Wisdom Bodhisattva (Yuehui pusa). Sun Suzhen's rise to power within the sect was accompanied by an interesting addition to the mythology of Jigong. In an apparent effort to provide Sun with divine authority, she was described as an incarnation of Jigong's wife, to whom he was supposedly married prior to taking orders.[74] Thus, just as his latter-day avatar Zhang Guangbi had a young wife, so the crazy god himself had to be supplied with one.

Following the Japanese defeat in World War II, the Unity Sect was accused by the Nationalists and the Communists alike of having cooperated with the occupation army. The Unity Sect had flourished in the Japanese-controlled areas, and its very success there made it suspect of collaboration.[75] After the establishment of the People's Republic, many leaders of Unity Sect branches found their way to Taiwan, but there, too, their relations with the ruling Guomindang party remained ambiguous for some time. One reason was the lingering suspicion of collaboration with the Japanese; another may have been the traditional mistrust, inherited from the imperial regimes, of all sectarian activities.[76] Nonetheless, by the early 1980s, the relations between the Unity Sect and the ruling Guomindang party had improved significantly. For one thing, the government could not ignore the growing popularity of the sect on the island. For another, they were favorably impressed with the Unity Sect's pro-Guomindang teachings. As Song Guangyu has pointed out, in their study sessions, Unity Sect teachers tend to quote not only Confucius and Mencius but also Sun Yat-sen, Chiang Kai-shek, and even the latter's son, the late President Chiang Ching-kuo. The government also found the Unity Sect's emphasis on the traditional values of loyalty and filiality very congenial. Thus the government has come to see in the Unity Sect "a reliable friend, a social force that could be trusted and made use of,"[77] and it abolished the designation of the sect as an illegal group, which, in any case, it had ignored for some time.[78]

The gradual improvement of relations with the government facilitated the Unity Sect's growth in Taiwan. The exact number of Unity Sect initiates is hard to ascertain because, as Jordan and Overmyer have pointed out, the Unity Sect is not a monolithic organization. Its more-or-less independent branches are often in competition with each other, and there are no unified registries of members.[79] According to one, in all likelihood exaggerated, estimate, by 1977 the number of Unity Sect members in Taiwan was four million. More realistic estimates suggest between 300,000 and 500,000 initiates by the early 1980s. Even these conservative assessments make the Unity Sect the largest religious denomination in Taiwan, surpassing the other large initiatory religion, Catholicism, by some 150,000 members.[80] In terms of social background, most Unity Sect members belong to the urban middle class, but some belong to society's highest echelons as well. In 1989 I participated in a Unity Sect gathering, which took place inside the Taipei headquarters of a large financial corporation. The president of this corporation—one of the largest on the island—is an ardent Unity Sect follower, and his economic empire actively supports sect activities.[81] As a religion in which Jigong occupies a central position in the pantheon, the Unity Sect, like the Association of the Orthodox Religion's Writing and Painting, reveals that the crazy god's cult in Taiwan is by no means limited to society's lower classes.

The Unity Sect's teaching revolves around the myth of the Eternal Mother, creator of humankind.[82] Like White Lotus religions in general, the Unity Sect venerates a supreme goddess, who sent her human descendants to inhabit the earth. This goddess was betrayed by her children, who forgot their heavenly origins, and sunk into sinful ways. In her great mercy, the heavenly mother has assigned numerous emissaries—including the founders of the Confucian, Taoist, and Buddhist traditions—the task of awakening her children to the fatal course of their actions. And yet the majority of humankind has ignored these warnings. Thus, human history is a relentless story of decline, as humankind strays further and further from its divine ancestry. This process of decline can be accurately divided into a three-stage scheme, known as the "Decline of the Law," which the sectarian tradition inherited from Chinese Buddhism. The last of the three stages is now upon us, and it is marked by catastrophic events, which make the search for salvation all the more urgent. Some Unity Sect members highlight this apocalyptic vision by references to a future savior, who, during the apocalypse, will lead the Unity Sect's initiates back to their heavenly mother. At least one Unity Sect informant, in Taipei, told John Kieschnick that, when the final days come, sect members will gather in their chapels (called "Buddha halls," or *Fotang*), where they have prepared food in advance. They would seal the doors behind them and smear them with chicken blood. As the apocalypse rages outside, the Unity Sect's initiates, shielded inside their chapels, will pay no heed to the screams of the helpless victims. Then, Jigong, the savior, will come and lead them all to heaven.[83]

Whom will Jigong save when the apocalypse strikes? What is the path to personal salvation in the Unity Sect? First, initiation into the sect is of primary significance. The initiation ritual in itself erases one's name from the registers of purgatory, thereby circumventing the possibility of punishment there.[84] Beyond this, each member has to apply himself or herself to moral and spiritual self-cultivation, which are understood in terms borrowed from the Chinese cultural heritage. The Unity Sect considers the Confucian, Taoist, and Buddhist traditions alike divine revelations by the Eternal Mother and it makes use of all three. Thus, for example, the sect's moral teachings are based on Confucian tenets, the Taoist classic *Daode jing* is used as a primer of spiritual cultivation, and, as in other sectarian movements, vegetarianism derives from the Buddhist tradition.[85] Since the Unity Sect considers these three traditions equally sacred, much time and energy are dedicated to their study. The sect publishes new editions of texts from the Confucian, Taoist, and Buddhist canons, and sect gatherings are usually dedicated not to rituals but to the study of these texts. Promoting the study of the Chinese classics, the "sect portrays itself as the chief hope for the restoration of Chinese culture itself."[86] Indeed, as David Jordan and Daniel Overmyer have pointed out, the sect's drawing power may derive largely from a present-day yearning for the restoration of traditional values. Like the Taiwanese morality books discussed above, the Unity Sect's response to the challenge of modernization is a reaffirmation of the Chinese cultural heritage.

Jigong's position in the Unity Sect's teachings was set forth by Jigong himself, in his incarnation as Zhang Guangbi. In his *Provisional Regulations* (*Zhanding fogui*), Zhang assigned Jigong the fourth-ranking position in the Unity Sect's hierarchy of divinities. The mad god is preceded only by the Eternal Mother, the Buddha Maitreya, and the Bodhisattva Guanyin. Trailing behind him are a multitude of other deities, including "all the celestial gods and saints" (*zhu tian shen sheng*); Jigong's wife, the Moon-Wisdom Bodhisattva; "all masters of the law" (*gewei falü zhu*; including Guangong, Lü Dongbin, and Yue Fei, who are listed by name), and the Kitchen God.[87] Jigong's high rank in the heavenly hierarchy is seen in Unity Sect rituals, in which he is usually the fourth named deity to which homage is paid. In the Unity Sect's initiation rites, for example, the order of obeisances to the gods runs the Eternal Mother, "all celestial gods and saints," the Buddha Maitreya, the Bodhisattva Guanyin, and Jigong.[88] In this initiation rite, as in most Unity Sect rituals, the crazy god is paid homage to as the "Living Buddha Jigong" (*Jigong huofo*), a title that illustrates the significance of the novel *Storyteller's Jigong* in the shaping of his twentieth-century cult. In this novel Jigong is referred to by this same title.[89]

Does Jigong's official ranking in the Unity Sect's hierarchy of divinities mirror his significance in the sect? The informant quoted above who described Jigong as the future savior seems to have assigned him a role (of future messiah) more significant than that suggested by his fourth ranking. In 1986, 1987, and again in 1991, I gained the impression from interviews of other Unity Sect members in Taipei that they, too, directed more of their religious fervor toward Jigong than toward other deities. The impression that Jigong looms larger in the believers' consciousness than all other Unity Sect's gods was also shared by Li Shiyu, who studied this sect in the 1940s. Li commented that "Jigong's prestige in the Unity Sect is almost equal to that of the Eternal Mother. So much so, that in most believers' eyes his position is even higher than hers."[90] One reason for Jigong's prominence is probably the complete fusion of his image with that of his avatar, Zhang Guangbi, who has contributed most to the shaping of the Unity Sect as it exists today. The sect's scriptures and rituals emphasize that Jigong and Zhang are one and the same. Both figures are addressed as "venerable teacher" (*shizun*), and both are referred to by at least twenty other honorific titles, including the Living Buddha Jigong, Jigong the Saintly Monk, the Miracle-Worker Great Master, the drunkard Crazy Ji, and the mad monk from Nanping.[91] (Nanping is the name of the hill on which the Jingci Monastery—where the historical Daoji resided—is located.)

One indication of Jigong's pre-eminent position in the Unity Sect's pantheon is his prominence in its literature. The Unity Sect produces its own scriptures and, in addition, makes use of Confucian, Taoist, Buddhist, and other sects' literature. The sect's own scriptures are usually composed through spirit-writing, the majority of which are attributed to Jigong. During Zhang Guangbi's life, some 80 percent of the Unity Sect's divine revelations (books and shorter pieces alike) were signed by the crazy god, and after Zhang's death, when he himself began possessing the brush under his divine persona's name, the number of pieces attributed to Jigong increased.[92] In his annotated catalogue of Unity Sect literature, published in 1948, Li Shiyu describes thirteen books authored in full, or in large part, by Jigong. (There are other scriptures to which the eccentric god contributed only short pieces.)[93] David Jordan and Daniel Overmyer analyze two other scriptures attributed to Jigong,[94] and in my collection is yet another composition by Jigong entitled *Jigong, the Living Buddha, Having Manifested Himself and Lectured on the Law: A Collection* (*Jigong huofo xianshen shuofa zhuanji*).[95] All these works are doctrinal and hortatory. They elaborate upon the sect's path of salvation and exhort people to follow it. Two books are catechisms, in which Jigong answers such theological queries as "What is the Way?" "What is the Unity Sect?" "What is the meaning of the three stages decline of the law?" and "Are 'spirit-written' texts composed by people or by real immortals and Buddhas?"[96] Two of the more interesting books are the Confucian classic, the *Great Learning*, and the canonical Buddhist *Diamond Sūtra*, to which the eccentric god has appended his own prefaces and commentaries.[97]

The Unity Sect books attributed to Jigong share one characteristic—by and large they do not feature him as a protagonist. Jigong may mention that he is the Eternal Mother's emissary, and the editor may record the sound of the crazy god's laughter (Ha, ha!), indicating that it is indeed Jigong who is possessing the brush.[98] But, usually, the spirit-written book provides very little, if any, information about its divine author. Here the difference between the novels *on*

Fig. 1. Jigong. Woodblock print in the 1569 edition of the *Recorded Sayings*. Note that his image lacks the iconographic emblems—the gourd, hat, fan, and patched garb—that characterize his twentieth-century representations.

Fig. 2. Visitors gather around the Jingci Monastery's well, from which, according to legend, the logs collected by Jigong miraculously emerged. Supposedly, one log is still visible at the bottom of the well (photograph by the author, December 1994).

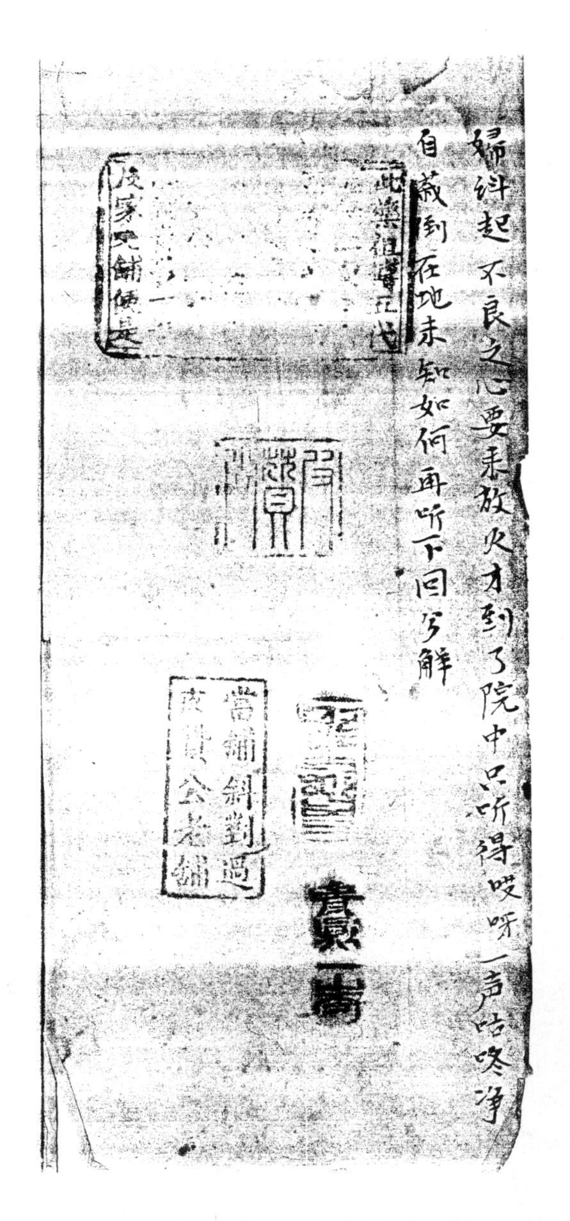

Fig. 3. Vendor's seals on vol. 32 of the *Jigong Drum-Song* manuscript in the Chewang Fu collection. The seal at the bottom left reads: "Mr. Pi Zan's old store, located at an angle across from the pawnshop." The blurred seal at the top suggests that the store in question also sold medicines (photograph courtesy Shoudu Library, Beijing).

Fig. 4. Shop's seal and reader's scribbles on vol. 34 of the *Jigong Drum-Song* manuscript in the Academia Sinica collection. The seal provides the shop's address and warns readers: "Men who tear or burn books, add writings, or change characters are robbers. Women [who do the same] are prostitutes." This warning did not prevent one reader from scribbling a riddle right over the seal. The marks on the right were probably made by the shopkeeper when calculating the fee owed him as a function of the number of days the book had been borrowed (photograph courtesy Institute for History and Philology, Academia Sinica, Taipei).

Fig. 5. Statue of Jigong at the Five-Hundred Arhat Hall of the Wuyou Monastery, Leshan, Sichuan. The statue, dated 1909, is the earliest in which Jigong is supplied, in addition to the wine cup and the fly whisk, with a fan and *two* gourds (one gourd is visible just under the palm of his right hand, the other is partially screened by the railing) (photograph by Izhak Sonenshtain, May 1995).

Fig. 6. Statue of the Mad Monk of the Yue Fei saga. Statue, dated 1909, at the Five-Hundred Arhat Hall of the Wuyou Monastery, Leshan, Sichuan. The mad monk carries a broom (with which he "sweeps away traitors" such as Qin Gui) and a pipe for fanning the fire (with which he stirs the nation into action). Note the similarity between his patched garb and the one worn by Jigong (photograph by Izhak Sonenshtain, May 1995).

Fig. 7. Jigong (on the right) in a puppet television serial by Huang Junxiong. Unlike traditional handpuppets, Huang Junxiong's puppets can move their eyes and lips. They are also larger than the classical puppets and show up better on television screens (photograph courtesy Huang Junxiong).

Fig. 8. Lin Guoxiong as Jigong in a 1980s television serial produced by Yashi Television, Hong Kong.

Fig. 9. Chen Shengzai as Jigong in a Minghuayuan *gezaixi*-opera performance, Gaoxiong, Taiwan, August 1989. Note the orchestra in the background.

Fig. 10. The spirit-medium Chen Wenshan, in a trance, as Jigong, Pingdong county, southern Taiwan, 1980 (photograph courtesy Chen Wenshan).

Fig. 11. An advertisement for a Jigong gambling shrine distributed to pilgrims during the Goddess Mazu's birthday festival, Beigang, Taiwan, April 1987. The inscription in the middle reads: "Wealth and Honors Depend on Heaven, for Windfalls Rely on the Help of Gods and Buddhas: Jigong the Living Buddha Instructs Us."

Fig. 12. A Jigong medium in trance writing numbers for Everybody's Happy bettors. Note his colorful garb, wine gourd, and fan. Pingdong county, Taiwan, June 1987 (photograph by the author).

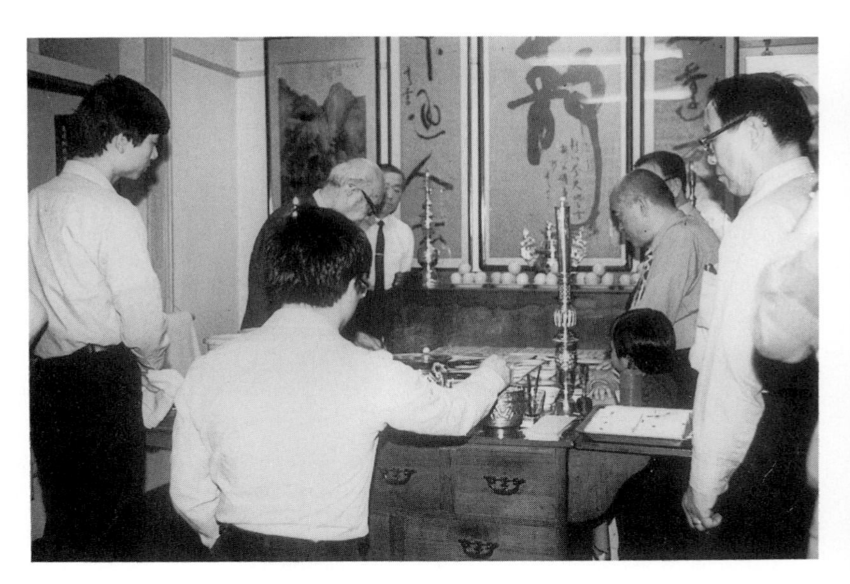

Fig. 13. Spirit-writing séance at the Taipei offices of the Association of the Orthodox Religion's Writing and Painting, April 1987. The devotee kneels and contemplates a question. On the left side of the offering table, the medium-painter, Mr. Li Shouqi, draws a painting considered an answer (photograph by the author).

Fig. 14. Spirit-writing séance at the Taipei offices of the Association of the Orthodox Religion's Writing and Painting, April 1987. Mr. Li Shouqi, in a trance, paints an answer to a devotee's silent question (photograph by the author).

Fig. 15. A self-portrait of Jigong produced by the automatic spirit-painting technique. Painting in the Taipei offices of the Association of the Orthodox Religion's Writing and Painting (photograph by the author, April 1987).

Fig. 16. A statue of Jigong in the Five Dragons Mountain, Phoenix Mountain Temple in Gaoxiong county, Taiwan. This 61-foot statue (note the cars at its base) is the tallest statue of Jigong on the island. It was completed in 1967 (photograph by the author, January 1987).

Fig. 17. Jigong's image in a 1987 comic-strip version of his stories. The inscription, "Wherever there is injustice, there I am," mirrors the tone of social protest that has been characteristic of this crazy saint's lore since the *Storyteller's Jigong*'s publication. From *Jigong gushi* (Jigong stories) (Shanghai: Renmin meishu, 1987).

Fig. 18. Jigong in an early twentieth-century lithographic edition of the *Drunken Puti*, by the Shanghai publisher Chenhe ji shu. Note the patched robe, fan, and gourd.

Fig. 19. Jigong in an early twentieth-century lithographic edition of the *Storyteller's Jigong*, by the Shanghai publisher Chenhe ji shu. Note that even in this relatively late print, Jigong wears neither a patched robe nor a small hat and carries neither a fan nor a gourd. (Photograph courtesy Harvard-Yenching Library, Cambridge, Mass.)

Fig. 20. The fan, not even mentioned in the novels on Jigong, becomes a flying carpet in this comic-strip edition of *Jigong gushi* (Jigong stories) (Shanghai: Renmin meishu, 1987).

Jigong, and the scriptures *by* him could not be greater. Novels depict the god's personality; sectarian literature (at least in this instance) assumes the readers' familiarity with it. Indeed, Zhang Guangbi may have chosen Jigong to deliver the Unity Sect's message of salvation precisely because of this crazy god's popularity in fiction, drama, and oral literature. Once he had been adopted into the sect's pantheon, it was unnecessary to elaborate upon this newcomer's personality, since sect members, like the population at large, had already been introduced to it. In this respect, the Unity Sect's scriptures are similar to the morality books discussed above, which assume their audiences' familiarity with Crazy Ji and use him to voice their moral message only.

Spirit-writing is not the only medium of communication between Jigong and his Unity Sect devotees. Spirit-mediumship is practiced in the sect as well. In January 1991, at a Unity Sect branch office in Taipei, I was shown a video-recording of a medium's performance. The medium wore the same colorful, patched garb worn by non-Unity Sect Jigong mediums, and she carried the same iconic gourd and fan they do. However, the purpose of her performance was entirely different. Most mediums in Taiwan function as oracles and answer the personal questions of individual clients. By contrast, her performance was integrated into the sect's doctrinal teachings. Her words were written on a blackboard to be used in a lecture. This Unity Sect medium was female, and, according to sect informants (and as attested by photographs included in one of the sect's publications), most of the sect's other mediums are women as well.[99] In this they differ from non-sectarian Jigong mediums in Taiwan, who are usually male. Interestingly, in some Unity Sect's gatherings, young girls—usually twelve to fifteen years old—are possessed by the gods, for, as one informant put it, children's purity is conducive to divine revelation.[100] The primacy of women in Unity Sect's mediumship can be interpreted as one manifestation of their importance in this and other White Lotus–type sects, in general. These sects worship the Eternal Mother, creator of the world, and women have often played an important role in their religious organizations, as evinced by Sun Suzhen, who, under the divine title Moon-Wisdom Bodhisattva, controlled the Unity Sect.

In addition to his appearance in the possessed body of spirit-mediums, Crazy Ji's likeness is also captured on film by Unity Sect cameras. Photography of gods amounts to an obsession in Unity Sect circles, to judge from the volume *Collection of the Immortals', Buddhas', and Saints' Traces* (*Xian fo sheng ji zhuanji*), which is entirely dedicated to such pictures. Some photographs in this volume show the gods as revealed in the night sky, or in broad daylight. Others, taken during spirit-writing and spirit-possession séances, reveal rays of light, usually red, that supposedly trace the deity's descent into the medium's body. (Such rays of light could have been produced by combining a long exposure time with a movable flashlight, or they could have been drawn during developing.) The *Collection of the Immortals', Buddhas', and Saints' Traces* includes quite a few photographs of Jigong. The earliest was taken in Shanghai in 1934. Another reveals Jigong's likeness in a pattern of clouds above the Chiang Kai-shek memorial in Taipei.[101] A third photograph, taken at a Unity Sect chapel in Malaysia, shows the burning of a memorial offered to Heaven. According to the accompanying caption, Jigong's likeness is detectable in the flames of the burnt offering:

> In March 1984, Initiator (*dianchuan shi*)[102] Huang of the Auspicious-Heavens Branch traveled together with the Manager of the Liang Chapel, Lecturer Cai, to Malaysia. On the eve of their departure, Lecturer Cai prayed to the Living Buddha, the Old Master [i.e., Jigong], to provide them with spiritual assistance. The Living Buddha, the Old Master, communicated with her through the *sancai* [i.e., spirit-writing][103] and said: "Don't worry. I will travel with you." Indeed, after they started the ceremonies at Mrs. Yi Baolin's chapel [in Malaysia], exactly when Initiator Huang was making the offering of the written memorial to Heaven, the image of the Living Buddha Jigong was manifested in the burnt memorial. In the [enclosed] photograph's far left, at the bottom of the window curtain, to the right of the offering candle, we can see the Living Buddha, the Old Master, wearing his pointed monk hat, and his loose monk robe. Facing the camera, his appearance is easygoing and carefree. This proves that if we adhere to the Buddha Mind, and conduct Buddha deeds, the Living Buddha, the Old Master, will always be near us.[104]

Jigong's role in the Unity Sect adds a new dimension to his multivalent personality as, among other things, a divine adviser to gamblers and a spokesman for conservative denunciations of gambling. The Unity Sect has assigned Crazy Ji yet another task: the promotion of vegetarianism. Unity Sect members adhere to a "pure mouth" (*qingkou*) regime that prohibits the consumption of meat, wine, and cigarettes. Here the discrepancy between the divine bon vivant and his Unity Sect devotees could not be greater. As portrayed in novels, Jigong delights in nothing better than wine and dog meat. Aware of this discrepancy, Unity Sect members have tried to transform their divine patron's image so that he adheres to their own dietary regulations. All the sect's members I interviewed insisted that Jigong's portrayal in the novels is false. Jigong does not eat meat, nor does he drink wine, they claimed. According to one informant, Jigong's gourd holds medicine, not wine; according to another, the gourd contains a "Zen potion." John Kieschnick overheard a particularly interesting apologia on behalf of the eccentric god. In the course of one Unity Sect dinner in Taipei, a child asked the meeting organizer why they were eating vegetarian food when Jigong eats meat. "He only pretends to eat it," explained the leader of this Unity Sect event. "When no one is watching, he turns his head and vomits. Then the animals he has eaten emerge alive from his mouth."[105]

The Unity Sect's apologetics for Jigong's antinomian behavior resembles that employed by the Buddhist establishment, which also incorporated this crazy deity from the popular religion. In 1995, at a Buddhist monastery on Mount Wutai in Shanxi, I was offered the exact same apologia for Jigong's diet as that overheard by John Kieschnick. "Jigong," a Buddhist monk told me, "vomits alive the animals he has eaten." The appearance of this legend in twentieth-century Buddhist and Unity Sect circles attests to the continuity of the Chinese religious tradition. An identical explanation for the violation of dietary laws is given in Buddhist literature as early as the seventh century. In *Continuation of the Biographies of Eminent Monks* (*Xu Gaoseng zhuan*), Daoxuan (596–667) tells of a monk named Ācārya Xiang (Xiang Sheli) who tried on numerous occasions to convert his fellow townspeople to vegetarianism. Finally he joined them for a lavish picnic of meat and wine. After eating and drinking with them, he stood up to vomit by a ditch: "The chicken meat that emerged cried out and flew off. The mutton that came out galloped away. Wine and food came out chaotically, until it just about filled the ditch to the top with fish and ducks swimming about in profusion. All of the people sighed and vowed to abandon their practice of killing animals."[106] The ability to vomit living animals has been attributed to Jigong in fiction as early as the seventeenth century. In *Jigong's Complete Biography*, Wang Mengji set out to refute the antinomian traits attributed to his protagonist in other works of fiction, including Jigong's supposed breach of the monastic dietary laws.

Wang explains that the animals supposedly eaten by the crazy saint emerge from his mouth alive.[107]

Iconography

The sources examined in the preceding pages indicate that the Jigong cult underwent a significant transformation around the turn of the twentieth century. The earliest evidence of Jigong's role in spirit-possession cults, spirit-writing, morality books, and sectarian religion dates from 1900 or later, as do the earliest references to the cult in places as distant from each other as Liaoning, Taiwan, Thailand, and Malaysia. It is therefore likely that Jigong became the object of a cult throughout the Chinese cultural area no earlier than the twentieth century. Another area of inquiry that will corroborate this hypothesis is iconography. Presumably in a polytheistic religious setting a god must have recognizable iconic traits before his cult can become widespread. If worshipers are unable to identify a deity's visual image, this would suggest that he is not a popular object of worship. Of course, popular deities may have several iconic representations. The Bodhisattva Guanyin, for example, is variously embodied as the Water and Moon Guanyin, the White-Robed Guanyin, and the Guanyin of the South Sea, among others. However, each of these distinct iconographic representations has been standardized. In other words, a god probably needs at least one fixed iconic form before his or her cult can be described as popular. Discovery of the date that a standard iconography for Jigong emerged would aid in determining the date his cult became widespread.

In his standard iconographic image, Jigong is dressed in a long robe (usually black covered with brightly colored patches). The clownish robe is supplemented by a comedian's pointed hat, usually inscribed with the character *fo* (Buddha). The eccentric god holds a tattered fan in one hand, and carries a gourd, which serves as his wine jug, in the other. This iconographic image is evident in the overwhelming majority of Jigong's visual representations, whether religious or theatrical, and can be found in both proselytizing literature and vernacular fiction. Mediums possessed by the crazy god and actors portraying his image on the commercial stage wear the same outfit, which is equally shared by the god's representations in temple iconography and in children's comic strips (compare Figs. 7–10 and 16–17). Thus, Jigong's iconography provides further evidence of the intimate relation between religion and drama, entertainment and ritual, in the history of his cult.

When did a standard iconography for Jigong appear? Sixteenth- and seventeenth-century novels on Jigong describe icons of him in the houses of the laity. But these, along with all other visual vestiges of his early popular cult in Zhejiang, no longer survive. Two types of sources do, however, provide evidence of Jigong's early iconography as well as its development over time: illustrations in the novels (woodblock prints and, by the early twentieth century, lithographic prints); and icons (mostly statues) in Buddhist temples. The latter represent a secondary development in the history of the cult—its appropriation by the monastic establishment, which is discussed in the next section. Here I will examine them from an iconographic standpoint only.

To the best of my knowledge, the earliest extant icon of Jigong in a Buddhist monastery is a statue at the Five-Hundred Arhat Hall of the Temple of the Azure Clouds (Biyun si) on the outskirts of Beijing. Designed in 1748, this statue differs markedly from Jigong's present-day iconography. The crazy saint, who is perched on one of the beams that support the ceiling, is wearing neither a patched robe nor a hat, and he carries neither a fan nor a gourd. Instead he holds a wine pot, and he is wearing a childish apron, leading the local tour-guides (accustomed to Jigong's present-day iconography) to describe him as the "baby Jigong."[108] Sculptured about a hundred years later, in 1851, a Jigong image at the Five-Hundred Arhat Hall of the Temple of Precious Light (Baoguang si) near Chengdu, Sichuan, is slightly closer to the crazy god's present representation. Here Jigong wears a small hat and a robe with colorful patches. (The robe may be evidence of the influence of opera on Jigong's iconography: in several forms of regional drama, beggars are costumed in colorfully patched black gowns.) In this statue, Jigong's wine pot has been replaced by a winecup. A painting of Jigong, dated 1895, preserved at the Lingyin Monastery in Hangzhou adds an emblem crucial to the crazy saint's later iconography—his fan.[109] And about a decade later, Jigong's other emblem—his gourd—makes its first known appearance: an expressive statue, dated 1909, at the Arhat Hall of the Wuyou Monastery in Leshan, Sichuan, is an interesting hybrid of the earlier images such as that in Temple of Precious Light and new icons. Here Jigong still holds the winecup, but the artist has also supplied him with a fan, two gourds, and a fly whisk (see Fig. 5).[110] The winecup, fly whisk, and extra gourd disappear only in the second half of this century, leaving the fixed iconography of one gourd, fan, pointed hat, and patched robe.[111]

Like the sculptors who molded the early Jigong statues, book illustrators from the sixteenth through the late nineteenth centuries imagined the crazy saint in a form completely different from his present-day image. For example, the artist who illustrated the 1569 edition of the *Recorded Sayings* chose an earring, bare feet, and a bristle of hair on Jigong's head (which according to Buddhist law is supposed to be shaved) to express the saint's eccentricity (see Fig. 1). As with Buddhist statuary, the first signs of a quintessential Jigong iconography emerge in book illustration only around the turn of the twentieth century. The iconic fan, gourd, small hat, and a patched garb appear for the first time in lithographic editions of novels on Jigong, which were published for the most part in Shanghai. Not all these editions are dated, but they were probably published between 1890 and 1930, given the lithographic technique of printing as well as the place of publication. One early edition in which Jigong wears a patched robe and wields a fan was published around 1910. This is an edition of one of the *Storyteller's Jigong*'s sequels.[112] In another lithographic edition, of the novel *Drunken Puti*, Jigong has a gourd as well (Fig. 18). However, even in these early twentieth-century prints, Jigong's iconography is still far from fixed. In the illustration from the *Storyteller's Jigong*'s sequel, the crazy saint carries a wine pot, rather than a gourd, and in the *Drunken Puti* print, he has a large straw hat as well as a rolled mat, both of which were to disappear from later representations. In some twentieth-century editions, just as in the sixteenth-century *Recorded Sayings*, Jigong bears none of his present-day emblems. For example, in a beautiful print from an early twentieth-century edition of the *Storyteller's Jigong*, the saint has long hair, but he wears neither a patched garb nor a hat, and carries neither a fan nor a gourd (Fig. 19).

Thus, statues in Buddhist monasteries, as well as woodblock and lithographic prints, reveal that the first traits of a recognizable Jigong iconography emerged around the turn of the twentieth century and did not become standardized until the 1950s. This visual evidence tallies well with the information, presented above, that the last decade of the Qing dynasty represents a watershed in the growth and spread of Jigong's cult. I have been arguing that the publication of the *Storyteller's Jigong* played a crucial role in this dramatic development, and yet the iconographic evidence examined here reveals that even as this novel created a greater need for a fixed iconography of Jigong (by making this deity so much more popular), it did not shape the iconography itself. Visual logic dictates iconographic representation, and often its requirements are not met by written narratives. Jigong's gourd, for example, is not mentioned in any novel. Furthermore, in the *Storyteller's Jigong*, the crazy saint's archenemies, the Taoist master-sorcerers, employ the gourd as their weapon of choice. Why then did a gourd become an integral part of Jigong's iconography? The answer lies in the need to represent visually this insouciant deity's love of wine. We have seen that both a pot and a cup had been used to address this need, but unlike the gourd, they do not benefit from a lengthy tradition ascribing to them magic powers.

Another piece of evidence that visual representation could shape Jigong's image in ways unforeseen by the written novels is the crazy saint's fan. No novel associates a fan with Jigong. And yet once it became part of his iconography, visual artists employed it in the creation of new narratives on him. The fan was transformed into a magic wand, which, in a lithographic edition of *Drunken Puti*, emanates fire and, in a comic strip published in 1987, serves as Jigong's flying carpet (see Figs. 18 and 20). Here iconography spurred a narrative development—Jigong flying on a magic fan—not foreshadowed by the novels, which do not even associate the eccentric saint with this accessory. Thus, narrative art follows its own visual logic to develop aspects of Jigong's myth that were not shaped by novels.

Appropriation by the Monastic Establishment

The historical Daoji did not occupy an important position in the monastic community of his time, and his name is barely mentioned in contemporary Buddhist sources. He never held an official post in a monastery, nor did he ever receive an official title. The earliest signs of his posthumous veneration come from the laity, not from the clergy. These were the laymen who "sorted Daoji's *śarīra* remains and stored them below the Twin Peak."[113] Likewise, it was the laity who transformed Daoji into a literary and dramatic hero, celebrating his adventures in oral and written fiction as well as in drama. Under pressure from the laity, however, the attitude of the monastic community toward Daoji changed. The same monastic establishment that in his own time had treated this eccentric monk with suspicion eventually admitted him into its gallery of saints. Literary and iconographic evidence alike points to the gradual acceptance of Jigong by the monastic establishment. The crazy saint's hagiography, often extracted from novels about him, was gradually incorporated into Buddhist literature, and his sculpted image became a common feature of many Buddhist monasteries.

The earliest indication that the monastic establishment had accepted Daoji is the inclusion of his name in "Transmission of the Lamp" texts, which contain biographies of eminent masters of the Chan lineage. In some cases these texts provide only a master's name, but no biography is attached. Works in this genre written during Daoji's lifetime or shortly thereafter do not include a biography of him; in fact, they do not even mention his name. Neither the *Jiatai Period Record of the Universal Transmission of the Lamp* (*Jiatai Pu deng lu*; 1204) nor the *Five Lamps Compendium* (*Wudeng huiyuan*; 1253) lists him among the famous monks of his generation, indicating that Daoji's Buddhist contemporaries did not conceive of him as an important figure. By contrast, Ming period "Transmission of the Lamp" chronicles do mention him, under his nickname Crazy Ji, albeit with no biographical detail. Both Juding's (?–1404) *Continuation of the Transmission of the Lamp Record* (*Xu Chuandeng lu*) and Wenxiu's (1345–1418) *Supplement to the Five Lamps Compendium* (*Wudeng huiyuan buyi*) insert Jigong's name among the eminent masters in Huiyuan's lineage. (Juding specified that Jigong's "Recorded [Sayings]" have not survived.)[114] The title by which both works refer to Jigong, "scribe" (*shuji*), may indicate the growth of popular lore on this crazy saint. To judge from the one contemporary source on the historical Daoji, Jujian's *Collected Prose*, this eccentric monk never held the official position of a scribe in a Buddhist monastery, even though his literary skills were outstanding.[115]

Unlike the Ming period records, monastic histories written during the Qing include biographies of Jigong. The histories in question are those of the two Hangzhou monasteries associated with the historical Daoji, the Lingyin Monastery (where he was ordained) and the Jingci Monastery (where he passed away) (see Map 1, p. 27). The earliest of these histories is Sun Zhi's *History of the Lingyin Monastery* (*Lingyin si zhi*; 1663; revised version 1671).[116] Jigong's biography in this history probably derives from the novels about him. Sun Zhi emphasized that Jigong's antinomian behavior led to conflicts between him and the monastery's superintendent, and that the abbot invariably sided with his "crazy" disciple. In this context, he quotes the novel *Recorded Sayings*: "The Way of Chan is broad. Can't it encompass one crazy monk?"[117] Sun Zhi also noted that Jigong performed many miracles, but he did not give specific examples. In addition to a biography of Jigong, the *History of the Lingyin Monastery* includes two literary pieces attributed to this eccentric saint, a poem and a fund-raising petition. Since neither is included in the novels about Jigong, they may possibly be authentic.[118]

A wealth of information about Jigong is included in Jixiang's 1805 *History of the Jingci Monastery* (*Jingci si zhi*; hereafter *Jingci History*),[119] where the information about the crazy saint is divided, with some repetition, among several chapters.[120] A chapter on eminent monks includes a biography of Jigong, and a chapter entitled "Miscellaneous Records" narrates in detail some of this crazy saint's most famous miracles. Finally, a chapter on famous sites includes biographical sketches of Jigong, appended to the descriptions of the monastery's Arhat hall, where a statue of him was located, and the monastery's well. The latter figures in the famous legend first recorded in the seventeenth-century novels *Drunken Puti* and *Jigong's Complete Biography* (see Fig. 2).[121]

According to Jixiang's *Jingci History*, Jigong was an eccentric monk who transgressed monastic regulations by eating meat and drinking wine. Nonetheless, he was one of the 500 arhats of Mount Tiantai, and his divine nature was revealed in his miraculous birth; he was conceived after his mother dreamed that she swallowed rays of the sun. During his sojourn on earth, Jigong displayed his supernatural powers in a wide array of miracles. Jixiang does not shy away from incorporating into his history some of the most blatant magical feats attributed to Jigong in the novels celebrating him. The Jigong of the *Jingci History* appears in the empress dowager's dream, and convinces her to make a contribution to the Jingci Monastery, orders the corpse to remove itself from the street in front of a dumpling store, revives dead snails, and cremates a cricket, which then appears in midair as a youth clad in green.

Jixiang's biography of Jigong is based on the novels on this eccentric saint. All the miracles he attributes to Jigong appear either in the sixteenth-century *Recorded Sayings* or in the seventeenth-century *Drunken Puti* and *Jigong's Complete Biography*. In addition, these novels served as a source for other sections of Jixiang's monastic history. Several chapters of the *Jingci History* reproduce literary pieces that celebrate the monastery or literary works by its monkish residents. These chapters include seven pieces attributed to Jigong, all of them borrowed from the *Recorded Sayings*.[122] Jixiang even relied on that novel for biographical information on figures other than Jigong. A character named Dehui figures prominently in the *Recorded Sayings* and its sequels as the abbot of the Jingci Monastery. To the best of my knowledge, he is not mentioned in any Buddhist source of the Song, Yuan, or Ming periods and is therefore most likely the fictional invention of the *Recorded Sayings'* author. Nonetheless, Jixiang, who relied heavily on the *Recorded Sayings*, inserted a biography of Dehui into the chapter on abbots of the *Jingci History*. Thus a fictional character was enshrined in the official history of a Buddhist monastery. Jixiang's biography of Dehui consists of little more than the latter's valedictory poem, which is borrowed verbatim from the *Recorded Sayings*; he acknowledges that "Dehui's origins are unknown."[123]

Jixiang's reliance on the *Recorded Sayings* illustrates the significant role of vernacular fiction in shaping the monastic understanding of Jigong. The bulk of the *Recorded Sayings*, Text B, derives from oral literature, and it mirrors popular beliefs regarding the eccentric miracle worker. Nonetheless, this novel's version of Jigong's life was sanctioned by the monastic establishment and incorporated, at least in part, into monastic histories. The influence of popular fiction on the monastic attitude toward the crazy saint is likewise revealed in a full-length hagiography written by a member of the clergy that derives from a novel. Entitled *Crazy Ji's Original Biography* (*Jidian benzhuan*), this seventeenth-century hagiography is now lost. However, an extant preface by the Lingyin Monastery monk Jiexian (fl. 1667) makes it clear that this hagiography was extracted from a novel, most likely the *Recorded Sayings*:

> Crazy Ji lived in Hangzhou. There is a work of fiction (*xiaoshuo*) regarding his life there. Its language is somewhat unpolished, but its contents are entirely true. My disciple Jutang[124] deleted its vulgar passages and compiled an *Original Biography* (*Benzhuan*), which is distributed to clergymen and laymen alike. It is also a charming new story of the Lingyin and Jingci monasteries.[125]

The monastic reliance on popular fiction culminated with the Buddhist canonization of novels on Jigong. During the first decade of the twentieth century, the *Recorded Sayings* was incorporated into *The Great Japanese Continuation of the Canon*. Thus, a novel that derived, in large part, from oral lore became part of canonical Buddhist literature. Shortly thereafter, in the early 1930s, the Shanghai Buddhist Studies Publishing Company issued its own edition of the seventeenth-century *Drunken Puti*. This development took place after the publication of the best-selling *Storyteller's Jigong*, which the Buddhist Studies preface rejects as inaccurate. By contrast, the preface presents the long-forgotten *Drunken Puti* as a "truthful" account of Jigong's life. Thus, against the background of a new novel's success, an old work of fiction is being presented as a reliable historical source. Upholding the Buddhist dietary rules, this preface warns its readers lest they try to imitate the novel's eccentric protagonist. Much like Unity Sect informants, the preface emphasizes that what an all-powerful saint may do, ordinary people should not do. After all, the preface reminds its readers:

> After he eats dead animals' [flesh], Jigong is capable of vomiting them alive. But if you [the reader] eat dead animals, you are still incapable of vomiting them in their original form.[126] How could you possibly imitate Jigong and eat meat? He [Jigong] drinks wine and is then able to cover Buddhist statues with gold,[127] and he caused innumerable logs of wood to emerge from a well. You drink wine, and still the water in the well will not move. How could you imitate him?[128]

Thus, vernacular fiction gradually shaped the monastic perception of Jigong. In the first stage, passages from sixteenth- and seventeenth-century novels were incorporated into the histories of the Lingyin and Jingci monasteries. In the second stage, a Buddhist hagiography of Jigong was extracted from one of these novels, and, in the third stage, the novels *Recorded Sayings* and *Drunken Puti* themselves were canonized by the Buddhist establishment. Here it need be noted, however, that the earliest of these novels, the *Recorded Sayings*, may have itself been influenced by Buddhist sources. Even though the bulk of this novel (Text B) derives from oral literature and mirrors the popular perception of Jigong, Text A portrays Jigong as an enlightened monk, rather than a miracle worker, and it may reflect a monastic conception of him. It is also possible, though unlikely, that some of the literary pieces attributed to Jigong in this novel derive from monastic sources. We know that the historical Daoji was a gifted writer, and at least one poem of his is preserved in a collection dating from 1302.[129] According to Lang Ying, one of Daoji's fund-raising petitions was preserved in the Dafo Monastery, and the *History of the Lingyin Monastery* attributes to this eccentric monk a poem and a petition that are not included in any of the novels about him.[130] It is therefore conceivable that some of the literary pieces ascribed to Daoji in the *Recorded Sayings*, primarily fund-raising petitions, derive from monastic sources, which attributed them to him.[131]

Buddhist iconography, like Buddhist literature, indicates a gradual acceptance of the eccentric saint Jigong by the monastic establishment. By the sixteenth century at the latest, a statue of Jigong had been placed in the Five Hundred Arhat Hall of the Jingci Monastery,[132] and in Qing times his image became a common feature of such halls throughout China (see Fig. 5). Five hundred arhat halls are stately structures found only in rich monasteries, such as the Temple of the Azure Clouds near Beijing, the monastic complex at the Summer Palace in Chengde, and the Temple of Precious Light in Chengdu, Sichuan.[133] They contain statues of the 500 Mahāyāna saints, the arhats, usually arrayed in rows along the walls, and they are major tourist attractions. The placement of Jigong's statue in these halls indicates a certain ambivalence in the attitude of the monastic establishment toward him. In these halls he is not one of the 500 arhats, and his image is not placed among theirs. Rather, his statue is placed in one of the hall's cross-aisles or even on one of the beams that support the ceiling.[134] Crouching there, this smiling saint looks like one of those gargoyles whose grotesque figures lurk above the somber ambience of medieval cathedrals. Thus set apart from the crowd of saints, Jigong is much more visible than they are. The average visitor cannot distinguish the arhats, whose pseudo-Sanskrit names mean nothing to most Chinese. However, he does recognize the lovable Jigong, who, according to popular lore, lost his seat in the hall because he arrived late.[135]

In most arhat halls, Jigong is venerated side by side with another latecomer to the Chinese Buddhist pantheon—the "mad monk" (*feng heshang* or *fengseng*) of the Yue Fei saga (see Fig. 6).[136] As noted above, this eccentric saint (who has no personal name) shares significant similarities with Jigong, and his legend exerted a significant influence on the latter's portrayal in the *Storyteller's Jigong*. Unlike Jigong, however, the mad monk of the Yue Fei story cycle is not a historical figure, and in this case the clergy admitted into its gallery of saints a figure invented by storytellers and playwrights. In the arhat halls, where the two eccentrics are venerated side by side, one is referred to as the Mad Monk (*fengseng*), the other by his nickname Crazy Monk (*dianseng*).

In recent years, the Jigong cult at the Lingyin and Jingci monasteries in Hangzhou has been revived. Together with the Jigong temple on Hupao Hill—a popular temple not managed by the Buddhist clergy—the two monasteries are active sites of pilgrimage for Jigong devotees. At the Jingci Monastery, pilgrims are shown the well from which the logs miraculously emerged (see Fig. 2), and they make offerings to the crazy saint in front of a new statue of his (dated 1985). They are also asked to donate money for the construction of a large Jigong Hall. At the Lingyin Monastery, pilgrims pay homage to an 1896 painting of Jigong, which is surrounded by stone-carved images of the eighteen—rather than the 500—arhats. In both temples, peddlers sell to pilgrims and tourists statues of the crazy saint, amulets bearing his name, and a large variety of toys and mementos shaped in his image.[137]

The hustle and bustle of lay devotees making offerings to Jigong at a Buddhist temple reveals that the distinction between Jigong's popular and monastic cults is not clear-cut. Spirit-mediums possessed by Jigong certainly differ from learned monks, but these two groups of religious specialists often serve the same lay clientele, and the growing significance of Jigong within the monastic religion certainly enhanced his popular cult. In north China, for example, the earliest evidence of Jigong's popular cult dates from the Boxer Uprising in 1900. But a hundred years before that date, statues of the eccentric saint could be found in two Buddhist monasteries there—the Temple of the Azure Clouds in Beijing, and the monastic complex in the Summer Palace in Chengde.[138] These visual images probably helped transmit knowledge of Jigong to the Beijing region. Thus, in the history of the Jigong cult, the interaction between Buddhism and the popular religion has not been one-sided. To borrow a term from Paul Katz's study of the god Wen Qiong, Buddhist and popular perceptions of Jigong mutually "reverberate."[139] Once it appropriated the crazy saint, the monastic community helped spread his cult, and shape his image.

The interaction between the laity's piety and monastic beliefs, between popular literature and canonical scripture, that characterizes Jigong's posthumous career is not unique. Other eccentric miracle workers who while alive occupied the fringes of the monastic community were posthumously admitted into this community's gallery of saints. As we have seen in Chapter 2, the monastic establishment was willing to accept the laity's verdict regarding their sanctity. Indeed, at least in one instance, the Buddhist establishment admitted into its pantheon of divinities a mad monk who was not even a historical figure. This was the eccentric protagonist of the Yue Fei saga, who, as far as we know, was the product of storytellers' and playwrights' imagination.

One eccentric miracle worker who rose particularly high in the Buddhist pantheon of divinities is the Cloth-Bag Monk (Budai heshang). This obese and jolly wonder worker, who was never ordained as a Buddhist monk, enjoyed posthumous veneration by the laity, who regarded him as an incarnation of the Buddha Maitreya. The Buddhist establishment eventually accepted this verdict, and thus bestowed upon the Cloth-Bag Monk an elevated position in its supernatural hierarchy. Indeed the obese image of this eccentric miracle worker has become a permanent feature of Buddhist monasteries throughout China. An indication of his elevated position in the Buddhist pantheon is that Cloth-Bag's images in Buddhist monasteries are usually guarded by divine attendants. Statues of the jolly Cloth-Bag are surrounded by the fearful images of the Heavenly Kings of the Four Quarters (Si tianwang; Sanskrit: Caturmahārājas).[140]

Conclusion

Over the course of the twentieth century, the Jigong cult underwent, simultaneously, processes of dissemination and diversification. The veneration of the crazy god spread through such geographically distinct regions as the north China plains, Taiwan, and Malaysia. The cult proliferated among diverse social groups, including possessed anti-Christian rebels in north China, socially marginal gamblers in Taiwan, and the Chinese business elite in Malaysia. The cult took a diversity of forms: temple worship, spirit-possession, spirit-writing, and spirit-painting, and it was adopted by diverse religious groups ranging from the Unity Sect to the Buddhist monastic establishment (which, as early as the sixteenth century, had incorporated Crazy Ji into its gallery of saints). This geographic, social, and religious diversity is related to a multivocality of meaning. Different congregations of believers variously interpret the crazy god's image according to their own ideological agendas. Thus, whereas peasant rebels in north China and socially marginal outlaws in Malaysia amplify the eccentric god's rebellious traits, authors of morality books transform this jolly deity into the mouthpiece for a conservative and a puritanical ethos. In certain localities Jigong's name has been invoked simultaneously by those transgressing accepted norms and by those struggling to preserve them. Indeed, the crazy god has served as a rallying symbol for competing social groups and radically different ideologies.

Historians and anthropologists alike have been intrigued by the question of the carnival's social significance: Does the upside-down world of the carnival prompt a real questioning of the existing order? Or, on the contrary, by allowing society to let off steam, does it strengthen prevailing norms and hierarchies? If the eccentric god Jigong is considered representative of a carnivalesque dimension in Chinese religion, then, in China, these possibilities are not mutually exclusive. On the one hand, the rebellious god has served as a mouthpiece for the most conservative ideologies; on the other hand, given the right historical circumstances, his divine example could be used by those trying to change the existing order. Thus, the Boxers in north China, gamblers in Taiwan, and members of the black societies in Malaysia have perceived the potential for resistance embodied in Jigong's image, and they have utilized it equally to justify their rebellious or socially marginal activities.

From another, theological, perspective, the diverse modes of behavior followed by Jigong devotees throw an interesting light on the question of *imitatio dei* (the imitation of god). Whereas some devotees do follow the example of the eccentric god, and behave as befitting him, others do not. At least some believers, then, perceive a sharp dichotomy between what is permissible to them and what is allowed their object of worship. These believers remain somber and reverential throughout séances, in which their object of worship, embodied in the person of the possessed medium, behaves outrageously. Evidently, some forms of craziness are permissible to the gods alone.

CONCLUSION

The God's Laughter

Chinese religion has no name because it does not exist as an independent entity. The body of religious beliefs and practices we now call Chinese religion, or Chinese popular religion, is inseparable from the culture that has served as the vehicle for its transmission. The Chinese laity learns about the gods not by reciting canonical scriptures but, in most cases, by reading vernacular fiction, listening to storytellers, and watching plays. The interplay of these three media—written fiction, oral fiction, and drama—has been the primary mechanism that spread the cults of the gods, and shaped their images in late imperial and modern times. Written fiction, which was expressed in a more or less standardized vernacular, crossed regional and linguistic boundaries and served as a source for regional forms of oral literature and drama. The latter, performed in regional dialects, reached every segment of society in every locality. The history of the Jigong cult exemplifies the intimate relation between the evolution of a deity's veneration and the growth of fiction on him or her. In any particular locality, this crazy god became the object of a religious cult following the emergence of regional lore on him, which itself derived from novels. Thus Jigong first came to be venerated in north China following the emergence of oral narratives on him there (which were based, in part, on novels written in Hangzhou), and he became the object of a nationwide cult following the publication of the *Storyteller's Jigong*, which had an enormous impact on the growth of oral and written fiction, as well as drama, on him throughout China.

To argue that vernacular fiction has played an important role in the transmission of cults and the shaping of images of the gods is not to say that all novels portray all deities in the same light. Jigong's image varies significantly from one novel to another, reflecting the tastes and beliefs of individual authors, the evolution of this god's cult, and even the development of the vernacular genre itself. For instance, the *Recorded Sayings* was pieced together from two different texts, which mirror different types of belief in the crazy god, and the novelist Wang Mengji attempted to cleanse Crazy Ji of the antinomian traits attributed to him in all other works of fiction. The multivocality of the eccentric god's image grows even more resonant when we take into account his portrayal in genres other than fiction. Jigong's iconography followed its own visual logic to shape the god's image in ways unforeseen by the novels on him. Thus, for example, the gourd, which is an indispensable element of Jigong's iconography, is not even mentioned in the literature celebrating him. On the contrary, in some novels it serves as his archenemies' magic weapon.

The diversity in Jigong's fictional representations has been echoed by the multifarious uses to which his cult has been put. The rebellious saint's potential for cultural and political resistance has been perceived by the Boxers in north China, gamblers in Taiwan, and members of secret societies in Malaysia, all of whom have chosen him as a tutelary deity. At the same time, a yearning for the restoration of traditional values in Taiwan and Malaysia alike has led to the crazy god's revealing, through spirit-writing techniques, a large body of ethical literature, which condemns the activities of the groups mentioned above. Sectarian religions, as well as the Buddhist establishment, have added further hues to the multicolored picture of Jigong's cult. Members of the Unity Sect and the Buddhist clergy alike have attempted to transform the crazy deity's image so that it adheres to their own dietary rules. Sometimes they argue that fictional accounts of Jigong's life are inaccurate, challenging, for example, his fictional image as a guzzler of wine. Or they explain away his carnivorous tendencies, contending that whatever animals Jigong eats, he then vomits out alive.

One element, however, is common to all representations of Jigong, in fiction and religious practice alike—his laughter. Be it a novel on Jigong, or a spirit-written morality book attributed to him, an actor playing the eccentric god's role on the stage, or a medium possessed by him—the eccentric god always laughs. Spirit-written texts attributed to Crazy Ji are punctuated with the sound of his laughter, indicating that it was indeed the playful god who possessed the brush, and visual representations—book illustrations, children's comic strips, and statues alike—always depict a smiling Jigong. But why does Jigong laugh? Throughout this book, I have examined Jigong's personality from the perspective of its impact on society. Defiant deities such as Jigong, I have suggested, offer members of society liberation and relief (albeit in most cases temporary) from accepted social and cultural norms, and given the right historical circumstances, they may also provide the necessary symbolic resources for rebellion. But from a theological perspective, from the perspective of the religious sentiments of the individual worshipper, what does it mean that this god laughs? What is the believer's response to the god's humor?

Jigong is of course not the only humorous Chinese god. Chinese iconography and myth alike feature several deities who delight in laughter. The messianic Buddha of the future, Maitreya, whose obese image welcomes visitors to Chinese Buddhist monasteries, is always grinning, and in one of the most dramatic scenes of the *Journey to the West*, the Buddha Śākyamuni bursts into laughter: Monkey (Sun Wukong) and his fellow pilgrims have traveled thousands of miles from China to the Western Paradise to obtain the Buddhist scriptures. On their way back to China, the pilgrims discover, to their horror, that the scriptures given them by the Buddha's attendants Ānanda and Kāśyapa are blank, whereupon they rush back to paradise and complain angrily to the Buddha. It turns out that Ānanda and Kāśyapa had wanted a bribe for the scriptures; this demand had outraged the pilgrims—after all they had journeyed to paradise on the express order of the Buddha Śākyamuni himself to bring the Buddhist scriptures to China. Their refusal to pay had led the greedy attendants to cheat them. The Buddha finds this incident hilarious, and suppressing a chuckle, he explains to the furious pilgrims that "these blank texts are actually true, wordless scriptures, and they are just as good as those with words. However, those creatures in your Land of the East [China] are so foolish and unenlightened that I have no choice but to impart to you now the texts with words."[1] Thereupon he orders his naughty attendants to hand a copy of the written scriptures to the pilgrims.

Do the pilgrims find the Buddha's laughter amusing, or infuriating? Does his laughter liberate the pilgrims and help them realize that empty scriptures are as true as written ones? Or does Śākyamuni's laughter mock the hardships that the pilgrims have endured while fulfilling the Buddha's order that they bring the canon to China? On the allegorical level, the Buddha's amused response to the pilgrims' complaints is indeed liberating. It suggests to the pilgrims, as well as the readers, that the journey to enlightenment should be perceived as an internal quest of the mind rather than an external journey after a body of scriptures. But as Andrew Plaks has pointed out, in the *Journey to the West*, "the difficulty of reconciling a total vision of existence *sub specie aeternitatis* with the time-bound moral sensitivity of the mimetic artist often produces a compromise that is uneasy, problematical, or even tragic in tone."[2] In other words, the Buddha's laughter may be philosophically enlightening, but it is doubtful that the pilgrims find it amusing. The pilgrims, who, in this instance, stand for the human person in his encounter with the divine, do not necessarily join the god in laughing.

Another example is perhaps more pertinent to Jigong's laughter. It comes not from the realm of myth but from that of ritual. It concerns a form of divination so widespread in China that it is almost inseparable from the act of worship itself. In most Chinese temples, questions to the gods are posed in the following manner: the believer faces the gods' statues and ponders a question, for which he or she is beseeching from the gods a "yes" or "no" answer. The questioner holds two wooden divination blocks in the shape of a crescent moon, which are usually known in Chinese as *bei* or *jiao*. One side of each block is flat; the other is rounded. When dropped on the ground, the blocks may land in one of three combinations: one block rounded side up, the other flat side up (which is taken as a positive answer); both rounded side up (a negative answer); and both boards flat side up. This last position is known as the "laughing blocks" (*xiaobei*), and most informants explain that the gods are amused by the question.[3] Why is it that the gods find a question funny, and what is perhaps more significant, what impact does their amused response have on the oracle-seeker?

Of course, this question cannot be answered with certainty, because responses to the gods' laughter vary. But it is my subjective impression that many find the gods' amused response soothing. The gods' laughter relieves the anxiety that prompted the question in the first place. In this respect, the gods' amusement may resemble that of a parent who finds some of his or her child's concerns funny. Rather than mocking him, the parent's laughter may assuage the child's worries and suggest that they will disappear naturally. To the person who consults the gods, like the child who confides in an adult, an amused response may indicate that the question itself is not significant or that either a yes or a no answer would prove equally satisfactory. If this interpretation is correct and if it applies to Jigong, then to those who read novels on him, watch him on stage, or worship him in temples, the crazy god's laughter is soothing.

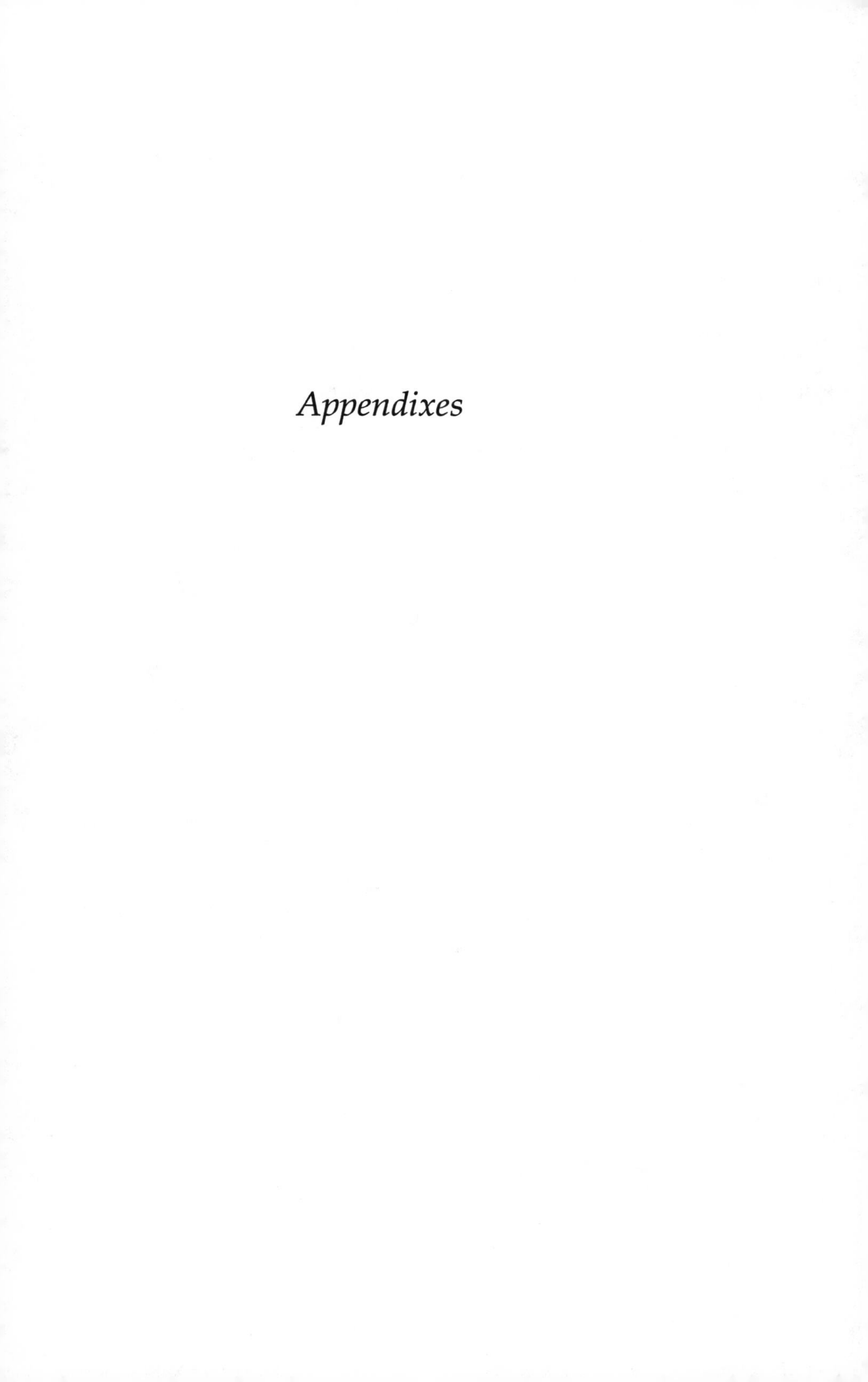

Appendixes

APPENDIX A

Extant Written, and Transcribed Oral, Fiction on Jigong

1569 *Qiantang hu yin Jidian Chanshi yulu* 錢塘湖隱濟顛禪師語錄 (The recorded sayings of the recluse from Qiantang Lake, the Chan master Crazy Ji). Earliest edition, dated 1569, at the Naikaku bunko Library. It gives the author as Shen Mengpan 沈孟柈 of Renhe 仁和 (in Hangzhou prefecture). The publisher is given as Sixiang gaozhai 四香高齋 (Lofty studio of four fragrances). Photographic reprint in *Guben xiaoshuo congkan,* series no. 8, vol. 1, pp. 1–140. Punctuated edition, which follows the 1569 edition, in ZZ, section 2, case no. 26, *ce* 1, pp. 1a-23b.

The 1569 edition was followed by two late Ming editions. One forms part of Feng Menglong's 馮夢龍 (1574–1646) tripartite collection *Sanjiao ounian* 三教偶拈 (Chance selection on the three doctrines) (copy at the Sōkōdō collection of the Tōyō bunka kenkyūjo, Tokyo University; photographic reprint in *Guben xiaoshuo congkan,* series no. 4, vol. 5.) Two Qing editions of this novel also survive.

The *Recorded Sayings* was probably pieced together from two different texts. The first (Text A) is written in a relatively elevated vernacular, and it draws heavily upon Buddhist lore. It portrays Jigong as an enlightened Chan master, and it probably represents a monastic understanding of this saint. The second (Text B), written in a simple vernacular and interspersed with evidence of the Wu dialect, probably derives from oral literature. It portrays Jigong as an incarnate deity endowed with salvational powers. This understanding of Jigong was probably prevalent among the sixteenth-century Hangzhou laity.

1668 — *Jigong quanzhuan* 濟公全傳 (Jigong's complete biography), preface 1668 (copies at the Dalian Municipal Library and the Beijing Library [missing the title page and preface]; fragmentary copy at the Chinese Academy of Social Sciences).

The novel was authored by Wang Mengji 王夢吉, who is probably also the author of *Doupeng xianhua* 豆棚閒話 (Idle talk under the bean arbor), a seventeenth-century collection of short stories. Wang Mengji's source was the *Recorded Sayings,* but he substantially transformed and enlarged it. His sophisticated novel, which is accompanied by a running commentary, represents a sustained effort to mitigate Jigong's antinomian behavior and present him as a Buddhist teacher and moral exemplar. Nonetheless, the narrator also censures the Buddhist establishment of his time severely. Thus *Jigong's Complete Biography* mirrors the Buddhist devotionalism of the laity, not the monastic community.

Before 1673 — *Zui puti* 醉菩提 (Drunken puti). Dating based on its relation to the collection *Xihu jiahua* 西湖佳話 (Charming stories of West Lake; 1673), which derives from it. Earliest reference to the novel (dated 1707) can be found in a Japanese list of imported books, *Hakusai shomoku* 舶載書目. Earliest extant edition (dated 1721) at the Beijing Library. Reference here is to the photographic reprint of the Baoren tang 寶仁堂 edition, in vol. 73 of *Guben xiaoshuo jicheng. Drunken Puti* had been the most popular novel on Jigong until its eclipse in the early twentieth century by the *Storyteller's Jigong*. At least twenty late Qing editions of this novel survive. In recent years several editions of *Drunken*

Puti have been distributed in Taiwanese temples as edifying literature. One of these (dated 1983) is even accompanied by a commentary, attributed to Jigong himself, written by the automatic spirit-writing technique of the planchette (see Appendix D).

The earliest extant edition, like most later ones, attributes the novel to Tianhua Zang Zhuren 天花藏主人 (Master of the Heavenly Flower Repository), known to us as a prolific author of scholar and beauty romances. However, the earliest written reference to the novel, in the *Hakusai shomoku*, gives the author as Molang Zi 墨浪子 (Ink-Crazy Master) and attributes to Tianhua Zang Zhuren the novel's preface only. Three later editions likewise attribute the novel to Molang Zi. The available information does not permit us to conclude whether Tianhua Zang Zhuren or Molang Zi authored the novel. It is even possible that both pseudonyms refer to the same person.

The *Drunken Puti* follows the *Recorded Sayings* story line closely. However, it embellishes it with lively narrative detail.

1673 "Nanping zuiji" 南屏醉跡 (Drunken traces at Nanping). A short story in the collection *Xihu jiahua* 西湖佳話 (Charming stories of West Lake) (photographic reprint of the 1673 edition in vol. 37 of *Guben xiaoshuo jicheng*).

Charming Stories of West Lake celebrates the religious and cultural lore of West Lake in the outskirts of Hangzhou. Its author is given, like the *Drunken Puti*'s author in several editions, as Molang Zi 墨浪子.

The story "Drunken Traces at Nanping" was collated from several episodes in the *Drunken Puti*, which must therefore have been written before 1673.

1791 "Nanping shan Daoji zhuang feng" 南屏山道濟裝瘋 (Daoji feigns madness at Nanping Mountain). A short story in chapter nine of Chen Shuji's 陳樹基 collection *Xihu shiyi* 西湖拾遺 (Anecdotes of West Lake) (photographic reprint of the 1791 edition in *Guben xiaoshuo jicheng*).

"Daoji Feigns Madness" does not represent a new development in the fiction on Jigong, since it was copied almost verbatim from the *Xihu jiahua* story "Drunken Traces at Nanping."

Before 1859 *Jigong zhuan* 濟公傳 (hereafter *Jigong Drum-Song*). Two manuscripts, one complete, the other fragmentary, of one and the same prosimetric drum-song (*shuochang guci* 說唱鼓詞) narrative on Jigong survive. The original titles appearing on these manuscripts are *Jigong zhuan* and *Jigong an* 案. The complete manuscript, in 110 volumes, belongs to the Chewang Fu 車王府 collection (original at the Shoudu tushuguan, Beijing; photographic edition, cases 269–79). The fragmentary manuscript, in 20 volumes, is in the Academia Sinica "popular performance literature" (*suqu* 俗曲) collection (microfilm edition, reel 83).

Prosimetric drum-song is a form of oral literature popular in north China from the mid- through the late Qing. The *Jigong Drum-Song* is a more or less accurate transcription of an oral prosimetric drum-song. Manuscript transcriptions of oral literature were either sold, or rented out, to interested readers in nineteenth-century Beijing. The *Jigong Drum-Song*'s complete manuscript bears the seal of the shop that sold it. The fragmentary manuscript was put together from three different manuscripts, which carry the seals of three different rental shops. A reader's comment, dated 1859, on one of the rented manuscripts shows that the *Jigong Drum-Song* must have been transcribed before that date.

The rich Beijing patois in which the *Jigong Drum-Song* is written leaves no doubt that not only was this text rented out in Beijing (as evinced by the shops' seals) but the oral narrative it represents was originally performed there as well. Thus, the *Jigong Drum-Song* attests to the growth of indigenous Jigong lore in Beijing. However, this lore was not unrelated to the earlier Hangzhou narrative tradition regarding Jigong. Several episodes in the *Jigong Drum-Song* were borrowed from the novel *Drunken Puti*, which itself derived from the Hangzhou oral literature recorded in the *Recorded Sayings*.

1898–1900 *Pingyan Jigong zhuan* 評演濟公傳 (The storyteller's life of Jigong; abbreviated in this book as *Storyteller's Jigong*). This 240-chapter novel was originally published in two parts of 120 chapters each. The earliest known edition of the first dates from 1898; of the second from 1900. Both these editions are now lost, but their prefaces, as appended to later editions of the novel, survive. (See, for example, the 1911 editions of both sequels by the Shanghai publisher Cui Wen Zhai 萃文齋; copy in the Zhejiang Library.) The earliest extant edition of the entire novel, by the Jian Qing zhai 簡青齋 publishing house, dates from 1906 (copy at the Zhejiang Library). Reference here is to the 1991 Zhejiang guji edition, entitled, like most recent editions of this novel, *Jigong zhuan*.

The prefaces to the now lost 1898 and 1900 editions attribute the novel's publication to the Tianjin publishing house Zhuzi shanfang 煮字山房 and ascribe its authorship to Guo Xiaoting 郭小亭. The latter is probably Guo Guangrui 郭廣瑞 (*zi* given as Xiaoting 筱亭 or 曉亭), author of the slightly earlier novel *Yongqing shengping* 永慶昇平 (Everlasting blessings and peace; 1892).

The Storyteller's Jigong represents a watershed in the development of fiction on this saint. This is the first novel on Jigong that was not written in Zhejiang and did not derive, directly or indirectly, from Hangzhou oral literature. Instead the *Storyteller's Jigong* is a more or less accurate rendition of oral narratives in the *pingshu* 評書 genre, which were performed in Beijing during the late nineteenth century. These *pingshu* narratives derived for their part from the *guci* oral narratives represented in the *Jigong Drum-Song*, and they may have been influenced also by Beijing opera. (However, the Beijing *guci* narratives that served as the *Storyteller's Jigong*'s ultimate source are related to an earlier novel on Jigong, the *Drunken Puti*.)

The *Storyteller's Jigong* has had an enormous impact on the development of Jigong's lore and cult during the twentieth century. It inspired an avalanche of sequels and served as a source for an enormous body of dramatic adaptations, ranging from Taiwanese puppet theater and Cantonese opera to television serials and movies.

1900–1926 Thirty-eight sequels to the *Storyteller's Jigong*, totaling 1,515 chapters, are published; see Appendix B.

Ca. 1920s(?) *Huitu guci Jigong quanzhuan* 繪圖鼓詞濟公全傳 (The complete, illustrated *guci* version of Jigong's life); lithographic edition by the Shanghai publisher Jinzhang tushu 錦章圖書 (copy in the Academia Sinica collection; photocopy in the Harvard-Yenching Library). Preliminary comparison suggests that this drum-song narrative is not directly related to either the *Storyteller's Jigong* or the *Jigong Drum-Song*. Future research might possibly determine whether *The Complete Guci Version* is a transcription of an oral drum-song or only simulates the latter's form and was originally written for a reading audience.

1987 *Jigong hou zhuan* 濟公后傳 (Biography of Jigong, continued) (Beijing: Zhongguo quyi, 1987); based on the *pingshu* oral narratives of the contemporary storytellers Yang Zhimin 楊志民 and his disciple Guo Tianen 郭天恩.

1987 *Jigong hou zhuan xu* 續 (Sequel to the *Biography of Jigong, Continued*) (Beijing: Zhongguo quyi, 1987); based on the *pingshu* oral narratives of the contemporary storytellers Yang Zhimin and his disciple Guo Tianen.

1987 *Jigong waizhuan* 濟公外傳 (The untold biography of Jigong), 2 vols. (Harbin: Beifang wenyi, 1987). Stories on Jigong compiled by Jiang Sha 江沙 et al.

APPENDIX B

The Thirty-eight Sequels to the "Storyteller's Jigong"

Thirty-eight sequels to Guo Xiaoting's *Storyteller's Jigong* were published between 1905 and 1926. With three exceptions, each sequel is 40 chapters long (the exceptions have 35, 39, or 41 chapters). The sequels were published in lithographic editions by several different, mostly Shanghai, publishers, who vied with each other and pirated each other's works.

Even though only 38 sequels were published, their titles create the misimpression that there are 40 sequels. The *Storyteller's Jigong* itself was originally published in two parts, the second of which is titled in some editions *Jigong Stories: Second Collection* (*Jigong zhuan erji* 濟公傳二集). The first sequel to the novel was therefore titled *Jigong Stories: Third Collection* (*Jigong zhuan sanji*). The editors of the second sequel to the novel entitled their sequel *The Fourth Sequel to Jigong Stories* (*Sixu* 四續 *Jigong zhuan*). The third sequel was then titled *Fifth Sequel to Jigong Stories*, and so on. In the following bibliographical notes, I refer to the sequels by their actual sequence rather than by their current title. Thus, for example, by "thirty-eighth sequel," I am referring to the novel titled the *Fortieth Sequel to Jigong Stories* (*Sishixu* 四十續 *Jigong zhuan*).

Complete Sets of the Sequels

The Republican period Shanghai publisher Jiaojing shanfang 校經山房 issued at least thirty-seven of the thirty-eight sequels in lithographic editions (many of these sequels were published for the first time by this publisher). A complete set, together with the missing sequel, in another publisher's edition, is available at the Hangzhou University Library. A partial set is available at the Zhejiang Library (which is also located in Hangzhou). In 1991 the Hangzhou publisher Zhejiang guji issued a 12-volume set that contains the *Storyteller's Jigong* and all 38 sequels. It is titled *Jigong zhuan xilie xiaoshuo* 濟公傳系列小說.

The first nine sequels are also available in a three-volume set published in 1991 as part of the series *Zhongguo shenguai xiaoshuo daxi* 中國神怪小說大系 (Jilin: Jilin wenshi chubanshe). The titles of the three volumes are (1) *Wanshi qiguan* 頑世奇觀 (Miraculous sights of playing in the world); (2) *Diantuo mishi* 顛陀迷史 (The crazy ascetic's bewitching history); and (3) *Mo ying xian zong* 魔影仙蹤 (Ghosts' shadows, immortals' traces).

Dating the Sequels

The following is a list of sequels of which an early dated edition survives, or for which we have information on such an edition. These dates of the known editions enable us to infer the publication dates of the other sequels as well. For example, the twelfth sequel must have been published either in late 1910, or in early 1911, judging by the publication dates of the eleventh and thirteenth sequels.

Sequel no.	*Publication date*
1	There existed a 1905 edition of the *Storyteller's Jigong*, to which this sequel was appended, creating a 280-chapter work. See *Shinmatsu Minsho shōsetsu mokuroku* 清末民初小說目錄 item no. J038 (the date given for item J039, in reality, applies to the first sequels only), and *Zhongguo tongsu xiaoshuo zongmu tiyao*, p. 808.
2	Author Ge Xiaonong's 葛嘯儂 preface, dated 1908, appended to an edition by the Shanghai publisher Jiaojing shanfang (copy at the Tianjin Municipal Library).
3	1908 edition by the Shanghai publisher Puxin shuju 普新書局 (copy at the Zhejiang Library).
4	1909 edition by the Shanghai publisher Puxin shuju (copy at the Zhejiang Library).

5	Author Keng Yusheng's 坑余生 preface, dated 1909, appended to two later editions of this sequel: the 1913 edition by the Shanghai publisher Zhenhua shuju 振華書局 (copy at the Zhejiang Library), and the 1913 edition by the Shanghai publisher Lianshi shuju 鍊石書局 (copy at the Hangzhou University Library).
9	1910 edition by the Shanghai publisher Jiaojing shanfang (copies at the Zhejiang Library and the Hangzhou University Library).
11	1910 edition by the Shanghai publisher Jiaojing shanfang (copy at the Tianjin Municipal Library).
13	1911 edition by the Shanghai publisher Jiaojing shanfang (copy in the author's possession).
14	1911 edition by the Shanghai publisher Jiaojing shanfang (copy at the Tianjin Municipal Library).
22	1917 edition by the Shanghai publisher Jiaojing shanfang (copies at the Zhejiang Library and the Hangzhou University Library).
31–36	1923 editions of all six sequels by the Shanghai publisher Jiaojing shanfang (copies at the Hangzhou University Library).
37–38	1926 editions of both these sequels by the Shanghai publisher Jiaojing shanfang (copies at the Hangzhou University Library).

APPENDIX C

Extant Pre-Twentieth-Century Plays on Jigong

ca. 1670	*Drunken Puti* (*Zui puti* 醉菩提); *chaunqi* play by Zhang Dafu 張大復. Manuscript edition; photographic reprint in *Guben xiqu congkan sanji* 古本戲曲叢刊三集 (Beijing, 1957). The play is based on the novel *Recorded Sayings* and (probably) the novel *Drunken Puti* as well.
ca. 1770	*Drunken Puti* (*Zui puti* 醉菩提); four scenes of a Kunqu play of this title preserved in an anthology entitled *Zhui baiqiu* 綴白裘 (Piecing together a white fur coat; 1777), which was edited by (pseudonym) Wanhua zhuren 玩花主人 and continued by Qian Peisi 錢沛思. The play is based on the novel *Drunken Puti* and does not derive from Zhang Dafu's play of the same title. Reference here is to the *Zhui baiqiu* edition collated by Wang Xieru 汪協如 (Beijing: Zhonghua shuju, 1955).
(probably) second half of the nineteenth century	The *Zhao Family's Mansion* (*Zhaojia lou* 趙家樓). Beijing Opera play in three extant, and practically identical, manuscripts. Two at the Academia Sinica collection (microfilm edition, reels 205 and 208), and one in the Chewang Fu collection (original at the Beijing University Library; photographic edition, case no. 30, vol. 1). One of the two manuscripts currently in the

Academia Sinica collection (in reel 205) originally belonged to the Chewang Fu collection as well.

The play corresponds to the same episode in the *Jigong Drum-Song* (Chewang Fu MS, vols. 87–88) and in the *Storyteller's Jigong* (chaps. 68–70).

(probably) second half of the nineteenth century	The *Ma Family's Lake* (*Majia hu* 馬家湖). Beijing Opera play. Manuscript belonging to the Chewang Fu collection (original at the Beijing University Library; photographic edition. case no. 24, vol. 4). The play corresponds to the same episode in the *Jigong Drum-Song* (Chewang Fu MS, vols. 83–84) and in the *Storyteller's Jigong* (chaps. 89–101).
1898	*The Dabei Tower* (*Dabei lou* 大悲樓). Beijing Opera play. Manuscript (dated 1898) in the Academia Sinica collection (microfilm edition, reel 209). The play corresponds to, but also differs from, the same episodes in the *Jigong Drum-Song* (Chewang Fu MS, vol. 22) and the *Storyteller's Jigong* (chap. 3).

APPENDIX D

Literature on, and by, Jigong Distributed in Taiwanese Temples

This list includes some of the literature on Jigong distributed in Taiwanese temples during the 1980s. It is not exhaustive, and it does not include the voluminous Unity Sect literature attributed to this deity. Some of the items I collected myself; others I have not seen but they are described in chap. 16 of Zheng Zhiming's *Zhongguo shanshu yu zongjiao*. Another item of which I have not seen the original has been translated by Laurence G. Thompson in his "The Moving Finger Writes." Items in both these categories are marked by an *.

Publication date	*Novels*
1981	*Jidian Chanshi da zhuan* 濟顛禪師大傳 (The great biography of the Chan master Crazy Ji). Taipei: Buddhist Publications. This is a photographic reprint of a *Drunken Puti* edition, published in 1932 by the Shanghai Buddhist Studies Publishing Company. In addition to this novel, it includes also excerpts from the hagiographic collection *Chanhai shizen ji* 禪海十珍集 (Ten treasures from the Chan sea). This book differs from all other items on the list in that it was sold, not distributed.
1981	*Nanping huofo Jigong Chanshi zhuan* 南屏活佛濟公禪師傳 (Biography of the living Buddha from Nan-

	ping, the Chan master Jigong). Author given as Fakong 法空. Taipei: Wanyou shanshu 萬有善書. Written in a simple vernacular, this new biography of Jigong derives from the novel *Drunken Puti.*
1982	*Jidian seng zhuan* 濟顛僧傳 (The biography of the monk Crazy Ji). Taipei: Longyi 隆藝. This is also a photographic reprint of the *Drunken Puti* edition that was published in 1932 by the Shanghai Buddhist Studies Publishing Company.
1983 (rpt. 1986)	*Jigong huofo zhengzhuan* 濟公活佛正傳 (The authoritative biography of the living Buddha Jigong). Taizhong: Shengde tang 聖德堂. This edition of the seventeenth-century novel *Drunken Puti* is accompanied by chapter-by-chapter commentary, attributed to Jigong himself, compiled by the spirit-writing technique. The publisher, Shengde tang, issued also a spirit-writing morality book attributed to Jigong, titled *Shengdao youji* 聖道遊記 (Journey along the saintly road; 1985).

Spirit-Written Morality Books Attributed to Jigong

The "Journey" Books

1978 (and reprints)	*Diyu youji* 地獄遊記 (A journey to purgatory). Taizhong: Shengxian tang 聖賢堂. Principal wielder of the *fuji* writing implement given as Yang Zanru 楊贊儒.
1981 (and reprints)	*Tiantang youji* 天堂遊記 (A journey to paradise). Taizhong: Shengxian tang. Principal wielder of the *fuji* writing implement given as Yang Zanru 楊贊儒.
1981	*Yangjian shan'e youji* 陽間善惡遊記 (A journey to this world's good and bad deeds). Gaoxiong: Lingyin ci shan tang 靈陰慈善堂.(*)
1983	*Renjian youji* 人間遊記 (A journey in the human world). Taizhong: Shengxian tang.(*)
1982	*Yinguo youji* 因果遊記 (A journey following the law of retribution). Gaoxiong: Lingyin ci shan tang.(*)

1982	*Jiuyang guan youji* 九陽關遊記 (A journey to Jiuyang Pass). Taizhong: Chongsheng tang 重生堂.
1983 (and reprints)	*Daoji youji* 道濟遊記 (Daoji's journey). Yuanlin: Lingde tang 靈德堂.
1984	*A-bi diyu youji* 阿鼻地獄遊記 (A journey to Avici Hell). Taizhong: Shengtian gong 聖天宮.(*)
1984	*Jile shijie youji* 極樂世界遊記 (A journey to the paradise world). Taizhong: Shengtian tang 聖天堂.(*)
1985	*Shengdao youji* 聖道遊記 (Journey along the saintly road). Taizhong: Shengde tang.(*)
1985	*Yuanling yuan youji* 原靈園遊記 (A journey to the Yuanling Garden). Taizhong: Chongsheng tang.(*)
1986	*Lianhua foguo youji* 蓮花佛國遊記 (A journey to the Lotus Flower Buddha Land). Taizhong: Chongsheng tang.(*)

Other Spirit-Written Morality Books Attributed to Jigong

1972	*Xiudao zhinan* 修道指南 (Directions for cultivating the Tao). Taizhong: Shengxian tang. Translated in Laurence Thompson, "The Moving Finger Writes." In this early work, Jigong does not occupy center stage and is but one of several deities who descend to possess the brush.(*)
1982	*Chudao lunhui ji* 畜道輪迴記 (Record of animal transmigration). Taizhong: Shengde tang.(*)
1984 (and reprints)	*Sanjiao shengxun* 三教聖訓 (The saintly instructions of the three religions). Jilong: Qiqing tang 啓清堂. In this work Jigong is but one of many deities who descend to possess the brush.
1986 (and reprints)	*Shuizu xiudao ji* 水族修道記 (Record of aquatic animals' cultivation of the Way). Taizhong: Sanhou gong 三候宮.
1988	*Yifeng huasu* 移風化俗 (Changing behavior, transforming norms). Taizhong: Chongsheng tang.

1988 (and reprint) *Xian zhen bao yu* 賢眞寶玉 (The worthies' and perfected ones' precious jade). Pingdong: Xian she chang xian tang 賢社昌賢堂. In this work Jigong is but one of many deities who descend to possess the brush.

Liturgical Texts

1966 *Jigong huofo xingshi zhenjing* 濟公活佛醒世眞經 (The living Buddha Jigong's true scripture for awakening the world). Yilan: Yilan yinshuaju. The text, which was composed by the automatic spirit-writing technique, opens with several invocations followed by a lecture on self-cultivation, attributed to Jigong himself. Despite its early date of publication, this text was distributed by the Jigong temple in the Shilin suburb of Taipei as late as 1986.

1978 *Yusuo zhenjing* 玉瑣眞經 (The true scripture of the jade chain). Published by the Taipei Jigong temple, the Lingyuan si 靈源寺. The text opens with psalms for the offering of water and incense, followed by various invocations for the cleansing of the mouth, mind, and body; for pacifying the earth god; and for purifying the altars of heaven, earth, and the gods. (This appears to be a common sequence in Taiwanese liturgical texts; cf. Jordan and Overmyer, *The Flying Phoenix*, p. 74.) The scripture itself, attributed to Jigong, opens with an autobiography that alludes to episodes narrated in the novel *Drunken Puti*, and is followed by a lecture on self-cultivation and enlightenment.

n.d. *Yusuo baochan* 玉瑣寶懺 (Precious repentance of the jade chain). Like the two preceding texts, the bulk of this scripture is attributed to Jigong himself. It is available in an undated edition, which includes also the preceding *Yusuo zhenjing* and another text, entitled *Mingjue jing* 明覺經 (The luminous perception scripture).

Reference Matter

Abbreviations

Jidian yulu	*Qiantang huyin Jidian chanshi yulu*
SKQS	*Wenyuange siku quanshu*
T.	*Taishō shinshū daizōkyō*
ZZ	*Dai Nihon zokuzōkyō*

Notes

For complete author names, titles, and publication data on works cited here in short form, see the Works Cited, pp. 289–311. For a list of the abbreviations used here, see p. 247.

Preface

1. See Patrick Hanan, *Chinese Vernacular Story*, pp. 12–13.

2. See especially Andrew Plaks, *Four Masterworks of the Ming Novel.*

3. It is possible to emphasize the underlying unity of the Chinese religious experience, the differences between its manifestations in diverse social settings notwithstanding (which is the approach I take here), or to highlight the differences that have existed between diverse classes in their expression of "Chinese culture" or "Chinese religion" without denying underlying similarities. For the latter approach, see, e.g., David Johnson, "Communication, Class, and Consciousness in Late Imperial China."

Introduction

1. For the role of the state in the transmission of the Mazu (Tianhou) cult, see James L. Watson, "Standardizing the Gods: The Promotion of T'ien Hou ('Empress of Heaven') Along the South China Coast, 960–1960." For a survey of recent scholarship on the transmission of deities' cults, see Meir Shahar and Robert Weller, "Introduction: Gods and Society in China," pp. 22–30.

2. Both David Johnson ("The City-God Cults of T'ang and Sung China") and Valerie Hansen (*Changing Gods in Medieval China, 1126–1276*, pp. 164–66) highlight the significance of merchants in the dissemination of deities' cults. Hansen also emphasizes the significance of government officials, see ibid.

Barend Ter-Haar ("The Genesis and Spread of Temple Cults in Fukien," pp. 387–88) notes the significance of migrants.

3. On the significance of drama in the shaping of popular beliefs, see, among other studies, David Johnson, "Actions Speak Louder Than Words: The Cultural Significance of Chinese Ritual Opera"; Piet van der Loon, "Les Origines rituelles du théâtre chinois"; Kristofer Schipper, "The Divine Jester: Some Remarks on the Gods of the Chinese Marionette Theater"; and Barbara E. Ward, "Not Merely Players: Drama, Act and Ritual in Traditional China."

4. See, among other studies, Ann Swann Goodrich, *Peking Paper Gods: A Look at Home Worship*; and Po Sung-nien and David Johnson, *Domesticated Deities and Auspicious Emblems: The Iconography of Everyday Life in Village China*.

5. Chinfa Lien, "Language Adaptation in Taoist Liturgical Texts."

6. Cao Xueqin and Gao E, *Honglou meng* 43.599. I have altered David Hawkes's translation slightly; see Cao Xueqin, *The Story of the Stone*, 2: 357.

7. Paul Ropp (*Dissent in Early Modern China*, p. 53) translates *jiao* in this context as "teaching," which lends this passage a different thrust: as a "teaching," fiction shapes moral values and behavioral patterns, not religious beliefs. However, as Confucianism, Buddhism, and Taoism evince, *jiao* as religion and *jiao* as teaching are not mutually exclusive.

8. Qian Daxin, *Qianyan tang wenji* 17.282.

9. Tao Chengzhang, *Jiaohui yuanliu kao* la.

10. Wu Yong, *Gengzi xishou congtan*, 4: 463.

11. Pu Songling, *Liaozhai zhiyi* 11.1459; trans. from Judith Zeitlin, *Historian of the Strange: Pu Songling and the Chinese Classical Tale*, p. 167.

12. Pu Songling, 11.1462; trans. from Zeitlin, pp. 167–68. I substitute "efficacy" for Zeitlin's "spiritual power."

13. Willem A. Grootaers, "The Hagiography of the Chinese God Chen-Wu"; see also Gary Seaman, *The Journey to the North: An Ethnohistorical Analysis and Annotated Translation of the Chinese Folk Novel "Pei-yu-chi."*

14. See, respectively, Huang Huajie, *Guangong de ren'ge yu shen'ge*, pp. 100–122; Ursula-Angelika Cedzich, "The Cult of the Wu-t'ung/Wu-hsien in History and Fiction: The Religious Roots of the *Journey to the South*"; Glen Dudbridge, *The Legend of Miao-shan*, pp. 51–58; Li Xianzhang, "Yi *Sanjiao soushen daquan* yu *Tianfei niangma zhuan* wei zhongxin lai kaocha Mazu chuanshuo"; Paul Katz, "Enlightened Alchemist or Immoral Immortal? The Growth of Lü Dongbin's Cult in Late Imperial China"; and Danielle Éliasberg, *Le Roman du pourfendeur de démons: traduction annotée et commentaire*, pp. 49–74.

15. Sun Kaidi, *Zhongguo tongsu xiaoshuo shumu*, pp. 187–207.

16. Liu Ts'un-yan (*Buddhist and Taoist Influences on Chinese Novels*, vol. 1, *The Authorship of the "Fengshen yen-i"*) suggested that the *Enfeoffment of the Gods* was written by Lu Xixing, whose dates he established as 1519–78/79. However, Nicholas Koss ("The Relationship of the *Hsi-yu chi* and *Feng-shen*

yan-i") has shown convincingly that the novel must have been written after 1592.

17. For a general survey, see Dudbridge, *Legend of Miao-shan*, pp. 52–54, 60–61.

18. See Richard von Glahn, "The Enchantment of Wealth: The God Wutong in the Social History of Jiangnan."

19. For a comparison of the *Enfeoffment of the Gods*'s protagonists with the deities currently worshipped in Taiwan, see Zeng Qinliang, *Taiwan minjian xinyang yu "Fengshen yanyi" zhi bijiao yanjiu.*

20. Henri Maspero, "The Mythology of Modern China," p. 86.

21. Admittedly, Guangong and Song Jiang displayed supernatural powers following their deaths; the authors note that they responded to worshippers' requests. Throughout the bulk of the narrative, however, they are depicted as humans.

22. Paul Katz highlights the multivocality of Lü Dongbin in his "Enlightened Alchemist or Immoral Immortal?" He also discusses the multivocality of another deity, Wen Qiong, in "Wen Ch'iung: The God of Many Faces." Prasenjit Duara ("Superscribing Symbols: The Myth of Guandi, Chinese God of War") shows how the state tried to reform the often rebellious popular image of Guangong. See also the survey of relevant studies in Shahar and Weller, "Introduction," pp. 15–16.

23. Cedzich; see also von Glahn.

24. On deities and tensions within the family, see Steven Sangren, "Female Gender in Chinese Religious Symbols: Kuan Yin, Ma Tsu, and the 'Eternal Mother' "; see also his "Myths, Gods, and Family Relations."

25. Katz ("Enlightened Alchemist or Immoral Immortal?") contrasts the humorous and irreverent depictions of the immortal Lü Dongbin in works of fiction to the somber portrayals of this saint in the *Daoist Canon*.

26. Hanan, *Chinese Vernacular Story*, pp. 12–13.

27. See the essays in Meir Shahar and Robert Weller, eds., *Unruly Gods: Divinity and Society in China.*

28. Mikhail Bakhtin, *Rabelais and His World*, pp. 4, 11.

29. Emmanuel Le Roy Ladurie, *Carnival in Romans*; see also Peter Burke, *Popular Culture in Early Modern Europe*, pp. 199–204.

30. Walter Burkert, *Greek Religion*, p. 4.

31. See Philip Lutgendorf, *The Life of a Text: Performing the Rāmcaritmānas of Tulsidas.*

32. C. K. Yang, *Religion in Chinese Society*, pp. 294–98.

Chapter 1

1. *Beixian wenji*; Jujian's collected writings also include an anthology of poems entitled *Beixian shiji*. A combined edition of his *wenji* and *shiji*, dated 1374, is preserved in the Naikaku bunko in Tokyo; Daoji's biography is in *ce*

7, *juan* 10. The *Beixian wenji* only is also included in the *SKQS*, where it is entitled *Beixian ji*; Daoji's biography can be found in 1183: 159–60. Jujian's biography of Daoji is also included in ZZ, section 2, case no. 26, *ce* 1, 23a–b, where it is appended to the *Jidian yulu*. Sun Kaidi was the first modern scholar to discover Daoji's biography in the *Beixian wenji*; see his *Riben Dongjing Dalian tushuguan suojian Zhongguo xiaoshuo shumu*, p. 131. I know of no other Song period references to Daoji. The "Recorded Sayings" of the Song monk Puyan (1156–1226) include a poem about Daoji, which Sawada Mizuho believed to throw light on the historical figure. Since, however, Puyan's "Recorded Sayings" were compiled as late as 1694 (in Japan), I think the poem cannot be taken as authentic; see *Yun'an Puyan Chanshi yulu*, 327a–b; and Sawada Mizuho, "Saiten sui bodai ni tsuite," p. 185. On the historical Daoji, as well as the early evolution of his fictional character, see also Vincent Durand-Dastès, "Le Bouddha ivre du Lac de L'ouest: Les premières étapes de la légende du bonze Ji-le-Fou (Ji Gong) XIIème –XVIIIème siecle. Choix de textes présentés, traduits et annotés." For some of the relevant sources for the study of Daoji's human and posthumous career, see also Lai Yonghai, *Jigong heshang*. As far as the historical Daoji is concerned, however, Lai's is an uncritical study that relies heavily on novels on Daoji.

2. On Jujian, see Daguan, ed., *Beixian Jujian Chanshi yulu* 64b–84b; Juding (?–1404), *Xu chuandeng lu*, 51: 2077a; see also the entry "Kokan," in Zengaku daijiten hensanjo, ed., *Zengaku daijiten*, 1: 330.

3. The cult of *śarīra*, or holy relics, most notably of the Buddha Śākyamuni himself, was prevelant in Buddhism throughout its history. The term *śarīra* denotes both the relics of an uncremated body and those left after cremation. In the case of Chinese monks, the term gradually came to denote mainly the latter kind; see the entry "Shari," in Mochizuki Shinkō, *Bukkyō daijiten*, 3: 2185–88; and the entry "Shari," in Zengaku daijiten hensanjo, 1: 477. On *śarīra* reliquaries, see Nara kokuritsu hakubutsukan, *Busshari no shōgon*.

4. In the Naikaku bunko edition and in the later ones as well, the nickname "Jidian" follows the title in smaller characters.

5. Jujian seems to refer to small, marble-like relics that are sometimes left after cremation and, according to some modern scholars, are gallstones. They occasionally sparkle and were held as proof of the deceased's sanctity.

6. This is Li Bangchan (?–1130), who held various high positions in the central government of the Northern Song during its final years; see *Song shi* 352.11120–21.

7. This is the renowned abbot of the Lingyin Monastery, Huiyuan (1103–76); see Zhengshou, *Jiatai Pu deng lu* (1204), 116b–117b; see also the entry "Eon," in Zengaku daijiten hensanjo, 1: 90.

8. I take Jujian's *xinjiao* 信腳 as equivalent to *xingjiao* 行腳, the common term for a wandering monk.

9. Yandang shan; Jujian has for *dang* the character 宕 instead of the more commonly used 蕩.

10. I substitute *yuan* 院 for *wan* 皖.

11. In Chan terminology the term *yaoshi* has the specialized meaning of "evening meal." Yet since here the reference is to "old and sick monks," I assume that Jujian is using the term in its literal meaning: medicine.

12. Zujue, a Huayen master, resided at the Zhongyan Monastery in Meizhou prefecture, Sichuan. For a brief biography, see Ruxing, *Da Ming gaoseng zhuan* (1617), 50: 902a, 921c–922b. Ruxing does not attribute to him the kind of antinomian behavior Jujian describes in the case of Daoji.

13. *Qianzhu,* literally "thousand pillars"—this expression stands for stately palaces; see, e.g., Su Shi's (1036–1101) poem "Jingchun jian he," in *Su Shi shiji* 11.539.

14. *Zuo tuo li wang*—this is a common expression in the Chan tradition; see, e.g., Dōgen (1200–1253), *Fu kan zazen gi,* 82: 2. Death in the meditation posture was seen as the mark of the holy man.

15. The series of images that follow describes the beauty of the sparkling *śarīra* left after the cremation of Daoji. *Bi bu sui* is an allusion to the precious jade disc that Lin Xiangru (fl. ca. 275 B.C.E.) threatened to smash if the Qin king did not pay for it; see Sima Qian (ca. 145–ca. 85 B.C.E.), *Shiji* 81.2439–41.

16. According to a legend often cited in Chinese poetry, the shark man's (*jiaoren*) tears are pearls; see *Shu yi ji* 2.634–65. *Śarīra* remains were also sometimes referred to as pearls.

17. Here Jujian uses the pearls metaphor in an allusion to Bai Juyi's (772–846) poem "Pipa yin"; see *Bai Juyi ji,* 1: 242.

18. See the entry "Jyōkai," in Mochizuki, 3: 2218–19. For the role of the Ten Novice Precepts in the ordination of Chan monks in particular, see Theodore G. Foulk, "The 'Chan School' and Its Place in the Buddhist Monastic Tradition," pp. 78–84.

19. See the entry "Gokai," in Mochizuki, 2: 1118–20.

20. See, e.g., the poems of Shams al-Dîn Muhammad Hâfiz (ca. 1320–ca. 1390) in *Hafiz of Shiraz: Thirty Poems,* esp. p. 30.

21. See, respectively, Gershon G. Scholem, "Redemption Through Sin"; and Daniel H. H. Ingalls, "Cynics and Pasupatas: The Seeking of Dishonor."

22. For example, all the poems attributed to Daoji in the monastic history of the Jingci Monastery, the *Jingci si zhi* (1805), are taken from a sixteenth-century novel about him, the *Jidian yulu;* see Chapter 6 below.

23. See, respectively, the two fund-raising petitions (*huayuan shu*) in Lang Ying (b. 1487), *Qixiu leigao,* 2: 475; and *Lingyin si zhi* 6b.21b. Lang Ying claimed that the former was preserved in the Dafo Monastery in Daoji's own handwriting. See also the poem "Jiuli song," in *Lingyin si zhi* 8.31b.

24. Meng Zongbao, *Dongxiao shiji,* in Bao Tingbo (1728–1814), ed., *Zhibuzu zhai congshu* (1872 ed.), collection no. 11, *ce* 41, 8.2a–b. Li E included this poem in his *Songshi jishi* (preface dated 1746), 93.2254–55.

25. *Pingming fa*; this is an allusion to Liu Xiang's (77–6 B.C.E.) poem "Feng fen" (Encountering trouble) in *Chu ci* 16.164.

26. Axis Mundi (Tianzhu) was the original name of the Dongxiao Monastery; see Deng Mu, *Dongxiao tu zhi* (1305), 6.76.

27. This is a mountain in the vicinity of Dongxiao Monastery; the road leading to it bends nine times, for which reason it was named "Nine Locks Mountain" (Jiusuo shan); see Deng 2.14.

28. "Clouds root" (*yungen*) is a common metaphor for a mountain peak; see, e.g., Guanxiu (?–912), "Zeng Fanggan shi," in *Quan Tang shi* 829.9345.

29. (*Scripture*) *of the Yellow Court* (*Huangting* [*jing*]) and *Inner Effulgences* (*Neijing*); Daoji is probably referring in both instances to the fourth-century version of the Taoist classic *Huangting jing*, the *Huangting neijing jing* (Scripture of the inner effulgences of the Yellow Court).

30. The immortals' island Penglai, in the east, and the Weak River (Ruoshui), in the west, figure in Taoist fantastic geography.

31. "Nine Transformations" (*jiuzhuan*) is the name of an immortality pill, which is produced through nine refinements.

32. This is Su Shi (Su Dongpo), who authored at least one poem on the Dongxiao Monastery; see "Dongxiao gong," in Su Shi, 10.503–4.

33. The Dadi cave is the most famous of the many caves surrounding the Dongxiao Monastery. It is one of the Taoist Cave-Heavens (*dongtian*), in which the immortals were believed to reside; see Deng 3.23–24.

34. *Shiru*, lit. "stone-milk," is the Chinese term for stalactite.

35. On the association of gibbons and cranes in Chinese poetry, see R. H. van Gulik, *The Gibbon in China: An Essay in Chinese Animal Lore*, pp. 38–39, 53–54.

Chapter 2

1. The term "shamanistic substratum" was coined by Piet van der Loon (p. 168).

2. On Chinese spirit-mediums in Taiwan and Southeast Asia, see Alan J. A. Elliott, *Chinese Spirit Medium Cults in Singapore;* and David K. Jordan, *Gods, Ghosts, and Ancestors: The Folk Religion of a Taiwanese Village*, pp. 67–74. On the spirit-medium as an example of a holy fool, see also Michel Strickmann, "Holy Fools," pp. 1–2.

3. According to such Taoist hagiographies as "A Record of Huan the Perfect One's Ascent to Immortality" ("Huan zhenren sheng xian ji"); see Strickmann, "Holy Fools," esp. pp. 9–13.

4. A. C. Graham, trans., *Chuang-tzu: The Inner Chapters*, p. 79.

5. Liu I-ch'ing, *A New Account of Tales of the World*, p. 374.

6. Etienne Balazs, "Nihilistic Revolt or Mystical Escapism," p. 237.

7. For a discussion of these two types of political madness, see Lawrence

A. Schneider, *A Madman of Ch'u: The Chinese Myth of Loyalty and Dissent*, esp. pp. 14–15.

8. Trans. from Stephen Owen, *The Great Age of Chinese Poetry: The High Tang*, p. 109. For the concept of the eccentric poet during the Tang, see ibid., esp. pp. 109–43.

9. See *Xin Tang shu* 202.5764.

10. E. Zürcher, "Eschatology and Messianism in Early Chinese Buddhism," pp. 53–54.

11. See the Dunhuang text of the *Liuzu tan jing*, in Philip Yampolsky, ed. and trans., *The Platform Sutra of the Sixth Patriarch*, esp. sections 3 (p. 2) and 8 (p. 4), and Yampolsky's translation on pp. 128, 131–32.

12. For a general survey, see Heinrich Dumoulin, *Zen Buddhism: A History*, 1: 166–70.

13. See ibid., 1: 163.

14. *On luohan* paintings, see *Luohan hua*; Helmut Brinker, *Zen in the Art of Painting*, pp. 63–66; and Richard K. Kent, "Depictions of the Guardians of the Law: Lohan Painting in China," pp. 183–213. On Bodhidharma paintings, see Brinker, pp. 85–92.

15. Brinker, p. 76; for a survey of the "three sages"' paintings, see ibid., pp. 70–82.

16. Michel Strickmann, *Mantras et mandarins: Le buddhisme tantrique en Chine*, pp. 55–56, 243–90. On Tantrism during the Tang, see also Chou I-liang, "Tantrism in China." Stephen Teiser (*The Ghost Festival in Medieval China*, pp. 107–8) has pointed out Tantric elements in the ghost-festival. Glen Dudbridge (*The "Hsi-yu chi": A Study of Antecedents to the Sixteenth-Century Chinese Novel*, pp. 18–21) notes the influence of Tantric mythology on one of the *Journey to the West*'s supernatural protagonists, Sha Heshang.

17. See James A. Robinson's translation from the Tibetan of Abhayadatta's *Caturaśīti-siddha-pravṛtti*, entitled *Buddha's Lions: The Lives of the Eighty-Four Siddhas*, pp. 236–39.

18. See Zhipan, *Fozu tongji* (1271), 49: 390c. See also Ferdinand Lessing, *Yung-ho-kung*, p. 27.

19. See John Kieschnick, *The Eminent Monk: Buddhist Ideals in Medieval Chinese Hagiography*, pp. 67–111.

20. See Huijiao, *Gaoseng zhuan*, chaps. 9–10, 50: 383–95; Daoxuan, *Xu Gaoseng zhuan*, chaps. 25–26, 50: 643–78; Zanning, *Song Gaoseng zhuan* (988), chaps. 18–22, 50: 820–855.

21. Daoyuan, *Jingde chuandeng lu*, vol. 51, chap. 27, 433b–434a. For another chapter on miracle workers in "transmission of the lamp" literature, see *Jiatai Pu deng lu*, *ZZ*, section 2, part 2, case no. 10, *ce* 2, chap. 24, 165a–170b.

22. See, e.g., the biography of the mad monk (*feng heshang*) Miaoying in Qian Yueyou, ed., *Xianchun Lin'an zhi* (ca. 1270), 91.15a–b.

23. Li Fang (925–96), ed., *Taiping guangji*, chaps. 87–98, 1: 566–657; *Gujin tushu jicheng, shenyi* section, chaps. 125–202, 49: 1337–50: 2078.

24. See, respectively, *Shenseng zhuan*, 50: 948–1015; and *Zhoudian xianren zhuan*, 1: 6. Since Zhu Yuanzhang referred to Zhoudian as an immortal (*xian*), the latter was classified in later hagiographic collections as a Taoist, rather than a Buddhist, saint. See, e.g., Zhang Wenjie, *Guang lie xian zhuan* 7.22b–24b.

25. For a study of a miracle worker who was *not* an itinerant eccentric, see A. F. Wright, "Fo-t'u-teng, a Biography."

26. See Hansen, *Changing Gods*, pp. 44–45.

27. See Holmes Welch, *The Practice of Chinese Buddhism*, p. 16.

28. However, the "forest monks" did not transgress Buddhist law; see Stanley Tambiah, *The Buddhist Saints of the Forest and the Cult of Amulets*. On the *hijiri*, see Kyoko Motomochi Nakamura, *Miraculous Stories from the Japanese Buddhist Tradition;* and Ichiro Hori, "On the Concept of *Hijiri* (Holy-Man)."

29. From *The Questions of King Milinda*, quoted in Tambiah, p. 14.

30. For a survey of miracle workers' supernatural powers, see Li Fengmao, "Huijiao *Gaoseng zhuan* ji qi shenyi xingge."

31. See Chikusa Masaaki, "Sōdai baichō kō" (originally 1979), in his *Chūgoku Bukkyō shakaishi kenkyū*, pp. 64–65. See also Valerie Hansen, Review of *Chūgoku Bukkyō shakaishi kenkyū* and "Sō Gen Bukkyō ni okeru an dō" by Chikusa Masaaki; and Hansen, *Changing Gods*, pp. 41–42.

32. Huijiao, 50: 390b–392b.

33. Similar mortuary miracles were incorporated also into the hagiographies of Bodhidharma, Budai heshang, and Daoji; see Chapter 3 of this book.

34. Zanning, 50: 848b–c.

35. See, e.g., Daoyuan, 51: 434b; and Nianchang, *Fozu lidai tongzai* (1344), 49: 652a. For a translation of Daoyuan's biography of Cloth-Bag Monk, see Helen B. Chapin, "The Ch'an Master Pu-Tai"; on Budai heshang, see also Lessing, pp. 21–37.

36. Zhengshou, *ce* 2, 165b–66a. The similarities between Yuxian and Daoji were pointed out by Sawada, "Saiten sui bodai," pp. 194–96.

37. Hong Mai, *Yi Jian zhi* 9.78–79.

38. See Chikusa Masaaki, "Sō Gen Bukkyō ni okeru an dō," pp. 6–10; and Hansen, Review, p. 106.

39. See, e.g., Li Fang, ed., *Taiping yulan* (983), chap. 35, 1: 167. See also Alvin P. Cohen, "Coercing the Rain Deities in Ancient China," p. 247 and note 9.

40. Hansen, *Changing Gods*, p. 45. Hansen discusses Huiji as an example of the similarity between uneducated Buddhist and Taoist practitioners. My observations on this point owe much to hers.

41. Zheng Tingyu, *Budai heshang ren zi ji*; for a translation into French, see Li Tche-houa, *"Le Signe de patience" et autres pieces du théâtre des Yuan*, pp. 29–134.

42. See "Liang Wudi lei xiu gui jile," in Feng Menglong, *Gujin xiaoshuo*, pp. 562–69. On the historical Baozhi, see Huijiao, 50: 394–95. Ono Shihei ("Saiten setsuwa no seiritsu," pp. 197–201) has noted the similarities between Baozhi and Daoji (as well as the identity of Baozhi and Zhigong).

43. See Chapter 3 of this book. On the historical Liaoyuan, see the entry "Ryogen" in Zengaku daijiten hensanjō, p. 1283.

44. Chen Li-li, trans., *Master Tung's Western Chamber Romance*, pp. 45–61.

45. *Shuihu quanzhuan* 4.64 and 119.1790–91.

46. *Jin Ping Mei cihua* 49.221–25; and Clement Egerton, trans., *The Golden Lotus*, 2: 309–11.

47. See Cao Xueqin, *The Story of the Stone*, 1: 47–55 and 5: 358–61.

48. On the Eight Immortals in Yuan drama, see Wilt Idema and Stephen H. West, *Chinese Theater, 1100–1450: A Source Book*, pp. 299–311. For a translation of one play, "Chung-li of the Han Leads Lan Ts'ai-ho to Enlightenment," see Idema and West, pp. 312–43. There are several late Ming and Qing novels on the Eight Immortals; see, e.g., *Baxian chuchu dong youji*; Yang Erceng, *Han Xiangzi quanzhuan* (1623); and Wang Xiangxu, *Lüzu quanzhuan* (1662). The play *Budai heshang ren zi ji* is closely related to the Eight Immortals plays; see Idema and West, p. 305. The *Han Xiangzi quanzhuan* shares common motifs with the earliest extant novel on Daoji; see Chapter 3 of this book. On one of the Eight Immortals, Lü Dongbin, in drama and fiction alike, see Katz, "Enlightened Alchemist or Immoral Immortal?"

49. For example, an early seventeenth-century story, "Magistrate Wang Burns the Treasure Lotus Monastery," tells of a monastery frequented by barren women beseeching offspring. A skillful magistrate discovers that the monastery's therapeutic powers are due not to the efficaciousness of its icons but to the sexual prowess of its resident monks. They rape the women in their sleep, and the latter are too ashamed to tell about it. See "Wang dayin huofen Baolian si," in Feng Menglong, *Xingshi hengyan*. On the story's dating, see "HY 39" in Patrick Hanan, *The Chinese Short Story: Studies in Dating, Authorship, and Composition*, p. 245. Another story about a lascivious monk is the Yuan or early Ming "The Monk with the Love Letter" ("Jiantie heshang"), in *Qingpingshan tang huaben*. On this story, see Hanan, *Chinese Vernacular Story*, pp. 40–43.

Chapter 3

1. On the *taozhen* genre, see Ye Dejun, "Song, Yuan, Ming jiangchang wenxue," pp. 648–57; Chen Ruheng, *Shuoshu shihua*, pp. 115–18; and Hanan, *Chinese Short Story*, pp. 139–40.

2. Tian Rucheng, *Xihu youlan zhiyu* 20.368.

3. On the *taozhen* topics and Ming vernacular fiction, see Hanan, *Chinese Short Story*, pp. 139–40.

4. *Fei fan fei xian;* a similar expression, *fei sheng fei fan* (neither saint nor mortal), appears in a song attributed to the eccentric holy man Budai heshang in Nianchang, *Fozu lidai tongzai* (1344), 49: 652a.

5. The "Forest of Thorns" (*jingji lin*) is a common metaphor in Chan literature for the realm of ignorance and delusion; see, e.g., Shoujian, ed., *Yunmen Kuangzhen Chanshi guanglu* (preface dated 1076), 47: 554b.

6. Like the "Forest of Thorns," the "Diamond Circle" (*jin'gang quan*) stands in Chan literature for the prison of passion and delusion; see, e.g., Chongxian (980–1052) and Keqin (1063–1135), *T.* no. 2003, vol. 48, section 78, 205b.

7. *Bikong liao tian;* the expression stands in Chan literature for intellectual conceit, see Zengaku daijiten hensanjo, p. 1042c, s.v. It is also worth noting, however, that the arhats (*luohan*) are often depicted in Chinese art with long protruding noses. Chinese artists, it appears, delighted in exaggerating the foreign features of these originally non-Chinese Buddhist saints; see, e.g., the *luohan* paintings by Gou Longshuang (fl. 1067–85) and Liu Songnian (fl. 1174–1224) in *Luohan hua*, pp. 8–13; see also Chapter 2 of this book.

8. *Luo zhi ru yunyan*; this is a quote from Du Fu's poem "Yinzhong baxian ge" in *A Concordance to the Poetry of Tu Fu*, 2: 23. For a translation, see William Hung, *Tu Fu: China's Greatest Poet*, pp. 51–52.

9. *Chang'anshi shang jiujia mian;* again this is a quote from Du Fu's "Yinzhong baxian ge"; see *A Concordance to the Poetry of Tu Fu*, 2: 22.

10. *Yan ru tui chan*; cf. Pi Rixiu's (ca. 834–ca. 883) portrayal of Bai Juyi in his poem "Bai tai zhuan": *Chushi si gu he, yirong tong tui chan*, in *Quan Tang shi* 608.7018.

11. This is the number of relics said to have been left by the Buddha Śākyamuni.

12. Tian Rucheng, 14.275.

13. See Chapter 2 and Chapter 3, notes 8 and 9, of this book; on Zhang Xu, see *Xin Tang shu* 202.5764.

14. For the relationship between the "Honglian" and "Liu Cui" stories and the *Jidian yulu*, see below. For a general survey of the Honglian and Liu Cui lore, see Sawada Mizuho, "Kōren Ryūsui," in his *Sō Min Shin shōsetsu sōkō*, pp. 23–49; on Honglian and Liu Cui in Ming vernacular fiction, see Hanan, *Chinese Short Story*, pp. 142–47; and Hanan, *Chinese Vernacular Story*, pp. 70–71.

15. See Chao Li, comp., *Chao shi Baowentang shumu*, chap. 2, p. 129.

16. Chen Shan's preface to the *Qixiu leigao*'s sequel, the *Qixiu xugao*, makes it clear that the former was published before 1566; see Lang, 2: 752.

17. Lang, 2: 475. The piece attributed to Jidian may possibly be authentic; see Chapter 1 of this book, and note 23 to that chapter. The *Qixiu leigao* passage was first noted by Sawada, "Saiten sui bodai ni tsuite," p. 188.

18. See the list of the *Jidian yulu* editions in Ōtsuka Hidetaka, *Zōho Chūgoku tsūzoku shōsetsu shomoku*, pp. 255–56.

19. The Naikaku bunko has a copy. A photographic reprint is available in *Guben xiaoshuo congkan*, series no. 8, 1: 1–140. The punctuated edition in the *Dai Nihon zokuzōkyō* follows the text of the 1569 edition; see ZZ, section 2, case no. 26, *ce* 1, la–23b. Subsequent references are to the ZZ edition, since the photographic edition is occasionally illegible. See also Appendix A.

20. A copy is preserved at the Sōkōdō collection of the Tōyō bunka kenkyūjo, Tokyo University. A photographic reprint is available in *Guben xiaoshuo congkan*, series no. 4, vol. 5. The other late Ming edition was dated by Lu Gong to the Chongzhen period (1628–44). A copy, missing the title page and the first page, is preserved at the Chinese Academy of Social Sciences in Beijing. Typeset reprints are available both in Lu Gong, ed., *Ming Qing pinghua xiaoshuo xuan*, pp. 236–88; and in Lu Gong and Tan Tian, eds., *Guben pinghua xiaoshuo ji*, pp. 1–62. (In the Lu and Tan reprint, the missing first page, copied from a later edition of the novel, has been added.)

21. Two copies of this edition, which I have not seen, survive: one at the Kunaichō shoryōbu library in Tokyo, the other at Tenri University Library; see Sun, *Riben Dongjing*, pp. 132–34; and Ōtsuka, p. 256. The other Qing edition attributes the novel to the "Yunlin-si [i.e., the Lingyin Monastery in Hangzhou] resident Liu Tong." A copy is preserved at the Beijing Library.

22. According to Juding (51: 679a), no "recorded [sayings]" of Jidian survived.

23. The *Jidian yulu*'s title in Feng Menglong's edition is *Jidian luohan Jingci si xiansheng ji* (The luohan Jidian manifests his divinity at the Jingci Monastery).

24. Unlike the *Jidian yulu*, however, the *Dongpo Foyin yulu* is not an extended narrative, but a series of mostly unrelated jokes and epigrams attributed to its protagonists, Su Shi and Foyin. A manuscript edition of the *Dongpo Foyin yulu* is preserved in the Naikaku bunko. The same work exists also under the title of *Dongpo wenda lu*. The latter carries a preface by Zhao Kaimei, dated 1601, and is preserved in two collections: Zhao Kaimei, ed., *Dongpo zazhu liu zhong*, preface dated 1602 (copy in National Central Library, Taipei); and Chen Jiru (1558–1639), ed., *Baoyantang miji*, 1606–1620 ed. (copy in Harvard-Yenching Library). The date of the *Dongpo Foyin yulu* is unclear. Although it contains some material that may date from the Song, it was probably compiled later, see Sun, *Riben Dongjing*, p. 142; Zhang Zhenglang, "*Wenda lu* yu 'shuo canqing,'" pp. 2–3; and Wang Ch'iu-kuei, "On 'Shuo Ts'an-Ch'ing,'" p. 74. Only Zhang Zhenglang argues that the *Dongpo Foyi lu* was compiled during the Song.

25. For a general survey see Dudbridge, *Legend of Miao-shan*, pp. 52–54, 60–61.

26. They are, respectively, (1) *Damo chushen chuandeng zhuan*, Wanli ed.; (2) *Tang Zhong Kui quanzhuan*, Wanli ed.; (3) *Tianfei niangma zhuan*; (4) *Nan*

hai Guanshiyin pusa chushen xiuxing zhuan, Wanli ed.; (5) *Beifang Zhenwu zushi Xuantian Shangdi chushen zhizhuan*, Wanli ed.; (6) *Huaguang Tianwang zhuan*, Wanli ed. On these novels, see, respectively, (1) Sawada Mizuho, "Darumaden shōsetsu," pp. 169–76; (2) Éliasberg, pp. 49–62; (3) Li Xianzhang; (4) Dudbridge, *Legend of Miao-shan*, pp. 51–58; (5) Seaman, *Journey to the North*; and (6) Cedzich.

27. See Dudbridge, *Legend of Miao-shan*, pp. 44–50, 56–58.

28. See ibid., pp. 58–61; and Li Xianzang, respectively.

29. Seaman, *Journey to the North*, p. 20; see *Beifang Zhenwu zuzhi Xuantian Shangdi chushen zhizhuan* 4.26b–29a.

30. The *Huaguang Tianwang zhuan* is distributed in Taiwanese temples; see Cedzich, p. 4. This is also the case with the seventeenth-century novel on Jidian, *Zui puti*, see Chapter 4 of this book.

31. The mad monk from the Yue Fei cycle is conceived of as an incarnation of the Bodhisattva Kṣitigarbha (Dizang wang). In the Yuan play he is referred to as the "Witless Novice" (Dai Xingzhe), but he is not identified by a personal name; see Kong Xueshi (1260–1341), *Dong chuang shifan*, 8: 78–91. He probably figured also in another Yuan play, by Jin Renjie (?–1329), of the same title and, presumably, the same topic. This play is now lost. On both plays, see Fu Xihua, *Yuandai zaju quanmu*, pp. 93–94, 221–22. The image of this eccentric Hangzhou monk was further developed in the Ming period play *Jingzhong ji* 2.27a–35a. This play's authorship is unknown; see Fu Xihua, *Mingdai chuanqi quanmu*, pp. 451–52. He figured also in at least two Ming period novels: Xiong Damu, *Da Song zhong xing yanyi*, pp. 850–62; and *Yue Wumu jing zhong zhuan* (earliest edition probably 1626), Qing ed. at the Beijing Library, 63.25b. On the evolution of fiction on Yue Fei, see also Zheng Zhenduo, "Yue zhuan de yanhua," pp. 360–68.

32. See Chapter 5 of this book.

33. The stories are included, respectively, in (1) *Qingpingshan tang huaben*, pp. 136–54; (2) Feng Menglong, *Xingshi hengyan*, 1: 241–49; (3) Feng Menglong, *Gujin xiaoshuo*, pp. 428–41; and (4) Feng Menglong, *Jingshi tongyan*, pp. 80–89. A fifth story, which shares some common motifs with the preceding four, is "Liannü Achieves Buddhahood in the Bridal Sedanchair" ("Huadeng jiao Liennü cheng Fo ji"), in *Qingpingshan tang huaben*, pp. 193–206. For these stories, see Hanan, *Chinese Short Story*, pp. 148–51; and idem, *Chinese Vernacular Story*, pp. 70–72.

34. The play is included in Zang Maoxun, ed., *Yuanqu xuan*, 4: 1335–52. On its relation to the short story of the same title, see Hanan, *Chinese Short Story*, pp. 143–44.

35. This mark of the Wu dialect has been for the most part erased in all later editions of the novel.

36. See Hanan, *Chinese Vernacular Story*, p. 8; and William O. Hennessey, trans., *Proclaiming Harmony*, p. x.

37. It is interesting that the narrator chose to include the Guoqing Monastery in his hagiography of Jidian, since that monastery also figures prominently in the legend of three other famous eccentrics, the Three Sages of Tiantai Mountain; see Chapter 2 of this book.

38. On the cult of arhats in China, see Wen Fong, *The Lohans and a Bridge to Heaven*, pp. 17–43; Thomas Watters, "The Eighteen Lohan of Chinese Buddhist Temples"; and Bai Huawen, "Zhongguo de luohan."

39. See, e.g., the *luohan* paintings by Liu Guandao (fl. 1270–1300), Wu Bin (fl. 1568–1627), and Ding Yunpeng (ca. 1547–after 1628), in *Luohan hua*, pp. 16, 27–35; see also Kent, p. 190; and Chapter 2 of this book.

40. *Ershisi zun dedao luohan zhuan*, Wanli ed.

41. In the case of Lu Zhishen, however, it is not the narrator but the rascals of the vegetable garden who refer to him as an arhat; see *Shuihu quanzhuan* 7.112.

42. On the legend of the Tiantai Mountain's arhats, see Fong, esp. pp. 17–24.

43. See Edward Conze's translation of Ashvaghosha's *Buddhacarita* in his *Buddhist Scriptures*, p. 53.

44. See, e.g., the miraculous conceptions of Mazu, Zhong Kui, and Xuantian Shangdi in, respectively, *Tianfei niangma zhuan*, p. 22; Éliasberg, p. 53; and *Beifang Zhenwu* 2.3b; see also Seaman's translation of the last in his *Journey to the North*, p. 88.

45. Huiran, comp., *Zhenzhou Linji Huizhao chanshi yulu*, 47: 504c, trans. Irmgard Schloegl in *The Zen Teaching of Rinzai: The Record of Rinzai*, pp. 78–79. I substitute Chinese readings for Schloegl's Japanese readings of names.

46. Huiran, 47: 503b; trans. Schloegl, pp. 67–68. For the term *zei*, see also the "recorded sayings" of Pang Yun (ca. 740–808), *Pang jushi yulu* 28a–b. For an English translation, see Ruth Fuller Sasaki et al., trans., *The Recorded Sayings of Layman Pang: A Ninth-Century Zen Classic*, pp. 49–50 (this translation has "thief" for *zei*).

47. *Shuihu quanzhuan* 4.73.

48. Still preserved today, the Cool-Spring Pavilion is located outside the Lingyin Monastery's main gate.

49. According to a local Hangzhou tradition, a supernatural monkey inhabited the Summoning-the-Monkey Cave south of the Lingyin Monastery; see Meir Shahar, "The Lingyin si Monkey Disciples and the Origins of Sun Wukong."

50. The *yinqing* is a portable percussion instrument used in Buddhist monasteries to signal the various stages of ceremonies; for this reason it is called the "leading *qing*" (see the entry "yinkin" in Zengaku daijiten hensanjo, 1: 55).

51. See the song "Heshang" in Feng Menglong, *Shan'ge*, p. 36.

52. *Shuihu quanzhuan* 4.64, 66, 68, and 72.

53. Yanagida Seizan, "The 'Recorded Sayings' Texts of Chinese Chan Buddhism," p. 190.

54. See the Dunhuang text edited by Yampolsky, esp. sections 5–10, pp. 2–5, and Yampolsky's translation, pp. 128–33. Shenxiu is referred to in *The Platform Sutra* as *shangzuo*. Another term for head monk is *zuozhu*.

55. This is the name of a rod used for disciplinary purposes in Chan monasteries; see the entry "shippei" in Zengaku daijiten hensanjo, 1: 454.

56. In the *Gaoseng zhuan*, Huijiao (50: 393a, 394b, 389b) refers to three miracle workers by the title *gong*. These are Shaoshi (referred to as Shigong), Baozhi (referred to as Zhigong), and Shegong. Zanning (50: 848c) refers to the eccentric saint Budai heshang by the title *gong* as well.

57. The 1569 edition is the only one to have a reference to the Lingyin Monastery here; cf. *Jidian yulu* 16b, to Feng Menglong, *Sanjiao ounian*, section 2, p. 57b; Lu, p. 273; and Lu and Tan, p. 44.

58. See the seventeenth-century novel *Zui puti* (Baoren tang ed.), 15.1a–5b; see also Chapter 4 of this book.

59. The term *huofo* is a Chinese translation of a term common in Tibetan and Mongolian Buddhism *(sprul sku and hutuktu, or hobilgan,* respectively), where it is used in reference to religious leaders such as the Dalai Lama (of Tibet) and the rJe btsun dam pa hutuktu (of Outer Mongolia); see "Katsubutsu," in Nakamura Hajime, ed., *Bukkyōgo daijiten*, p. 180. In Chinese vernacular fiction, the laity use it as a respectful term of address to monks. See *Shuihu quanzhuan* 5.82 for its use in regard to Lu Zhishen.

60. See Chapter 4 of this book.

61. See Juding, 51: 679; and Wenxiu (1345–1418), *Wudeng huiyuan buyi*, p. 458b.

62. See Yang Erceng, *Han Xiangzi quanzhuan*.

63. As Stephen Owen describes Li Bai in *Great Age of Chinese Poetry*, p. 109.

64. *A Concordance to the Poetry of Tu Fu*, 2: 22; trans. Stephen Owen, *Great Age of Chinese Poetry*, p. 109.

65. *Shuihu quanzhuan* 119.1791.

66. In this case there are a few textual inaccuracies in the ZZ edition; cf. the 1569 edition, photographic reprint in *Guben xiaoshuo congkan*, series no. 8, 1: 81.

67. Juliet Bredon, *Peking: A Historical and Intimate Description of Its Chief Places of Interest*, p. 252.

68. Wang Tieqiang; this was the nickname of the historical Wang Yanzhang. See *Xin Wudai shi* 32.347.

69. *Jidian yulu* 19a. The "dream of Nanke" (*Nanke meng*) is a reference to the tale of a man who was appointed magistrate of Nanke prefecture, only to wake up and realize that the prefecture and the whole kingdom to which it belonged were part of an anthill by the side of which he happened to fall asleep; see Li Fang, *Taiping guangji* 475.3910–15.

70. The color black stands here for a monk's robe.

71. The reference to Maitreya is particularly appropriate since he was commonly worshipped as his comical manifestation of Budai heshang.

72. *Pilu ding shang mian;* the same expression appears also in the Hangzhou story "Yueming heshang du Liu Cui," in Feng, *Gujin xiaoshuo,* p. 433. A common expression in Chan literature is *Pilu ding shang xing* (walk on Vairocana's head); see, e.g., *Biyan lu,* vol. 48, section 99, 222b–223b. Since the Buddha Vairocana stands for the whole of reality, one could conceivably walk or sleep on his head.

73. On the role of Buddhist clergy in funerary rites in late imperial and modern times, see Susan Naquin, "Funerals in North China: Uniformity and Variation," pp. 40–41, 46, 59, 62; and Welch, pp. 179–205.

74. Tian Rucheng, 14.275.

75. See James Watson and Evelyn S. Rawski, *Death Ritual in Late Imperial and Modern China.*

76. "Green-clad youths" appear in Chinese religion in a variety of both Buddhist and non-Buddhist contexts: A green-colored incarnation of the Buddhist deity Jin'gang tongzi is called Qingyi tongzi; the *Taiping guangji* (981) includes a story about a swallow transformed into a "youth clad in green" *(qingyi tongzi);* and each of the two late Ming hagiographic collections entitled *Soushen ji* includes a biography of a deity called "Qingyi shen" (Green-clad deity); see, respectively, the entry "kongō dōji" in Mochizuki, 2: 1344–45; Li Fang, *Taiping guangji* 46.3776–77; and *Huitu sanjiao,* pp. 316, 433.

77. See Naquin, "Funerals in North China," pp. 42, 48; and James L. Watson, "Funeral Specialists in Cantonese Society," pp. 127–28.

78. See Hansen, *Changing Gods,* pp. 54–55, 62–64.

79. Ibid., pp. 63–64.

80. See his essay in Qian Yueyou 73.15b.

81. Robert P. Hymes, *Statesmen and Gentlemen: The Elite of Fu-chou, Chiang-hsi, in Northern and Southern Sung,* p. 181.

82. See Kenneth Dean, *Taoist Ritual and Popular Cults of South-East China,* pp. 134, 144.

83. Cf. *Jidian yulu* 21a to T. W. Rhys Davids, trans., *The Questions of King Milinda,* pp. iv, 3, 21–22. See also Edward J. Thomas, *The Life of Buddha as Legend and History,* p. 149.

84. See Daoyuan, 51: 220b. Mortuary miracles involving shoes appear in Buddhist hagiographic literature as early as the sixth century. See the hagiographies of Beidu and Shaoshi in Huijiao, 50: 392b and 393a, respectively. For the miracle involving Budai heshang's shoes, see Zhipan, 49: 390c. See also Lessing, pp. 28–29.

85. See *Beifang Zhenwu* 4.26a; and *Huaguang* 4.28a.

86. *Sanguo zhi tongsu yanyi* 16.22b.

87. *Shuihu quanzhuan* 120.1818.

88. Of course, a monk is not supposed to have hair at all.

89. The image of a carefree eccentric who rides his donkey facing backward appears frequently in Chinese poetry.

90. See Lessing, p. 24.

91. Cf. *Jidian yulu* 7a–7b to *Shuihu quanzhuan* 4.71.

92. *Shuihu quanzhuan* 4.71.

93. Ibid. 4.66.

94. It is worth noting that the portrayal of Jidian in Text A is also reminiscent of Lu Zhishen; see above.

95. See Zang Maoxun, 4: 1335–52.

96. See above.

97. These are the two immortals' islands, Penglai and Yingzhou.

Chapter 4

1. See Ōtsuka, pp. 147–50; and *Zhongguo tongsu xiaoshuo zongmu tiyao*, p. 364. Reference here is to the photographic reprint of the Baoren tang edition, in vol. 73 of *Guben xiaoshuo*. The complete title of this edition is *Jidian dashi wanshi qiji, Zui puti quanzhuan*. The author is given as Tianhua Zang Zhuren, and the preface is signed Taohua An Zhuren. Other *Zui puti* editions are also entitled: *Jigong quanzhuan, Jigong zhuan, Dushi jinsheng*, or *Jieda huanxi*.

2. See Yves Robert, trans., *L'Ivresse d'éveil: faits et gestes de Ji Gong le moine fou*; and Ian Fairweather, trans., *The Drunken Buddha*. Fairweather's translation is inaccurate. For scholarly discussion, see Ono, "Saiten setsuwa no seiritsu," pp. 186–91; and Zhou Chunyi, "Jigong xingxiang zhi wancheng ji qi shehui yiyi," pp. 546–47.

3. This edition (nine lines per page, twenty characters per line) is preserved at the Beijing Library.

4. A copy is preserved at the Institute of Literature of the Chinese Academy of Social Sciences. This edition has been reissued several times. At least two photographic reprints of it have been distributed by Taiwanese temples (see Appendix D). In addition, it also served as the source for a typeset edition of the novel entitled *Jidian seng zhuan*, which was published in 1987 by the Zhejiang Buddhist Association.

5. The reference here is to the photographic reprint of the 1673 edition in vol. 37 of *Guben xiaoshuo jicheng*. See also the 1985 typeset edition by the Zhejiang wenyi chubanshe, which is based on the former. Yves Robert's (p. 30) tentative suggestion is made in general terms only.

6. See, respectively, *Xihu jiahua*, chaps. 1, 4, 16. On the *Xihu jiahua*, see Hanan, *Chinese Vernacular Story*, p. 208.

7. Cf., respectively, *Xihu jiahua* 9.3b–5a to *Zui puti* 7.1 a–2b; 9.5a–11a to 9.5a–10.4b; 9.11a–12b to 11.5b–9a; 9.12b–13b to 12.2b–4a; 9.13b–25a to 13.8b–14.13a; 9.25a–28b to 16.7b–17.2a; and 9.28b–29b to 19.5b–6a.

8. Cf., e.g., *Xihu jiahua* 9.4a to *Zui puti* 7.1b, and 9.12a–b to 11.8a–b.

9. See Glen Dudbridge, "The Hundred-Chapter *Hsi-yu chi* and Its Early Versions."

10. *Xihu jiahua*, story no. 15 was adapted from *Jingshi tongyan*, story no. 28; the twelfth story was adapted from the first story in *Xihu erji*. See Hanan, *Chinese Vernacular Story*, p. 242, notes 3 and 2, respectively.

11. Cf. *Xihu jiahua* 4.5b–9b to *Jigong quanzhuan* 11.2a–6b.

12. See Lin Chen, *Ming mo Qing chu xiaoshuo shulu*, pp. 85–98, 242–301. See also Su Xing, "Tianhua Zang Zhuren ji qi caizi jiaren xiaoshuo," pp. 9–26.

13. See *Hakusai shomoku*, 6: 14. In addition to the *Drunken Puti* edition listed under the year 1707, the *Hakusai shomoku* lists what was probably yet another edition of this novel under the year 1754; see 40: 17–18.

In the *Hakusai shomoku*, Molang Zi is said to be from West Lake; in the *Charming Stories* he is said to be from Suzhou. A similar pseudonym, Molangxian Zhuren of the Three Wu, appears on the Qing novel *Hai liefu bailian zhenzhuan* (copy at the Bibliothèque Nationale). The subject matter of this novel is the celebrated martyrdom, said to have occurred in 1667, of a chaste wife; see Tan Zhengbi, *Guben xijian xiaoshuo huikao*, pp. 372–74; and Hanan, *Chinese Vernacular Story*, p. 242 note 1. Hanan (ibid.) suggests that the pseudonym Molang Zi was fashioned after that of Feng Menglong's associate, Molang Zhuren, in the collection *Xingshi hengyan* (1627).

14. These are the 1880 Laoer you tang edition, preserved at the Beijing University Library, and two other Qing editions: one (in six vols., ten lines per page, 22 characters per line) at the Beijing Library; the other at the Institute for Humanistic Studies of Kyoto University. On the Kyoto edition, see *Kyōto daigaku, Jimbun kagaku kenkyūjo kanseki mokuroku*, p. 698. See also Sun Kaidi, *Zhongguo tongsu xiaoshuo shumu*, p. 200; and Gu Xinyi's preface to the *Zui puti*, pp. 1–2.

15. Lin Chen (pp. 92, 288, 290) questioned Tianhua Zang Zhuren's authorship of the *Drunken Puti* on the basis of the differences between this novel, which is concerned with religious lore, and Tianhua Zang's other novels, which are concerned for the most part with romantic love. On the same grounds, he also questioned Tianhua Zang's authorship of the novel *Liang Wudi xilai yanyi*.

16. With minor exceptions, the *Zui puti* refers to the eccentric saint as Jigong only after his physical death at 20.1b.

17. *Jidian yulu* 11a.

18. *Zui puti* 10.2b–4a. See also Ono Shihei's Japanese translation and discussion in "Saiten setsuwa no seiritsu," pp. 188–91.

19. See *Zui puti* 14.4b–9b, 15.1a–5b, 15.7b–8b, 16.5b–7a, and 16.9b–17.2a.

20. Zhou Chunyi, p. 547.

21. See the hagiography of Ācārya Xiang (Xiang Sheli) in Daoxuan, 50: 657b; see also Kieschnick, p. 55.

22. See *Jidian yulu* 16b. This miracle is also mentioned in *Jigong quanzhuan* 32.9b–10a, where it is dismissed as absurd.

23. See *Jigong quanzhuan* 29.4b–10a.

24. One copy is preserved at the Dalian Municipal Library and another (missing the title page and preface) at the Beijing Library. There is also a fragmentary copy at the Institute of Literature of the Chinese Academy of Social Sciences. A photocopy reproduction of the Dalian copy is available at the Harvard-Yenching Library. The novel has never received scholarly attention.

25. *Jushi* can mean either "Buddhist layman" or "recluse." The unmistakable Buddhist topic of the novel suggests the former.

26. Another caption, on the title page, adds "Collated by the Man of the [Buddhist] Way, from the Western Lodge (*xishu*)."

27. See, repectively, Patrick Hanan, *The Invention of Li Yu*, pp. 134–36; and Ellen Widmer, *The Margins of Utopia: "Shui-hu hou-chuan" and the Literature of Ming Loyalism*, pp. 79–80. In the case of Dong Yue's *Supplement to the Journey to the West* (*Xiyou bu*), no attempt is made to distinguish the author from the commentator by means of a separate pseudonym.

28. The comment is based on the graphic similarity between *dian* 顛 (crazy) and *zhen* 眞 (true or sincere). *Jidian yulu* 5a.

29. The *Jigong quanzhuan* comment is slightly different from the *Jidian yulu* original. It reads: *dian zhe zhenzhen zhi yi.*

30. See *Doupeng xianhua*. On the *Doupeng xianhua* editions, see Hanan, *Chinese Vernacular Story*, p. 240 note 1.

31. See Hanan, *Chinese Vernacular Story*, pp. 191, 240 note 3.

32. See ibid., pp. 191–92.

33. See, e.g., *Doupeng xianhua*, pp. 24, 104, 109.

34. See Hanan, *Chinese Vernacular Story*, pp. 20, 191–207.

35. The term is used by Hanan (ibid., p. 195) in reference to *Idle Talk*.

36. Tea is served during the summer. In wintertime soup is served instead. Jigong is invited to manage this arbor, and for a while, he resides in it. However, no mention is made of stories being told there. Another tea arbor is mentioned at 30.lb–2b.

37. The stories have been selected from *Jidian yulu* 8a–19a. The storyteller also mentions several episodes from *Jidian yulu* 20b–21a, but he does not narrate them in detail.

38. It is noteworthy that Wang Mengji borrowed verbatim several pages from the *Xihu erji*. These provide historical background on the establishment of the Southern Song capital in Hangzhou, as well as descriptions of West Lake sites and amusements. Cf., respectively, *Jigong quanzhuan* 1.4a–b to *Xihu erji* 1.20; 1.4b to 2.32; 1.5b to 2.32; 1.8b–9b to 2.37; and 2.1a–b to 2.32–33.

39. See *Jidian yulu* 2a, 3a–b.

40. See the description of the headless man in *Doupeng xianhua*, p. 145; trans. in Hanan, *Chinese Vernacular Story*, pp. 199–200.

41. Jigong and the reader learn of their death only in chapter 21; see *Jigong quanzhuan* 13.5b–6b and 21.2a–b.

42. *Jidian yulu* 6b and 17a.

43. Apparently the abbot Dehui did not perish in the fire. Rather, he returned in his physical body to Tiantai Mountain, which denotes either the physical mountain in Zhejiang province or the arhats' supernatural abode at that same place; see *Jidian yulu* 14a.

44. See Chapter 3 of this book, as well as above in this chapter.

45. See *Zui puti* 16.5b–7a.

46. Cf. *Jidian yulu* 5a–b; on Lingyin Monastery monkey lore, see Shahar, "The Lingyin si Monkey Disciples," esp. p. 204 and note 32.

47. On the history of the "monkey of the mind" metaphors, see Dudbridge, *Hsi-yu chi*, pp. 167–76.

48. The parable is included in Shen Yue, *Song shu* 89.2231.

49. See the anti-Buddhist stories in *Doupeng xianhua* 6.67–78.

50. See Dudbridge, *Hsi-yu chi*, pp. 167–76.

51. See, e.g., the dream interpreted by Jigong's disciple Fanhua at 32.9a–b.

52. The play is included in *Guben xiqu congkan sanji*.

53. All of Zhang Dafu's surviving plays are included in ibid. On these, see Zhou Miaozhong, *Qingdai xiqu shi*, pp. 24–30; Zhuang Yifu, *Gudian xiqu cunmu huikao*, pp. 1219–28; and Zhao Jingshen, *Ming Qing qu tan*, pp. 181–87.

54. See, e.g., the play *Haichao yin* on Guanyin. The play is discussed briefly in Dudbridge, *Legend of Miaoshan*, pp. 68–69.

55. Cf., respectively, the play *Zui puti* 2.47b to *Jidian yulu* 22a–b, and 2.18b to 8a. The poem is included also in the novel *Zui puti* 7.8b, but it is significantly altered there. The play follows the *Jidian yulu* version. Beyond the general similarities between Jidian and the eccentric monk of the Yue Fei story cycle, I find no evidence to support Zhou Miaozhong's (p. 28) suggestion that the Yuan period play *Dong chuang shi fan* influenced Zhang Dafu's play.

56. Zhou Chunyi, pp. 547–49.

57. Cf. the play *Zui puti* 2.43a, the novel *Zui puti* 10.4a, and *Jidian yulu* 11a.

58. Cf. the *Jidian yulu* 19a, the novel *Zui puti* 17.8b–9a, and the play *Zui puti* 2.11 a–b.

59. Zhang Dafu's approximate dates can be inferred from references made in his works to his friends Feng Menglong (1574–1646) and Niu Shaoya (ca. 1564–after 1651). These show that he was alive for quite some time after Niu had passed away. See Zhou Miaozhong, pp. 25–26.

60. There are several instances where Zhang Dafu is quoting a poem that appears in an identical form in the *Jidian yulu* and in the novel *Zui puti*. In these cases it cannot be ascertained which source he is using.

Chapter 5

1. I am aware of only one piece of fiction on Jigong written during the eighteenth or early nineteenth century. This is a short story entitled "Daoji Feigns Madness at Nanping Mountain" ("Nanping shan Daoji zhuang feng"), in chapter 9 of Chen Shuji, *Xihu shiyi* (preface dated 1791) (see Appendix A). This story does not represent a new development in Jigong lore, since it was copied almost verbatim from the *Xihu jiahua* story, which itself has been collated from episodes in the novel *Zui puti*.

2. Reference here is to the 1991 Zhejiang guji edition entitled *Jigong zhuan*, in vols. 1–2 of *Jigong zhuan xilie xiaoshuo*.

3. The editors of the 1991 Zhejiang guji edition of the *Pingyan Jigong zhuan* (entitled *Jigong zhuan*) list nineteen late Qing and Republican period editions of the novel, eighteen of them by Shanghai publishers; see *Jigong zhuan*, 1: 2. I know of at least two other Republican period Shanghai editions not included in the Zhejiang guji list; these are the Jiujing zhai edition (in Zhou Chunyi's possession, photocopy in my possession) and the Tianbao shuju edition at the Zhejiang Library. Among recent editions, see, e.g., the 1983 Taipei Sanmin shuju edition (also entitled *Jigong zhuan*) and the 1991 Zhejiang guji edition.

4. See the complete twelve-volume edition of *The Storyteller's Life of Jigong* and all its sequels published by Zhejiang guji in 1991 under the title *Jigong zhuan xilie xiaoshuo*. See Appendix B for the dating of the sequels.

5. See *Jigong hou zhuan*, by Yang Zhimin and Guo Tianen (1987); *Jigong hou zhuan xu*, by Yang Zhimin and Guo Tianen, ed. Zhang Xi (1987); and *Jigong waizhuan*, by Jiang Sha et al. (1987).

6. The dated (1898) preface to the first part is appended both to a 1911 edition by the Shanghai publisher Cuiwen zhai (copy at the Zhejiang Library) and to an undated edition, in which the text is rearranged in 60 chapters, by the Shanghai publisher Jiaojing shanfang (copy at the Hangzhou University Library). The same preface is also appended to two other editions of the novel, where its original (1898) date has been replaced by the publication dates of these editions. These are the 1906 edition by the Jianqing zhai publishing house (copy at the Zhejiang Library; typeset reprint of the preface, now dated 1906, in Tan Zhengbi and Tan Xun, comps., *Pingtan tongkao*, pp. 55–56); and the 1913 edition by the Shanghai publisher Jiujing zhai (copy in Zhou Chunyi's possession; photocopy in my possession).

The dated (1900) preface to the second part is appended to a 1911 edition by the Shanghai publisher Cuiwen zhai (copy at the Zhejiang Library). Like the 1898 preface, this preface, too, is also appended to other editions of the novel, where its original date is replaced by those editions' publication dates. These are the 1906 edition by the Jianqing zhai publishing house (copy at the Zhejiang Library; typeset reprint of the preface in Tan Zhengbi and Tan Xun, p. 56), and the 1912 edition by Jiujing zhai (copy in Zhou Chunyi's possession; photocopy in my possession).

According to the editors of the series *Zhongguo shenguai xiaoshuo daxi* (Chinese fiction on the supernatural), there existed an early Guangxu (1875–1908) edition of the *Storyteller's Jigong*, which they have not seen (see their preface to the sequels to the *Storyteller's Jigong* in *Wanshi qiguan*, p. 1). However, they do not cite their source, and I am not aware of any evidence that such an edition existed.

7. This is the Jianqing zhai edition at the Zhejiang Library. There existed also a 1905 edition of the novel, which is still listed in the Tianjin Library's catalogue, even though it is no longer to be found in its collection (according to the librarians it was probably lost during the Cultural Revolution). See also *Zhongguo tongsu xiaoshuo zongmu tiyao*, p. 808.

8. Known to us to have published at least one other work (in 1891): an edition of Fan Tengfeng's (fl. 17th century) *Wufang yuanyin*; see Yang Shengxin, *Zhongguo banke zonglu*, p. 366.

9. On lithographic printing in China, see Perry Link, *Mandarin Ducks and Butterflies: Popular Fiction in Early Twentieth-Century Chinese Cities*, pp. 81–83. See also Zhang Jinglu, *Zhongguo jindai chuban shiliao erbian*, pp. 356–57, 368.

10. See the two dictionaries of the Beijing dialect: Xu Shirong, *Beijing tuyu cidian*; and Qi Rushan, *Beijing tuhua*. I am grateful to my friend Zhang Ping for his help in identifying Beijing vocabulary in this novel.

11. The preface is signed by one Lou Jiangshi. In the 1906 Jianqing zhai and 1913 Jiujing zhai editions, where the preface's original date (1898) is changed to these editions' respective dates, his name is changed to Yao Pinhou; see above note 6.

12. Some scholars trace the origins of the *pingshu* genre as far back as the early Qing. It is unclear, however, when this genre evolved into the form familiar from the late nineteenth century; see Yun Youke, *Jianghu congtan*, pp. 41–99; and *Tianqiao yilan*, ed. Zhang Cixi and Zhao Xianhuan, pp. 53–59; see also the entry "pingshu" in *Zhongguo xiqu quyi cidian*, ed. Shanghai yishu yanjiusuo, p. 685; and Chen Ruheng, pp. 153–56.

13. On storytelling teashops, see Yun, pp. 55–56, 60–64; *Tianqiao yilan*, pp. 53–59; *Beijing wangshi tan*, ed. Beijingshi weiyuanhui wenshi ziliao yanjiu weiyuanhui, pp. 16–17; and H. Y. Lowe, *The Adventures of Wu: The Life Cycle of a Peking Man*, pp. 154–58.

14. *Chuan hua* as in *chuan hua qigai* (smallpox-scarred beggar); see Yun, pp. 50, 79. On Jigong's popularity in Beijing *pingshu*, see also *Tianqiao yilan*, pp. 55, 57.

15. Yun, pp. 65, 79–80; see also *Tianqiao yilan*, p. 55. Regarding Shuang Houping's dates, see also Yun, pp. 55–56; *Tianqiao yilan*, pp. 56–57; and the entry "Shuang Houping" in *Zhongguo xiqu quyi cidian*, p. 735. Hai Wenquan remained active through the early 1930s.

16. The word *xuan* (balcony) appeared in the names of several storytelling teashops; see Yun, pp. 55–56. On Liu Jiye's performances in the Cuckold's Teashop, see ibid., pp. 61–62; on Jigong Li, see ibid., p. 82.

17. Yun, p. 80; for Yun's explanation of the expression *dou baofu*, see ibid., p. 79.

18. Lowe, p. 158. H. Y. Lowe published his Beijing memoir in English. He refers to his protagonist in the third person, but his work is most likely autobiographical.

19. Yun, p. 87.

20. A copy of *Yongqing shengping* is available at the Beijing University Library; see the reprint edition (which includes the author's original preface), ed. Cao Yibing.

21. Admittedly, the preface of *Everlasting Blessings and Peace* writes "Xiaoting" with the character *xiao* 筱, rather than *xiao* 小, as in the prefaces to the now lost, early editions of the *Storyteller's Jigong*. However, the 1892 edition of *Everlasting Blessings and Peace* is itself inconsistent. Another preface to the same edition, signed by one Fan Shouyan, writes the author's style-name with the character *xiao* 曉 (This preface is not reproduced in the 1988 reprint edition by the Baowen tang, Beijing). The early editions of the *Storyteller's Jigong* do not survive, and only their prefaces as appended to later editions do. It is not impossible that the publishers of the latter erred in copying Guo's style-name. In any event, the large number of orthographic errors in the surviving editions of both novels make it highly probable that the "Xiaoting" of the *Storyteller's Jigong* is the same as that of *Everlasting Blessings and Peace*.

22. See, e.g., Cao Yibing's concern with the novel's ideological bent in his introduction to *Yongqing shengping*.

23. Taking into account the large number of orthographic errors in this edition, I am amending *guci* 古詞 to *guci* 鼓詞. The *guci* genre of oral literature is discussed below.

24. Yun, p. 76.

25. See *Jigong hou zhuan* and *Jigong hou zhuan xu*.

26. On the *guci* genre, see Zhao Jingshen, *Guci xuan*; Li Jiarui, *Beiping suqu lüe*, pp. 9–12; and Ye, pp. 681–82.

27. Quoted in Li Jiarui, *Beiping suqu lüe*, p. 10.

28. On the differences between *guci* and *dagu*, see Zhao Jingshen, *Guci xuan*, esp. pp. 1, 17. On the *dagu* genre, see, among others, Zhao Jingshen, *Dagu yanjiu*; see also the autobiography of the drum-singer Zhang Cuifeng, which was written down by Liu Fang (Zhang Cuifeng herself was illiterate): Zhang Cuifeng, *Dagu shengya de huiyi*; this autobiography has been translated into English by Rulan Chao Pian, under the title "My Life as a Drum Singer: The Autobiography of Jang Tsueyfeng"; see also Catherine Stevens, "Peking Drumsinging."

29. *Guci* narratives were published, however, during the twentieth century. A lithographic edition of a *guci* narrative on Jigong is preserved at the Institute of History and Philology of the Academia Sinica, Taipei, Taiwan. It is entitled *Huitu guci Jigong quanzhuan* and was published by the Shanghai publisher Jinzhang tushu (a photocopy of this edition is available at the Harvard-Yenching Library). A preliminary comparison suggests that this *guci* narrative is not directly related to either the *Storyteller's Jigong* or the *guci* narrative that served as the latter's source (see below in text). Another *guci* narrative on Jigong was published during the Republican period by the Shanghai publisher Dacheng shuju; see this publisher's advertisement appended to its 1927 edition of the novel *Xiayi fengyue zhuan* (A tale of chivalrous love) (copy in Zhou Chunyi's possession); see also Zhou Chunyi, p. 552.

30. A large number of Baiben Zhang's and other vendors' manuscripts are preserved at the popular performance-literature (*suqu*) collection of the Academia Sinica, Taipei, Taiwan. (The complete title of this collection is: *Zhongyang yanjiuyuan, Lishi yuyan yanjiusuo suocang suqu.*) This collection also includes original catalogues issued by these vendors listing the manuscripts they carried and their prices. Multivolume prosimetric narratives could cost up to 4,000 coins. The collection is available on microfilm in several Western libraries. The catalogues can be found in the table-of-contents reel.

Baiben Zhang's and other vendors' manuscripts are also available in the Sōkōdō collection at the Institute of Eastern Culture of Tokyo University; see Nagasawa Kikuya, "Sōritsu nijūshūnen kinen Sōkōdō bunko tenran mokuroku," 4: 395–96.

On "Baiben Zhang" manuscripts, see Fu Xihua, "Baiben Zhang xiqu shuji kaolüe," pp. 317–29. See also Stevens, pp. 22–24.

31. At least eighteen *guci* manuscripts in the Academia Sinica collection carry the seals of rental shops. On these shops, see Qi Rushan, "Guci xiaodiao," p. 10; see also the illustrations in Fu, "Baiben Zhang," pp. 330–31. Judging by its seals, one of the shops that rented out the *guci* narrative on Jigong, the Yonglong zhai, also rented out vernacular fiction; see *Jigong zhuan guci*, in *Zhongyang yanjiuyuan*, reel 83, vol. 47.

32. The *zidishu* genre was performed mostly by artists of Manchu ethnicity; for this reason the genre is sometimes rendered in English as "Manchu ballads." (The term *zidi* refers to adult men who were eligible for, but not yet appointed to, posts in the bannermen garrisons.) Most scholars consider *zidishu* a sub-genre of *dagu,* which, as noted above, is itself closely related to *guci;* See Zhao, *Guci xuan*, p. 15; and Ye, p. 682.

33. See Stevens, p. 250. The store in question is the Delighting in Virtue Hall (Leshan tang). The advertisement appears on this store's original catalogue, which is preserved in the *Zhongyang yanjiuyuan*, table-of-contents reel.

34. It needs to be pointed out that none of the manuscripts in the so-called Chewang Fu collection bears this name. Thus, the assumptions that—(1) all the manuscripts in question came from one source, and (2) this source was the private collection of, or was located at, the Chewang Fu—rely solely on the testimony of the book vendors who sold these manuscripts to Ma Yuqing and Shen Yinxian. Scholars have debated the identity of Prince Che; most believe that he was a Mongol prince, and that the residence in question was his Beijing one. Guan Dedong, for example, suggests that Prince Che was Chebudeng Zhabu, who became chief of the Mongol League in 1771. However, it needs to be emphasized that the identity of Prince Che has no bearing on the dating of the manuscripts ascribed to his mansion. Even if all the so-called Chewang Fu manuscripts did come from one source, and even if this source was indeed Prince Che's Mansion—the manuscripts are still attributed to the mansion, not the prince, and were probably collected by a later occupant of the residence. In any event, most scholars believe that most of the Chewang Fu manuscripts were collected in the mid-nineteenth century. One text in the collection bears the date 1855, and the oral and dramatic genres represented in the collection did not flourish before the nineteenth century. The bulk of the Chewang Fu collection is available in a photographic reprint edition entitled *Qing Menggu Chewang fu cang quben*.

On the Chewang Fu collection, see Lei Mengshui, "Shulin suoji," p. 107; see also Wang Jisi's, Guan Dedong's, and Jin Peilin's prefaces (especially Jin's) to *Qing Menggu Chewang fu*; see also Liu Fu's preface to Liu Fu and Li Jiarui, *Zhongguo suqu zongmu gao*, p. 1.

35. The *guci* narrative on Jigong is in cases 269–79 of *Qing Menggu Chewang fu*. In this photographic edition, two original volumes are bound into one. Thus instead of 110 volumes, there are 55 only (5 in each case). Here I cite the original edition; thus, for example, by vol. 110 I refer to the second section of vol. 55 in the photographic edition.

There are 31 other *guci* narratives in manuscript form in the Chewang Fu collection (*Qing Menggu Chewang fu*, cases 76–290).

Some Chewang Fu manuscripts are available at Zhongshan University in Guangzhou, at the Sōkōdō collection of the Institute of Eastern Culture, Tokyo University, and in the Academia Sinica collection. The latter are included in the microfilm edition of the Academia Sinica collection (*Zhongyang yanjiuyuan*). They are identified by the character *che* (as in Chewang Fu), which was inscribed on them by this collection's editors, Liu Fu and Li Jiarui; see Liu Fu and Li Jiarui, p. 2.

36. The *Jigong Drum-Song* manuscript is included in *Zhongyang yanjiuyuan*, reel no. 83. Volumes 34–41, 44, 48–51, and 53 were rented out by the Everlasting Harmony Studio; vols. 45, 46, and 47 by the Everlasting Abundance Studio; and vols. 42, 43, and 52 by the Abundant Blessings Studio.

37. *Jigong Drum-Song,* in *Zhongyang yanjiuyuan,* reel 83, vol. 36; see also Zhou Chunyi. Another *guci* manuscript in the *Zhongyang yanjiuyuan* collection bears the date 1862, and yet another the date 1884; see, respectively, *Feng jian* (The sword's point), in *Zhongyang yanjiuyuan,* reel 75, vol. 26; and *Longqing shengping* (Abundant blessings and a time of peace), in *Zhongyang yanjiuyuan,* reel 75, vol. 5.

38. Some of these words are included in Xu Shirong's and Qi Rushan's dictionaries of the Beijing dialect. I am grateful to my friends Zhang Ping and Shang Quan for their help in identifying these Beijing patois words.

39. *Jigong Drum-Song,* in *Zhongyang yanjiuyuan,* reel 83, vol. 35.

40. The price of a single rented volume (of a multivolume *guci* narrative) appears to have ranged between 30 and 40 coins. The above-mentioned reader's complaint, dated 1859, suggests a price of 40 coins; another reader complains that at other stores he could get two volumes for 60 coins, whereas this one volume cost him 40. See *Jigong Drum-Song,* in *Zhongyang yanjiuyuan,* reel 83, vol. 36.

41. *Jigong Drum-Song,* Chewang Fu MS, vols. 31–43, 85–86, 99–106.

42. Cf. *Jigong Drum-Song,* Chewang Fu MS, vol. 18; and *Jigong zhuan,* chaps. 8–11.

43. Cf. *Jigong Drum-Song,* Chewang Fu MS, vol. 46, and *Jigong zhuan,* chaps. 165–66.

44. Cf., respectively, *Jigong Drum-Song,* Chewang Fu MS, vol. 44, to *Jigong zhuan,* chaps. 20–21; and *Jigong Drum-Song,* Chewang Fu MS, vols. 87–88, to *Jigong zhuan,* chaps. 68–70.

45. See *Tianqiao yilan,* p. 57.

46. Cf., respectively, *Zui puti* 1.7b–8b to *Jigong Drum-Song,* Chewang Fu MS, vol. 61; *Zui puti* 15.1a–5b to *Jigong Drum-Song,* Chewang Fu MS, vol. 110; and *Zui puti* 14.4b–9b to *Jigong Drum-Song,* Chewang Fu MS, vol. 110. The second miracle is also alluded to, but not narrated in the *Jidian yulu* 16b, and it is dismissed as absurd in *Jigong quanzhuan* 32.9b–10a. The third miracle is also narrated in *Jigong quanzhuan* 29.4b–10a; see also Chapter 4 of this book.

47. On nineteenth- and twentieth-century martial-arts fiction, see Chen Pingyuan, *Qiangu wenren xiake meng,* pp. 42–204; Wang Hailin, *Zhongguo wuxia xiaoshuo shilüe,* pp. 99–120, 134–261; Ning Zongyi, *Zhongguo wuxia xiaoshuo jianshang cidian;* and James J. Y. Liu, *The Chinese Knight-Errant,* pp. 116–21, 124–37.

48. For the term "military romance," see C. T. Hsia, "The Military Romance: A Genre of Chinese Fiction."

49. On the differences and similarities between martial-arts fiction and the military romance (especially the *Water Margin*), see Chen Pingyuan, pp. 47–55. Chen refers to the military romance as "heroic tales" (*yingxiong chuanqi*).

50. Y. W. Ma outlines the differences between late Qing martial-arts

novels and earlier courtcase fiction. Nonetheless, he classifies those martial novels in which the heroes are presented as an official's underlings as courtcase fiction; see his "Kung-an Fiction: A Historical and Critical Introduction," pp. 241–56. On the differences between martial-arts fiction and courtcase fiction, see also Chen Pingyuan, pp. 43–47; and James J. Y. Liu, p. 118. On Baogong in Yuan drama, see George A. Hayden, *Crime and Punishment in Medieval Chinese Drama: Three Judge Pao Plays*; on Baogong in Ming and early Qing vernacular stories, see Patrick Hanan, "*Judge Bao's Hundred Cases* Reconstructed"; and idem, *Chinese Vernacular Story*, pp. 72-74.

51. On the sources of *Three Heroes*, see Li Jiarui, "Cong Shi Yukun de *Longtu gongan* shuo dao *Sanxia wuyi*"; and Susan Blader, "*Sanxia wuyi* and Its link to Oral Literature." On nineteenth-century martial-arts fiction and oral literature, see also Chen Pingyuan, pp. 61–62; Wang Hailin, p. 108; and Y. W. Ma, pp. 255–56; see also *Zhongguo xiqu quyi cidian*, pp. 790, 792.

52. See Chapter 3 of this book and note 59 to that chapter.

53. See Yun, pp. 191–200; and James J. Y. Liu, pp. 53, 210 note 6.

54. Yun, p. 201.

55. Ibid., p. 202.

56. Ibid., pp. 192–93.

57. Wang Hailin, pp. 104–6.

58. *Jigong zhuan*, chaps. 54, 55, 58, 59.

59. Ibid. 70.346, 164.218–19.

60. See Chen Pingyuan, pp. 136–38.

61. See James J. Y. Liu, p. 118; and Y. W. Ma, p. 246 and note 98.

62. See *Jigong zhuan*, chap. 47 and 54.266.

63. Ibid., chap. 72.

64. See ibid. 46.227, 60.293, 90.441.

65. See *Sanxia wuyi*; see also James J. Y. Liu, p. 119.

66. *Jigong zhuan* 68.334. Here this modern edition of the novel is incomplete; cf. the 1913 Jiujing zhai edition (copy in Zhou Chunyi's possession; photocopy in my possession), 3:7a.

67. *Jigong zhuan* 68.337, 70.345.

68. Cf., e.g., ibid. 50.248, 68.336, and 70.344 with *Sanxia wuyi* 12.98.

69. Yun, p. 191.

70. Ibid., p. 195.

71. See ibid., p. 196; see also Xu Shirong, p. 554.

72. See also *Jigong zhuan* 53.190.

73. See, respectively, ibid. 90.438, 90.441, and 96.469.

74. See, respectively, ibid. 91.443 and 96.468.

75. *Shuihu quanzhuan* 16.233–36; on the use of sedatives and poison in martial-arts fiction, see also Chen Pingyuan, pp. 94–95.

76. The Lu Zhishen cycle occupies chaps. 3–8 of the *Shuihu quanzhuan*. The monk's nickname, Tattooed-Faced (Huamian), in the *Storyteller's Jigong* differs slightly from Lu Zhishen's; see *Jigong zhuan* 75.368. In the *Storyteller's*

Jigong this is Fayuan, who uses the first-person pronoun *sajia;* see ibid. 165.223–24. On Lu Zhishen and the *Recorded Sayings,* see Chapter 3 of this book.

77. Cf. *Jigong zhuan* 13.54, and *Shuihu quanzhuan* 5.85.

78. See, e.g., *Jigong zhuan* 90.439.

79. See, respectively, ibid. 91.443 and 97.471.

80. See, respectively, ibid. 72.356 and 92.448.

81. See Tzvetan Todorov, "The Typology of Detective Fiction," p. 47.

82. See *Jigong zhuan,* chaps. 76 and 91.

83. See, respectively, ibid., chaps. 71, 73 and 77, 91, 94.

84. Philip A. Kuhn, *Soulstealers: The Chinese Sorcery Scare of 1768,* p. 95.

85. Baoyu and his cousin Wang Xifeng are the victims of such sorcery; see Cao Xueqin, *The Story of the Stone* 25.498.

86. See the Han period account in *Wuyue Chunqiu zuzi suoyin* 4.9.

87. See Rolf A. Stein, *The World in Miniature: Container Gardens and Dwelligs in Far Eastern Religious Thought,* pp. 58–77.

88. See, e.g., *Fengshen yanyi* 48.327, 84.591.

89. *Jidian yulu* 17b; see also Chapter 3 of this book.

90. Chen Pingyuan, pp. 95–96.

91. On Tantric mantras in medieval China, see Strickmann, *Mantras et Mandarins;* on the syllable *oṃ* in such mantras, see ibid., p. 65. Regarding the formula *jiji rulü lingchi,* see *Hanyu dacidian,* 7: 458.

92. The spell *oṃ maṇi padme hūṃ* is used to imprison Sun Wukong in the mountain crevasse, which serves as his home for 500 years; see Anthony Yu, trans., *The Journey to the West,* vol. 1, chap. 14, p. 299 (whereas the formula *jiji rulü lingchi,* "Act promptly, as ordered by the law," appears in Tang Xianzu's *Mudanting*).

93. Anthony Yu, vol. 2, chap. 47, p. 364.

94. See Emily M. Ahern, "The Power and Pollution of Chinese Women," pp. 193–214; see also Gary Seaman, "The Sexual Politics of Karmic Retribution."

95. See Susan Naquin, *Shantung Rebellion: The Wang Lun Uprising of 1774,* pp. 100–101. Apparently the Taipings engaged in the same practice; see ibid., pp. 198–99; see also Joseph W. Esherick, *The Origins of the Boxer Uprising,* p. 54.

96. Kuhn, p. 224.

97. Ibid., p. 1.

98. *Yongging shengping* 12.75–13.78.

99. See Esherick, pp. 55, 96–98, 104–9.

100. Trans. from ibid., p. 105.

101. *Jigong zhuan* 75.369; see also ibid. 92.451, where it is explained that the only means of defeating a practitioner of the armor of the golden bell are to burn him, bury him alive, or boil him.

102. Ibid. 165.223; see Esherick, pp. 57–59.

103. Esherick, esp. pp. 329–31.

104. See Qian Cai, *Shuo Yue quanzhuan*. The earliest extant edition of the *Shuo Yue quanzhuan* is dated 1798. However, the novel was written earlier; its preface is dated *jiazi*, which probably refers to 1684 or 1744. During the Qianlong reign (1736–95) the novel was banned. Nevertheless at least 21 extant editions attest to its popularity during the late Qing and the Republican periods; see Ōtsuka, p. 229; *Zhongguo tongsu xiaoshuo zongmu tiyao*, p. 418; and the preface to Qian Cai, p. 3. On the *Shuo Yue quanzhuan*'s antecedents, see Chapter 3, note 31, of this book.

105. See Chapter 3 of this book.

106. The historical Qin Gui did have an adopted son named Qin Xi, but he never occupied the premiership. As noted above, the son's given name was written with the fire radical (Qin Xi 秦熺). The novel's misspelling of his name (Qin Xi 秦喜) indicates its reliance on an oral source.

107. During the nineteenth century, the Yue Fei cycle was performed in several northern genres of oral literature, including *bajiaogu, zidishu,* and the *zidishu* narratives in Shi Yukun's style; see the texts reprinted in Du Yingtao, *Yue Fei gushi xiqu shuochang ji*. See also the *zidishu* manuscript *Quan sao Qin*, and the Shi Yukun-style *zidishu* manuscript *Fengbo ting* in the Chewang Fu collection (*Qing Menggu Chewang fu*, case 297, vols. 4–6, and case 215, vols. 1–6, respectively). (Fengbo ting is the name of the pavilion under which, according to tradition, Yue Fei and son were murdered on Qin Gui's order.) On the play *Fengseng sao Qin* in Beijing opera, see Ceng Bairong, *Jingju jumu cidian*, pp. 739–40.

108. The Hubei *Hanju* actor Li Chunsen performed both a play on Jigong entitled *Capturing the Consumption Insect* (*Shou laochong*) and a play on the Yue Fei cycle's monk entitled, like most regional plays on this eccentric saint, *The Mad Monk Sweeps Away [Premier] Qin*; see the first two pages of illustrations in *Zhongguo difang xiqu jicheng*, Hubei volume. In the summer of 1989 I interviewed the Taiwanese handpuppeteer Xu Wang, who told me that he uses the same puppet for Jigong and for the mad monk of the Yue Fei cycle. Even so, Xu Wang emphasized that these are two distinct figures.

109. The original is in the *Doctrine of the Mean*, chap. 14; see James Legge, trans., *The Chinese Classics*, 1: 395.

110. See Le Roy Ladurie; and Burke, pp. 199–204.

111. Tun Li-ch'en, *Annual Customs and Festivals in Peking*, p. 14.

112. *Jidian yulu* 11a.

113. The three *Zhaojia lou* manuscripts are practically identical, suggesting that they were copied from the same source. Two manuscripts are in the Academia Sinica collection (reels 205 and 208), and one belongs to the Chewang Fu collection (original at the Beijing University Library; *Qing Menggu Chewang Fu*, case no. 30, vol. 1). One of the two *Zhaojia lou* manuscripts currently in the Academia Sinica collection (in reel 205) originally belonged to the Chewang Fu collection (see note 35 to this chapter).

The play *Zhaojia lou* is listed in three nineteenth-century catalogues of the Baiben Zhang manuscript shop. The Baiben Zhang manuscript version of the play was probably different from the extant one; whereas the extant manuscript versions of the play are in one volume each, the Baiben Zhang version was in four volumes. According to one catalogue, its price was 6,000 cash. The catalogues are preserved in the Academia Sinica collection (*Zhongyang yanjiuyuan*, table-of-contents reel).

114. The *Majia hu* manuscript belongs to the Chewang Fu collection (the original is at the Beijing University Library; *Qing Menggu Chewang Fu*, case no. 24, vol. 4). The *Dabei lou* manuscript is in the Academia Sinica collection (*Zhongyang yanjiuyuan*, reel 209).

115. This is the 1898 preface; see note 6 to this chapter for its location.

116. Cf. *Jigong zhuan*, chap. 3, *Jigong Drum-Song* (Chewang Fu MS, vol. 22) and the *Dabei lou* manuscript. In the novel and the *Jigong Drum-Song* alike, it is one (or several) of Jigong's fellow monks, rather than Hua Yunlong, who attempts unsuccessfully to burn him. The play also differs from the novel and the *guci* narrative in that the Bodhisattva Guanyin appears in it. In the novel "Dabei lou" is written 大碑樓, whereas in the play and the *guci* narrative, it is written 大悲樓.

117. Cf. *Jigong zhuan*, chaps. 68–70; *Jigong Drum-Song*, Chewang Fu MS, vols. 87–88; and the *Zhaojia lou* manuscripts.

118. Cf. *Jigong zhuan*, chaps. 89–101; *Jigong Drum-Song*, Chewang Fu MS, vols. 83–84, and the *Majia hu* manuscript. (In the *Jigong Drum-Song*, Majia hu is referred to as the Majia zhai 馬家寨.)

119. These are the plays *White Water Lake (Baishui hu)* and *Primordial Heaven Mountain* (*Gutianshan*); they correspond, respectively, to *Jigong zhuan*, chaps. 132–35, and 90–94. The four other new plays are the *Double-Heads Mystery (Shuangtou an)*, the *Compassionate Clouds Temple* (*Ciyun guan*), the *Eight-Trigrams Furnace* (*Bagua lu*), *The Eight Devils Try Crazy Ji (Bamo lian Jidian)*; these plays correspond respectively to *Jigong zhuan*, chaps. 109–10, 182–200, 205–10, and 233–37. Another twentieth-century play, *The Buddha Manifested in the Cave* (*Dongfang xianfo*), concerns the battle between Jigong and Hua Yunlong, but its plot differs from that of the novel. The twentieth-century versions of the play *Dabei Tower*, now named *Burning the Dabei Tower* (*Huoshao Dabei lou*), are closer to the novel than the nineteenth-century manuscript version. On these plays, see Ceng, pp. 757–59.

120. One of these *wusheng* actors was the renowned Yang Xiaolou (1878–1938); see Ceng, pp. 757–58; see also Wu Tongbing and Zhou Yaxun, eds., *Jingju zhishi cidian*, pp. 288 and 499–500.

121. See Ceng, pp. 759–62.

122. When I interviewed Xu Wang in the summer of 1989, he listed ten different plays of his on Jigong: *Inviting Weituo* (*Qing Weituo*), *Jigong Subdues Premier Qin* (*Jigong shou Qinxiang*), *Jigong Subdues the Precocious Child* (*Jigong shou shentong*), *Compassionate Clouds Temple* (*Ciyun guan*), *Xiaoxitian*, *The*

Eight Devils Try Crazy Ji (*Bamo lian Jidian*), *Capturing Hua Yunlong* (*Zhua Hua Yunlong*), *Capturing Liu Xiangmiao* (*Zhua Liu Xiangmiao*), *Subduing the Peach-Flower Spirit* (*Shou Meihua jingren*), and *Pingyang zhuan* (in the last play Jigong is apparently a minor figure only). Xu Wang does not use detailed scripts but only brief synopses. He kindly allowed me to photocopy several of the latter; see also Lü Lizheng, *Budaixi biji*, pp. 89, 98, 180, 204.

123. See Chen Longting, "Dianshi budiaxi de fazhan yu bianqian"; see also Lü, pp. 84–85.

124. I am grateful to Chen Changhui for her simultaneous translation of Taiwanese into Mandarin during these interviews.

125. This information tallies well with Lü Lizheng's (p. 89) findings that Xu Tianfu created his Jigong plays in the 1930s.

126. See Jiang Wuchang, "Taiwan budaixi jianshi," pp. 101–2.

127. See Lü, p. 98.

128. By "novel," Xu Wang and Huang Haidai probably refer to the 280-chapter edition of the *Storyteller's Jigong*, which includes the first sequel to the novel. The repertoires of both artists include the play *Xiaoxitian*, which is based on this sequel.

129. These are the plays *Compassionate Clouds Temple* (*Ciyun guan*) and *The Eight Devils Try Crazy Ji* (*Bamo lian Jidian*), which figure in Beijing opera under the same titles; see note 122 to this chapter.

130. Cf. *Jigong zhuan*, chap. 113.

131. Liang Peijin's catalogue of Cantonese opera scripts, the *Yueju jumu tongjian*, is arranged chronologically. It lists no plays on Jigong for the period before 1911, one play for the period 1911–19, and six plays for the period 1920–36; see Liang, items 8891–96.

132. The play *The Zhao Family's Mansion* has been performed in Hebei *bangzi*, Anhui *Huiju*, and Hunan *Xiangju*; the play *The Ma Family's Lake* has been performed in Hebei *bangzi*. It is possible that these plays spread to these genres through the influence of Beijing opera, in which they both figure; see Ceng Bairong, pp. 757–58.

133. One actor who performed this play was Li Chunsen (see note 108 to this chapter); the original episode is in *Jidian yulu* 17b.

134. In the summer of 1989, video rental shops in Taiwan carried at least three movies on Jigong: *The New Living Buddha Jigong* (*Xin Jigong Huofo*), *Jigong Wreaks Havoc in Court* (*Jigong da nao gongtang*), and *The True and False Jigong* (*Zhen jia Jigong*). Jean DeBernardi (pers. comm.) tells me that a Jigong movie enjoyed great popularity in Malaysia during the 1970s.

135. The Mandarin-speaking Taiwanese series, entitled the *Muddle-Headed Immortal* (*Hutu shenxian*), was produced by Taishi Television; the Taiwanese-speaking series, entitled *Big and Little Jigong* (*Daxiao Jigong*), was produced by Huashi Television. The mainland and Hong Kong serials alike were titled *The Living Buddha Jigong* (*Jigong huofo*); the latter was produced

by Hong Kong Asia Television (Xianggang Yashi). Like the preceding list of movies on Jigong, this list of television serials is probably incomplete.

136. The Gem-Cassia (Zhubao gui) *gezaixi* opera troup from Jiayi, Taiwan, performed a play entitled the *Big and Little Jigong Story* (*Daxiao Jigong zhuan*) in the 1990 local drama competition in Taiwan; I am grateful to Jiang Wuchang for a photocopy of the script. The theme of a big and a small Jigong is already present in the serial *Muddle-Headed Immortal*, which started airing in 1986, several months before the 1987 television serial *Big and Little Jigong*.

137. See Wang Songshan, p. 81.

138. For a brief introduction to the *gezaixi* genre, see ibid., pp. 66–74; see also "Gezaixi."

139. See Wang Songshan, pp. 69, 95.

140. On the Minghuayuan Company, see Huang Meiying, "Sandai tongtang de Minghuayuan"; and Wang Songshan, pp. 82–83, 95–102; Wang Songshan refers to Chen Shengdian as the company's general manager. But when I interviewed him in 1989, it was Chen Shengfu who held this position.

141. This is a temple for Taiziye Zhongtan yuanshuai. But the Minghuayuan Company also performs plays on Jigong in the latter's own temples, such as the Five Dragons Mountain, Phoenix Mountain Temple (Wulong shan fengshan si) in Gaoxiong; see Wang Songshan, illustrations 15, 17, and 18.

142. Chen Shengfu kindly gave me a photocopy of the script.

143. On this Taiwanese tradition, and its sources, see Katz, "Enlightened Alchemist or Immoral Immortal?"

144. See also Huang Meiying, pp. 103–4.

Chapter 6

1. Jujian, *Beixian wenji*, *SKQS*, 1183: 160 and 159; see also Chapter 1 of this book.

2. See *Jidian yulu* 22b, *Zui puti* 20.2a, *Jigong quanzhuan* 34.11a. The Jingci Monastery's history, the *Jingci si zhi* (3.260, 10.679) also points to Hupao Hill as the site of Jigong's stūpa; see also *Xihu zhi*, by Fu Wanglu (*jinshi* 1715) and Li Wei (?–1738), 23.29b. Wu Zhijing (fl. ca. 1600; *Wulin fan zhi*, p. 219) is probably wrong in arguing that Jigong's remains were enshrined at the Jingci Monastery; he contradicts all the above sources.

3. A Buddhist monastery variously called Dinghui si and Hupao si was located on Hupao Hill. It no longer survives, however, and it is not clear to me whether Jigong's stūpa was located within its precincts. In his history of the Dinghui Monastery, Abbot Shengguang (*Hupao Dinghui si zhi*) does not mention a Jigong stūpa.

4. See Clarence Day, *Chinese Peasant Cults: Being a Study of Chinese Paper Gods*, pp. 32, 48–49. Unfortunately, Day identifies Jigong wrongly as the ec-

centric miracle worker Baozhi (?–514), about whom see Chapter 2 of this book and note 42 to that chapter.

5. Information gathered during visits to Hupao in 1992 and 1994.

6. See, e.g., *Qiantang xianzhi* (1609), *waiji* section 9.a; Wu Zhijing, 588.218–19; and *Hangzhou fuzhi* 171.17a; see also Tian Rucheng, 14.275.

7. Chuandeng, *Tiantai shan fangwai zhi* 5.11b; see also *Tiantai xianzhi* 11.19a; *Tiantai shan fangwai zhiyao* 4.10b; and Yu Changlin et al., *Taizhou fuzhi* 140.8a.

8. See Li Jie, "Jigong guli: Tiantai Shiqiangtou." On the Jigong cult in Tiantai county, see also Zhu Fengao, *Tiantai shan fengwu zhi*, pp. 47–49.

9. The temple is located on the second floor of a building, next to a structure called the "Jigong Pavilion" (Jigong ting). The neighborhood in which it is located was originally an independent village called Shiqiangtou.

10. Information gathered during visits to the temple in 1992 and 1994. According to a pamphlet distributed by the temple, as well as a stele dated 1990 inside it, the temple originated in the Song period, when a shrine dedicated to Jigong was built there. However, I have found no evidence to support this claim in either the extant gazetteers or the novels on Jigong.

11. One Jigong temple in Taiwan that considers itself a branch temple of the Jigong Hall is the large Five Dragons Mountain, Phoenix Mountain Temple (Wulong shan fengshan si) in Gaoxiong. Donald Sutton has videotaped the temple's delegation to the Jigong Hall, as it returned in procession from Mount Tiantai to Gaoxiong. He kindly allowed me to examine this recording. On the social functions of "division of incense" temple networks, see Kristofer Schipper, "The Cult of Pao-sheng Ta-ti and Its Spread to Taiwan: A Case Study of *Fen-hsiang*."

12. *Jidian yulu* 23a.

13. See Chapter 3 of this book.

14. *Jidian yulu* 17b, 18b; see also the same episode in *Zui puti* 16.7a–b, 17.3b–4b.

15. *Jidian yulu* 20b; see also the same episode in *Zui puti* 18.5b.

16. *Jigong quanzhuan* 32.4a; the icon was obtained at the Jingci Monastery; see also ibid. 29.4a–b, 25.9a–11a, 30.1b, and 36.1a.

17. I am grateful to Eric Cohen of the Hebrew University, who provided photographs of a Thai-Chinese medium possessed by Jigong. The photographs were taken on Oct. 18, 1996, during a festival celebrated by the Hokkien-speaking Overseas Chinese community on Phuket island in the southern part of Thailand; on the Jigong cult in Malaysia, see below.

18. Many of these mediums cannot speak Mandarin, and the interviews were conducted with the help of my friend Huang Chunsen, who provided simultaneous Taiwanese-Mandarin translation.

19. In the religious ceremonies of the Unity Sect (Yiguan dao) in Taiwan, however, most Jigong mediums are women.

20. On spirit-mediums in Taiwan, see Jordan, pp. 67–86. On the Fujianese origins of Taiwanese mediumship, see J. J. M. de Groot, *The Religious*

System of China, 6: 1269–94; see also Dean, esp. pp. 64–66, 181–82, 229–30. For a detailed study of Singaporean mediums, see Elliot.

21. See Jordan, p. 71; cf. the similar accounts in Groot, 6: 1272, and Elliot, p. 46.

22. I am grateful to Vincent Durand-Dastès, who provided me with a fund-raising petition—signed by You Benchang—for this temple. I do not know if construction of the temple, which was supposed to begin in March 1993, did indeed take place.

23. On the medium as oracle, see Jordan, pp. 70–78.

24. There were other variations; see Jiang Renxiu et al., *Dajiale dubo zhi yanjiu*, pp. 3–8; see also Robert P. Weller, *Resistance, Chaos and Control in China: Taiping Rebels, Taiwanese Ghosts and Tiananmen*, pp. 139–40.

25. See Weller, p. 140; and Jiang Renxiu, p. 1.

26. Quoted in Hu Taili, "Shen gui yu dutu: Dajiale duxi fanying zhi minsu xinyang."

27. I collected two editions of this poem, in the spring and summer of 1987. In one edition, the poem is dated 1986.

28. Quoted in Hu.

29. For a study of this ghost's temple and cult, see Weller, pp. 124–68.

30. See Hu; and Weller, esp. pp. 139–42.

31. Jean DeBernardi, "The God of War and the Vagabond Buddha," p. 330.

32. Ibid., p. 328.

33. For a general survey of the deities worshipped by the Boxers, see Jerome Ch'en, "The Nature and Characteristics of the Boxer Movement: A Morphological Study"; and Esherick, esp. p. 329 (Esherick does not mention Jigong).

34. See Sawara Tokusuke and Ou-yin, "Quanluan jiwen," 1: 156.

35. Luo Dunrong, "Quanbian yuwen," 2: 961; see also ibid., 2: 960. The Tang monk, Zhu Bajie, Sha Monk, Sun Wukong, and Erlang all figure in the *Journey to the West;* Ma Chao and Huang Hansheng are characters in *Romance of the Three Kingdoms.*

36. Quoted in Liu Yitong, "Min jiao xiangchou dumen wenjian lu," 2: 188. I follow the partial translation in Jerome Ch'en, pp. 292–93. On Jigong in the Boxer movement, see also Liu Mengyang, "Tianjin Quanfei bianluan jishi," 2: 8.

37. Spirit-writing is also known as *fuji* (wielding the winnowing basket); on its history and current practice, see David Jordan and Daniel Overmyer, *The Flying Phoenix: Aspects of Chinese Sectarianism in Taiwan*, esp. pp. 36–88; and Xu Dishan, *Fuji mixin di yanjiu*. See also Laurence G. Thompson, "The Moving Finger Writes: A Note on Revelation and Renewal in Chinese Religion"; and Gary Seaman, *Temple Organization in a Chinese Village*, pp. 66–69, 82–94. For a translation of Wenchang's autobiography, see Terry F.

Kleeman, *A God's Own Tale: The Book of Transformations of Wenchang, the Divine Lord of Zitong.*

38. This is the *Precious Book of the Jade Regulations* (*Yulü baojuan*); see Jordan and Overmyer, pp. 46–49.

39. See Jordan and Overmyer, pp. 46–49, 55–57.

40. See Cynthia J. Brokaw, *The Ledgers of Merit and Demerit: Social Change and Moral Order in Late Imperial China*, p. 234.

41. David Jordan and Daniel Overmyer (pp. 16–20, 57–63) have coined the term "Motherist sectarianism" to refer to this sectarian tradition.

42. See ibid., pp. 19, 57–63.

43. Xu Dishan, p. 99.

44. Day, p. 49.

45. One and a half million copies were distributed in Taiwan, and another million and a half in Hong Kong, Singapore, and Malaysia; see Song Guangyu, "*Diyu youji* suo xianshi de dangqian shehui wenti," p. 116.

46. See Song Guangyu's (ibid.) analysis of the social problems mirrored in the morality book *Journey to Purgatory*.

47. See Jordan and Overmyer, esp. pp. 12–13; and Zheng Zhiming, *Zhongguo shanshu yu zongjiao*, pp. 445–49.

48. See Zheng Zhiming, pp. 417–19; see also Appendix D of this book.

49. On these spirit-writing congregations, see Jordan and Overmyer, pp. 79–81; and Seaman, *Temple Organization*, esp. pp. 65–81. These groups need to be distinguished from large sectarian movements such as the Unity Sect. First, they are much smaller in scope and number of followers. They are centered on one temple only and have no branch temples. Second, the salvational element of Motherist sectarianism is absent in their teachings. They propagate traditional Confucian ethics only.

50. *Diyu youji* 37.109–10.

51. Ibid. 37.110.

52. Ibid.

53. Ibid. 16.57–58.

54. Ibid. 16.58.

55. Ibid. 32.98; see also Song Guangyu, "*Diyu youji* suo xianshi de dangqian shehui wenti," p. 119.

56. *Tiantang youji* 33.165.

57. *Jidian yulu* 7b; see also Chapter 3 of this book.

58. See Chapter 5 of this book.

59. *Diyu youji* 35.104; see also 35.105 and 26.84–85.

60. See Tan Chee-beng, *The Development and Distribution of Dejiao Associations in Malaysia and Singapore: A Study on a Chinese Religious Organization*, pp. 8, 37, and 42 note 5, and plates 8 (p. 30) and 21 (page 53).

61. Translated in Stephen F. Teiser, "'Having Once Died and Returned to Life': Representations of Hell in Medieval China," p. 448; see also Hansen,

Changing Gods, pp. 54–55, for Hong Mai's story of a self-portrait by Lü Dongbin.

62. A small number of Li's paintings are also signed by Guanyin, Lü Dongbin, Yue Fei, and Guangong. Jordan and Overmyer (p. 77) mention that Sun Yat-sen also figures in Taiwanese spirit-writing cults.

63. See ibid., esp. pp. 16–20.

64. Susan Naquin, "The Transmission of White Lotus Sectarianism in Late Imperial China," pp. 255–56.

65. The former term is used by Naquin in ibid.; the latter is used by Jordan and Overmyer, e.g., p. 59.

66. See Naquin, *Shantung Rebellion*.

67. See Ma Xisha and Han Bingfang, *Zhongguo minjian zongjiao shi*, pp. 1092–167.

68. Ibid., pp. 1150–67.

69. See Li Shiyu's annotated bibliography of Unity Sect publications, in his *Xianzai Hua bei mimi zongjiao*, item no. 5, p. 99; Li Shiyu lists at least ten other Unity Sect books attributed to Wang Jueyi, usually under the latter's *hao* of Beihai Laoren.

70. It is interesting that despite the sect's claim for ancient origins, some Unity Sect publications describe Wang Jueyi as the founder of the sect; see Fan Kaiyin, *Yiguan dao de jianxin cheng*, pp. 25–28. Some Unity Sect publications, including Fan Kaiyin's book, refer to Wang Jueyi under the name Wang Ximeng, which does not appear in Qing period sources.

71. On Zhang Guangbi, see Li Shiyu, pp. 34–35 and 48–50; see also Jordan and Overmyer, pp. 216–17.

72. The date 1928 is given in Li Shiyu, p. 32. On Zhang Guangbi's proselytizing activities, see also Song Guangyu, *Tiandao gouchen: Yiguan dao diaocha baogao*, pp. 122–29.

73. Zhang's death was followed by a succession struggle between Sun Suzhen and Zhang's other wife, Madame Liu. In this struggle Sun Suzhen gained the upper hand, and today most Unity Sect followers consider her the sect's "mistress." Nonetheless, some of the sect branches established by Madame Liu revere her as their authority and are angered by the excessive veneration of Sun Suzhen apparent in most other branches; see Jordan and Overmyer, pp. 218–21. Sun Suzhen lived her later years in seclusion in Taizhong; see Song, *Tiandao gouchen*, p. 133.

74. See Li Shiyu, p. 49.

75. The Unity Sect did maintain amicable relations with the Chinese puppet government, which the Japanese established in Nanking in 1940; see Jordan and Overmyer, pp. 216–17.

76. See ibid., pp. 240–45.

77. Song, *Tiandao gouchen*, p. 42; on the gradual rapprochement between the Unity Sect and the ruling Guomindang, see also Jordan and Overmyer, pp. 247–49.

78. One exception is the charges leveled against the Unity Sect leader in Tainan, Wang Shou, during the late 1970s; see Jordan and Overmyer, pp. 241–45.

79. Ibid., p. 221.

80. See Song, *Tiandao gouchen*, pp. 1, 19.

81. I was asked not to disclose the name of the corporation in question.

82. This brief outline of the sect's teachings is based primarily on Jordan and Overmyer, pp. 257–63.

83. John Kieschnick, pers. comm., summer 1995. The interview itself took place in 1991. This specific informant felt that the apocalypse is imminent. She had one home in Taipei and another in the United States (in Virginia). In preparation for the possibility that the apocalypse might strike while she is at the latter, she financed the construction of a chapel there as well.

84. See Jordan and Overmyer, pp. 213 and 222.

85. On vegetarianism in the Unity Sect, see Song, *Tiandao gouchen*, pp. 91–94.

86. Jordan and Overmyer, p. 258; see also p. 237.

87. See Song, *Tiandao gouchen*, p. 43; see also Willem A. Grootaers, "Une Société secrete moderne: I-Koan-Tao. Bibliographie annotée."

88. See Jordan and Overmyer, pp. 302 and 236; see also Li Shiyu, pp. 77–78; Grootaers, "Une Société secrete moderne," pp. 336–37; and Song, *Tiandao gouchen*, p. 50.

89. This title was applied to Jigong twice in the *Recorded Sayings*, but it gained currency only in the *Storyteller's Jigong*.

90. Li Shiyu, p. 50.

91. See the list of titles in ibid., p. 50.

92. See ibid.; and Jordan and Overmyer, p. 252 note 2.

93. See Li Shiyu's annotated bibliography, items 20, 23, 36, 38, 45, 50, 67, 78, 107–10, 114.

94. See Jordan and Overmyer, pp. 252 and 255.

95. *Jigong huofo xianshen shuofa zhuanji*.

96. See item 20 in Li Shiyu; see also Jordan and Overmyer, pp. 251–53.

97. See items 36 and 78 in Li Shiyu. Grootaers describes an edition of the *Prajñāpāramitā Hṛdaya* sūtra with commentaries attributed to several other deities, including Guangong and Wendi; see item no. 31 in his "Une Société secrete moderne."

98. See, e.g., the chapter from the *Bai yang bao fa* (Precious raft of the White Yang [Period]); quoted in Li Shiyu, p. 75.

99. I interviewed a few Unity Sect's devotees in 1986 and again in 1989 and 1991 (all in Taipei); see also the photographs in *Xian fo sheng ji zhuanji*, pp. 62–63 and 43.

100. For photographs of children possessed by deities (but not Jigong) during Unity Sect's gatherings, see *Xian fo sheng ji zhuanji*, pp. 22–27, 65.

101. See ibid., pp. 85 and 60–61, respectively; see also the photographs on pp. 39 and 83.

102. The term "initiator" is applied to any sect official who has been authorized to conduct the initiation ritual; see Song, *Tiandao gouchen*, p. 77; see also Jordan and Overmyer, p. 222.

103. The Unity Sect's technical term for spirit-writing, *sancai* (literally "three talents"), alludes to the three people who operate the writing implement: the one who draws the characters (and has "divine talent"), the one who reads them out loud (and has "human talent"), and the one who records them (and has "earthly talent"); see Song, *Tiandao gouchen*, p. 77.

104. *Xian fo sheng ji zhuanji*, p. 45.

105. John Kieschnick, pers. comm., summer 1995. The dinner took place in 1991.

106. Daoxuan, 50: 657a; translated in Kieschnick, p. 55.

107. *Jigong quanzhuan* 31.1a–7b. The ability to vomit living animals is also attributed to Jigong in the seventeenth-century *Zui puti* (16.5b–7a). However, in that novel it serves no apologetic purpose and is meant only to demonstrate Jigong's magic powers. See also Chapter 4 to this book.

108. Information gathered during a visit to the monastery in April 1995; see also the photograph in *Biyun si luohan tang*, p. 261.

109. Information on this painting was gathered during visits to the Lingyin Monastery in June 1992 and December 1994. The 1888 edition of the *Jingci si zhi* (3.8a) includes a woodblock illustration of Jigong in which he also carries a fan. According to an accompanying inscription, this illustration is based on a stone relief, carved in 1758, at the Jingci Monastery, which derives from an earlier, Song period work. The claim for a Song period antecedent is most likely unfounded. But if this illustration is based on an eighteenth-century stone relief, this would mean that at least one artist, in Hangzhou, associated Jigong with a fan at that time (the illustration includes none of the other emblems now associated with Jigong).

110. Information on the dating of the arhat halls at the Baoguang and Wuyou monasteries was gathered during visits in May 1995.

111. See, e.g., the Jigong statue, dating from 1985, in the main hall of the Jingci Monastery in Hangzhou.

112. This edition, of which I have a copy, is the fourth sequel to the *Storyteller's Jigong*, and is entitled *The Sixth Continuation of the Jigong Story* (*Liuxu Jigong zhuan*). (On the discrepancy between the title and the actual sequence of each of the *Storyteller's Jigong*'s sequels, see Appendix B.) The first edition of the third sequel was published in 1908, and the first dated edition of the fourth in 1909. In all likelihood, this edition of the fourth sequel postdates the latter.

113. Jujian, p. 159; see Chapter 1 of this book.

114. See, respectively, Juding, 51: 679a; and Wenxiu, p. 458b. Wenxiu also quotes a *gāthā* attributed to Daoji.

115. See Chapter 1 of this book.

116. *Lingyin si zhi* 3b.9b.

117. Cf. ibid. to *Jidian yulu* 5a.

118. *Lingyin si zhi* 8.31b, 6b.21b. See also Chapter 1 of this book and note 24 to that chapter.

119. Jixiang's *Jingci si zhi* is based on two earlier histories of the monastery, Dahuo's *Nanping Jingci si zhi* (ca. 1625) and Zhuanyu's *Jingci xu zhi*. The former is preserved at the Library of Congress. I have not seen these histories.

120. See *Jingci si zhi* 3.6b–9a, 10.11b–13b, 22.4b–5a.

121. See *Zui puti* 14.4b–9b and *Jigong quanzhuan* 29.4b–10a. See also Chapter 4 of this book.

122. Cf., respectively, *Jingci si zhi* 1.9a–b to *Jidian yulu* 15a–b, 18.28b to 18a, 19.3a to 17b, 19.3a–b to 18b, 25.3a to 13a, and 25.3a to 20a. The earliest piece is a fund-raising petition, which is included in a chapter on the monastery's sites rather than in one of the chapters dedicated to works of literature. These literary pieces are also included, with some changes, in *Zui puti*, but the *Jingci si zhi* follows the *Jidian yulu* versions.

123. *Jingci si zhi* 8.21 a. The poem was borrowed from the *Jidian yulu* 14a. It is included also in *Zui puti* 13.1b.

124. I assume that the nonstandard character [illegible] should be pronounced "ju."

125. Jiexian, "Jidian benzhuan xu," in Shen Hengbiao, *Yunlin si xuzhi*, 25: 4.8b–9b. The *Yunlin si xu zhi* includes several other pieces by Jiexian, who is also the author of the *Chanmen duanlian shuo* (1661). On Jiexian, see *Lingyin si zhi* 3b.30a–b.

126. In the *Drunken Puti*, Jigong eats three pigeons and then vomits them alive; see *Zui puti* 16.5b–7a.

127. This legend is dismissed as absurd in *Jigong quanzhuan* 36.4a–b; see also Chapter 4 of this book.

128. *Zui puti*, under the title *Jidian chanshi dazhuan*, p. 19. The 1932 Foxue shuju edition is available in yet another Taiwanese photographic reprint (dated 1981), and it also served as the source for a typeset edition that was published by the Zhejiang Buddhist Association in 1987; see Appendix D.

129. For a translation of this poem, see pp. 28–29.

130. See, respectively, Lang, 2: 475; and *Lingyin si zhi* 8.31b, 6b.21b.

131. Another literary piece in the *Jidian yulu* (1a) that may have been borrowed from a monastic source is the eulogy in his honor printed on this novel's front page, preceding the text. Prior to the compilation of the *Jidian yulu*, this eulogy was quoted by Tian Rucheng (14.275) in his *Xihu youlan zhiyu*, and by the early nineteenth century at the latest it was inscribed on a stone tablet in the Jingci Monastery (*Jing si zhi* 3.8b–9a). For a translation of the eulogy, see p. 50.

132. See Lang, 2: 457; and *Jingci si zhi* 3.6b–9a.

133. Some Buddhist monasteries in which there are arhat halls with Jigong figures are (1) Biyun si, in the outskirts of Beijing (whose arhat hall was built in 1748); (2) the monastery complex in the Summer Palace in Chengde (built in 1774, but no longer extant); (3) Baoguang si, in the outskirts of Chengdu, Sichuan (built in 1851); (4) Wuyou si, in Leshan, Sichuan (built in 1909); (5) The Jie chuang lü si, (also known as the Xiyuan si), in Suzhou (date of arhat hall uncertain); (6) Puhua si, on Mount Wutai in Shanxi Province (Jigong's statue, dated 1982, is located in the Eighteen Arhats Hall). The dates of the arhats halls of the items 1, 3, 4, and 6 were established during visits to them in spring 1995. On item no. 1, see also *Biyun si luohan tang*, p. 261. On item no. 2, see Li Bingxin, ed., *Wai ba miao*, p. 156. For general information on Jigong in 500-arhat halls, see also J. Prip-Møller, *Chinese Buddhist Monasteries: Their Plan and Its Function as a Setting for Buddhist Monastic Life*, p. 121; and Bai Huawen, p. 67.

134. This is the case in the Biyun si (near Beijing) and in the Puhua si (on Mount Wutai in Shanxi).

135. See Bai Huawen, p. 67.

136. Buddhist monasteries in whose arhat halls Jigong is venerated side by side with the mad monk include items 1, 2, 4, and 5 in note 133 to this chapter; see also Ma Shutian, *Huaxia zhu shen*, p. 507.

137. Information gathered during visits to these temples in summer 1992 and fall 1994.

138. The Biyun si arhat hall was built in 1748, the arhat hall in the Summer Palace complex in 1774; see note 133 to this chapter.

139. See Katz, "Wen Ch'iung," pp. 216–19.

140. See Chapter 2 of this book.

Conclusion

1. Wu Chengen, 98.1111; trans. Anthony Yu, 4: 393.

2 Andrew Plaks, "Allegory in the *Hsi-yu Chi* and *Hung-lou Meng*," pp. 172–73.

3. See Jordan, p. 61; and Richard J. Smith, *Fortune-tellers and Philosophers: Divination in Traditional Chinese Society*, p. 235. This is also the explanation I was given by informants in Taiwan.

Works Cited

For a chronological list of works of fiction and drama on Jigong, as well as a list of spirit-written texts attributed to him, see Appendixes A–D.

Ahern, Emily Martin. "The Power and Pollution of Chinese Women." In Margery Wolf and Roxane Witke, eds., *Women in Chinese Society*. Stanford: Stanford University Press, 1975.

Bai Huawen 白化文. "Zhongguo de luohan" 中國的羅漢 (Chinese arhats). *Wenshi zhishi* 文史知識, no. 37 (1984): 62–67.

Bai Juyi 白居易. *Bai Juyi ji* 白居易集 (Collected writings of Bai Juyi). Ed. Gu Xuejie 顧學頡. Beijing: Zhonghua shuju, 1979.

Bakhtin, Mikhail. *Rabelais and His World*. Trans. Hélèn Iswolsky. Bloomington: Indiana University Press, 1984.

Balazs, Etienne. "Nihilistic Revolt or Mystical Escapism." In idem, *Chinese Civilization and Bureaucracy*, pp. 226–54. Trans. H. M. Wright. New Haven: Yale University Press, 1964.

Baxian chuchu dongyou ji 八仙出處東遊記 (The origins of the Eight Immortals and their journey to the east). Wanli ed. Photographic rpt., in *Guben xiaoshuo jicheng* (q.v.), vol. 70.

Beifang Zhenwu zushi Xuantian Shangdi chushen zhizhuan 北方眞武祖師玄天上帝出身志傳 (The chronicle of the incarnations of the True Warrior from the North, the Patriarch, Emperor of the Dark Heavens). Wanli ed. Photographic rpt., in *Guben xiaoshuo jicheng* (q.v.), vol. 71.

Beijing lishi ditu ji 北京歷史地圖集 (Historical atlas of Beijing). Hou Renzhi 侯仁之, gen. ed. Beijing: Beijing chubanshe, 1988.

Beijing wangshi tan 北京往事談 (Talks on things past in Beijing). Beijingshi weiyuanhui wenshi ziliao yanjiu weiyuanhui 北京市委員會文史資料研究委員會, ed. Beijing: Beijing chubanshe, 1988.

Biyan lu 碧巖錄 (The blue cliff record). By Chongxian 重顯 and Keqin 克勤. *T.* no. 2003.

Biyun si luohan tang 碧雲寺羅漢堂 (The arhat hall at the Temple of the Azure Clouds). Beijing: Beijing shi teyi gongsi, Huace zu, 1979.

Blader, Susan. "*San-hsia wu-yi* and Its Link to Oral Literature." *CHINOPERL Papers* 8 (1978): 9–38.

Bredon, Juliet. *Peking: A Historical and Intimate Description of Its Chief Places of Interest.* 2d ed. London: T. Werner Laurie, n.d. [1924].

Brinker, Helmut. *Zen in the Art of Painting.* Trans. George Campbell. London: Arkania, 1987.

Brokaw, Cynthia J. *The Ledgers of Merit and Demerit: Social Change and Moral Order in Late Imperial China.* Princeton: Princeton University Press, 1991.

Burke, Peter. *Popular Culture in Early Modern Europe.* New York: Harper and Row, 1978.

Burkert, Walter. *Greek Religion.* Trans. by John Raffan. Cambridge: Harvard University Press, 1985.

Cao Xueqin. *The Story of the Stone.* Trans. David Hawkes; vols. 4 and 5, ed. Gao E and trans. John Minford. 5 vols. Middlesex, Eng.: Penguin, 1973–86.

Cao Xueqin 曹雪芹 and Gao E 高鶚. *Honglou meng* 紅樓夢 (The dream of the red chamber). 3 vols. Beijing: Renmin, 1985.

Cedzich, Ursula-Angelika. "The Cult of the Wu-t'ung/Wu-hsien in History and Fiction: The Religious Roots of the *Journey to the South.*" In D. Johnson, ed., *Ritual and Scripture* (q.v.).

Ceng Bairong 曾白融. *Jingju jumu cidian* 京劇劇目辭典 (Dictionary of Chinese opera scripts). Beijing: Zhongguo xiju, 1989.

Chao Li 晁瑮, comp. *Chao shi Baowentang shumu* 晁氏寶文堂書目 (Catalogue of Mr. Chao's Baowentang Library). Shanghai: Gudian wenxue, 1957.

Chapin, Helen B. "The Ch'an Master Pu-Tai." *Journal of the American Oriental Society* 53 (1933): 47–52.

Ch'en, Jerome. "The Nature and Characteristics of the Boxer Movement: A Morphological Study." *Bulletin of the School of Oriental and African Studies* 23, no. 2 (1960): 287–308.

Chen Li-li, trans. *Master Tung's Western Chamber Romance.* Cambridge: Cambridge University Press, 1976.

Chen Longting 陳龍廷. "Dianshi budaixi de fazhan yu bianqian" 電視布袋戲的發展與變遷 (The development and transformation of television hand-puppetry). *Minsu quyi* 民俗曲藝 67–68 (1990): 84–87.

Chen Pingyuan 陳平原. *Qiangu wenren xiake meng* 千古文人俠客夢 (Dreams of knight-errantry by literati throughout history). Beijing: Renmin, 1992.

Chen Ruheng 陳汝衡. *Shuoshu shihua* 說書史話 (History of Chinese oral literature). Beijing: Zuojia, 1958.

Chen Shuji 陳樹基. *Xihu shiyi* 西湖拾遺 (Anecdotes of West Lake). 1791. Photographic rpt., in *Guben xiaoshuo jicheng* (q.v.).

Chikusa Masaaki 竺沙雅章. "Sōdai baichō kō" 宋代賣牒考 (The sale of Buddhist ordination certificates during the Song). 1979. Rpt. in idem, *Chūgoku Bukkyō shakaishi kenkyū* 中國佛教社會史研究 (Researches on the social history of Chinese Buddhism). Kyoto: Dōhōsha, 1982.

———. "Sō Gen Bukkyō ni okeru an dō" 宋元佛教における庵堂 (Hermitages in Buddhism during the Song and Yuan). *Tōyōshi kenkyū* 東洋史研究 46, no. 1 (1987): 1–28.

Chou I-liang. "Tantrism in China." *Harvard Journal of Asiatic Studies* 8 (1945): 241–332.

Cohen, Alvin P. "Coercing the Rain Deities in Ancient China." *History of Religions* 17 (1978): 244–64.

A Concordance to the Poetry of Tu Fu. Ed. William Hung. 2 vols. Harvard-Yenching Sinological Index Series, Supplement no. 14.

Conze, Edward, ed. and trans. *Buddhist Scriptures*. Middlesex, Eng.: Penguin, 1959.

Chu ci 楚辭 (Songs of Chu). Congshu jicheng, 1st series. Changsha: Shangwu yinshuguan, 1939.

Chuandeng 傳燈. *Tiantai shan fangwai zhi* 天台山方外志 (Gazetteer of the spiritual world of Tiantai Mountain). Author's preface dated 1601. Rpt.—1894.

Daguan 大觀, ed. *Beixian Jujian chanshi yulu* 北磵居簡禪師語錄 (The recorded sayings of the Chan master Beixian Jujian). ZZ, section 2, case no. 26, *ce* 1.

Dai Nihon zokuzōkyō 大日本續藏經 (The great Japanese continuation of the Buddhist Canon). 750 *ce*, in 150 cases. Kyoto: Zōkyō shoin, 1905–12.

Damo chushen chuandeng zhuan 達摩出身傳燈傳 (Damo's background and his transmission of the lamp). Wanli ed. Photographic rpt., in *Guben xiaoshuo jicheng* (q.v.), vol. 76.

Daoxuan 道宣. *Xu Gaoseng zhuan* 續高僧傳 (Continuation of the *Biographies of Eminent Monks*). *T.* no. 2060.

Daoyuan 道原. *Jingde chuandeng lu* 景德傳燈錄 (Jingde period *Record of the Transmission of the Lamp*). *T.* no. 2076.

Day, Clarence. *Chinese Peasant Cults: Being a Study of Chinese Paper Gods*. Shanghai: Kelly and Walsh, 1940.

Dean, Kenneth. *Taoist Ritual and Popular Cults of South-East China*. Princeton: Princeton University Press, 1993.

DeBernardi, Jean. "The God of War and the Vagabond Buddha." *Modern China* 13, no. 3 (1987): 310–32.

Deng Mu 鄧牧. *Dongxiao tu zhi* 洞霄圖志 (Illustrated gazetteer of the Dongxiao Monastery). Congshu jicheng, 1st series. Shanghai: Shangwu yinshuguan, 1936.

Diyu youji 地獄遊記 (A journey to purgatory). 1978. Rpt.—Taizhong: Shengxian tang, 1986.

Dōgen 道元. *Fu kan zazengi* 普勸坐禪儀 (General presentation of the principles of sitting in mediation). *T.* no. 2580.

Dong Yue 董說. *Xiyou bu* 西遊補 (Supplement to the *Journey to the West*). Chongzhen (1628–43) ed. Photographic rpt.: Shanghai: Shangwu yinshuguan, 1955.

Dongpo jushi Foyin chanshi yulu wenda 東坡居士佛印禪師語錄問答 (The dialogues and recorded sayings of the lay devotee [Su] Dongpo and the Chan master Foyin). MS in the Naikaku Bunko Library, Tokyo. The same work under the title *Dongpo wenda lu* 東坡問答錄 (Record of [Su] Dongo's conversations) is included also in (1), *Dongpo zazhu liu zhong* 東坡雜著六種, ed. Zhao Kaimei 趙開美. Preface dated 1602. Copy in National Central Library, Taipei; and (2) *Baoyantang miji* 寶顏堂秘笈, ed. Chen Jiru 陳繼儒. 1606–20 ed. Copy in Harvard-Yenching Library, Cambridge, Mass.

Doupeng xianhua 豆棚閒話 (Idle talk under the bean arbor). Author given as Aina jushi 艾衲居士. Eighteenth-century Hanhailou ed. Rpt.—Shanghai: Zazhi, 1935. Also, Shanghai: Guji, 1983 (based on the 1935 ed., without the original commentary).

Du Yingtao 杜穎陶. *Yue Fei gushi xiqu shuochang ji* 岳飛故事戲曲說唱集 (A selection of stories, plays, and oral pieces on Yue Fei). Shanghai: Gudian wenxue, 1957.

Duara, Prasenjit. "Superscribing Symbols: The Myth of Guandi, Chinese God of War." *Journal of Asian Studies* 47, no. 4 (1988): 778–95.

Dudbridge, Glen. *The "Hsi-yu chi": A Study of Antecedents to the Sixteenth-Century Chinese Novel*. Cambridge: Cambridge University Press, 1970.

———. "The Hundred-Chapter *Hsi-yu chi* and Its Early Versions." *Asia Major*, n.s. 14, no. 2 (1969): 141–91.

———. *The Legend of Miao-shan*. Oxford Oriental Monographs, no. 1. London: Ithaca Press, 1978.

Dumoulin, Heinrich. *Zen Buddhism: A History*. Trans. James W. Heisig and Paul Knitter. New York: Macmillan, 1988.

Durand-Dastès, Vincent. "Le Bouddha ivre du Lac de L'ouest: Les premières étapes de la légende du bonze Ji-Le-Fou (Ji Gong) XIIème–XVIIIème siècle. Choix de textes présentés, traduits et annotés." M.A. thesis, Université Paris III, 1986.

Egerton, Clement, trans. *The Golden Lotus*. 4 vols. London: Routledge, 1939.

Éliasberg, Danielle. *Le Roman du pourfendeur de démons: traduction annotée et commentaire*. Paris: Collège de France, Institut des Hautes Études Chinoises, 1976.

Elliott, Allan J. A. *Chinese Spirit Medium Cults in Singapore*. 1955. Rpt.—Taipei: Southern Materials Center, 1984.

Ershisi shi jiaodian ben 二十四史校典本 (Collated edition of the Twenty-Four Histories). Beijing: Zhonghua, 1974.

Ershisi zun dedao luohan zhuan 二十四尊得道羅漢傳 (Biographies of twenty-four arhats who have attained the way). Wanli ed. Photographic rpt. in

Guben xiaoshuo jicheng (q.v.), vol. 67. Typeset ed. in *Fozu pusa luohan zhuan* (q.v.).

Esherick, Joseph W. *The Origins of the Boxer Uprising*. Berkeley: University of California Press, 1987.

Fairweather, Ian. *The Drunken Buddha*. Brisbane: University of Queensland Press, 1965.

Fan Kaiyin 樊開印. *Yiguan dao de jianxin cheng* 一貫道的艱辛程 (The arduous journey of the Unity Sect). Taipei: Sanyang, 1987.

Feng Menglong 馮夢龍. *Gujin xiaoshuo* 古今小說 (Stories old and new). Beijing: Renmin wenxue, 1958.

———. *Jingshi tongyan* 警世通言 (Common words to warn the world). Beijing: Zuojia, 1956.

———. *Sanjiao ounian* 三教偶拈 (Chance selection on the three doctrines). Late Ming ed., copy in the Sōkōdō collection of the Tōyō Bunka Kenkyūjo, Tokyo University. Photographic rpt: *Guben xiaoshuo congkan* (q.v.), series no. 4, vol. 4.

———. *Shan'ge* 山歌 (Mountain songs). Shanghai: Chuanjingtang shu, 1935.

———. *Xingshi hengyan* 醒世恒言 (Constant words to awaken the world). 1956. Rpt.—2 vols. Beijing: Renmin wenxue, 1984.

Fengshen yanyi 封神演義. Author given as Xu Zhonglin 許仲琳. Shanghai: Shanghai guji, 1991.

Fong, Wen. *The Lohans and a Bridge to Heaven*. Freer Gallery of Art Occasional Papers 3, no. 1. Washington. D.C.: Freer Gallery of Art, 1958.

Foulk, Theodore G. "The 'Chan School' and Its Place in the Buddhist Monastic Tradition." Ph.D. diss., University of Michigan, 1987.

Fozu pusa luohan zhuan 佛祖菩薩羅漢傳 (Biographies of Buddhas, bodhisattvas, and arhats). Zhongguo shenguai xiaoshuo daxi. Chengdu: Bashu shushe, 1989.

Fu Xihua 傅惜華. "Baiben Zhang xiqu shuji kaolüe" 百本張戲曲書籍考略 (Preliminary investigation of Baiben Zhang opera and performance literature texts). In *Zhongguo jindai chuban shiliao, erbian* 中國近代出版史料二編 (Historical materials on publishing in modern China, vol. 2), ed. Zhang Jinglu. Shanghai: Qunlian, 1954.

———. *Mingdai chuanqi quanmu* 明代傳奇全目 (A comprehensive catalogue of Ming *chuanqi*). Beijing: Renmin wenxue, 1959.

———. *Yuandai zaju quanmu* 元代雜劇全目 (A comprehensive catalogue of Yuan *zaju*). Beijing: Zuojia, 1957.

"Gezaixi" 歌仔戲 (Taiwanese opera). *Minsu quyi* 民俗曲藝 20 (Oct. 1982): 56–58.

Goodrich, Ann Swann. *Peking Paper Gods: A Look at Home Worship*. Monumenta Serica Monograph Series 23. Nettetal: Steyler Verlag, 1991.

Graham, A. C., trans. *Chuang-tzu: The Inner Chapters*. 1981. Rpt.—London: Unwin Paperbacks, 1986.

Groot, J. J. M. de. *The Religious System of China: Its Ancient Forms, Evolution, History, and Present Aspect, Manners, Customs, and Social Institutions Connected Therewith.* 1892–1910. Rpt.—Taipei: Ch'eng-wen, 1969, 6 vols.

Grootaers, Willem A. "The Hagiography of the Chinese God Chen-Wu." *Folklore Studies* 11, no. 2 (1952): 139–81.

———. "Une Société secrete moderne: I-Koan-Tao. Bibliographie annotée." *Folklore Studies* 5 (1946): 316–52.

Guben xiaoshuo congkan 古本小說叢刊 (Old editions of fiction series). Ca. 100 vols. Beijing: Zhonghua, 1990– .

Guben xiaoshuo jicheng 古本小說集成 (Collection of old editions of fiction). 160 vols. Shanghai: Guji, 1990.

Guben xiqu congkan sanji 古本戲曲叢刊三集 (Old editions of drama, third series). Beijing: Wenxue guji, 1957.

Gujin tushu jicheng 古今圖書集成 (Comprehensive collection of ancient and modern charts and writings). Ed. Jiang Tingxi 蔣廷錫, et al. 1725. Rpt.—1934; photographic rpt., in 79 vols. Taipei: Dingwen, 1977.

Gulik, Robert Hans van. *The Gibbon in China: An Essay in Chinese Animal Lore.* Leiden: Brill, 1967.

Hâfiz, Shams al-Dîn Muhammad. *Hafiz of Shiraz: Thirty Poems.* Trans. Peter Avery and John Heath-Stubbs. London: John Murray, 1952.

Hakusai shomoku 舶載書目 (List of books brought by boat). Ed. Ōba Osamu 大庭脩. Edo period. Photographic rpt.—Osaka: Kansai University, 1972.

Hanan, Patrick. *The Chinese Short Story: Studies in Dating, Authorship, and Composition.* Cambridge: Harvard University Press, 1973.

———. *The Chinese Vernacular Story.* Cambridge: Harvard University Press, 1981.

———. *The Invention of Li Yu.* Cambridge: Harvard University Press, 1988.

———. "Judge Bao's Hundred Cases Reconstructed." *Harvard Journal of Asiatic Studies* 40, no. 2 (1980): 301–23.

Hangzhou fuzhi 杭州府志 (Gazetteer of Hangzhou prefecture). By Gong Jiajun 龔嘉俊 and Li Rong 李榕. 1922. Photographic rpt. in *Zhongguo fangzhi congshu* (q.v.), no. 199.

Hansen, Valerie. *Changing Gods in Medieval China, 1126–1276.* Princeton: Princeton University Press, 1990.

———. Review of *Chūgoku Bukkyō shakaishi kenkyū* and "Sō Gen Bukkyō ni okeru andō," by Chikusa Masaaki. *Bulletin of Sung-Yuan Studies* 20 (1988): 99–108.

Hanyu dacidian 漢語大詞典 (The big dictionary of the Chinese language). Luo Zhufeng 羅竹風, gen. ed. Shanghai: Hanyu dacidian chubanshe, 1991.

Hayden, George A. *Crime and Punishment in Medieval Chinese Drama: Three Judge Pao Plays.* Harvard East Asian Monographs, no. 82. Cambridge: Harvard University, Council on East Asian Studies, 1978.

Hennessey, William O., trans. *Proclaiming Harmony.* Michigan Papers in Chinese Studies, no. 41. Ann Arbor: University of Michigan, 1981.

Hong Mai 洪邁. *Yi Jian zhi* 夷堅志 (Yi Jian's record). Ed. He Zhuo 何卓. 4 vols. Beijing: Zhonghua, 1981.

Hori, Ichiro. "On the Concept of *Hijiri* (Holy-Man)." *Numen* 5 (1958): 128–60, 199–232.

Hsia, C. T. "The Military Romance: A Genre of Chinese Fiction." In *Studies in Chinese Literary Genres*, ed. Cyril Birch. Berkeley: University of California Press, 1974.

Hu Taili 胡台麗. "Shen gui yu dutu: Dajiale duxi fanying zhi minsu xinyang" 神鬼與賭徒－大家樂賭戲反映之民俗信仰 (Gods, ghosts, and gamblers: the religious dimension of Everybody's Happy). Paper presented at the Second International Conference on Sinology, Academia Sinica, Taipei, Dec. 1986.

Huaguang Tianwang zhuan 華光天王傳 (Biography of the heavenly king Huaguang). Wanli ed. Photographic rpt. in *Guben xiaoshuo jicheng* (q.v.), vol. 70. (Later editions of this novel are usually entitled *Nanyou ji* 南遊記 [Journey to the south].)

Huang Huajie 黃華節. *Guangong de ren'ge yu shen'ge* 關公的人格與神格 (Guangong's human and divine personality). Taipei: Shangwu yinshuguan, 1967.

Huang Meiying 黃美英. "Sandai tongtang de Minghuayuan" 三代同堂的明華園 (The Minghuayuan: three generations under the same roof). *Minsu quyi* 民俗曲藝 26 (1983): 99–106.

Huijiao 慧皎. *Gaoseng zhuan* 高僧傳 (Biographies of eminent monks). *T.* no. 2059.

Huiran 慧然, comp. *Zhenzhou Linji Huizhao chanshi yulu* 鎮州臨濟慧照禪師語錄 (The recorded sayings of the Chan master Linji Huizhao of Zhenzhou). *T.* no. 1985.

Huitu guci Jigong quanzhuan 繪圖鼓詞濟公全傳 (The complete, illustrated *guci* version of Jigong's life). Lithographic ed. Shanghai: Jinzhang tushu, n.d. [20th c.]. Copy at the Institute of History and Philology, Academia Sinica, Taipei. Photocopy at the Harvard-Yenching Library, Cambridge, Mass.

Huitu sanjiao yuanliu soushen daquan 繪圖三教源流搜神大全 (The illustrated great compendium of the deities throughout the history of the three religions). Ed. Wang Qiugui 王秋桂. Taipei: Lianjing, 1970.

Hung, William. *Tu Fu: China's Greatest Poet*. Cambridge: Harvard University Press, 1952.

Hymes, Robert P. *Statesmen and Gentlemen: The Elite of Fu-chou, Chiang-hsi, in Northern and Southern Sung*. Cambridge: Cambridge University Press, 1986.

Idema, Wilt, and Stephen H. West. *Chinese Theater, 1100–1450: A Source Book*. München Ostasiatische Studien, no. 27. Weisbaden: Franz Steiner, 1982.

Ingalls, Daniel H. H. "Cynics and Pasupatas: The Seeking of Dishonor." *Harvard Theological Review* 55 (1962): 281–98.

Jian Bozan 翦伯贊 et al., eds. *Yihe tuan* 義和團 (The Boxers United in Righteousness). Shanghai: Shenzhou guoguang, 1951.

Jiang Renxiu 姜仁脩 et al. *Dajiale dubo zhi yanjiu* 大家樂賭博之研究 (Research into the Everybody's Happy gambling). Taizhong: Taizhong difang fayuan, Jiancha chu, 1987.

Jiang Wuchang 江武昌. "Taiwan budaixi jianshi" 台灣布袋戲簡史 (A brief history of Taiwanese handpuppetry). *Minsu quyi* 民俗曲藝 67–68 (1990): 88–129.

Jiexian 戒顯. *Chanmen duanlian shuo* 禪門鍛鍊說 (On forging oneself in the way of Chan). In *ZZ*, section 2, case no. 17, *ce* 5.

Jigong gushi 濟公故事 (Jigong stories). Comic book ed. Shanghai: Renmin meishu, 1987.

Jigong hou zhuan 濟公後傳 (Biography of Jigong, continued). By Yang Zhimin 楊志民 and Guo Tianen 郭天恩. Beijing: Zhongguo quyi, 1987.

Jigong hou zhuan xu 濟公後傳續 (Sequel to the *Biography of Jigong, Continued*). Narrated by Yang Zhimin 楊志民 and Guo Tianen 郭天恩. Ed. Zhang Xi 張璽. Beijing: Zhongguo quyi, 1987.

Jigong huofo xianshen shuofa zhuanji 濟公活佛現身說法傳輯 (Jigong, the living Buddha, having manifested himself and lectured on the law: a collection). Brought to press by Zhou Chao 周超, Taipei, 1987. Another edition of the same work: Taipei: Zhengyi shanshu, n.d.

Jigong huofo zhengzhuan 濟公活佛正傳 (The authoritative biography of the living Buddha, Jigong). Taizhong: Shengde zazhishe, 1983.

Jigong quanzhuan 濟公全傳 (Complete biography of Jigong). By Wang Mengji 王夢吉. Preface dated 1668. Copy in the Dalian Municipal Library; another (missing the title page and preface) in the Beijing Library. Photocopy of the Dalian copy in the Harvard-Yenching Library, Cambridge, Mass.

Jigong waizhuan 濟公外傳 (The untold biography of Jigong). By Jiang Sha 江沙, et al. 2 vols. Harbin: Beifang wenyi, 1987.

Jigong zhuan 濟公傳 (Jigong's biography). Original title: *Pingyan Jigong zhuan* 評演濟公傳 (The storyteller's life of Jigong). By Guo Xiaoting 郭小亭. 1898–1900. Rpt.—*Jigong zhuan xilie xiaoshuo* (q.v.). vols. 1–2.

Jigong zhuan 濟公傳 (Jigong's biography). Author (mistakenly) given as Wang Mengji 王夢吉. Taipei: Sanmin, 1983.

Jigong zhuan 濟公傳 (Jigong's biography). Title also given as *Jigong an* 濟公案. Two manuscripts of this same *guci* narrative, referred to as *Jigong Drum-Song*, survive. One, complete, in *Qing Menggu Chewang fu cang quben* (q.v.), cases 269–79; the other, fragmentary, in *Zhongyang yanjiuyuan, Lishi yuyan yanjiusuo suocang suqu* (q.v.), reel 83.

Jigong zhuan xilie xiaoshuo 濟公傳系列小說 (Jigong's biographical fiction series). 12 vols. Hangzhou: Zhejiang guji, 1991.

Jingci si zhi 淨慈寺志 (History of the Jingci Monastery). Ed. Jixiang 際祥.

1805. 2d ed. 1888. Photographic rpt.—*Zhongguo Fosi zhi huikan* (q.v.), series no. 1, vols. 17–19.

Jingzhong ji 精忠記 (Record of utmost loyalty). Jiguge 汲古閣 ed. Photographic reprint in *Guben xiqu congkan chuji* 古本戲曲叢刊初集 (Old editions of drama, first series), vol. 38. Shanghai: Shangwu yinshuguan, 1954.

Jin Ping Mei cihua 金瓶梅詞話 (The prosimetric narrative of *The Plum in the Golden Vase*). 3 vols. Taipei, 1981.

Johnson, David. "Actions Speak Louder Than Words: The Cultural Significance of Chinese Ritual Opera." In idem, ed., *Ritual Opera Operatic Ritual: "Mu-lien Rescues His Mother" in Chinese Popular Culture*, pp. 1–45. Publications of the Chinese Popular Culture Project, no. 1. Berkeley: University of California, Institute for East Asian Studies, 1989.

———. "The City-God Cults of of T'ang and Sung China." *Harvard Journal of Asiatic Studies* 45 (1985): 363–457.

———. "Communication, Class, and Consciousness in Late Imperial China." In idem et al., *Popular Culture* (q.v.).

Johnson, David, ed. *Ritual and Scripture in Chinese Popular Religion: Five Studies*. Publications of the Chinese Popular Culture Project, 3. Berkeley: University of California, Institute for East Asian Studies, 1994.

Johnson, David; Andrew J. Nathan; and Evelyn S. Rawski, eds. *Popular Culture in Late Imperial China*. Berkeley: University of California Press, 1985.

Jordan, David K. *Gods, Ghosts, and Ancestors: The Folk Religion of a Taiwanese Village*. Berkeley: University of California Press, 1972.

Jordan, David K., and Daniel Overmyer. *The Flying Phoenix: Aspects of Chinese Sectarianism in Taiwan*. Princeton: Princeton University Press, 1986.

Juding 居頂. *Xu chuandeng lu* 續傳燈錄 (Continuation of the *Transmission of the Lamp Record*). *T*. no. 2077.

Jujian 居簡. *Beixian wenji* 北磵文集 (Beixian's Collected Prose Writings). 1374 ed., which includes also his *shiji* 詩集, Copy in the Naikaku Bunko Library, Tokyo. The *wenji* only is included in *SKQS*, vol. 1183.

Katz, Paul. "Enlightened Alchemist or Immoral Immortal? The Growth of Lü Dongbin's Cult in Late Imperial China." In Shahar and Weller, eds., *Unruly Gods* (q.v.).

———. "Wen Ch'iung: The God of Many Faces." *Hanxue yanjiu* 8, no. 1 (1990): 183–219.

Kent, Richard K. "Depictions of the Guardians of the Law: Lohan Painting in China." In *Latter Days of the Law: Images of Chinese Buddhism, 850–1850*, ed. Marsha Weidner. Kansas: Spencer Museum of Art (in association with the University of Hawai'i Press), 1994.

Kieschnick, John. *The Eminent Monk: Buddhist Ideals in Medieval Chinese Hagiography*. Kuroda Institute Studies in East Asian Buddhism, no. 10. Honolulu: University of Hawai'i Press, 1997.

Kleeman, Terry F. *A God's Own Tale: The Book of Transformations of Wenchang, the Divine Lord of Zitong*. Albany: State University of New York Press, 1994.

Kong Xueshi 孔學詩. *Dong chuang shifan* 東窗事犯 (The eastern window plot). In vol. 8 of *Yuanren zaju quanji* 元人雜劇全集 (The complete collection of *zaju* by Yuan period authors). Shanghai: Zazhi gongsi, 1926.

Koss, Nicholas. "The Relationship of the *Hsi-yu chi* and *Feng-shen yan-i*." *T'oung pao* 65, no. 4–5 (1979): 143–65.

Kyōto daigaku, Jimbun kagaku kenkyūjo kanseki mokuroku 京都大學人文科學研究所漢籍目錄 (Catalogue of Chinese books at the Institute for Humanistic Studies, Kyoto University). Kyoto: Kyōto daigaku, Jimbun kagaku kenkyūjo, 1979.

Kuhn, Philip A. *Soulstealers: The Chinese Sorcery Scare of 1768*. Cambridge: Harvard University Press, 1990.

Lai Yonghai 賴永海. *Jigong heshang* 濟公和尚 (The monk Jigong). Xiandai foxue 現代佛學 series. Taipei: Dongda tushu, 1994.

Lang Ying 郎瑛 (b. 1487). *Qixiu leigao* 七修類稿 (Draft notes on seven categories of learning). 1959. Rpt.—2 vols. Shanghai: Zhonghua, 1961.

Le Roy Ladurie, Emmanuel. *Carnival in Romans*. Trans. Mary Feeney. New York: George Braziller, 1980.

Legge, James, trans. *The Chinese Classics*. 5 vols. Oxford University Press. Rpt.—Hong Hong: Hong Kong University Press, 1960.

Lei Mengshui 雷夢水. "Shulin suoji" 書林瑣記 (Bibliographical trifles). In *Xuelin manlu* 學林漫錄 (Extensive records of scholarship), vol. 9. Beijing: Zhonghua, 1984.

Lessing, Ferdinand. *Yung-ho-kung*. Sino-Swedish Expedition Publication no. 18. Stockholm, 1942.

Li Bingxin 李秉新, gen. ed. *Wai ba miao* 外八廟 (The eight outer monasteries). Shijiazhuang: Hebei wenshi, 1992.

Li E 厲鶚, et al., eds. *Songshi jishi* 宋詩記事 (Recorded occasions in Song poetry). Shanghai: Guji, 1983.

Li Fang 李昉, ed. *Taiping guangji* 太平廣記 (Extensive records compiled during the Taiping period). 5 vols. Beijing: Renmin wenxue, 1959.

———. *Taiping yulan* 太平御覽 (Imperial digest compiled during the Taiping period). Song ed. Photographic rpt.—4 vols. Shanghai: Zhonghua, 1960.

Li Fengmao 李豐楙. "Huijiao *Gaoseng zhuan* ji qi shenyi xingge" 慧皎高僧傳及其神異性格 (Huijiao's *Biographies of Eminent Monks* and its dimension of miracle working). (*Zhengzhi daxue*) *Zhonghua xueyuan* 政治大學中華學院, no. 26 (1982): 123–37.

Li Jiarui 李家瑞. *Beiping suqu lüe* 北平俗曲略 (A survey of popular performances in Beiping). 1933. Rpt.—Beijing: Zhongguo quyi, 1988.

———. "Cong Shi Yukun de *Longtu gongan* shuo dao *Sanxia wuyi*" 從石玉崑的龍圖公案說道三俠五義 (From Shi Yukun's *Longtu's Cases* to

Three Heroes and Five Altruists). *Wenxue jikan* 文學季刊, no. 2 (Apr. 1934): 393–97.

Li Jie 李傑. "Jigong guli: Tiantai Shiqiangtou" 濟公故理：天台石牆頭 (Jigong's native village: Shiqiangtou near Tiantai). *Shijie ribao* 世界日報, Jan. 23, 1995.

Li Shiyu 李世瑜. *Xianzai Hua bei mimi zongjiao* 現在華北秘密宗教 (Contemporary secret religions in north China). Chengdu: Huaxi xiehe daxue, 1948.

Li Tche-houa. *"Le Signe de patience" et autres pièces du théatre des Yuan*. Paris: Gallimard, 1963.

Li Xianzhang 李獻章. "Yi *Sanjiao soushen daquan* yu *Tianfei niangma zhuan* wei zhongxin lai kaocha Mazu chuanshuo" 以三教搜神大全與天妃娘媽傳爲中心來考察媽祖傳說 (Using the *Compendium of the Three Religions' Deities* and *The Biography of the Heavenly Consort and Mother* as primary sources to investigate Mazu lore." Trans. Li Xiaoben 李孝本. Rpt. in *Huitu sanjiao* (q.v.).

Liang Peijin 梁沛錦. *Yueju jumu tongjian* 粵劇劇目通檢 (Index to Cantonese opera scripts). Hong Kong: Sanlian, 1985.

Lien, Chinfa. "Language Adaptation in Taoist Liturgical Texts." In Johnson, ed., *Ritual and Scripture* (q.v.).

Lin Chen 林陳. *Ming mo Qing chu xiaoshuo shulu* 明末清初小說述錄 (Notes on late Ming and early Qing fiction). Nanjing: Chunfeng wenyi chubanshe, 1988.

Lingyin si zhi 靈隱寺志 (History of the Lingyin Monastery). Ed. Sun Zhi 孫志. 1663 ed. Rev. version by Xu Zeng 徐增, 1671 ed. Copy in Harvard-Yenching Library, Cambridge, Mass. 2d ed., 1888; photographic rpt. in *Zhongguo Fosi zhi huikan* (q.v.), series no. 1, vol. 23.

Link, Perry. *Mandarin Ducks and Butterflies: Popular Fiction in Early Twentieth-Century Chinese Cities*. Berkeley: University of California Press, 1981.

Liu Fu 劉復 and Li Jiarui 李家瑞. *Zhongguo suqu zongmu gao* 中國俗曲總目稿 (Draft of a comprehensive index to Chinese popular performance literature). Beiping, 1932.

Liu I-ch'ing. *A New Account of Tales of the World*. Trans. Richard B. Mather. Minneapolis: University of Minnesota Press, 1976.

Liu, James J. Y. *The Chinese Knight-Errant*. London: Routledge and Kegan Paul, 1967.

Liu Mengyang 劉孟揚. "Tianjin Quanfei bianluan jishi" 天津拳匪變亂紀事 (Record of the Boxer upheaval in Tianjin). In Jian Bozan et al., eds., *Yihe tuan* (q.v.).

Liu Ts'un-yan. *Buddhist and Taoist Influences on Chinese Novels*, vol. 1, *The Authorship of the "Feng-shen yen-i."* Wiesbaden: Kommissionverlag, 1962.

Liu Yitong 劉以桐. "Min jiao xiangchou dumen wenjian lu" 民教相仇都門聞見錄 (An eyewitness account of the hostility between the people and the church in Beijing). In Jian Bozan et al., eds., *Yihe tuan* (q.v.).

Loon, Piet van der. "Les Origines rituelles du théâtre chinois." *Journal Asiatique* 265 (1977): 141–68.

Lowe, H. Y. (Lu Xingyuan 盧興源). *The Adventures of Wu: The Life Cycle of a Peking Man*. 1940–41. Rpt.—Princeton: Princeton University Press, 1983.

Lu Gong 路工, ed. *Ming Qing pinghua xiaoshuo xuan* 明清平話小說選 (A collection of Ming and Qing *pinghua xiaoshuo*). Shanghai: Gudian wenxue, 1958.

Lu Gong 路工 and Tan Tian 譚天, eds. *Guben pinghua xiaoshuo ji* 古本平話小說集 (Collection of old editions of *pinghua xiaoshuo*). Beijing: Renmin wenxue chubanshe, 1984.

Lü Lizheng 呂理政. *Budaixi biji* 布袋戲筆記 (Notes on the handpuppet theater). Banqiao: Taiwan fengwu, 1991.

Luo Dunrong 羅惇曧. "Quanbian yuwen" 拳變餘文 (Further stories of the Boxer incident). In *Gengzi shibian wenxue ji* 庚子事變文學集 (Literary works concerning the 1900 incident), ed. A Ying 阿英, 2: 959–85. Beijing: Zhonghua, 1959.

Luohan hua 羅漢畫 (Luohan paintings). Taipei: Guoli gugong bowuyuan, 1990.

Lutgendorf, Philip. *The Life of a Text: Performing the Rāmcaritmānas of Tulsidas*. Berkeley: University of California Press, 1991.

Ma Shutian 馬書田. *Huaxia zhu shen* 華夏諸神 (Chinese gods). Beijing: Beijing Yanshan, 1990.

Ma Xisha 馬西沙 and Han Bingfang 韓秉方. *Zhongguo minjian zongjiao shi* 中國民間宗教史 (A history of Chinese popular religion). Shanghai: Renmin, 1992.

Ma, Y. W. "Kung-an Fiction: A Historical and Critical Introduction." *T'oung Pao* 65, no. 4–5 (1979): 200–259.

Maspero, Henri. "The Mythology of Modern China." In idem, *Taoism and Chinese Religion*, trans. Frank A. Kierman, pp. 75–196. Amherst: University of Massachusetts Press, 1981.

Meng Zongbao 孟宗寶. *Dongxiao shiji* 洞霄詩集 (Collected poems on the Dongxiao Monastery). In *Zhibuzu zhai congshu* 知不足齋叢書 (Collected books from the Insufficient Knowledge Studio), ed. Bao Tingbo 鮑廷博. 1872 ed. Collection no. 11, *ce* 41.

Mochizuki Shinkō 望月信亨, ed. *Bukkyō daijiten* 佛教大辭典 (The big dictionary of Buddhism). 3d ed. 10 vols. Kyoto: Sekai seiten kankō kyōkai, 1954–71.

Nagasawa Kikuya 張澤規矩也. "Sōritsu nijūshūnen kinen Sōkōdō bunko tenran mokuroku" 創立二十週年紀念雙紅堂文庫展覽目錄 (Catalogue of the exhibition commemorating the twentieth anniversary of the founding of the Sōkōdō Library). In idem, *Nagasawa Kikuya chosakushu* 張澤規矩也著作集 (Collected works of Nagasawa Kikuya), vol. 4. Tokyo: Kyushu shoyin, 1982–89.

Nakamura Hajime 中村元, ed. *Bukkyōgo daijiten* 佛教語大辭典 (The big dictionary of Buddhist terminology). Tokyo: Tōkyō shoseki, 1981.

Nakamura, Kyoko Motomochi. *Miraculous Stories from the Japanese Buddhist Tradition*. Harvard-Yenching Institute Monograph Series, vol. 20. Cambridge: Harvard University Press, 1973.

Nanhai Guanshiyin pusa chushen xiuxing zhuan 南海觀世音菩薩出身修行傳 (The chronicle of the incarnations and the self-cultivation of the bodhisattva Guanshiyin of the Southern Sea). Wanli ed.; photographic rpt. in *Guben xiaoshuo jicheng* (q.v.), vol. 76. Typeset version in *Fozu pusa luohan zhuan* (q.v.).

Naquin, Susan. "Funerals in North China: Uniformity and Variation." In Watson and Rawski, eds., *Death Ritual* (q.v.).

———. *Shantung Rebellion: The Wang Lun Uprising of 1774*. New Haven: Yale University Press, 1981.

———. "The Transmission of White Lotus Sectarianism in Late Imperial China." In Johnson et al., eds., *Popular Culture* (q.v.).

Nara kokuritsu hakubutsukan 奈良國立博物館. *Busshari no shōgon* 佛舍利の莊嚴 (The worship of the Buddha's relics and the art of the reliquary). Kyoto: Dōhōsha, 1983.

Nianchang 念常. *Fozu lidai tongzai* 佛祖歷代通載 (Comprehensive record of the successive generations of buddhas and patriarchs). *T.* no. 2036.

Ning Zongyi 寧宗一. *Zhongguo wuxia xiaoshuo jianshang cidian* 中國武俠小說鑒賞辭典 (A connoisseur's dictionary of Chinese martial-arts fiction). Beijing: Guoji wenhua, 1992.

Ono Shihei 小野四平. "Saiten setsuwa no seiritsu" 濟顛說話の成立 (The formation of fiction on Crazy Ji). 1966. Rpt. in idem, *Tampen hakuwa* (q.v.).

———. [*Chūgoku kinsei ni okeru*] *Tampen hakuwa shōsetsu no kenkyū* 中國近世における短片白話小說の研究 (Studies of vernacular short stories [from late imperial China]). Tokyo: Hyōronsha, 1978.

Ōtsuka Hidetaka 大塚秀高. *Zōho Chūgoku tsūzoku shōsetsu shomoku* 增補中國通俗小說書目 (Supplement to the *Catalogue of Chinese Popular Fiction*). Tokyo: Kifuku shoin, 1987.

Owen, Stephen. *The Great Age of Chinese Poetry: The High Tang*. New Haven: Yale University Press, 1981.

Pang jushi yulu 龐居士語錄 (The recorded sayings of the lay devotee Pang). Comp. Yu Di 于頔. *ZZ*, section 2, case no. 25, *ce* 1.

Pian, Rulan Chao, trans. "My Life as a Drum Singer: The Autobiography of Jang Tsueyfeng (As Told to Liou Fang)." *CHINOPERL Papers* 13 (1984–85): 7–106.

Plaks, Andrew. "Allegory in the *Hsi-yu Chi* and *Hung-lou Meng*." In *Chinese Narrative: Critical and Theoretical Essays*, ed. A. Plaks. Princeton: Princeton University Press, 1977.

———. *The Four Masterworks of the Ming Novel*. Princeton: Princeton University Press, 1987.

Po Sung-nien and David Johnson. *Domesticated Deities and Auspicious Emblems: The Iconography of Everyday Life in Village China*. Publications of the Chinese Popular Culture Project, 2. Berkeley: University of California, Institute for East Asian Studies, 1992.

Prip-Møller, J. *Chinese Buddhist Monasteries: Their Plan and Its Function as a Setting for Buddhist Monastic Life*. 1937. Rpt.—Hong Kong: Hong Kong University Press, 1982.

Pu Songling 浦松齡. *Liaozhai zhiyi* 聊齋志異 (Liaozhai's records of the strange). Ed. Zhang Youhe 張友鶴. Shanghai: Guji, 1962.

Qi Rushan 齊如山. *Beijing tuhua* 北京土話 (Beijing patois). Beijing: Beijing Yanshan, 1991.

———. "Guci xiaodiao" 鼓詞小調 (*Guci* and folk songs). In idem, *Qi Rushan quanji* 齊如山全集 (Collected writings of Qi Rushan), vol. 5. Taipei, 1964.

Qian Cai 錢彩. *Shuo Yue quanzhuan* 說岳全傳 (The complete story of Yue Fei). Shanghai: Shanghai guji, 1979.

Qian Daxin 錢大昕. *Qianyan tang wenji* 潛研堂文集 (Collected writings from the Qianyan Hall). Ed. Lü Youren 呂友仁. Shanghai: Guji, 1989.

Qian Yueyou 潛說友, ed. *Xianchun Lin'an zhi* 咸淳臨安志 (Gazetteer of Lin'an compiled during the Xianchun period [1265–74]). 1830. Photographic rpt. in *Zhongguo fangzhi congshu* (q.v.), no. 49.

Qiantang hu yin Jidian chanshi yulu 錢塘湖隱濟顛禪師語錄 (The recorded sayings of the recluse from Qiantang Lake, the Chan master Crazy Ji). 1569 ed. Copy in Naikaku Bunko Library, Tokyo; photographic rpt. in *Guben xiaoshuo congkan* (q.v.), series no. 8, vol. 1. Punctuated ed. in ZZ, section 2, case no. 26, *ce* 1.

Qiantang xianzhi 錢塘縣志 (Gazetteer of Qiantang county). 1609. 1893 ed.; photographic rpt. in *Zhongguo fangzhi congshu* (q.v.), no. 192.

Qing Menggu Chewang fu cang quben 清蒙古車王府藏曲本 (Performance-literature manuscripts from the residence of the Qing Mongolian Prince Che). Photographic rpt., with prefaces by Wang Jisi 王季思, Guan Dedong 關德棟, and Jin Peilin 金沛霖. 1,700 vols. in 315 cases. Beijing: Shoudu tushuguan, Beijing guji, 1991. Also available on microfilm.

Qingpingshan tang huaben 清平山堂話本 (*Huaben* stories from the Qingpingshan Hall). Ed. Tan Zhengbi 譚正璧. Shanghai: Gudian wenxue, 1957. (Under this modern title are collected the extant stories of Hong Pian 洪楩. Originally published under the title *Liushijia xiaoshuo* 六十家小說 [Sixty stories].)

Qiu Dezai 仇德哉. *Taiwan miao shen zhuan* 台灣廟神傳 (Deities in Taiwanese temples). 1979. Rpt.—Douliu: Xintong, 1985.

Quan Tang shi 全唐詩 (Complete poetry of the Tang). Ed. Peng Dingqiu 彭定求 (1645–1719). 12 vols. Beijing: Zhonghua shuju, 1960.

Rhys Davids, T. W., trans. *The Questions of King Milinda*. Oxford: Oxford University Press, 1890.

Robert, Yves, trans. *L'Ivresse d'éveil: faits et gestes de Ji Gong le moine fou*. Paris: Les Deux Océans, 1989.

Robinson, James A., trans. *Buddha's Lions: The Lives of the Eighty-Four Siddhas. Translation from the Tibetan of Abhayadatta's "Caturasīti-siddha-pravrtti."* Berkeley: Dharma Publishing, 1979.

Ropp, Paul S. *Dissent in Early Modern China: "Ju-lin wai-shih" and Ch'ing Social Criticism*. Ann Arbor: University of Michigan Press, 1981.

Ruxing 如惺. *Da Ming gaoseng zhuan* 大明高僧傳 (*Biographies of Eminent Monks*, compiled during the Ming dynasty). *T.* no. 2062.

Sangren, P. Steven. "Female Gender in Chinese Religious Symbols: Kuan Yin, Ma Tsu, and the 'Eternal Mother.'" *Signs* 9, no. 1 (1983): 4–25.

———. "Myths, Gods, and Family Relations." In Shahar and Weller, eds., *Unruly Gods* (q.v.).

Sanguo zhi tongsu yanyi 三國志通俗演義 (The popular romance of the Three Kingdoms). 1522 ed. Photographic rpt.—8 vols. Beijing: Renmin, 1975.

Sanxia wuyi 三俠五義 (Three heroes and five altruists). Taipei: Heluo tushu, 1970.

Sasaki, Ruth Fuller; Yoshitaka Iriya; and Dana R. Frazer, trans. *The Recorded Sayings of Layman Pang: A Ninth-Century Zen Classic*. New York: Weatherhill, 1971.

Sawada Mizuho 澤田瑞穗. *Bukkyō to Chūgoku bungaku* 佛教と中國文學 (Buddhism and Chinese literature). Tokyo: Kokusho kankōkai, 1975.

———. "Daruma-den shōsetsu" 達摩傳小說 (Fiction on Boddhidharma). 1964. Rpt. in idem, *Bukkyō to Chūgoku bungaku* (q.v.).

———. "Saiten sui bodai ni tsuite" 濟顚醉菩提について (On Jidian, the drunken *puti*). 1960. Rev. version in idem, *Bukkyō to Chūgoku bungaku* (q.v.).

———. *Sō Min Shin shōsetsu sōkō* 宋明清小說叢考 (Collected studies of Song, Ming, and Qing fiction). Tokyo: Kenbun shuppan, 1982.

Sawara Tokusuke 佐原篤介 and Ou-yin 漚隱, pseud. "Quanluan jiwen" 拳亂紀聞 (Recorded stories from the Boxer Rebellion). In Jian Bozan et al., eds., *Yihe tuan* (q.v.).

Schipper, Kristofer. "The Cult of Pao-sheng Ta-ti and Its Spread to Taiwan: A Case Study of *Fen-hsiang*." In *Development and Decline of Fukien Province in the 17th and 18th Centuries*, ed. E. B. Vermeer. Leiden: Brill, 1990.

———. "The Divine Jester: Some Remarks on the Gods of the Chinese Marionette Theater." *Bulletin of the Institute of Ethnology, Academia Sinica* 21 (1966): 81–96.

Schloegl, Irmgard, trans. *The Zen Teaching of Rinzai: The Record of Rinzai*. Berkeley: Shambhala, 1976.

Schneider, Lawrence A. *A Madman of Ch'u: The Chinese Myth of Loyalty and Dissent*. Berkeley: University of California Press, 1980.

Scholem, Gershon G. "Redemption Through Sin." In idem, *The Messianic Idea in Judaism*, pp. 78–141. New York: Schoken, 1971.

Seaman, Gary. *The Journey to the North: An Ethnohistorical Analysis and Annotated Translation of the Chinese Folk Novel "Pei-yu-chi."* Berkeley: University of California Press, 1987.

———. *Temple Organization in a Chinese Village*. Asian Folklore and Social Life Monographs, vol. 101. Taipei: Orient Cultural Service, 1978.

———. "The Sexual Politics of Karmic Retribution." In *The Anthropology of Taiwanese Society*, ed. Emily Martin Ahern and Hill Gates, pp. 381–96. Stanford: Stanford University Press, 1981.

Shahar, Meir. "The Lingyin si Monkey Disciples and the Origins of Sun Wukong." *Harvard Journal of Asiatic Studies* 52 (1992): 193–224.

Shahar, Meir, and Robert Weller. "Introduction: Gods and Society in China." In Shahar and Weller, eds., *Unruly Gods* (q.v.).

Shahar, Meir, and Robert Weller, eds. *Unruly Gods: Divinity and Society in China*. Honolulu: University of Hawai'i Press, 1996.

Shen Hengbiao 沈鑅彪. *Yunlin si xuzhi* 雲林寺續志 (The history of the Yunlin [i.e., Lingyin] Monastery, continued). 1829. 2d ed. 1888; photographic rpt. in *Zhongguo Fosi zhi huikan* (q.v.), series no. 1, vol. 25.

Shen Yue 沈約. *Song shu* 宋書. In *Ershisi shi jiaodian ben* (q.v.).

Shengguang 聖光. *Hupao Dinghui si zhi* 虎跑定慧寺志 (History of the Dinghui Monastery on Hupao Hill). MS dated 1900. Photographic rpt. in *Zhongguo Fosi zhi huikan* (q.v.), series no. 1, vol. 28.

Shenseng zhuan 神僧傳 (Biographies of saintly monks). Compiled by the Yongle emperor. Preface dated 1417. *T.* no. 2064.

Shinmatsu Minsho shōsetsu mokuroku 清末民初小說目錄 (Catalogue of late Qing and early Republican Chinese fiction). Ed. Shinmatsu shōsetsu kenkyūkai 清末小說研究會. Osaka: Chūgoku bungei kenkyūkai, 1988.

Shoujian 守堅, ed. *Yunmen Kuangzhen chanshi guanglu* 尣門匡眞禪師廣錄 (The extensive records of the Chan master Yunmen Kuangzhen). *T.* no. 1988.

Shuihu quanzhuan 水湖全傳 (Water margin). 3 vols. Beijing: Renmin wenxue, 1954. Rpt.—2 vols. Taipei: Wannianqing, 1979.

Shu yi ji 述異記 (Records of marvels). In SKQS, vol. 147.

Sima Qian 司馬遷. *Shi ji* 史記 (Records of the historian). Beijing: Zhonghua shuju, 1959.

Smith, Richard J. *Fortune-tellers and Philosophers: Divination in Traditional Chinese Society*. Boulder, Colo.: Westview, 1991.

Snellgrove, D. L. trans. *The Hevajra Tantra: A Critical Study*. 2 vols. London: Oxford University Press, 1959.

Song Guangyu 宋光宇. "*Diyu youji* suo xianshi de dangqian shehui wenti" 地獄遊記所顯示的當前社會問題 (Current social problems reflected in the *Journey to Purgatory*). In *Minjian xinyang yu shehui yantaohui lunwenji* 民間信仰與社會研討會論文集 (Colloquium on popular religion and society), ed. Taiwan sheng, Minzheng ting 台灣省民政廳. Taizhong: Donghai daxue, 1982.

———. *Tiandao gouchen: Yiguan dao diaocha baogao* 天道鉤沈: 一貫道調查報告 (Fishing in the depths of the Celestial Way: Report of investigations into the Unity Sect). Taipei: 1983.

Song shi 宋史 (Song history). Ed. Tuo Tuo 脫脫 (1313–55) et al. Beijing: Zhonghua shuju, 1977.

Stein, Rolf A. *The World in Miniature: Container Gardens and Dwellings in Far Eastern Religious Thought*. Trans. Phyllis Brooks. Stanford: Stanford University Press, 1990.

Stevens, Catherine. "Peking Drumsinging." Ph.D. diss., Harvard University, 1973.

Strickmann, Michel. "Holy Fools." Davis Lecture, Oxford, May 1984.

———. *Mantras et mandarins: Le buddhisme tantrique en Chine*. Paris: Gallimard, 1996.

Su Shi 蘇軾. *Su Shi shiji* 蘇軾詩集 (Collected poetry of Su Shi). Beijing: Zhonghua, 1982.

Su Xing 蘇興. "Tianhua Zang Zhuren ji qi caizi jiaren xiaoshuo" 天花藏主人及其才子佳人小說 (Tianhua Zang Zhuren and his scholar and beauty fiction). In *Caizi jiaren xiaoshuo shu lin* 才子佳人小說述林 (Collected essays on scholar and beauty fiction). Ming Qing xiaoshuo luncong, no. 2. Nanjing: Chunfeng wenyi, 1985.

Sun Kaidi 孫楷弟. *Riben Dongjing Dalian tushuguan suojian Zhongguo xiaoshuo shumu tiyao* 日本東京大連圖書館所見中國小說書目提要 (Catalogue of Chinese fiction I have seen in the Dalian Library and in libraries in Tokyo, Japan). Beiping: Guoli Beiping tushuguan, 1931.

———. *Zhongguo tongsu xiaoshuo shumu* 中國通俗小說書目 (Catalogue of Chinese popular fiction). Rev. ed. Beijing: Renmin wenxue, 1982.

Taishō shinshū daizōkyō 大正新修大藏經 (The great Buddhist canon compiled during the Taishō period). 100 vols. Tokyo: Taishō issaikyō kankōkai, 1924–32.

Tambiah, Stanley Jeyaraja. *The Buddhist Saints of the Forest and the Cult of Amulets*. Cambridge Studies in Social Anthropology, no. 49. Cambridge: Cambridge University Press, 1984.

Tan Chee-beng. *The Development and Distribution of Dejiao Associations in Malaysia and Singapore: A Study on a Chinese Religious Organization*. Singapore: Institute of Southeast Asian Studies, 1985.

Tan Zhengbi 譚正璧. *Guben xijian xiaoshuo huikao* 古本稀見小說匯考 (Studies of early editions and rare works of fiction). Hangzhou: Zhejiang wenyi, 1984.

———. *Huaben yu guju* 話本與古劇 (*Huaben* stories and classical plays). Shanghai: Gudian wenxue, 1957.

Tan Zhengbi 譚正璧 and Tan Xun 譚尋, comps. *Pingtan tongkao* 平彈通考 (General research into *pinghua* and *tanci*). Beijing: Zhongguo quyi, 1985.

Tang Zhong Kui quanzhuan 唐重馗全傳 (Complete biography of Zhong Kui of the Tang period). Wanli ed. Photographic rpt. in *Guben xiaoshuo jicheng* (q.v.), vol. 68.

Tao Chengzhang 陶成章. *Jiaohui yuanliu kao* 教會源流考 (Researches into the history of religious sects). In *Jindai mimi shehui shiliao* 近代秘密社會史料 (Materials on modern secret societies), ed. Xiao Yishan 蕭一山. 1935; rpt., Taiwan: Wenhai chubanshe, 1965.

Teiser, Stephen F. *The Ghost Festival in Medieval China*. Princeton: Princeton University Press, 1988.

———. "'Having Once Died and Returned to Life': Representations of Hell in Medieval China." *Harvard Journal of Asiatic Studies* 48, no. 2 (1988): 433–64.

Ter-Haar, Barend. "The Genesis and Spread of Temple Cults in Fukien." In *Development and Decline of Fukien Province in the 17th and 18th Centuries*, ed. E. B. Vermeer. Leiden: Brill, 1990.

Thomas, Edward J. *The Life of Buddha as Legend and History*. London: Kegan Paul, 1931.

Thompson, Laurence G. "The Moving Finger Writes: A Note on Revelation and Renewal in Chinese Religion." *Journal of Chinese Religions* 10 (1982): 92–147.

Tian Rucheng 田如成. *Xihu youlan zhiyu* 西湖遊覽志餘 (Supplement to the *Guide to the West Lake*). Beijing: Zhonghua, 1958.

Tianfei niangma zhuan 天妃娘媽傳 (The biography of the Heavenly Consort and Mother). Shanghai: Guji, 1990.

Tianqiao yilan 天橋一覽 (A tour of the Tianqiao district). Ed. Zhang Cixi 張次溪 and Zhao Xianhuan 趙羨渙. Beijing: Zhonghua, 1936.

Tiantai shan fangwai zhiyao 天台山方外志要 (Essentials of the *Gazetteer of the Spiritual World of Tiantai Mountain*). Ed. Qi Zhaonan 齊召南. 1767 ed. Copy in Harvard-Yenching Library, Cambridge, Mass.

Tiantai xianzhi 天台縣志 (Gazetteer of Tiantai county). Ed. Li Deyao 李德燿 et al. 1683 ed. Copy in Harvard-Yenching Library, Cambridge, Mass.

Tiantang youji 天堂遊記 (A journey to paradise). 1981. Rpt.—Taizhong: Shengxian tang, 1987.

Todorov, Tzvetan. "The Typology of Detective Fiction." In idem, *The Poetics of Prose*. Trans. Jonathan Culler. Ithaca: Cornell University Press, 1977.

Tun Li-ch'en. *Annual Customs and Festivals in Peking*. Trans. Derk Bodde. Peiping: Henri Vetch, 1936.

von Glahn, Richard. "The Enchantment of Wealth: The God Wutong in the Social History of Jiangnan." *Harvard Journal of Asiatic Studies* 51, no. 2 (1991): 672–75.

Wang Ch'iu-kuei. "On 'Shuo Ts'an-Ch'ing.'" *Asia Major*, 3d ser., 1, no. 2 (1988): 65–76.

Wang Hailin 王海林. *Zhongguo wuxia xiaoshuo shilüe* 中國武俠小說史略 (A brief history of Chinese martial-arts fiction). Taiyuan: Beiyue wenyi, 1988.

Wang Songshan 王嵩山. *Banxian yu zuoxi: Taiwan minjian xiqu renleixue yanjiu lunji* 扮仙與作戲台灣民間戲曲人類學研究論集 ("Acting immortals" and performing plays: collected anthropological essays on Taiwanese popular drama). Taipei: Daoxiang, 1988.

Wang Xiangxu 王象旭. *Lüzu quanzhuan* 呂祖全傳 (The complete fictionalized biography of Patriarch Lü). 1662 ed. Copy in Harvard-Yenching Library. 1859 ed.; photographic rpt. in *Guben xiaoshuo jicheng* (q.v.), vol. 21.

Wanshi qiguan 頑世奇觀 (Miraculous sights of playing in the world). In *Zhongguo shenguai xiaoshuo daxi* (q.v.).

Ward, Barbara E. "Not Merely Players: Drama, Act and Ritual in Traditional China." *Man*, n.s. 14, no. 1 (1979): 18–39.

Watson, James. "Funeral Specialists in Cantonese Society: Pollution, Performance, and Social Hierarchy." In Watson and Rawski, eds., *Death Ritual* (q.v).

———. "Standardizing the Gods: The Promotion of T'ien Hou ("Empress of Heaven") Along the South China Coast, 960–1960." In Johnson et al., eds., *Popular Culture* (q.v.).

Watson, James, and Evelyn S. Rawski, eds. *Death Ritual in Late Imperial and Modern China*. Berkeley: University of California Press, 1988.

Watters, Thomas. "The Eighteen Lohan of Chinese Buddhist Temples." *Journal of the Royal Asiatic Society*, April 1898, pp. 329–47.

Welch, Holmes. *The Practice of Chinese Buddhism*. Cambridge: Harvard University Press, 1967.

Weller, Robert P. *Resistance, Chaos and Control in China: Taiping Rebels, Taiwanese Ghosts and Tiananmen*. Seattle: University of Washington Press, 1994.

Wenxiu 文琇. *Wudeng huiyuan buyi* 五燈會元補遺 (Supplement to the *Five Lamps Compendium*). In idem, *Zengji Xu Chuandeng lu* 增集續傳燈錄 (Collected supplements to the *Record of the Transmission of the Lamp*), chap. 6. ZZ, section 2, part 2, case no. 15, *ce* 5.

Wenyuange Siku quanshu 文淵閣四庫全書 (All the books from the four treasuries stored at the Wenyuan Hall). 1782. Photographic rpt.—1,500 vols. Taiwan: Shangwu, 1983–86.

Widmer, Ellen. *The Margins of Utopia: "Shui-hu hou-chuan" and the Literature of Ming Loyalism*. Harvard East Asian Monographs, 128. Cambridge: Council on East Asian Studies, 1978.

Wolf, Arthur P. "Gods, Ghosts and Ancestors." In *Religion and Ritual in Chinese Society*, ed. Arthur P. Wolf, pp. 131–82. Stanford: Stanford University Press, 1975.

Wright, A. F. "Fo-t'u-teng, a Biography." *Harvard Journal of Asiatic Studies* 11 (1948): 321–71.

Wu Cheng'en 吳承恩. *Xiyou ji* 西遊記 (Journey to the west). 2 vols. Beijing: Zuojia, 1954.

Wu Tongbin 吳同賓 and Zhou Yaxun 周亞勛, eds. *Jingju zhishi cidian* 京劇知識辭典 (Dictionary of Beijing opera studies). Tianjin: Tianjin renmin, 1990.

Wu Yong 吳永. "Gengzi xishou congtan" 庚子西狩叢談 (Reminiscences of the imperial progress to the west in 1900). Recorded by Liu Zhixiang 劉治襄. In Jian Bozan et al., eds., *Yihe tuan* (q.v.).

Wuyue Chunqiu zhuzi suoyin 吳越春秋逐字索引 (A concordance to the *Wuyue Chunqiu*). Ed. Liu Dianjue 劉殿爵 and Chen Fangzheng 陳方正. Xianggang Zhongwen daxue, Zhongguo wenhua yanjiusuo xian-Qin liang Han guji zhuzi suoyin congkan 香港中文大學中國文化研究所先秦兩漢古籍逐字索引叢刊, no. 5. Hongkong: Shangwu yinshuguan, 1993.

Wu Zhijing 吳之鯨. *Wulin fan zhi* 武林梵志 (Gazetteer of Buddhist monasteries in Wulin [Hangzhou]). In *SKQS*, vol. 588.

Xian fo sheng ji zhuanji 仙佛聖蹟專集 (Collection of the immortals', buddhas', and saints' traces). Huang Jinchang 黃金昌, ed. Enl. ed. Taipei: Mingde, 1986.

Xihu erji 西湖二集 (Second collection of West Lake stories). By Zhou Ji 周楫 (*zi*: Zhou Qingyuan 周清源). 2 vols. Hangzhou: Zhejiang renmin, 1981.

Xihu jiahua 西湖佳話 (Charming stories of the West Lake). By Molang Zi 墨浪子. 1673 ed.; photographic rpt.—*Guben xiaoshuo jicheng* (q.v.), no. 37, 2 vols. Typeset ed.: Hangzhou: Zhejiang wenyi, 1985.

Xihu zhi 西湖志 (Gazetteer of West Lake). By Fu Wanglu 傅王露 and Li Wei 李衛. Preface dated 1735. Rpt.—1878.

Xin Tang shu 新唐書 (New Tang history). Ouyang Xiu 歐陽修 et. al., comps. In *Ershisi shi jiaodian ben* (q.v.).

Xin Wudai shi 新五代史 (New history of the Five Dynasties). Ouyang Xiu 歐陽修 et. al., comps. In *Ershisi shi jiaodian ben* (q.v.).

Xiong Damu 熊大木. *Da Song zhong xing yanyi* 大宋中興演義 (The romance of the upsurge in the middle of the Great Song [dynasty]). 1552 ed. Photographic rpt., in *Guben xiaoshuo congkan* (q.v.), series no. 1, no. 37.

Xu Dishan 許地山. *Fuji mixin di yanjiu* 扶箕密信底研究 (Researches into the spirit-writing superstition). 1940. Rpt.—Taipei: Shangwu yinshuguan, 1966.

Xu Shirong 徐世榮. *Beijing tuyu cidian* 北京土語辭典 (Dictionary of Beijing patois). Beijing: Beijing chubanshe, 1990.

Yampolsky, Philip, ed. and trans. *The Platform Sutra of the Sixth Patriarch.* New York: Columbia University Press, 1967. (This edition includes also the original text, titled: *Liuzu tan jing* 六祖壇經.)

Yanagida Seizan. "The 'Recorded Sayings' Texts of Chinese Chan Buddhism." Trans. John R. McRae. In *Early Ch'an in China and Tibet*, ed. Whalem Lai and Lewis R. Lancaster, pp. 185–205. Berkeley Buddhist Studies Series. Berkeley: University of California Press, 1983.

Yang, C. K. *Religion in Chinese Society*. Berkeley: University of California Press, 1961.

Yang Erceng 楊爾曾. *Han Xiangzi quanzhuan* 韓湘子全傳 (The complete biography of Han Xiangzi). 1623 ed. Rpt.—Henan: Zhongzhou guji, 1989.

Yang Shengxin 楊繩信. *Zhongguo banke zonglu* 中國版刻綜錄 (A comprehensive record of Chinese publishers). Xianyang: Shaansi renmin, 1987.

Ye Dejun 葉德均. "Song, Yuan, Ming jiangchang wenxue" 宋元明講唱文學 (Prosimetric literature of the Song, Yuan, and Ming periods). In idem, *Xiqu xiaoshuo congkao* 戲曲小說叢考 (Collected studies on drama, performance literature, and fiction). Beijing: Zhonghua, 1979.

Yongqing shengping 永慶昇平 (Everlasting blessings and peace). By Guo Guangrui 郭廣瑞 (*zi* Xiaoting 筱亭). 1892 Baowentang 寶文堂 ed.; copy in Beijing University Library. Rpt.—Cao Yibing 曹亦冰, ed., Beijing: Baowentang, 1988.

Yu, Anthony, trans. *The Journey to the West*. 4 vols. Chicago: University of Chicago Press, 1977–83.

Yu Changlin 喻長霖 et al. *Taizhou fuzhi* 台州府志 (Gazetteer of Taizhou prefecture). 1936 ed. Photographic rpt. in *Zhongguo fangzhi congshu* (q.v.).

Yue Wumu jing zhong zhuan 岳武穆精忠傳 (The record of Yue Wumu's utmost loyalty). Ed. Zou Yuanbiao 鄒元標. Qing ed.; copy in Beijing Library.

Yun Youke 雲游客. *Jianghu congtan* 江湖叢談 (Collected talks on the itinerant life). Beijing: Zhongguo quyi, 1988.

Yun'an Puyan chanshi yulu 運菴普巖禪師語錄 (The recorded sayings of the Chan master Yun'an Puyan). Ed. Yuanjing 元靖 et al. *ZZ*, section 2, case no. 26, *ce* 4.

Zang Maoxun 臧懋循, ed. *Yuanqu xuan* 元曲選 (Collection of Yuan plays). 4 vols. Beijing: Zhonghua, 1961.

Zanning 贊寧. *Song Gaoseng zhuan* 宋高僧傳 (*Biographies of Eminent Monks*, compiled during the Song period). *T.* no. 2061.

Zeitlin, Judith. *Historian of the Strange: Pu Songling and the Chinese Classical Tale*. Stanford: Stanford University Press, 1993.

Zeng Qinliang 曾勤良. *Taiwan minjian xinyang yu "Fengshen yanyi" zhi bijiao yanjiu* 台灣民間信仰與封神演義之比較研究 (A comparative study of Taiwanese popular beliefs and the *Enfeoffment of the Gods*). Taipei: Huazheng, 1985.

Zengaku daijiten hensanjo 禪學大辭典編纂所, comp. *Zengaku daijiten* 禪學大辭典 (The big dictionary of Zen studies). 3 vols. Tokyo: Taishūkan, 1978.

Zhang Cuifeng 張翠鳳. *Dagu shengya de huiyi* 大鼓生涯的回憶 (Reminiscences of my life as a drum-singer). Transcribed by Liu Fang 劉芳. Taipei: Zhuanji wenxue, 1966.

Zhang Dafu 張大復. *Zui puti* 醉菩提 (Drunken *puti*). MS; photographic rpt. in *Guben xiqu congkan sanji* (q.v.).

Zhang Jinglu 張靜廬. *Zhongguo jindai chuban shiliao erbian* 中國近代出版史料二編 (Historical materials on publishing in China in recent times, second compilation). Shanghai: Qunlian, 1954.

Zhang Wenjie 張文介. *Guang lie xian zhuan* 廣列仙傳 (Extensive biographies of immortals). 1583 ed.; photographic rpt. in vol. 5 of *Zhongguo minjian xinyang ziliao huibian* 中國民間信仰資料彙編 (Collection of sources on Chinese popular beliefs), ed. Wang Qiugui 王秋桂 and Li Fengmao 李豐楙, vol. 5. Taipei: Xuesheng shuju, 1989.

Zhang Zhenglang 張政烺. "*Wenda lu* yu 'shuo canqing'" 問答錄與說參情 (The *Wenda lu* and *shuo canqing*). *Lishi yuyan yanjiusuo jikan* 歷史語言研究所集刊 17 (1948): 1–5.

Zhao Jingshen 趙景深. *Dagu yanjiu* 大鼓研究 (Researches on *dagu*). Shanghai: Shangwu yinshuguan, 1937.

———. *Guci xuan* 鼓詞選 (Selected drum-songs). Beijing: Zhonghua, 1959.

———. *Ming Qing qu tan* 明清曲談 (Discussions of Ming and Qing drama). Shanghai: Gudian wenxue, 1957.

Zheng Tingyu 鄭廷玉. *Budai heshang ren zi ji* 布袋和尚忍字記 (Record of Monk Budai's writing the character "endurance"). In *Yuanren zaju quanji* 元人雜劇全集 (The complete collection of *zaju* by Yuan period authors), vol. 3. Shanghai: Zazhi, 1936.

Zheng Zhenduo 鄭振鐸. "Yue zhuan de yanhua" 岳傳的演化 (The evolution of novels on Yue [Fei]). In idem, *Zhongguo wenxue lunji* 中國文學論集 (Collected essays on Chinese fiction). Shanghai: Kaiming, 1934.

Zheng Zhiming 鄭志明. *Zhongguo shanshu yu zongjiao* 中國善書與宗教 (Chinese morality books and religion). Taipei: Taiwan xuesheng, 1988.

Zhengshou 正受. *Jiatai Pu deng lu* 嘉泰普燈錄 (The Jiatai period record of the universal transmission of the lamp). *ZZ*, section 2, part 2, case no. 10, *ce* 1–2.

Zhipan 志磐. *Fozu tongji* 佛祖統紀 (Record of the lineages of Buddhas and patriarchs). 1271. *T.* no. 2035.

Zhongguo difang xiju jicheng 中國地方戲劇集成 (Collection of Chinese regional drama). Hubei vol. Ed. Zhongguo xijujia xiehui 中國戲劇家協會. Beijing: Zhongguo xiju, 1958.

Zhongguo fangzhi congshu 中國方志叢書 (Chinese local gazetteers series). Taipei: Chengwen, 1970– .

Zhongguo Fosi zhi huikan 中國佛寺志彙刊 (Chinese Buddhist monastic histories series). Series no. 1–2, 80 vols. Taipei: Mingwen, 1980. Series no. 3, 30 vols. Taipei: Danqing tushu, 1985.

Zhongguo shenguai xiaoshuo daxi 中國神怪小說大系 (The big series of Chinese fiction on the supernatural). Ca. 100 vols. Changchun and Chengdu: Jilin wenshi and Bashu shushe, 1989– .

Zhongguo tongsu xiaoshuo zongmu tiyao 中國通俗小說宗目提要 (Comprehensive catalogue and synopses of Chinese popular fiction). Ed. Jiangsu sheng shehui kexue yuan 江蘇省社會科學院. Beijing: Zhongguo wenlian, 1990.

Zhongguo xiqu quyi cidian 中國戲曲曲藝詞典 (A dictionary of Chinese drama and performance literature). Ed. Shanghai yishu yanjiusuo 上海藝術研究所. Shanghai: Shanghai cishu, 1981.

Zhongyang yanjiuyuan, Lishi yuyan yanjiusuo suocang suqu 中央研究院歷史語言研究所所藏俗曲 (Popular performance literature preserved at the Institute of History and Philology of the Academia Sinica). Microfilm ed.

Zhou Chunyi 周純一. "Jigong xingxiang zhi wancheng jiqi shehui yiyi" 濟公形象之完成及其社會意義 (The formation of the Jigong phenomenon and its social meaning). *Hanxue yanjiu* 漢學研究 8, no. 1 (June 1990): 535–62.

Zhou Miaozhong 周妙中. *Qingdai xiqu shi* 清代戲曲史 (A history of Qing period drama). Zhongguo gudai xiqu yanjiu congshu 中國古代戲曲研究叢書. Chengchow: Zhongzhou guji, 1987.

Zhoudian xianren zhuan 周顛仙人傳 (Biography of the immortal Crazy Zhou). By Zhu Yuanzhang 朱元璋. In *Jilu huibian* 紀錄彙編 (Collection of Records), ed. Shen Jiefu 沈節甫. 1617 ed. Photographic rpt. in *Song Yuan Ming shanben congshu shi zhong* 宋元明善本叢書十種. Shanghai: Shangwu yinshuguan, 1938.

Zhu Feng'ao 朱封鰲. *Tiantai shan fengwu zhi* 天台山風物志 (The sights of Tiantai Mountain). Hangzhou: Zhejiang daxue chubanshe, 1991.

Zhuang Yifu 莊一拂. *Gudian xiqu cunmu huikao* 古典戲曲存目彙考 (Collected researches on extant classical plays). Shanghai: Shanghai guji, 1982.

Zui puti 醉菩提 (Drunken *puti*). Complete title *Jidian dashi wanshi qiji, zui puti quanzhuan* 濟顛大師玩世奇跡醉菩提全傳. Baoren tang 寶仁堂 ed. Author given as Tianhua Zang Zhuren 天花藏主人. Original Preface signed by Taohua An Zhuren 桃花菴主人. Modern Preface by Gu Xinyi 顧歆藝. Photographic rpt. in *Guben xiaoshuo jicheng* (q.v.), vol. 73.

Zui puti 醉菩提 (Drunken *puti*). In *Zhui baiqiu* 綴白裘 (Piecing together a white fur coat), ed. Wanhua Zhuren 玩花主人 and Qian Peisi 錢沛思. 1777. Collated by Wang Xieru 王協如. Beijing: Zhonghua, 1955.

Zui puti 醉菩提 (Drunken *puti*). Shanghai: Chenhe ji shu, ca. 1910. Photographic rpt. in *Zui puti, Sanguo yin hekan* 醉菩提三國因合刊 (Combined reprint of *Zui puti* and *Sanguo yin*). Taipei: Tianyi, 1974.

Zui puti 醉菩提 (Drunken *puti*). Under the title *Jidian chanshi dazhuan* 濟顛禪師大傳 (Biography of the Chan master Crazy Ji). Shanghai: Foxue shuju, 1932. Photographic rpt.—Taipei: Fojiao chubanshe, 1981.

Zui puti 醉菩提 (Drunken *puti*). Under the title *Jidian seng zhuan* 濟顛僧傳 (Biography of the monk Crazy Ji). Shanghai: Foxue shuju, 1932. Rpt.—Hangzhou: Zhejiang sheng Fojiao xiehui, 1987.

Zürcher, E. "Eschatology and Messianism in Early Chinese Buddhism." In *Leiden Studies in Sinology*, ed. W. L. Idema, pp. 34–56. Leiden: E. J. Brill, 1981.

Glossary

Authors and books listed either in the Works Cited or in Appendixes A–D are not included in the following list. The entries are alphabetized letter by letter, ignoring word and syllable breaks, with the exception of personal names, which are ordered first under the surname and then under the given name.

age 阿哥
Aitai Tuo 哀駘它
an 庵
an mani bami hong 唵嘛呢叭咪吽
an shuoshu yanyi 按說書演義
apo 阿婆

Bagua lu 八掛爐
Baiben Zhang 百本張
Baigu renmo 百骨人魔
Bailian jiao 白蓮教
bailuan 拜鸞
Baishui hu 白水湖
"Bai tai zhuan" 白太傳
Bai yang bao fa 白陽寶筏
Baiyun guan 白雲觀
Baizhang 百丈
bajiaogu 八角鼓
Bamo lian Jidian 八魔煉濟顛
bangzi 梆子
banseng bansu 半僧半俗
baobiao 保鏢
Baogong 包公
Baoguang si 寶光寺
baojian 寶劍
baojuan 寶卷
Baosheng dadi 包生大帝
Baowen tang 寶文堂
Baoyu 寶玉
Baozhi 寶誌
Baxian 八仙
bei 杯
Beidu 杯度
Beihai Laoren 北海老人
Beiyu ji 北遊記
bian 編
biaoju 鏢局
bi bu sui 壁不碎
bikong liao tian 鼻孔撩天
Binqingshe 斌慶社

Biyun si 碧雲寺
Budai heshang 布袋和尚
budaixi 布袋戲

caizi jiaren 才子佳人
chang 唱
Chang'anshi shang jiujia mian 長安市上酒家眠
Changling 長齡
changpian xiaoshuo 長篇小說
chanshi 禪師
chapeng 茶棚
Chebudeng Zhabu 車布登扎布
Chen Chen 陳忱
"Chen Kechang duanyang xianhua" 陳可常端陽仙化
Chen Mingji 陳明吉
Chen Shan 陳善
Chen Shengdian 陳勝典
Chen Shengfa 陳勝發
Chen Shengfang 陳勝芳
Chen Shengfu 陳勝福
Chen Shengguo 陳勝國
Chen Shengshun 陳勝順
Chen Shengzai 陳勝在
Chewang Fu 車王府
Chicheng 赤城
Chifa wenshen 赤髮瘟神
chongbai 崇拜
chuan hua 串花
chuan hua qigai 串花乞丐
Chu Daoyuan 褚道緣
Chushi si guhe, yirong tong tuichan 處世似孤鶴, 遺榮同蛻蟬
Ciyun guan 慈雲觀
Cuiwen zhai 萃文齋

da 打
Dacheng shuju 大成書局
Dadi 大滌
Dafo [si] 大佛寺
dagu 大鼓
Dahuo 大壑
Dai Fengyi 戴鳳儀
Dai Xingzhe 呆行者
Dajiale 大家樂
Damo 達摩
Daoji 道濟
Daoming 道明
dashi 大師
da wan zhi gu shai lai 大碗只顧篩來
Da xiao Jigong 大小濟公
Dayu 大愚
Dehui 德輝
dejiaohui 德教會
Deng Zhimo 鄧志謨
dian 顛
dianchuan shi 點傳師
diandao 顛倒
dian seng 顛僧
Dian xie 顛寫
dian zhe nai zhen zi ye 顛者乃眞字也
Dian zhe zhenzhen zhi yi 顛者眞眞之義
Ding Baigui 丁伯桂
Ding Yunpeng 丁雲鵬
Dinghui si 定慧寺
Dizang(wang) 地藏王
dong chuang shifan 東窗事犯
Dong Jieyuan 董解元
Dongfang xianfo 洞房獻佛
Donglong 東隆
dongtian 洞天
Dongyouji 東遊記
Dongyuedi 東嶽帝
doubaofu 抖包袱
doufu tang 豆腐盪
Du Fu 杜甫
dudie 度牒
duo 咄
Dushi jinsheng 度世金繩

Erlang 二郎

Facong 法聰
Fan Shouyan 樊壽岩

Fan Tengfeng 樊騰風
Fanguang 梵光
Fangyuan 方圓
fashi 法師
fasi 法嗣
Fayuan 法元
fei fan fei xian 非凡非仙
Feijian ji 飛劍記
fei sheng fei fan 非聖非凡
Fengbo ting 風波亭
"Feng fen" 逢紛
Fenggan 豐干
feng heshang 瘋和尚
Feng jian 鋒劍
fengmo heshang 瘋魔和尚
fengseng 瘋僧
Fengseng sao Qin 瘋僧掃秦
Fengshen yanyi 封神演義
fenxiang 分香
fo 佛
foguang 佛光
Fohai 佛海
Fotang 佛堂
Foxin dushi 佛心度世
Foyin 佛印
"Foyin shi si tiao Qinniang" 佛印師四調琴娘
Fozu lidai tongzai 佛祖歷代通載
Fozu tongji 佛祖統記
fu 符
fuji (wielding the divination instrument) 扶乩
fuji (wielding the winnowing basket) 扶箕
fuluan 扶鸞
Fuzhou 覆舟

gaiyun 改運
Gan Jiang 干將
gantong seng 感通僧
Ge Caixia 葛彩霞
Ge Hong 葛洪
gewei falü zhu 各位法律主
gezaixi 歌仔戲
gong 公
gongan 公案
gongan xiaoshuo 公案小說
Gou longshuang 勾龍爽
gouzi 狗子
Guangong 關公
Guanxiu 貫休
Guanyin 觀音
guci 鼓詞
guduo 餶飿
gujin xiaoshuo 古今小說
Gulong 古龍
Guo Shengwang 郭聖王
Guo Xiaoting 郭小亭
Guoqing [si] 國清寺
Gutian shan 古天山

Hafuyuan 哈輔源
Haichao yin 海潮音
Hai liefu bailian zhenzhuan 海烈婦百鍊眞傳
Hai Wenquan 海文泉
Han Xiangzi 韓湘子
hanju 漢劇
Hanshan 寒山
Hanshanzi 寒山子
he 喝
"Heshang" 和尚
Hong Liansheng 洪連生
Hong Pian 洪楩
"Honglian" 紅蓮
"Hongqian nan Jidian" 紅倩難濟顚
Hongren 弘忍
Hu Weiguan 胡偉冠
Hua Heshang 花和尚
Hua Qingfeng 華清風
Hua Yunlong 華雲龍
"Huadeng jiao Liannü cheng Fo ji" 花燈轎蓮女成佛記
Huaguang 華光
Huamian 花面
Huan Kai 桓闓
Huang Haidai 黃海岱

Huang Hansheng 黃漢升
Huang Junxiong 黃俊雄
Huang Luzhi 黃魯直
Huang Wenfu 黃溫甫
Huang Xin 黃欣
Huangting jing 黃庭經
"Huanhun ji" 還魂記
"Huan zhenren sheng xian ji" 桓眞人升仙記
Huanzhulou zhu 還珠婁主
Huashi 華視
huayuanshu 化緣疏
Huiji 慧吉
huiju 徽劇
Huineng 慧能
Huiyuan 慧遠
huntun 餛飩
huofo 活佛
Huoshao Dabei lou 火燒大悲樓
Hupao 虎跑
huseng 胡僧
hushenfu 護身符
Hutu shenxian 糊塗神仙
Huyin 湖隱
Huyuan dong 呼猿洞

Jiang Zhenming 姜振名
jianghu hua 江湖話
Jianqing zhai 簡青齋
jiansi 監寺
"Jiantie heshang" 簡貼和尚
jianxiaxi 劍俠戲
jiao (divination blocks) 筊
jiao (religion; teaching) 教
Jiaojing Shanfang 校經山房
jiaoren 鮫人
Jiatai Pu deng lu 嘉泰普燈錄
Jidian 濟顛
Jidian benzhuan (xu) 濟顛本傳敘
Jidian dashi quanzhuan 濟顛大師全傳
Jidian luohan Jingci si xiansheng ji 濟顛羅漢淨慈寺顯聖記
Jidian seng zhuan 濟顛僧傳
Jie chuang lü si 戒幢律寺
Jieda huanxi 皆大歡喜
Jiepona Guangfan 揭波那光梵
Jiexian 戒顯
Jigong 濟公
Jigong da nao gongtang 濟公大鬧公堂
Jigong huofo 濟公活佛
Jigong leilei xian ying, shu bu neng jin 濟公累累顯應, 書不能盡
Jigong Li 濟公李
Jigong shou Qinxiang 濟公收秦相
Jigong shou shentong 濟公收神童
Jigong ting 濟公亭
Jigong yuan 濟公院
jiji rulü lingchi 急急如律令敕
Jin Renjie 金仁傑
Jin Yong 金庸
jin'gang quan 金剛圈
Jin'gang tongzi 金剛童子
"Jingchun jian he" 景純見和
Jingci [si] 淨慈寺
Jingci xu zhi 淨慈續志
jin'ge 錦歌
jingji lin 荊棘林
jingshi 淨室
jinguang 金光
Jingzhong zhuan 精忠傳
jinshen luohan 金身羅漢
jinzhong zhao 金鐘罩
jitong 乩童
Jiujing zhai 久敬齋
"Jiuli song" 九里松
jiurou heshang 酒肉和尚
Jiusuo shan 九鎖山
Jiuxian 酒仙
Jiuxian weng 酒仙翁
jiuzhuan 九轉
Jujian 居簡
jushi 居士
Jutang 蘜堂

kouzhan 口占
kuangquan 狂泉

Kunlun Zi 崑崙子

Laoer you tang 老二酉堂
"Leifeng ta" 雷峰塔
Leigong 雷公
Lengquan ting 冷泉亭
Leshan tang 樂善堂
Li Bai 李白
Li Bangchan 李邦產
Li Chunsen 李春森
Li Maochun 李茂春
Li Shouqi 李壽耆
Li Tianlu 李天祿
Li Wenhe 李文和
Li Yu 李漁
Li Zhiqing 李致清
"Liang Wudi lei xiu gui jile" 梁武帝累修歸極樂
Liang Wudi xilai yanyi 梁武帝西來演義
liantai benxi 連台本戲
Liaoyuan 了元
Lin Guoxiong 林國雄
Lin Xiangru 藺相如
Lin'an 臨安
ling 靈
lingguai xiaoshuo 靈怪小說
lingguang 靈光
Lingyin [si] 靈隱寺
Linhai 臨海
Linji Yixuan 臨濟義玄
"Liu Cui" 柳翠
Liu Guandao 劉貫道
Liu Haibao 劉海報
Liu Jiye 劉繼業
Liu Songnian 劉松年
Liu Tong 流通
Liu Xiang 劉向
Liushijia xiaoshuo 六十家小說
Liuzi zhenyan 六字眞言
Longfu zhai 隆福齋
Longqing shengping 隆慶昇平
Lou Jiangshi 婁江詩
Lü Dongbin 呂洞賓

Lu Xixing 陸西星
Lu Zhishen 魯智深
lülin 綠林
Luo Binwang 駱賓王
luohan 羅漢
luohan tang 羅漢堂
luo zhi ru yunyan 落紙如雲煙

Ma Chao 馬超
Ma Yuqing 馬隅卿
maiyi 賣藝
Mazu (Chan master) 馬祖
Mazu (popular deity) 媽祖
Meizhou 眉州
Miaoying 妙應
Minggong 明公
Minghuayuan 明華園
Molangxian Zhuren 墨浪仙主人
Molang Zhuren 墨浪主人
Molang Zi 墨浪子
Mo Taixu 莫太虛
Mulian 目連

Nankemeng 南柯夢
Nanping 南屏
Nanping Jingci si zhi 南屏淨慈寺志
Nanyou ji 南遊記
naoba 鐃鈸
Nazha 哪吒
Neijing 內經
neitai 內台
nian 念
Niu Shaoya 鈕少雅
nuo 儺

Pang Yun 龐蘊
Pengcheng 彭城
Penggong an 彭公案
Penglai 蓬萊
Pi Rixiu 皮日休
Pi Zan gong 皮贊公
piaoyou 票友
Pilu ding shang mian 毗盧頂上眠
Pilu ding shang xing 毗盧頂上行

ping bu ping 平不平
pinghua 平話
pingmingfa 平明發
pingshu 評書
pingshu chaguan 評書茶館
Pingyang zhuan 平陽傳
"Pipa yin" 琵琶引
Puhua 普化
Puhua si 普化寺
Puyan 普巖

Qianyang 前洋
Qianzhu 千柱
Qici 契此
qielan 伽藍
Qin Da 秦怛
Qin Gui 秦檜
Qin Shaoyou 秦少游
Qin Xi 秦喜
qing 情
Qing Weituo 請韋陀
qingkou 清口
Qingyi shen 青衣神
Qingyi tongzi 青衣童子
Qiu 邱
Qixia wuyi 七俠五義
qi yan ji xing 奇言畸行
Qu toutou Jidian quanzhuan 麴頭陀濟顛全傳
Qu toutuo zhuan 麴頭陀傳
Qu Yuan 屈原
Quan sao Qin 全掃秦

Renyi xuan 仁義軒
Ruan Ji 阮籍
Rujiao 儒教
Ruoshui 弱水
Ruzong shen jiao 儒宗神教

Saizhu'er 賽珠兒
sajia 洒家
sancai 三才
Sanguo yanyi 三國演義
Sanjiao yuanliu soushen daquan 三教源流叟神大全
sanmei (zhen) huo 三昧眞火
sanxian 三絃
Sha Heshang 沙和尚
Sha Seng 沙僧
shami jie 沙彌戒
shan'ge 山歌
Shang Tianzhu si 上天竺寺
shangzuo 上座
shanshu 善書
Shao Huafeng 邵華風
Shaolin 少林
Shaoshi 邵碩
Shegong 涉公
sheli 舍利
Shen Fanhua 沈梵化
Shen Yinmo 沈尹默
Shen Zhuhong 沈株宏
sheng hu 聖湖
sheng shui 聖水
shenquan 神拳
shen seng 神僧
Shenxiu 神秀
shenyi seng 神異僧
Shi Diancheng 士殿城
Shi Yukun 石玉崑
shidafu 士大夫
Shide 拾得
Shigong 碩公
Shigong an 施公案
shimu 師母
Shiqiangtou 石牆頭
shiru 石乳
shizun 師尊
Shoudu tushuguan 首都圖書館
shoujing 收驚
Shou laochong 收癆虫
Shou Meihua jingren 收梅花精人
shouzuo 首座
Shuang Houping 雙厚坪
Shuangtou an 雙頭案
Shuangyan 雙巖

"Shuangyu shanzhui" 雙魚扇墜
Shuihu houzhuan 水湖後傳
Shuihu zhuan 水湖傳
shuji 書記
shuochang guci 說唱鼓詞
shuoshu heshang 說書和尚
si 寺
Si tianwang 四天王
Song Jiang 宋江
sou 叟
Sun Cuifeng 孫翠鳳
Sun Guopei 孫國佩
Sun Suzhen 孫素眞
Sun Wukong 孫悟空

Taining 泰寧
Taishang laojun 太上老君
Taishi 台視
Taiziye Zhongtan yuanshuai 太子爺中檀元帥
tan 壇
tâng-ki (Hokkien) 童乩
Tao Hongjing 陶弘景
Taohua An Zhuren 桃花菴主人
taozhen 陶眞
Tianbao shuju 天寶書局
Tianfu Gong 天府公
Tianhou 天后
Tianhua Zang Zhuren 天花藏主人
Tianqiao 天橋
Tiantai 天台
Tiantan 天壇
Tianzhu 天柱
tongxin 童心
tu lü 禿驢

"Wang dayin huofen Baolian si" 汪大尹火焚寶連寺
Wang Jueyi 王覺一
Wang Lun 王倫
Wang Mengji 王夢吉
Wang Shou 王壽
Wang Tieqiang 王鐵鎗
Wang Ximeng 王希孟
Wang Yangming 王陽明
Wang Yanzhang 王彥章
Wangba chaguan 王八茶館
Wei Daipo 魏岱坡
wei fu bu ren 爲富不仁
Weituo 韋馱
Wenchang 文昌
wonong 我農
Wu 吳
Wu Bin 吳彬
Wudeng huiyuan 五燈會元
Wufang yuanyin 五方元音
Wugui yinfeng jian 五鬼陰風劍
wujie 五戒
"Wujie Chanshi si Honglian ji" 五戒禪師私紅蓮記
Wulong shan fengshan si 五龍山鳳山寺
wusheng 武生
Wusheng laomu 無生老母
Wutong 五通
Wuyou (si) 烏尤寺
wuxi 武戲
wuxia xiaoshuo 武俠小說
wu you bu ying 無有不應

xian 仙
Xiang Sheli 香闍梨
xiangju 湘劇
Xiangying jushi 香嬰居士
xiaobei 笑杯
xiaohua ben 笑話本
xiao renwu 小人物
xiaoshuo 小說
Xiaoxitian 小西天
Xiayi fengyue zhuan 俠義風月傳
xie 寫
Xie Yi 謝逸
Xiede Jigong 邪的濟公
Ximen Qing 西門慶
xingmu 醒木
Xingshi hengyan 醒世恆言

Xin Jigong huofo 新濟公活佛
xinyuan 心猿
xishu 西墅
Xiuyuan 修元
Xiyuan si 西園寺
Xiyou ji 西遊記
Xu Sheng 許盛
Xu Sun 許遜
Xu Tianfu 許天扶
Xu Wang 許王
xuan 軒
Xuantian shangdi 玄天上帝
xushu 敘述

Yan Huaxuan 閻華軒
Yandang shan 雁蕩山.
Yang Meng 楊猛
Yang Ming 楊明
Yang Xiaolou 楊小樓
yangkuang 佯狂
Yan'nan 燕南
Yan ru tui chan 奄如蜕蟬
Yanxian si 延賢寺
yanyi 演義
Yanzhou 兗州
Yao Pinhou 姚聘候
yaoshi 藥石
Yapian Xian 鴉片絃
ye heshang 野和尚
yeshi xiaoshuo 野史小說
yetai 野台
yi 咦
Yi dou shi bai pian 一斗詩百篇
Yiguan dao 一貫道
Yiguan tanyuantu shuo 一貫探源圖說
Yihuang 宜黃
yin 吟
Yin Biefeng 印別峰
yinghua shengxian 應化聖賢
yingxiong chuanqi 英雄傳奇
Yingzhou 瀛洲
yinhun zhen 陰魂陣
yinqing 引磬
"Yinzhong baxian ge" 飲中八仙歌
Yisi bugua 一絲不掛
Yonghe zhai 永和齋
Yonglong zhai 永隆齋
You Benchang 游本昌
"You Dongxiao" 游洞霄
you zhuanji yiben liu yu shi
有傳記一本流於世
yuan 院
Yuanhu 鴛湖
Yuanshui 鴛水
yuanxing 猿行
Yue Fei 岳飛
Yuehui pusa 月慧菩薩
yueju 粵劇
"Yueming heshang du Liu Cui"
月明和尚度柳翠
Yugan 餘干
Yuhang 餘杭
yulu 語錄
Yulü baojuan 玉律寶卷
Yun Fang 惲芳
yungen 雲根
Yunlin si 雲林寺
Yuxian 遇賢
yuyan 寓言

zaju 雜劇
Zaogong 灶公
zei 賊
zeixiang 賊相
"Zeng Fanggan shi" 贈方干詩
Zhanding fogui 暫定佛規
Zhang Guangbi 張光璧
Zhang Heshang 張和尚
Zhang Shifang 張士芳
Zhang Tianran 張天然
Zhang Wenhai 張文海
Zhang Xu 張旭
Zhanggong 張公
zhanglao 長老
Zhao Bin 趙斌
Zhaojia lou 趙家樓
zhen 陣
zheng zhuan 正傳

Zhengde Jigong 正的濟公
Zhengzong shuhua she 正宗書畫社
Zhen jia Jigong 眞假濟公
Zhenwu 眞武
zhewei 闍維
Zhigong (Baozhi) 支公
Zhigong 誌公
zhiguai 志怪
zhi gu shai lai 只顧篩來
Zhong Kui 鍾馗
zhongdao 衆道
Zhonglie xiao wuyi zhuan 忠烈小五義傳
Zhongyan 中巖
zhou 咒
Zhoudian 周顚
zhu 著
Zhu Bajie 豬八戒
Zhua Hua Yunlong 抓華雲龍
Zhua Liu Xiangmiao 抓劉香妙
zhuang 莊
Zhuanyu 篆玉
Zhubao gui 珠寶桂
zhubi 竹篦
Zhulin qixian 竹林七仙
zhu tian shen sheng 諸天神聖
zhuyu 著語
zidishu 子弟書
Zigu 紫姑
zimu yinhun sheng 子母陰魂繩
Ziran daoren 紫髯道人
Ziran kuangke 紫髯狂客
Ziwei dadi 紫微大帝
zongping 總評
Zujue 祖覺
zunxin 尊信
zuo 作
zuo tuo li wang 坐脫立亡
zuozhu 座主

Index

Harvard-Yenching Institute Monograph Series
(titles now in print)

11. *Han Shi Wai Chuan: Han Ying's Illustrations of the Didactic Application of the* Classic of Songs, translated and annotated by James Robert Hightower
21. *The Chinese Short Story: Studies in Dating, Authorship, and Composition,* by Patrick Hanan
22. *Songs of Flying Dragons: A Critical Reading,* by Peter H. Lee
23. *Early Chinese Civilization: Anthropological Perspectives,* by K. C. Chang
24. *Population, Disease, and Land in Early Japan, 645–900,* by William Wayne Farris
25. *Shikitei Sanba and the Comic Tradition in Edo Fiction,* by Robert W. Leutner
26. *Washing Silk: The Life and Selected Poetry of Wei Chuang (834?–910),* by Robin D. S. Yates
27. *National Polity and Local Power: The Transformation of Late Imperial China,* by Min Tu-ki
28. *Tang Transformation Texts: A Study of the Buddhist Contribution to the Rise of Vernacular Fiction and Drama in China,* by Victor H. Mair
29. *Mongolian Rule in China: Local Administration in the Yuan Dynasty,* by Elizabeth Endicott-West
30. *Readings in Chinese Literary Thought,* by Stephen Owen
31. *Remembering Paradise: Nativism and Nostalgia in Eighteenth-Century Japan,* by Peter Nosco
32. *Taxing Heaven's Storehouse: Horses, Bureaucrats, and the Destruction of the Sichuan Tea Industry, 1074–1224,* by Paul J. Smith
33. *Escape from the Wasteland: Romanticism and Realism in the Fiction of Mishima Yukio and Oe Kenzaburo,* by Susan Jolliffe Napier
34. *Inside a Service Trade: Studies in Contemporary Chinese Prose,* by Rudolf G. Wagner
35. *The Willow in Autumn: Ryūtei Tanehiko, 1783–1842,* by Andrew Lawrence Markus
36. *The Confucian Transformation of Korea: A Study of Society and Ideology,* by Martina Deuchler
37. *The Korean Singer of Tales,* by Marshall R. Pihl

38. *Praying for Power: Buddhism and the Formation of Gentry Society in Late-Ming China,* by Timothy Brook
39. *Word, Image, and Deed in the Life of Su Shi,* by Ronald C. Egan
40. *The Chinese Virago: A Literary Theme,* by Yenna Wu
41. *Studies in the Comic Spirit in Modern Japanese Fiction,* by Joel R. Cohn
42. *Wind Against the Mountain: The Crisis of Politics and Culture in Thirteenth-Century China,* by Richard L. Davis
43. *Powerful Relations: Kinship, Status, and the State in Sung China (960–1279),* by Beverly Bossler
44. *Limited Views: Essays on Ideas and Letters,* by Qian Zhongshu; selected and translated by Ronald Egan
45. *Sugar and Society in China: Peasants, Technology, and the World Market,* by Sucheta Mazumdar
46. *Chinese History: A Manual,* by Endymion Wilkinson
47. *Studies in Chinese Poetry,* by James R. Hightower and Florence Chia-Ying Yeh
48. *Crazy Ji: Chinese Religion and Popular Literature,* by Meir Shahar